**W9-BZR-403**

GEOFFREY CHAUCER was born (c. 1340) in London, England. The son of a wealthy and highly-connected vintner, he received a classical education prior to becoming a page at the court of King Edward III. As soldier, statesman, public official, and court poet, he remained in contact with the most important people of his time. Chaucer was sent on several diplomatic missions to Italy, where he read and was deeply influenced by the works of Dante, Petrarch, and Boccaccio. The Italian influence is evident in his masterpiece, CANTERBURY TALES, on which he worked intermittently for at least twenty years Chaucer died in 1400 and was buried in Westminster Abbey.

**DONALD R. HOWARD** is Professor of English at Stanford University. He has taught at Ohio State, The University of California, and Johns Hopkins. He was a Fulbright fellow to Italy in 1959–60, an American Council of Learned Societies fellow in 1963–64, a Guggenheim fellow in 1969–70, and a National Endowment for the Humanities fellow in 1977–78. He is the author of THE THREE TEMPTATIONS: MEDIEVAL MAN IN SEARCH OF THE WORLD (1966), THE IDEA OF THE CANTERBURY TALES (1976), and WRITERS AND PILGRIMS: MEDIEVAL PILGRIMAGE NARRATIVES AND THEIR POSTERITY (1980). He is the editor of the Signet Classic edition of TROILUS AND CRISEYDE.

*Geoffrey Chaucer*

# THE CANTERBURY TALES

## A Selection

Edited by Donald R. Howard
with the assistance of James Dean

*The Signet Classic Poetry Series*
GENERAL EDITOR: JOHN HOLLANDER

A SIGNET CLASSIC

SIGNET CLASSIC
Published by the Penguin Group
Penguin Books USA Inc., 375 Hudson Street,
New York, New York 10014, U.S.A.
Penguin Books Ltd, 27 Wrights Lane,
London W8 5TZ, England
Penguin Books Australia Ltd, Ringwood,
Victoria, Australia
Penguin Books Canada Ltd, 10 Alcorn Avenue,
Toronto, Ontario, Canada M4V 3B2
Penguin Books (N.Z.) Ltd, 182–190 Wairau Road,
Auckland 10, New Zealand

Penguin Books Ltd, Registered Offices:
Harmondsworth, Middlesex, England

Published by Signet Classic, an imprint of Dutton Signet,
a division of Penguin Books USA Inc.

First Signet Classic Printing, October, 1969

30 29 28 27 26 25 24 23

 REGISTERED TRADEMARK—MARCA REGISTRADA

Library of Congress Catalog Card Number: 71-85359

Printed in the United States of America

# Contents

# INTRODUCTION

It is a habit of modern criticism to praise writers for their originality, and Chaucer is often so praised. Dryden called him "the father of English literature"—for he was, if anyone, the initiator of an English literary tradition, and was the inventor of the English rhyming decasyllabic couplet. From the historical studies of the nineteenth and twentieth centuries we know now that Chaucer's style reflects many of the conventions of medieval poetry and rhetoric, and that his tales are based on folk tales or on narratives borrowed from Boccaccio, Petrarch, Nicholas Trivet, and so on. When we think about this "background," with its enormous element of convention and stereotype, it becomes harder to see what is original in him. Perhaps very little. Originality was not the virtue for medieval poets that it is for us; where we may scorn what is "derivative" in an author, the medievals would have praised his taste in choosing well. Nor did they romanticize their poets as moderns do. They were uninterested in a poet's "development" and did not seek out in his work clues to his personality or his private life. Moreover, writers themselves did not see the act of composition in quite the romantic way a modern writer might. Poets were called "makers" and were viewed more often as craftsmen than as creators or artists. In his earlier works, Chaucer often presents himself humorously as a bookish scholar and naïve pedant hovering over "old

books" and citing "authorities"—a mere scribe copying
and adapting with myopic diligence. What is missing in
this image of the poet, and what we must therefore re-
move from our minds, is the printing press; for it was
only that technological improvement—a century after
Chaucer's time—which let writers imagine themselves
initiating an unpredictable process of reproduction and
addressing a "public" of unseen readers.

In these respects Chaucer was somewhat ahead of his
time. More than other English writers of his age he saw
himself as an originator and creator, expecting a reputa-
tion and a measure of fame; in this he was more like his
Italian contemporary Petrarch, whom he names with
honor in the Clerk's Prologue. It has never been fashion-
able to call Chaucer a humanist, and it is true that he
was untouched by many of the fads which characterized
the incipient humanism of Italy in the fourteenth century.
Yet he knew about Petrarch and Boccaccio and knew
some of their works. Like them, he was interested in the
ancient world and in ancient writers. Like them, he was
concerned about the accurate preservation of texts (but
especially those of his own works): in one of his short
poems he scolds his scribe for making mistakes, and at
the end of *Troilus and Criseyde* begs copyists to take
care. Like them, too, he showed an interest in fame. In
his earlier *House of Fame,* though it depicts fame as
mere unpredictable noise not bestowed justly, he evinces
this interest; at the end of the *Troilus,* though he modestly
hopes that his work will be "subject to all poesy," he
wishes it a place in literary tradition; in the Prologue to
*The Legend of Good Women* and again in the Man of
Law's Prologue he puts into the mouths of characters
lists of his own works; and he gives a similar list in his
"Retraction," though disclaiming all such as "sounen into
sin."

He was perhaps also ahead of his time in the way he
envisaged his audience. Medieval writers sometimes used
the phrase "readers and hearers"—by which they meant,
probably, that their work would more often than not be
read aloud. Chaucer himself evidently read his works to

the court of Richard II—there is a manuscript drawing of him doing so, executed a few years after his death. Much has been made of the notion that he wrote his poems for oral delivery and thus conceived of them as performances before a court audience. Nevertheless, Chaucer seems to have imagined readers unknown to himself poring over his works. At the close of the *Troilus* he worries about the "diversity of our tongue"—that is, about whether speakers of other dialects would understand him and copy him correctly. And before the Miller's Tale he warns those who might be offended by its coarseness to "turn over the leaf and choose another tale." In this last he seems to have in mind the more characteristically modern reader—a solitary person with book in hand. But literacy was not in the least common, the possession of books was rare, and a "reading public" in the modern sense scarcely existed at all. Chaucer himself says he owned sixty books (an enormous private library for those days) and read in bed (a luxurious use of expensive candles); when he envisages other readers like himself, solitary men who own their own books, he has in mind something new and still unusual.

All of this is the Chaucer we know from his works— Chaucer the writer and man of letters. What kind of private person he was is entirely a matter of guesswork. The intimate sense of his personality which we get from his writings—the "Chaucerian" irony and wit, the close observation of detail, his tolerant interest in people—is possibly our best and worthiest knowledge of the man himself. Bits and scraps of documents give us some facts about his whereabouts and employment as a civil servant, although none of them state that this Geoffrey Chaucer was the poet. But it is safe to assume that poet and civil servant were the same. Had there been two men of the same name at court, it would have occasioned comment; and there is one passage (*The House of Fame*, lines 652–60) where he describes finishing his "rekenynges" and coming home only to sit at another book, like a hermit, until bleary-eyed. We can build up a picture of a young man from an upper-middle-class home, sent to a noble house and then abroad to be trained in the niceties of high-born conduct, for a time possibly a student at the Inns of Court, where he would have had training in law and finance. (There is a report from the sixteenth century that the old records of the Inner Temple showed he was fined two shillings for beating a Franciscan friar in Fleet Street.) He was employed by the Crown on various ambassadorial missions to France, Spain, Flanders, and Italy, and held various civil service posts—Clerk of the Customs, Clerk of the King's Works—to which he was appointed by the King. He was especially under the patronage of John of Gaunt. His marriage to Philippa Roet was apparently arranged through these alliances in a businesslike manner; he had two sons and possibly two daughters. He jokingly refers to himself in his early poems as an outsider to love; but he probably means by this —if he means anything serious—that his social position, that of an "esquire," made the aristocratic conventions of love inappropriate for him. It is true that as an important functionary and as court poet he mixed freely with titled aristocrats of the greatest importance; but it is also true that he was not fully their equal. His ironic detachment and self-humor probably spring in part from this relationship with an aristocratic audience.

When Chaucer writes "I" in *The Canterbury Tales* we have therefore a complex self-projection. Our first glimpse of him, in the second sentence of the General Prologue, is of a pilgrim: he has joined a group of twenty-nine other pilgrims at the Tabard Inn in Southwark and has spoken to all of them. Thus he is an observer, just one of a group—accurate, interested, reporting in close detail what he has seen and learned. As he proceeds in this role, we get an idea of his character, and it is that of an exceedingly naïve fellow. He thinks the pilgrims are all perfectly wonderful people and describes each with enormous enthusiasm, admiring them, in bourgeois fashion, for their appearance and their success—even when that success is in duplicity or thievery.

This unduly accepting observer is telling about the

beginning of a pilgrimage from which he has now re-
turned. No doubt he learned much more in a week or so
than he would have seen at first glance in the inn. Like
any returned traveler he must have picked up some gossip
along with the facts and made some guesses or surmises.
But as we get further into his descriptions of his fellow
pilgrims, we realize that he is reporting many more de-
tails than the average observer would normally see or
guess. He knows how the Friar goes about his daily
rounds, what he keeps concealed in his hood, how he
hears confessions. He knows how the Prioress behaved
in her convent and how the Summoner abused his office.
He even knows what the Monk *thinks* (it seems unlikely
that the Monk would have told all this) and hints broadly
that the Monk's "outriding" and hunting was in fact a
hunt for women. In short, though we started with a
pilgrim-observer returned from his travels and reporting
what he remembers, we end up with an almost omniscient
observer and reporter who knows their thoughts and
secrets.

Obviously behind this observer stands the poet himself,
who can imagine and write down what he pleases. Indeed
the first voice we hear, in the opening sentence of the
General Prologue, is the poet's. The familiar lines, "Whan
that April with his showres soote/The drought of March
hath perced to the roote," are not "realistic observation,"
though often so described, but rely on learning and poetic
convention. We are not told that the flowers have blos-
somed, but that "the showers of April have penetrated
March's dryness, bathing the veins in such liquid as en-
genders flowers." We are not told that the winds blew,
but that "Zephyr with his sweet breath has breathed into
the sprouts." We are given astronomical measurements
for the position of the sun and are taught that birds sleep
at night with their eyes open as Nature directs them. The
pilgrimage itself is introduced with a generalization. What
we are getting here is *authority;* the poet's voice is steeped
in tradition, learning, science—all of it preserved in
books. When he turns to the pilgrims, we get (so he
says) *experience,* for the pilgrim-observer claims to be

telling us what he saw and heard. Authority plus experience—that is really the "method" of the General Prologue. To the medieval mind "authority" was a superior basis for knowledge. But it is hard not to feel that Chaucer shared somewhat the Wife of Bath's opinion:

> Experience, though noon auctoritee
> Were in this world, is right enough for me . . .
> (Wife of Bath's Prologue, 1–2)

The pilgrim-observer, who gives us experience, is naïve, wide-eyed, and uncritical. It is as if the poet has put on a mask—the mask of the fool. Imagine Chaucer reading the work aloud to a sophisticated upper-class audience and you catch this irony. Take the Monk. "There was this very fine Monk (he says), an outrider, who loved venery—a manly man, capable of being an abbot; he had many wonderful horses in his stable, and when he rode you could hear his bridle jingle in a whistling wind, as loud and clear as a chapel bell. Where he was in charge, the rule of St. Maur or St. Benedict, because old and rather strict—why, this monk let old things go by and held with the *new* world . . . " As the details mount up we get a most clear picture. The Monk is permitted to ride outside the monastery in order to take care of its business; but he derives far too much pleasure from this. He loves hunting (the sport of aristocrats), keeps fine horses, is handsomely dressed, even wearing a gold pin in the suspicious shape of a love-knot. "Venerie" (hunting) is likely a pun on "venereal" (having to do with Venus); "hunting" often suggested sexual escapades; the hare was and still is a symbol of lechery (he goes, moreover, "pricking" after hares). The pilgrim continues to be enthusiastic—he agrees wholeheartedly: "I said his opinion was good. Why should *he* study? Why should *he* work with his hands, as St. Augustine commanded? How shall the world be served?" The poet of course knows that the monk was violating his vows and was very far from admirable. We understand this without being told. As we continue to read the General Prologue, we come more and more to see evil in the pilgrims—the worst, the Summoner and Pardoner, are saved for the end. And because the pilgrim-observer remains uniformly enthusiastic and accepting, the irony becomes greater.

But Chaucer is not using this ironic device to *condemn* their abuses. From a Christian point of view, all men are sinners; the Christian, as St. Augustine had said, must "love the man but hate his sin." To condemn other men for their shortcomings would itself be a sin of pride. From this point of view, the pilgrim-observer is a kind of holy fool, and his generous, affable acceptance of everyone is a figure of Christian charity. But this charity is fragmented from the other side of Christian behavior—wisdom and knowledge, including self-knowledge—and is exaggerated in its simplicity. Certainly Chaucer is not recommending naïveté. He lets us see the abuses; and like him, we recognize them for abuses and must disapprove of them. The attitude, characteristic of the Christian Middle Ages, can be formulated like this: men themselves are God's creatures and therefore fundamentally good; the institutions they are connected with—monasticism, knighthood, labor, the professions and businesses—are only good or bad insofar as men use them well or ill. Thus, St. Francis' *ideal* was good; the way Friar Huberd of *The Canterbury Tales* practices that ideal is bad. Evil in men is the result of the Fall; with all men, as with Adam, it is the product of wrong choices; but it is parasitic and does not alter the fact of their goodness as creatures. When we see evil in others we are not supposed to click our tongues like puritans; we should love them as God's creatures and worry about our own sins first. Chaucer indeed ends *The Canterbury Tales* with the Parson's Tale (omitted in the present volume)—a sermon on penitence. And to this he adds his own act of penance.

In the General Prologue the pilgrims are described roughly in groups as they might have fallen together in the inn or on the road. The Knight, his son the Squire, and their Yeoman ride together. The clergy fall into a group: two nuns, a priest, a monk, and a friar. The

Sergeant of the Law and the Franklin, members of the upper bourgeoisie, are described one after the other. And various guildsmen and tradesmen fall into proximity, including Shipman, Doctor, and Wife of Bath. This is all realistic enough and reflects the makeup of fourteenth-century English society. But inserted among the rest are three *ideal* portraits, those of the Knight, the Parson, and the Plowman. These three are exactly what they should be in the light of medieval social ideals—the Knight a high-minded adventurer serving just causes, the Parson a humble parish priest who practices what he preaches, the Plowman a dutiful worker who "lives in peace and perfect charity." The three ideal portraits represent the medieval conception of the Three Estates—nobles, clergy, and commons. (Perhaps the Clerk is also an idealized figure representing a newer milieu sequestered from society, the universities. But, like the Squire, he is not yet fully a part of adult life and may stand apart in this way.)

Against this ideal is set the harsh reality. To the medieval mind things were arranged in hierarchies, and man's goal was perfection. On the other hand perfection was not absolutely attainable because of original sin and humanity in fact disposed itself into degrees of *im*perfection. While Chaucer thought of the class structure in ideal terms, the better part of the pilgrims come from the middle class, as Chaucer himself did, and this realistically describes conditions of fourteenth-century life; yet there is no idealized portrait of a middle-class pilgrim. The ideal, then, was rigid, hierarchical, and typically disposed into three parts; the reality was turbulent and many-faceted. As the result of the plague—the Black Death which swept England four times during Chaucer's lifetime—England was depopulated by at least a third. The result was a considerable social upheaval, a new demand for laborers, and therefore a new independence among the laboring classes. Chaucer begins his description of the pilgrims with the Knight, and begins the tales with the Knight's Tale. Both choices are appropriate—the man of highest rank *should* come first. But in the General Prologue this proper order by rank quickly falls apart; and in the tales the Host's good intentions are foiled when the drunken Miller butts in to "quite" the Knight's tale. Chaucer clearly intended to let the actualities of fourteenth-century life burst forth in this way; he even apologizes for doing so in the General Prologue:

> Also I pray you to foryive it me
> Al have I not set folk in hir degree
> Here in this tale as that they sholde stonde:
> My wit is short, ye may well understonde. (743–46)

There is, then, an intentional quality of haphazardness and randomness in the prologue and among the tales. For some time readers of the poem therefore considered the General Prologue a "portrait gallery" and the tales themselves a collection or anthology. In recent years critics have come to see in both a degree of arrangement and order, and hence a degree of unity. The General Prologue begins with the Knight, groups the pilgrims roughly by their livelihood, and ends with the most awesomely depraved of the pilgrims, the Summoner and Pardoner. The tales begin with the Knight, fall in some cases into dramatic units or juxtapositions, and end with the Parson's sermon. In spite of this evident planning, however, the randomness of the pilgrimage is pressed upon the reader in a gamelike way: quite literally the pilgrimage is a game —"I shall begin the game," declares the Knight before his tale, and after it the Host cries "the game is well begunne." It starts as a game of chance: at the end of the General Prologue the Host has them draw straws to see who will begin:

> Anon to drawen every wight began,
> And shortly for to tellen as it was,
> Were it by aventure, or sort, or cas,
> The sooth is this: the cut fill to the Knight.
>
> (842–45)

The real truth, as every reader can see, is that it was very far from "aventure," "sort," or "cas" (the three terms are as good as synonymous): behind the lucky accident, short of some sleight of hand by the Host, is the directing hand of Chaucer and the providential rightness of things. The game of chance seems to have hidden rules. But no sooner are these rules set up than they fall back into randomness: the Host calls next on the Monk, he being probably next in rank, but the Miller drunkenly intervenes. After him comes the Reeve, for reeves (farm managers) are natural enemies of millers; and besides, the two are exact opposites in temperament. The order of tales thus comes to be directed by inner forces of social conflict and interplay of character, by disagreement and aggression.

This tension between rule and chance reflects the medieval attitude toward the universe itself. God's Providence governed the universe, and all things worked according to a divine plan. But such a necessity in the nature of things could not be known to man's beclouded reason; neither did it limit man's free will to make moral choices. From man's point of view the universe therefore *seemed* haphazard; chance ("Fortune") seemed to govern the course of human affairs, and all earthly things seemed transitory, mutable, and untrustworthy. But behind this phenomenon of flux was the directing hand of Providence: hence, in the total order of things, every outcome was just and right. Life itself was a journey or pilgrimage in which men seemed to meander uncertainly toward the just certainties of the Last Things—death, judgment, heaven, and hell.

"Pilgrimage" was a perfect metaphor for human life conceived in this way, and Chaucer was aware of this when he chose a pilgrimage as the setting for the tales. Pilgrimages were often condemned by churchmen because of the self-indulgent holiday conduct of pilgrims; the Wife of Bath herself is a great joiner of pilgrimages, and knew, we find out, much about "wandering by the way." *The Way* was the controlling principle of pilgrimages, for they had a planned route and an ostensibly religious purpose. Egeus in the Knight's Tale articulates the pilgrimage metaphor when he says

This world nis but a thurghfare full of wo,
And we been pilgrims passing to and fro:
Deeth is an end of every worldly sore. (1989-91)

And at the end, the Parson introduces his sermon with these words:

—And Jesu for His grace wit me sende
To shewe you the way, in this viage,
Of thilke parfit glorious pilgrimage
That highte Jerusalem Celestial. (48-51)

Indeed the text of the Parson's sermon, from *Jeremiah* 6, deals with penitence as a means of choosing the Way, the right road in life:

Standeth upon the ways, and seeth and axeth of old paths (that is to sayn, of old sentences) which is the good way, and walketh in that way, and ye shall find refreshing for your souls.

While the pilgrimage to Canterbury must be under- stood thus as a metaphor, it is nonetheless real. Like the medieval pilgrimages themselves, it has both a quotidian and a spiritual dimension. From the simplest quotidian point of view it describes thirty pilgrims who meet at the Tabard and ride to Canterbury telling tales as they go; and seen this way the General Prologue is indeed a portrait gallery, and the tales a collection. The pilgrims are, by the Host's plan, each to tell two tales going and two returning, but they do not all tell even one, and there is no return voyage. Since Chaucer did not finish the work, it is almost always assumed that if he had there would have been one hundred twenty tales, half told on the way back to London. But is the work meant to be viewed with that much realism? In real life, the journey to the shrine of St. Thomas à Becket at Canterbury was a very popular pilgrimage. The pilgrims did really tell tales—a "Canterbury tale" came to mean a tall tale or lie. Thus a gamelike falseness and unreality are suggested

even by the realistic setting and straightforward title of
the work. We are, moreover, meant to suspend our dis-
belief in important particulars: we know that the pilgrims
did not tell their tales in rhyming couplets or stanzaic
forms, and that no one could *hear* a tale told to a group
of thirty while riding horseback through open country.
The pilgrims themselves suspend *their* disbelief and enter
upon an elaborate game in which an innkeeper assumes
leadership over a group composed in good part of his
betters; he has them hold up their hands in agreement
(line 783) before he has told them his plan! In short, the
world we enter upon is very far from the real world of the
everyday. It is a world of game, of carefree assent, a
topsy-turvy world where social rank is set aside, where
drawn straws turn out miraculously right "by aventure,
or sort, or cas"—a holiday atmosphere surging with dis-
cord and tension, its goal the Martyr's shrine.

This unreality points to the spiritual dimension of the
pilgrimage. At the outset we are with Chaucer the pilgrim
at the Tabard; when he tells us that he will describe each
pilgrim, we feel as if he must be describing them as he
first saw them in the inn. But in fact he describes them
as he saw them on the road—we get precise details about
their horses, how they rode, who rode with whom. Beyond
that, we get details of their private lives (the Franklin has
a "table dormant" at home, loves to serve food and drink
to his guests; the Prioress keeps little dogs in her abbey,
feeds them with roasted meat, milk, wastel bread) and
even details of their private thoughts (the Pardoner liked
best to sing the offertory because just after that he would
preach his sermon to win silver). Time is suspended in
this whole account. We have first a single point of time
(the night before the pilgrimage), then inner psycho-
logical time (what Chaucer remembers from the whole
journey), then a timeless and ubiquitous omniscience in
which Chaucer projects himself into their thoughts and
feelings at other times and in other places. In the same
way our normal sense of place is turned aside. We are at
the Tabard, then on the road, then back at the Tabard
planning the game; and during this sweeping view we are

taken into the Prioress' convent, the Monk's "celle," the Reeve's sly little world of livestock, garners, bins, and auditors. We are in that realm where thought and imagination permit us to project ourselves into the experience of others—in the author's mind and, with him, in the minds of the pilgrims. As we empathize with Chaucer, we join him in empathizing with them; and in this empathic realm time and place become malleable, existing only as they have or give meaning.

When *The Canterbury Tales* is seen in this way, its completeness is a relative matter. Chaucer the returned pilgrim could go on reciting the four tales each pilgrim told going and coming until he had told one hundred twenty tales, but the conception and design would stay the same. We are meant to see how life is a pilgrimage, and we see this by seeing into the author's consciousness. It is the nature of consciousness and of memory that we *could* see more; yet we could see the central conception without some of the tales we have. Memory is almost inexhaustible, and the completeness of memories relies on the structuring of details rather than on the accumulation of them. The one-way motion of the pilgrimage from London to Canterbury, which is what the text gives us, carries out the metaphor of life as a pilgrimage. If the return trip had been represented by more tales, this would not have altered the central conception unless the General Prologue were altered as well. It is hard not to imagine that such a return journey would have seemed anticlimactic, and it is entirely possible that Chaucer never meant to portray it. Not, of course, that we shouldn't be infinitely grateful if there were more; but what we have, as Dryden perceived, is God's plenty.

Moreover, the return journey does not go unacknowledged, for we see that the author has returned, like Dante, to recount his experience. What he tells is of a movement from tavern to cathedral, from home to shrine, from fellowship and chitchat to penance and retraction. Because the General Prologue prepares us in this way for the tales and their tellers as well as for the unidirectional shape of the pilgrimage, it must be regarded as one of

the great pieces of thematic writing. Like the great open-
ing "overture" of Proust's *A la Recherche du Temps
Perdu* it encapsulates and sets the nature and governing
principles of a work which could be indeterminately
shorter or longer, less or more detailed, without being the
less whole. It is perhaps for this reason that J. V. Cun-
ningham understood about the General Prologue that it
takes its character from the medieval dream-vision. In
it a structure of memories and received ideas takes shape
and, like consciousness itself, renders up the design of
the whole in vivid associations of feeling and perception.

The tales themselves can be read with pleasure sepa-
rately and at random; but the General Prologue accustoms
us to the conditions which make them parts of a design.
Each tale is told by a character we already know. These
characters are in relationships with each other—are mem-
bers of a single society who ally and clash. In addition,
the tales are being recounted by Chaucer himself, like an
actor recreating the roles of the storytellers and playing
all the parts.

This conception of a series of dramatic monologues
which itself tells a story was probably Chaucer's most
original stroke. Each tale, as it reflects the personality of
its teller, tells its own revealing story about the pilgrim
himself and thus contributes to the description of the
pilgrimage. Chaucer has often been praised as a dramatic
genius, and that he was. The dialogue in the tales has the
qualities of good drama, for the personages talk like indi-
viduals and reveal their characters in the way they talk.
The same is true of the pilgrims themselves. The Clerk's
discourse is idealistic and ironic; the Wife's ebullient and
nostalgic; the Miller's hardy, buoyant, and salacious; the
Reeve's acerb, self-pitying, and awesomely sly. If the
essence of drama is conflict, the pilgrimage is a wonder-
fully dramatic situation, for many of the pilgrims fall
quite spontaneously into disagreement. The Friar and
Summoner eye each other askance and tell outspoken
tales against each other—since both have their hands in
the pockets of ordinary layfolk, they are competitors.

There is no love lost between the Miller and Reeve. The Friar ruffles at the Wife's theological notions. And a whole group of tales makes up a discussion of marriage.

Beyond this dramatic excitement, the fully elaborated story of the pilgrimage reveals Chaucer's own mentality and, though very subtly, his opinions. This aspect of *The Canterbury Tales* has most engaged the attention of critics in recent years. It is the hardest problem because Chaucer's presence in the work is its most ambiguous element. Very possibly he did not want to seem too outspoken, but caution is not the reason he *gives;* and indeed in important matters—religion, politics, domestic harmony—his ideas were not at all radical. What he *says* is that he will tell the facts accurately. They are more daring and surprising than opinions, and it is for them that he makes a good-natured apology:

> But first I pray you of your curteisye
> That ye n'arette it not my villainye
> Though that I plainly speke in this mattere
> To telle you hir wordes and hir cheere,
> Ne though I speke hir wordes proprely.
> For this ye knowen also well as I:
> Whoso shall tell a tale after a man,
> He moot reherce as neigh as ever he can
> Everich a word, if it be in his charge—
> Al speke he never so rudelich and large—
> Or elles he moot tell his tale untrewe,
> Or feine thing, or finde wordes newe;
> He may not spare although he were his brother.
> He moot as well say oo word as another.
> Christ spak himself full brod in holy writ,
> And well ye wot no villainy is it.
> Eek Plato saith, whoso can him rede,
> The wordes mot be cosin to the deede. (725–42)

His use of "low" stories told by rude fellows is evidently what could have given offense to the gentlefolk of his audience. And before the Miller's contribution, which Chaucer calls a "churl's tale," he states his position:

And therefore every gentil wight, I praye,
Deemeth not, for God's love, that I saye
Of yvel entent, but for I mot reherse
Hir tales alle, be they bet or werse,
Or elles falsen some of my mattere.
And therefore, whoso list it not y-heere
Turn over the leef and chese another tale.
For he shall find enoughe, greet and smalle,
Of storial thing that toucheth gentilesse
And eek moralitee and holinesse.
Blameth not me if that ye chese amiss. (63–73)

In spite of this pose of objectivity, or perhaps because
of it, Chaucer's own views show through the tales. Prin-
cipally they do so by a process of accumulative *discredit-
ing*. No sooner do we get one point of view clearly in mind
than we are given some reasons to doubt it. The result is
a tentative, questioning spirit for which Chaucer is nor-
mally reckoned tolerant and ironic. This does not mean
he was without values, for he lets the profoundest values
of his civilization assert themselves in the most spontane-
ous and convincing way. One of those values, however,
was that placed upon the tentative and inquiring mind;
irony itself involves disinterestedness, openness, and
skepticism. Such a frame of mind is not thought "medi-
eval" by some, but I believe it was. The Church taught
that revealed truth was absolute, but this did not mean
that all Christians knew an absolute truth: man's reason
was clouded by ignorance, truth was not known abso-
lutely except to God, and many kinds of knowledge were
"forbidden" and unattainable to man. On the other hand,
Christians believed that "whatsoever things were written
aforetime were written for our learning" (*Romans* 15:4).
People had begun to believe in Chaucer's day that ex-
perience might be added to the canons of authority and
logic as a way of knowing truth. The universities, for
which Chaucer shows an affectionate regard, had evolved
a pedagogical method which relied largely on argument
and disputation; their sense of truth was far more dis-
cursive than we imagine it. Moreover, the growing power

of the middle-class professionals—men like the Sergeant of Law, the Franklin, and of course Chaucer himself—must have made manifest in fourteenth-century society a spirit of compromise, mutual concession, caution, and pragmatism. Whatever its sources and expressions, *The Canterbury Tales* evinces a conception of the variousness of worldly truth; we are reminded throughout that there is much to be said on all sides, and, at the end, that we are imperfect seekers of the perfect Way.

Chaucer's method of stating-and-discrediting thus sets up a kind of serial dialogue, which works at different levels and by different devices; and we shall see this most clearly if we pluck apart the strands for examination.

(1) Within individual tales, each reputedly told by a pilgrim, Chaucer sometimes lets his own voice discredit the tale. This is most notable in the Knight's Tale: we are kept in mind of Chaucer's presence behind the Knight's recital of his story. In reducing Boccaccio's epic, the *Teseida,* to a much shorter romance, Chaucer omitted vast stretches of the narrative. In summarizing or passing over these (the rhetorical device called *occupatio*), he comments on the unwieldiness of the story. At one point, for instance, occurs the line "But of that story list me not to write" (343). This is often treated as a mistake on Chaucer's part—obviously the Knight is not "writing," so the line seems a leftover from an early version before it was assigned to the Knight and included in *The Canterbury Tales*. If this were the only such line, the explanation would be valid; but there are others. For instance, telling of Palamon's imprisonment, Chaucer says,

> Who coude ryme in English proprely
> His martyrdom? Forsooth, it am not I.
> Therefore I pass as lightly as I may:
> It fill that in the seventh yeer, of May
> The thridde night, as olde bookes sayn
> (That all this story tellen more plain) . . . (601–06)

Indeed, throughout the Knight's Tale there is an undertone of ironic self-humor, sometimes in the form of exag-

geration—as where the two heroes fight ankle deep in
their own blood ("And in this wise I let hem fighting
dwelle," the poet adds)—and sometimes in comic relief
of a highly anticlimactic sort. An example of this last
occurs indeed at the climactic moment, the death of
Arcite:

> Dusked his eyen two and failed breeth—
> But on his lady yet cast he his eye.
> His laste word was: *"Mercy, Emelye!"*
> His spirit chaunged house and wente ther
> As *I* came never, I can not tellen wher;
> Therefore I stint—I nam no divinistre:
> Of soules find I not in this registre,
> Ne me ne list thilke opinions to telle
> Of hem, though that they writen where they dwelle.
> Arcite is cold, ther Mars his soule gie.
> Now wol I speken forth of Emelye.
>   Shright Emely . . . (1948–59)

It must be understood that this element in the tale does
not keep us from taking it seriously, does not discredit
the Knight personally, and does not turn the tale into a
parody. But it introduces an undertone of skepticism
toward the story and so toward the tradition of romance
and the body of aristocratic convention with which it was
intertwined.

(2) What we already know about a pilgrim sometimes
discredits his tale. The Miller is an excellent example. He
openly pokes fun at the Knight's tale, declaring outright
that he will "quite" (match, or repay) it. Not twenty
lines into his story he repeats a line out of the Knight's
Tale—"Alone, withouten any compaigny"—which the
Knight had used in a serious context (as the Miller, of
course, does not). His story, like the Knight's, is about
two suitors after a young woman who is in the custody
of an older man. But where the Knight's tale was of
princes and high love in ancient Athens, the Miller's is
about ordinary people and earthy love in present-day
Oxford. One lover is a young student at the university,

out for a lush time; the other, Absolon, is a clerk in minor orders, the sexton or janitor in the local parish, an affected bumpkin who has somehow picked up the clichés of courtly love. The "lady" is a skittish wench, age eighteen, described with very appropriate animal imagery borne out in her later conduct. And she is married to an old carpenter, uxorious, jealous, and dumb. In this atmosphere the conventions and language of courtly love, being utterly out of place, become artificial and ludicrous; and the situation is resolved in a Rabelaisian spirit complete with farts and hot pokers.

The buoyant quality of the tale gives us a very different view of medieval love conventions. But if the Miller discredits those conventions, his looseness of tongue, his drunkenness, and his churl's mentality, hilarious as they are, discredit him. We cannot say that this is what Chaucer thinks about high love, only that this is what the Miller thinks. Chaucer leaves it at that.

(3) Some tales discredit the tale preceding them. Just as the Miller's Tale "quites" the Knight's Tale, the tale following—the Reeve's—"quites" the Miller's. We know we are not meant to take the Miller's Tale as the last word, nor the Reeve's Tale either. What we get from the Reeve is another low-class point of view. The moment the Miller says he will tell a legend and life about a carpenter, the Reeve bristles paranoically: "Stint thy clappe!"—shut your mouth, he says, it's a sin and a folly to injure or defame anyone. When it is the Reeve's turn, he begins with a sly, self-pitying utterance about how old he is, intended to enlist the sympathy of the audience and disclaim any evil intent. He quickly gives himself the lie— he will "quite" the Miller right in his own churl's terms: "I pray to God his necke mote to-breke!" He is in fact burning up with a bitter anger and is bent on revenge. His last words are, "Thus have I quit the Miller in my tale."

The Reeve's story is again a tale of two clerks, and there are an eligible female and an older man as well. But now the clerks are from Cambridge, not Oxford; they speak a comic north-country dialect; and the rival older

man is, needless to say, a miller. In the darkest bedroom
in literary history one of the clerks climbs into bed with
the miller's daughter while the other tricks his wife into
climbing into bed with *him*. The wife, a haughty woman
who considers herself socially superior because she is a
priest's bastard child, doesn't know she is in the wrong
bed (the Reeve cannot resist commenting that she hadn't
had such a good time in years). During it all the drunken
husband snores away. At last the clerks are found out
and there ensues a battle; the wife hits her husband over
the head by mistake, and the clerks escape. It is as funny
a tale as the Miller's, but it has a less buoyant quality:
it reflects the sly, acerb spirit of the Reeve himself. To
the Miller, the "nice manners" of the Knight's Tale
seemed merely artificial and ridiculous, and he represented
them in the absurdly effete Absolon. But the Reeve's view
is different. The initial "nice manners" of the clerks
and of the miller and his wife just barely manage to hide
the ill will and guile of the miller and the suspicion of the
clerks. To the Reeve, "nice manners" are suspect; beneath
them he sees what is uppermost in his own character—a
sly meanness, a habit of distrust and guile. His is no more
a final view of love or manners than the Miller's had been;
but it is another view, a counterpart to the Miller's. The
next tale, the Cook's, might very well have presented still
another low-class view tending to discredit the others; but
alas Chaucer did not finish it.

(4) From these three tales we can see a further device
for presenting various views which partially discredit one
another: tales are arranged in groups. There are three
groups of this kind. One, which we have already dis-
cussed, is the sequence Knight-Miller-Reeve. A second,
less certainly intentional, includes Shipman, Prioress, Sir
Thopas, Melibee, Monk, and Nun's Priest. A third is the
so-called "marriage group."

Since the *Melibee* and the Monk's Tale are omitted in
the present volume, we may as well omit any detailed dis-
cussion of the group which includes them. Besides, the
grouping of these tales is greatly in debate. Perhaps, as
one critic suggests, they are about storytelling itself and

represent by turns the principles of "mirth" and "doctrine." The Shipman's Tale, intended as one of mirth, is consciously immoral; in it all that was sacred in medieval society—marriage, monastic vows, "brotherhood" among friends—is violated. The Prioress' Tale, intended as one of doctrine, is *un*consciously immoral; she tells a story of a supposed "ritual murder" by Jews—the ancient slander recently described in Malamud's *The Fixer*. Her unthinking, harsh anti-Semitism is an ironic contrast to the genteel manners and delicate sensibility ascribed to her in the General Prologue, and that contrast is profoundly sobering. *Sir Thopas,* told by Chaucer himself in his role of naïf, is a parody of a metrical romance and makes fun of the traditional literary knight-errant. But Chaucer then turns from mirth to doctrine and tells a serious tale in prose, the *Melibee*—a treatise, as it actually is, of high-minded advice about proper conduct for aristocrats. Then follows the Monk's tiresome recital of "tragedies."

The Nun's Priest's Tale, the last in this series, is remarkable—witty, satirical, profoundly intelligent. A mock-epic, its form satirizes the stylized conventions of medieval rhetoric. Its content satirizes the conventions of aristocratic conduct: its principle characters, a rooster and hen, talk to each other in the clichés of courtly love. It satirizes, too, almost every intellectual fashion of the later Middle Ages—the arguments about the meaning of dreams, the question of predestination versus free will, medieval medicine and astrology, anti-feminist doctrines, the citing of "authorities," the idea of Fortune. Even the Peasants' Revolt is brought in. Its technique is to build up pomposities to the point where they may be taken seriously, then pinprick them by reminding us that the pompous interlocutors are barnyard fowls. In the end, a sly fox captures the rooster by getting him to close his eyes and sing; but the rooster escapes by getting the fox to open his mouth and shout triumphantly at his pursuers. So the moral is simple: one should keep his eyes open and keep his mouth shut. Probably no advice could better be applied to the heady tales which have gone before. The Monk's Tale was surely pompous (the Monk himself was even described as a rooster in his prologue); the *Melibee* could be seen as pompous for its sententiousness, as could the Prioress' Tale for its naïve smugness. The spirit of the Nun's Priest, by contrast, perfectly involves that unpompous and ironic tentativeness which we call "Chaucerian." The Nun's Priest concludes by quoting St. Paul (Chaucer himself in his Retraction will quote the same text):

> But ye that holden this tale a follye
> As of a fox, or of a cock and hen,
> Taketh the moralitee, good men.
> For Saint Paul saith that all that written is
> To our doctrine it is y-writ, ywis:
> Taketh the fruit and let the chaff be stille. (618–23)

The "marriage group" has a clearer thematic unity. Since Kittredge first described this sequence critics have argued over its validity and differed about which tales should be included. Basically, the notion is this: the Wife of Bath initiates a discussion of marriage, arguing two points—that marriage is a desirable form of moral perfection, and that marriage can be happy only when the wife has the "maistrye," the upper hand. Her own prologue, with its account of her five husbands, illustrates the point admirably; and her tale is a grand wish-fulfillment of her yearning to be young again and to dominate her men. There are many ambiguities in her lusty and outspoken view which make her prologue and tale (in Root's phrase) a great human document. Among them is the fact that her fifth husband, the youngest and poorest of the lot, pleased her most, though he was the one who nearly gained power over her; and her tale ends with the lady obeying the husband with a surprising submissiveness.

The other tales (after an interruption, omitted here, by the Summoner and Friar) present radically different views. The Clerk, a young man studying at Oxford, is an idealist. He tells a noble tale of a wife, Griselda, who patiently submits to her husband's sadistic testing of her; it is too long to include in this volume, but the ending has been printed to show the heavy irony with which the Clerk admits that his ideals are never followed in these times. It is followed by the tale of the Merchant, an older man who has just had an unhappy brief marriage to a young woman. He tells the story of January, the foolish and self-willed old knight who after a lifetime of bachelorhood marries and is promptly cuckolded by a young toothsome lass, logically named May. The Merchant's view is one of total disillusionment and cynicism: the spiritual (and physical) blindness of old January reflects the Merchant's own self-contempt, and the moral of his tale is that happiness in marriage occurs only when the husband can let himself be utterly deceived.

So far then, after the Wife's proclamation, we have an idealistic view and a cynical one. According to Kittredge the debate was resolved by the Franklin, who shows the spirit of compromise characteristic of his class. At the beginning of his tale he outlines a kind of marriage based on mutual concession: the husband is to be "servant in love but lord in marriage"—i.e., he will have the position of superiority but in fact submit to the lady's will; she in turn will be a "humble, true wife"; and in this way they will attain happiness in marriage. There is something here to satisfy all the points of view so far represented. The remainder of the tale is elaborately bound up with the idea of keeping bargains and having "gentilesse." Kittredge believed, and probably most people agree, that this compromise was meant to be the last word on the subject and reflects Chaucer's own opinion. On this score I am skeptical: there is something faintly ludicrous about the Franklin's literal-minded characters and the fantastical situation they get involved in. This seems somewhat to discredit the neat finality of the Franklin's proposal; and indeed the Franklin's own character—he is ostentatious about his wealth and dreadfully keen on "gentilesse"—makes him an unlikely mouthpiece for serious views. His idea of marriage is different from the old conventional one of the aristocrats or from the ironic one we would expect of Chaucer. And the husband in his tale does in fact give stern orders to the wife when things get difficult. On the other hand, the value he puts upon mutual concession in marriage was to become the middle-class ideal, and still is. If Chaucer did not agree with it, he at least saw it coming.

If the Franklin's Tale is not meant to be a final word on marriage, Chaucer may have intended the Second Nun's Tale (here omitted) to serve that function. It is a statement of the Church's highest ideal of marriage, a chaste marriage in which neither partner has dominance but both submit themselves humbly to the will of God. How seriously Chaucer might have admired this ideal is open to question. It is a nun's conception of marriage, certainly, and its simple piety seems naïve: the husband rushes meekly off on the first night of his honeymoon to get baptized! On the other hand, the Second Nun, like the Nun's Priest, is a faceless figure about whom there is nothing to be discredited. Moreover, this kind of pietistic legend was popular in the Middle Ages and taken seriously. Such stories provided medieval men with ideals against which to measure their conduct. The unreality of the story does not render it absurd but puts it among those works which describe a potentially perfect life in an imperfect world.

(5) If Chaucer has any device for making affirmative statements, not discredited in any way, it is that of putting some tales in a position of finality. We have seen that the Nun's Priest's Tale stands in a final position and represents the disinterested, ironic view which one thinks of as characteristically Chaucerian. And we have seen that the marriage group ends with a tale—either the Franklin's or the Second Nun's—which suggests a final assertion. But the best example is the Parson's Tale, a long prose treatise on penitence which comes at the end of the whole work. It is told by the ideal Parson whose character has no flaw to discredit it, and the tale itself has in it no ironic or ludicrous qualities. This, clearly, is intended as sound "doctrine."

What I have been trying to describe is a principle of unity or wholeness in *The Canterbury Tales*. The work is complete in design but not in execution—the General Prologue provides us with a central conception of the whole, and the tales themselves show principles of grouping and ironic contrast which make them less a string of separate stories and more a structure or design. Part of our difficulty in seeing this design of the whole springs from our own preconceptions about wholeness. To us the unity of a work ought to be "organic"—every part and element should have a function which contributes to one total response. Our own aesthetic predilections are most easily seen, perhaps, in architecture: a modern building is thought good if it seems of a piece, a single conception which can be grasped and felt from any vantage point. Details in such a design must be functional and "integral," not decorative or extraneous. In the same way, our rhetoric is one of "logical" development, topic sentences, transitions, and beginning-middle-end organization. With respect to literature "organic unity" has been a major conception of criticism since the nineteenth century, and such an idea is reflected in book-trade jargon which seeks "development" and admires what "jells." We prefer a work with "an idea" and tend to scorn what seems "unnecessary" or "unmotivated." But it was not so in the Middle Ages.

The medievals admired detail, digression, and effulgence quite as much as they admired order. They liked details or images to have more than one possible meaning; they were not bothered but delighted by decorative detail which drew attention to itself; and they did not feel that details should be "consistent." On the contrary, they painted realistic and sometimes even lewd drawings in the margins of psalters and prayerbooks, covered their cathedrals with exquisite carvings often grotesque and earthy, and read romances whose intricate plots led the reader into mazes of happenstance. Their sense of order and structure involved hierarchy and multiplicity in a way that ours does not. They would not have understood what we mean by a "story-line," an "artistic whole," even "a work" or "a book." Their rhetoric was one of development by expansion, dilation, set descriptions, "apostrophes," and digressions. The kind of style they liked—it is sometimes called "gothic"—is not unfamiliar to us, for we continue to admire the gothic cathedrals for their effulgence of design and minutiae of detail as well as for their overall structure. And if we could manage to revive in ourselves something like the gothic sensibility, it would help us understand *The Canterbury Tales* as it was meant to be understood.

The medievals would not have seen a contradiction in the earthy content of some tales and the idealistic affirmations of others. To them it would have seemed natural and proper to end a work with a religious utterance; they would not have felt that it "cancelled out" anything. There is probably a parallel in Chaucer's Retraction. It is almost certainly authentic and would have been conventional. That Chaucer in "revoking" his secular works expected them to be destroyed or unread is out of the question; but he probably did mean that he wished, looking back, to be remembered and held accountable for those works which contained "moralitee and devocioun." Even so, he reminds us that the Bible says "All that is written is written for our doctrine." Probably from this viewpoint the medieval reader would have looked back upon the "enditings of worldly vanitees" with an understanding of their real, if limited, value. "Mirth" and "solace" would always give way before "doctrine" and "sentence"—in the end.

The best but most complicated example of our trouble in relating parts to the whole is the Pardoner's Tale. Of all the tales, it is the one hardest to find a place for. Evidently it was, at the time of Chaucer's death, in a manuscript fragment along with the Physician's Tale (which precedes it); but this fragment stands in no relation to any other, and can go in three possible places. (To us this seems regrettable and makes the work unfinished; to the medievals it would have seemed a more relative matter, for they were accustomed to unfinished works—their cathedrals and their manuscripts being notable examples.)

The Pardoner's Prologue and Tale are a sermon. He gives a demonstration of how he preaches in order to dupe

the "lewed" people and win silver from them. Arch-hypo-
crite, perverter of religion, preyer upon piety and sim-
plicity—all these abuses may justly be heaped upon him.
There is something monstrous and diabolical in his cynical
anti-sermon; yet it is a magnificent performance—one can
hardly fail to be delighted by his intelligence, his articu-
lateness, and his outrageous guile. He lures and challenges
us, almost mocks us, with his cleverness: he is at once
charming and abhorrent, comic and terrifying. The Host
addresses him derisively "thou bel amy"; the "gentils" cry
out that he must tell no ribaldry. From the General Pro-
logue we have learned of his immorality; but we have also
learned something far more revealing—what was, or so he
must have hoped, his secret. He is a eunuch. The entire
physical description suggests this in detail. Strange and
frightening he might seem to anyone, with his beardless
face, his stringy flaxen hair, his piping voice. To the
medievals eunuchry seemed a kind of abomination, and
they used it to symbolize the deprival of God's grace.
Hence the Pardoner's physical deformity is a symbol and
counterpart of his moral depravity. And his concealed
anguish and guilt is a deeper and more spiritual secret,
revealed only at the end of his tale.

In short, he is a grotesque figure—gargoyle-like, mis-
shapen, hideously comic. Yet he is here in *The Canterbury
Tales,* and his prologue and tale are among the best. He
tells the pilgrims, "For though myself be a full vicious
man,/A moral tale yet I you telle can." And this he does,
preaching convincingly against avarice—his purpose, of
course, to get fat offerings. His prologue is itself a con-
fession—or anti-confession, for in it he boasts of his evil.
His tale is, like his own story, one of divine retribution.
He is the portrait of a man wallowing with uneasy and
anguished braggadocio in his own depravity. But among
perverters of the Way, he is an artist, an evil genius.

When his sermon is over, a puzzling incident occurs.
"And lo, sirs, thus I preche," he ends, and adds what
seems a heartfelt blessing: "may Jesus Christ grant you
His pardon, for that is best, I will not deceive you." At
once, perhaps embarrassed by this outpouring of gener-

2

ous feeling, he turns about and tries to inveigle them into buying his pardons anyway! It is a master fraud's effort to administer a wondrous *coup de grace*—to confront, challenge, and swindle them all in a last glorious mockery. And, in this effort, he looks about and lights on the Host as an ally:

> For he is most envoluped in sinne.
> Come forth, sir Host, and offer first anon,
> And thou shalt kiss the relics everichon,
> Ye, for a grote! Unbuckle anon thy purs.
> (614–17)

But the Host, offended, hurls at him an enormous and gross insult—"I wish I had your balls in my hand, I'd cut them off." Needless to say he has hit the Pardoner's most vulnerable point, and the Pardoner lapses into angry silence. The Host avows that he will not "play" with an angry man. Then the Knight comes forth—the pilgrims are now laughing—and bids them embrace and be merry again. They do so, and the incident is allowed to lapse into the greater design of *The Canterbury Tales*. "Anon they kiste, and riden forth hir way."

Gross and outrageous as the Pardoner is, he seems in the end deflated, mysterious, and sad. Here Chaucer's urbane tolerance and his Christian charity meet. He condemns neither the Host for his cruelty nor the Pardoner for his depravity. We do not see the real feeling of either which lurks beneath the surface of their peacemaking. They become pilgrims again, seekers of the Way, on which the Parson in a true sermon is soon to counsel them. We are brought off at a distance, from which they are no longer "round" or realistic characters, but figures in a design. It is the most intense moment on the pilgrimage, and the final note of forgiveness, which is profoundly touching, matches the final penitential closing of *The Canterbury Tales* itself. Pardoners sell forgiveness, which is best. Yet the tale tricks every reader into the momentary sin of failing to pardon; a critic with such deep human understanding as Kittredge could conclude that the Pardoner was the "one lost soul" on the pilgrimage. But, as Chaucer makes us see, this is for God to decide. The two angry pilgrims embrace in a token of forgiveness *and riden forth hir way*. In that moment, if at any single point in the work, we catch the profoundly comic and forgiving spirit of Geoffrey Chaucer.

DONALD R. HOWARD
*The Johns Hopkins University*

# A GENERAL NOTE
# ON THE TEXT

The overall textual policy for the Signet Classic Poetry series attempts to strike a balance between the convenience and dependability of total modernization, on the one hand, and the authenticity of an established text on the other. Starting with the Restoration and Augustan poets, the General Editor has set up the following guidelines for the individual editors:

Modern American spelling will be used, although punctuation may be adjusted by the editor of each volume when he finds it advisable. In any case, syllabic final "ed" will be rendered with grave accent to distinguish it from the silent one, which is written out without apostrophe (e.g., "to gild refinèd gold," but "asked" rather than "ask'd"). Archaic words and forms are to be kept, naturally, whenever the meter or the sense may require it.

In the case of poets from earlier periods, the text is more clearly a matter of the individual editor's choice, and the type and degree of modernization has been left to his decision. But in any event, archaic typographical conventions ("i," "j," "u," "v," etc.) have all been normalized in the modern way.

JOHN HOLLANDER

# A NOTE ON THIS EDITION

The text, though eclectic, is indebted especially to *The Text of the Canterbury Tales,* ed. J. M. Manly and Edith Rickert (8 vols., Chicago, 1940), a work of inestimable value to all editors. Paragraphing and punctuation are my own.

The spelling is normalized, and made modern as far as is consistent with Middle English pronunciation. I have attempted, as much as common sense allows, to adopt uniform spellings for Middle English words rather than keep the helter-skelter variants of Middle English manuscripts. From such variants I have chosen that spelling most like standard modern spelling (e.g., *had* for "hadde," *find* for "fynd," *hert* for "herte"). Where Middle English had alternate pronunciations in Chaucer's dialect, I have often selected the pronunciation whose spelling approximates modern spelling (e.g., *saw,* not "sawgh"); but I have tried to preserve dialect doublets where Chaucer used them to good advantage. I have tried to introduce no spellings which are exclusively modern (thus *heer* rather than "hair," *greet* rather than "great," *throt* rather than "throat"); and to alter no spellings which could affect pronunciation (thus *wol* rather than "will," *namore* rather than "no more," *suster* rather than "sister").

The final *-e* is retained only under these conditions: (1) when it is pronounced (see pp. xli–xliii); (2) when the more nearly modern spelling ends in *-e* (as in *mine* or *have;* or in *there,* spelled in the modern way except when it means "where"); (3) when its omission might cause confusion with similar words or other pronunciations (thus *binethe,* because it looks more like modern "beneath," whereas *bineth* suggests a verb form); and (4) when it helps suggest the length of the preceding vowel (e.g., *speke,* not "spek" lest it suggest the pronunciation "speck").

Since perfect consistency is not possible, there remain in this text enough spelling variants to introduce the student to the mysteries of Middle English orthography. For example, words like *ordre* are so spelled when they seem to elide with the following word. Many old spellings are kept to preserve a rhyme or a prosodic effect. And of course variants like *land/lond, widow/widwe,* or *were/weren* themselves reflect variants in the speech of Chaucer's London.

I am much indebted to the principles and sentiments of E. T. Donaldson, *Chaucer's Poetry* (New York, 1958), pp. iii–vi, though I have gone further in simplifying spelling. My purpose was not to preserve the appearance of Middle English on the page, nor to enforce a needless consistency, but by eliminating as best I could any nonfunctional old spellings to make a Middle English text which the student or general reader can read with ease and pronounce with accuracy.

D. R. H.

# ON PRONOUNCING CHAUCER

Pronouncing Chaucer's English as he pronounced it preserves rhythm and rhymes and brings out the richness of sound which distinguishes his verse. Mispronounced with modern sounds, Chaucer's poetry loses much of its prosodical energy and variousness. Although we cannot know certainly what English sounded like in fourteenth-century London, we can make a reasonable reconstruction from such evidence as rhymes or puns, and from the overall history of English pronunciation. The spelling in the present text is normalized or standardized as an aid to reading and pronouncing. The following rules of thumb will help.

1. *Pronounce all consonants.* Spelling was not standardized in Chaucer's time but roughly phonetic: people wrote what they expected to hear. Thus *knight* was pronounced with a *k* at the beginning, and with *gh* pronounced like German *ch*. *Folk* had an *l* pronounced, and *write* a *w*. Note also that *ch* was always pronounced as in *church;* and *r* was trilled or flapped, as it is today in parts of Britain. In words of French origin, there are two exceptions: initial *h* (as in *honour*) was not pronounced, and *gn* (as in *sign*) was pronounced *n*.

2. *Pronounce final -e at the end of a line, and elsewhere as rhythm requires.* Chaucer probably did not pronounce final *-e* in everyday speech, but he used it for poetical

purposes. At the end of a line it is always pronounced. It has the reduced sound "uh" (as we pronounce the *e* in "m*e*chanic" or "wait*e*d"). There are other syllabic *e*'s, not final, which may be pronounced—e.g., bath*e*d, cropp*e*s, Eng*e*lond.

As an aid to learning how syllabic *e*'s work in the scansion of Chaucer's verse, the *e*'s which should be pronounced (but are not pronounced in modern English) have been marked in the General Prologue in the following manner:

> In all the orders four is none that kan
> So much of daliaunce and fair langagẹ.
> He haddẹ made full many a marriagẹ
> Of yongẹ women at his ownẹ cost;
> Unto his ordre he was a noble post.
> Full well beloved and familier was he
> With frankẹlains over all in his contree . . .

The careful reader can easily develop an "ear" for Chaucer's verse with this much assistance; more would be a crutch. Besides, such marking cannot be authoritative—there are too many variables. For one thing scholars disagree about the scansion; there is even a small minority who claim the verse scans without any pronounced *e*'s, and among the vast majority who agree that some *e*'s must be pronounced no two would agree on every line. It is not always certain where Chaucer meant to *write* a final *-e* since scribes who copied the manuscripts often added them indiscriminately. And not all those he *did* write have to be pronounced. The opening line is a good example:

> Whan that April with his showres soote

The manuscripts favor the spelling "Aprille,"* and a possible pronunciation of the word put the accent on the second syllable. Hence the line may read *Whán thăt Áprĭl*

---

* See Robert O. Evans, "Whan that Aprill(e)?," *Notes and Queries,* n.s. IV (1957), 234–37.

*wíth* . . . or *Whán thăt Ăprĭllĕ wíth* . . . (It may even read *Whán thăt Ăprĭllĕ wíth* . . . , for it is perfectly possible to have two short syllables in a metrical foot; here the *-e* would normally be dropped, but coming before the caesura it might have been pronounced in a very reduced way or as a plus-juncture.) For that matter we cannot be absolutely certain if Chaucer said *Whán thát* or *Whăn thát*. There are other variables as well. Some words may be pronounced in more than one way even in a single dialect (as was possibly the case with April/ Aprĭllĕ). Moreover, English has now, and likely had then, four degrees of stress, so that the "weak and strong" stresses of the verse support a more elaborate and variable stress according to the meaning of sentences and the emphasis a performer wants to give them. (Thus above there are maximum stresses on "April," "showres," and "soote.")\* Such interpretative emphasis sometimes affects a final *-e;* for example one can say *Yét hăd hé bŭt lítĕl góld ĭn cóffrĕ* (GP 298) or *Yĕt háddĕ hé* . . . The difference depends on whether you emphasize "yet" or "had," but if you emphasize "had" you need a weak syllable after it. Again, there is nothing to prohibit *two* weak syllables (*Yét háddĕ hé* . . .).

3. *Chaucer has six diphthongs.* A diphthong is two vowel sounds pronounced together as a continuing glide (not two letters in the spelling of a sound)—e.g., the "i" in modern *prize* is a diphthong ("ah-ee"), but "ea" in *meat* is not. In Modern English only some diphthongs are spelled with two letters; in Middle English nearly all were:

\* See M. Halle and S. J. Keyser, "Chaucer and the Study of Prosody," *College English,* XXVIII (1966), 187–219.

| Spelling | Middle English Example | Pronounced as in Modern English |
|---|---|---|
| ei, ey, ai, ay | vein, pain, may | "pie"; or better yet, a sound half way between "pie" and "pay": the vowel of "pat" plus the vowel of "be" |
| au, aw | cause, draw | "how" |
| ew | few, lewed, shew, beautee | the vowel of "bet" plus the vowel of "full." The sound occurs mainly in these four words. |
| ew, u | new, trew, knew cure | the vowel of "be" plus the vowel of "Luke." (Thus *cure* was pronounced as it is in Modern English.) |
| oi, oy | boy | "boy" |
| ou, ow | thought, know | the vowel of "ought" plus the vowel of "full" |

(Note: the spelling "ou" or "ow" was not always a diphthong, but sometimes a vowel pronounced like Modern English *root;* thus Middle English *house* would have been pronounced like "hoos.")

The ending -ion (-ioun) was always pronounced in two syllables.

4. *Pronounce vowels with their "continental" values,* as in German or French.

Vowels might be long or short. The distinction refers to the length of time they were held while pronounced, plus the quality of the sound (see chart below). Roughly, vowels were long in stressed syllables unless immediately followed by two or more consonants in the same word.*

---

* Exceptions: all vowels before *ld* are long, as are *i* and *o* before *mb*, and *i* and *u* before *nd*.

The spellings "e" and "o" each represent two vowel pronunciations, called "open" and "close" (referring to the relative position of the lips while articulating them). The following rules will decide which is which in most cases, though there are exceptions:

*Rule of thumb for close and open e*: go by the modern spelling. Words spelled with double *e* ("ee") in Modern English (or sometimes "ie" as in "thief") had close *e* in Middle English and were pronounced as in modern "bait"; other long *e*'s were open, and were pronounced as in modern "bed."

*Rule of thumb for close and open o:* go by the modern pronunciation. Words pronounced in Modern English like *hope, so,* etc. had open *o* in Middle English, and were pronounced as in modern "law"; other long *o*'s were close, and were pronounced as in modern "low."

The Middle English examples in the following table are from the opening lines of the General Prologue. The student would be well advised to memorize the famous lines as a means of practicing.

### LONG VOWELS

| Sound | | Middle English Example | Pronounced as in Modern English |
|---|---|---|---|
| | ā | bathed | "father" |
| close | ē | sweet | "bait" |
| open | ē | heeth | "bed" |
| | ī | inspired | "beet" |
| close | ō | roote | "low" |
| open | ō | open | "law" |
| | ū | shoures | "Luke" |
| [ü | | vertu | ; pronounced as in French *tu;* used for this vowel in words of French origin.] |

### SHORT VOWELS

| Sound | Middle English Example | Pronounced as in Modern English |
|---|---|---|
| ă | whan, hath | "part" |
| ĕ | { yonge hem | "even" "bet" |
| ĭ | his | "bit" |
| ŏ | londes, of | "bottle"* |
| ŭ | sunne | "full" |

## DISCOGRAPHY:

The only sure way to learn Chaucerian pronunciation is to hear it and imitate it. An excellent aid is phonograph records, of which there are a good many available. The present editor especially recommends the first two listed below. All are read in Middle English, and all but the last provide a printed text.

"Chaucer: The Canterbury Tales. The Prologue," read by Nevill Coghill, Norman Davis, John Burrow. Argo R G 401 (available in the US from McGraw-Hill).

"Chaucer: The Nun's Priest's Tale," read by John Burrow, Nevill Coghill, Lena Davis, Norman Davis. Includes also some of Chaucer's shorter poems. Argo R G 466 (available in the US from McGraw-Hill). [This and the preceding record are distinguished for the accuracy of the pronunciation and the excellence of the oral interpretation.]

"Chaucer: Two Canterbury Tales, the Miller's Tale and Reeve's Tale," read by J. B. Bessinger, Jr. Caedmon TC 1223.

"The Canterbury Tales," General Prologue, Prologue to the Parson's Tale, and Retraction, read by J. B. Bessinger, Jr. Caedmon TC 1151. [This and the preceding record are read with good scholarly accuracy but with rather less dramatic flair.]

* As pronounced in England and New England, i.e., rounded toward the sound in "bought," not as in American "bahttle."

"Chaucer's Canterbury Tales," the Nun's Priest's Tale and Pardoner's Tale, read by Robert Ross. Caedmon TC 1008. [The reader, an actor, gives a splendid performance; there are some mistakes in the pronunciation of Middle English, but they are easily overlooked.]

"Chaucer: Readings from 'Canterbury Tales'," General Prologue, Pardoner's Tale, Nun's Priest's Tale, and two shorter poems, read by Victor L. Kaplan. Folkways Records F L 9859. [Acceptable]

"A Thousand Years of English Pronunciation," a selection of readings by Helge Kökeritz. Educational Audio Visual, LE 7650/55. [Selections from *Beowulf* to the eighteenth century, illustrating the history of English pronunciation, read authoritatively by the great scholar of English phonology, though with a shadow of a Swedish accent. Contains a few selections from Chaucer.]

"Beowulf and Chaucer," read by Kökeritz and Pope. Educational Audio Visual, LE 5505. [Selections from General Prologue, Wife of Bath's Prologue, Prioress's Tale, *Troilus and Criseyde*—on one side of the record only.]

# CHRONOLOGY

| | |
|---|---|
| 1343 (?) | Born in London, son of John and Agnes Chaucer; had at least one sister, Catherine. Father and grandfather, wine merchants, both held public office, as Chaucer himself was to do. |
| | Schooling possibly at St. Paul's Cathedral School, London. By the time he reached maturity he knew Latin, French, and Italian. |
| 1357 | Served as a page in the household of Lionel, Earl of Ulster (the King's son) and Elizabeth, Countess of Ulster; this would have been a phase of his education. |
| 1359–60 | In France with the English army, was taken prisoner near Reims and released on ransom, to which the King contributed. Returned to England in May, then back to France during peace negotiations, serving as courier. |
| 1361–66 | Whereabouts unknown. He may have been for a time with Lionel in Ireland. He may also have been a student at the Inns of Court, where he would have received training in law and finance appropriate to his subsequent career as a public servant. |
| ? | Married Philippa Roet. They had a son Thomas, a younger son Lewis. There are records of an Elizabeth and an Agnes "Chaucy" in the circle of John of Gaunt, possibly daughters of the poet. |

1366    In Spain, probably on diplomatic mission.
1367    In the service of King Edward III; enrolled
        among the Esquires of the Royal Household.
        Beginning about this time and for the re-
        mainder of his life, Chaucer was in contact
        with the important people of his age, both
        on the continent and at home, among them
        the chief poets of his day.
1368    Abroad in the King's service.
1369    In France, in military service, probably with
        John of Gaunt on a campaign in Picardy.
        Throughout this period of his life Chaucer
        was under the protection of John of Gaunt.
        Gaunt's wife, the Duchess Blanche, died in
        this year; Chaucer's *Book of the Duchess*
        is an elegy to her.
1370    Abroad in the King's service.
        During these early years Chaucer wrote
        some of his shorter works, such as the *ABC*
        and lyrics based on French models. Prob-
        ably translated part of the *Romaunt of the
        Rose*.
1372–73 In Italy, to negotiate with Genoa about the
        use of an English port for commerce; visited
        Florence; undoubtedly bought some Italian
        books, among them Dante's *Divine Comedy*.
        From this period can be dated the influence
        of Italian literature on Chaucer. *The House
        of Fame* begun about this time, unfinished;
        *Anelida;* two tales later to show up in
        *Canterbury Tales* likely begun now—the
        legend of St. Cecilia (Second Nun's Tale)
        and the "tragedies" of the Monk's Tale.
1374    Took up residence in London at Aldgate
        (May).
        Appointed Controller of Customs and Sub-
        sidy of wools, skins, and hides in Port of
        London (June). Enjoyed great financial
        prosperity.

1376       On mission of secret service to the King.

1377       In Flanders on secret mission for the King; in France, in connection with negotiations for peace.

Coronation of Richard II (June 22). The new king confirmed Chaucer's office as Controller of Customs.

In France, evidently to negotiate a marriage between King Richard and the daughter of the King of France.

1378       In Italy (Lombardy) to secure help in the war with France. Probably from this trip he became acquainted with the work of Petrarch and Boccaccio.

1380       Released by one Cecily Chaumpaigne from legal action *"de raptu meo"*; it is not known whether *raptu* here means "rape" or "abduction" nor is it known what, if anything, Chaucer had to do with the case.

1380–86       *Parliament of Fowls* written; *Palamon* (the antecedent of the Knight's Tale); translation of Boethius. Was writing various poems and ballads and working on *Troilus and Criseyde*. Began *Legend of Good Women* possibly at request of the new queen, continued working on it for some years in a desultory way before abandoning it.

1382       Appointed Controller of the Petty Customs on wines and other merchandise.

1385       Received permission to have a deputy in the wool custom; appointed Justice of the Peace in Kent and took up at least partial residence there, probably at Greenwich.

1386–87       *Troilus and Criseyde* completed.

1386–89       Ended service in the Customs and left the house in Aldgate; the reason is unknown (the hostility of Gloucester toward the King's appointees has been suggested). Fell into debt.

1386        Appointed Knight of the Shire; sat in Par-
            liament only the one year, was not re-
            appointed. The office was evidently secured
            by the King's influence, but Gloucester and
            his adherents now began to gain control
            over the young King.

1387 (?)    Death of his wife.
            In Calais on official mission, its purpose
            unknown.
            During this period he was working on the
            General Prologue and the earlier Canterbury
            Tales. The idea of writing "some comedye"
            is mentioned at the end of *Troilus and
            Criseyde.*

1389–91     Richard II came of age; appointed Chaucer
            Clerk of the King's Works, an important
            office. He was in charge of royal palaces,
            chapels, parks, etc. Resigned commission in
            1391, his reason unknown. Had many work-
            men under him on various projects, handled
            large amounts of money. The government
            owed him a considerable sum when he
            turned in his accounts. In September 1390,
            was twice robbed and once assaulted by the
            same band of robbers, public funds being
            involved.

1391        Appointed Deputy Forester of the royal for-
            est of North Petherton; his son Thomas was
            later appointed to the same post.

1391–92     *Treatise on the Astrolabe.*

1393–1400   Worked on *The Canterbury Tales* plus a few
            minor poems, e.g., "Envoy to Bukton" (ca.
            1396), "Complaint to his Purse" (its envoy
            written in 1399, addressed to new King
            Henry IV). It is very difficult to determine
            the order in which *The Canterbury Tales*
            were written. Those written earlier were
            doubtless revised. Chaucer worked on a
            number of poems at once, leaving many

unfinished. There is evidence that he changed his mind several times about which pilgrim should tell which tale; and the order of the tales was never definitively settled.

1399    Coronation of Henry IV. Chaucer's annuities renewed, additional annuity of forty marks granted. Took long-term lease on house in garden of Westminster Abbey. Was engaged in "arduous and urgent matters" in the King's service.

1400    Died October 25; buried in "poet's corner," Westminster Abbey.

# SELECTED BIBLIOGRAPHY

### Editions

*Chaucer's Major Poetry.* Albert C. Baugh (ed.). New York: Appleton-Century-Crofts, 1963.

*Chaucer's Poetry: An Anthology for the Modern Reader.* E. Talbot Donaldson (ed.). New York: Ronald Press, 1958.

*The Text of the Canterbury Tales.* 8 vols. John M. Manly and Edith Rickert (eds.). Chicago: University of Chicago, 1940.

*The Works of Geoffrey Chaucer.* 2nd ed. F. N. Robinson (ed.). Boston: Houghton Mifflin, 1957.

### Collections

*Chaucer: Modern Essays in Criticism.* Edward Wagenknecht (ed.). New York: Oxford University Press, 1959.

*Chaucer Criticism: The Canterbury Tales.* Richard Schoeck and Jerome Taylor (eds.). Notre Dame, Ind.: University of Notre Dame Press, 1960.

*Discussions of the Canterbury Tales.* Charles A. Owen, Jr. (ed.). Boston: D. C. Heath and Company, 1961.

*Companion to Chaucer Studies.* Beryl Rowland (ed.). Toronto-New York-London: Oxford University Press, 1968.

*Chaucer and His Contemporaries: Essays on Medieval Literature and Thought.* Helaine Newstead (ed.). Greenwich, Conn.: Fawcett Publications, Inc., 1968.

*Chaucer's Mind and Art.* A. C. Cawley (ed.). Edinburgh and London: Oliver and Boyd, 1969.

Bibliography

*Chaucer.* Albert C. Baugh (comp.). New York: Appleton-Century-Crofts [in Goldentree Bibliographies in Language and Literature], 1968.

Criticism

Baldwin, Ralph. *The Unity of the Canterbury Tales.* (*Anglistica,* V). Copenhagen: Rosenkilde & Bagger, 1955.

Bowden, Muriel. *A Commentary on the General Prologue to the Canterbury Tales.* New York: Macmillan, 1948.

Bronson, Bertrand H. *In Search of Chaucer.* Toronto: University of Toronto Press, 1963.

*Chaucer Review: A Journal of Medieval Studies and Literary Criticism.* University Park, Pa.: Pennsylvania State University, 1966.

Coghill, Nevill. *The Poet Chaucer.* 2nd ed. London-New York-Toronto: Oxford University Press, 1967.

Cunningham, J. V. "The Literary Form of the Prologue to the *Canterbury Tales,*" *Modern Philology,* 49 (1952): 172–181.

Dempster, Germaine. *Dramatic Irony in Chaucer.* New York: Humanities Press, 1959 (reprint).

Donaldson, E. Talbot. "Chaucer the Pilgrim," *PMLA,* 69 (1954): 928–36.

Howard, Donald R. "Chaucer the Man," *PMLA,* 80 (1965): 337–43.

Jordan, Robert M. *Chaucer and the Shape of Creation.* Cambridge, Mass.: Harvard University Press, 1967.

Kellogg, Alfred L. "An Augustinian Interpretation of Chaucer's Pardoner," *Speculum,* 26 (1951): 465–81.

Muscatine, Charles. *Chaucer and the French Tradition.* Berkeley and Los Angeles: University of California, 1960.

Robertson, D. W., Jr. *A Preface to Chaucer.* Princeton, N.J.: Princeton University Press, 1962.

Ruggiers, Paul G. *The Art of the Canterbury Tales.* Madison and Milwaukee: University of Wisconsin Press, 1965.

Speirs, John. *Chaucer the Maker.* London: Faber & Faber, 1951.

## Language and Reference

Baugh, Albert C. *A History of the English Language.* 2nd ed. New York: Appleton-Century-Crofts, 1957.

Bryan W. F. and Dempster, Germaine. *Sources and Analogues of Chaucer's Canterbury Tales.* New York: The Humanities Press, 1958 (reprint).

Kökeritz, Helge. *A Guide to Chaucer's Pronunciation.* New York: Holt, Rinehart and Winston, 1961.

*Middle English Dictionary.* H. Kurath & S. Kuhn (eds.). Ann Arbor: University of Michigan, 1956– (in progress).

Mossé, Fernand. *A Handbook of Middle English.* James A. Walker (trans.). Baltimore: The Johns Hopkins Press, 1952.

Pyles, Thomas. *The Origins and Development of the English Language.* New York: Harcourt, Brace & World, 1964.

Tatlock, J. S. P. and Kennedy, A. G. *Concordance to the Complete Works of Geoffrey Chaucer.* Gloucester, Mass.: Peter Smith, 1963 (reprint).

### Collections of photographs

*Chaucer's World: A Pictorial Companion.* Maurice Hussey (ed.). Cambridge, England: Cambridge University Press, 1967.

*A Mirror of Chaucer's World.* Roger Sherman Loomis (ed.). Princeton, N.J.: Princeton University Press, 1965.

### Background

Bowden, Muriel. *A Reader's Guide to Geoffrey Chaucer.* New York: Noonday Press, 1966.

Brewer, D. S. *Chaucer in His Time.* London: Thomas Nelson, 1963.

Coulton, G. G. *Chaucer and His England.* New York: Russell & Russell, 1957 (reprint).

Curry, Walter Clyde, *Chaucer and the Mediaeval Sciences.* Rev. ed. New York: Barnes & Noble, 1960.

Hussey, Maurice, Spearing, A. C., and Winny, James. *An Introduction to Chaucer.* Cambridge, England: Cambridge University Press, 1965.

McKisack, M. *The Fourteenth Century, 1307–1399.* Oxford, England: Oxford University Press, 1959.

Rickert, Edith. *Chaucer's World.* C. C. Olsen and M. M. Crow (eds.). New York: Columbia University Press, 1948.

# SELECTED CANTERBURY TALES

# THE GENERAL PROLOGUE

Whan that April with his showres soote°
The drought of March hath perced to the roote
And bathed every vein in swich licour,°
Of which vertu° engendred is the flowr;
Whan Zephyrus,° eek,° with his sweete breeth          5
Inspired° hath in every holt and heeth°
The tender croppes,° and the yonge sunne
Hath in the Ram his halve course y-runne,°
And smalle fowles° maken melodye
That sleepen all the night with open ye          10
(So pricketh hem Nature in hir corages°),
Than longen folk to goon on pilgrimages,
And palmers for to seeken straunge strondes°
To ferne halwes,° kouth° in sundry londes:
And specially, from every shires ende          15
Of Engelond, to Canterbury they wende,
The holy blissful martyr° for to seeke
That hem hath holpen whan that they were seke.°

1 his showres soote its sweet showers   3 swich licour such moisture
4 of which vertu by whose power   5 Zephyrus the west wind, preva-
lent in spring according to tradition   5 eek also   6 Inspired
breathed into   6 holt and heeth wood and heath (i.e., land with
trees and land without trees)   7 croppes twigs   7–8 yonge sunne . . .
y-runne the sun at the beginning of its yearly course, past Aries
("the Ram"), the first sign of the Zodiac. "Half course" evidently
means the second half, which falls in April   9 fowles birds
11 corages hearts. So Nature urges them in their hearts to make
melody   13 palmers . . . strondes experienced pilgrims (long) to seek
out foreign shores   14 To ferne halwes to distant shrines   14 kouth
known   17 blissful martyr blessed martyr, St. Thomas à Becket,
murdered at Canterbury in 1170. As a saint he would be in eternal
"bliss." His shrine was the object of the most popular pilgrimage
18 seke sick

Befell that in that seson on a day,
20 In Southwerk at the Tabard° as I lay,
Redy to wenden° on my pilgrimage
To Canterbury, with full° devout corage,
At night was come into that hostelrye
Well nine and twenty° in a compaignye
25 Of sundry folk, by aventure° y-falle
In fellawship, and pilgrims were they alle
That toward Canterbury wolden° ride.
The chambres and the stables weren wide,°
And well we weren esed atte beste.°
30 And shortly, whan the sunne was to reste,
So had I spoken with hem everichon°
That I was of hir fellawship anon,°
And made forward° erly for to rise
To take our way, there as I you devise.°
35 But natheless,° while I have time and space,
Ere that I ferther in this tale pace,°
Me thinketh it accordant to resoun
To telle you all the condicioun°
Of ech of hem, so as it seemed me,
40 And which they weren, and of what degree,°
And eek in what array that they were inne;
And at a knight, than, wol° I first beginne:
A KNIGHT there was—and that a worthy man—
That fro the time that he first began
45 To riden out,° he loved chivalrye,

20 **Tabard** an inn in London just south of the Thames. It actually
existed. A tabard (short coat) would have been depicted on the
sign outside. The building burned down in 1676; there is a small
pub on the site today called by the same name  21 **wenden** go
22 **full** very  24 **well nine and twenty** as many as twenty-nine. There
would have been thirty pilgrims including Chaucer himself, but not
including the Host who tells no story (see line 814). By actual count
this makes twenty-nine, but the group is joined by the Canon's
Yeoman  25 **aventure** chance  27 **wolden** would, i.e., intended to
28 **wide** capacious  29 **well . . . beste** we were well entertained in
the best way  31 **with . . . everichon** with every one of them
32 **anon** right away  33 **And . . . forward** and (we) made an agree-
ment  34 **there . . . devise** as I shall describe for you  35 **natheless**
nevertheless  36 **pace** pass  38 **condicioun** position in society
40 **And . . . degree** and which was which, and of what social rank
42 **wol** will  45 **riden out** go on knightly expeditions, i.e., to wars,
crusades, etc.

Trouth and honour, freedom and curteisye.°
Full worthy was he in his lordes werre,°
And thereto had he riden, no man ferre,°
As well in Christendom as in hethenesse,°
And ever honoured for his worthinesse.                50
At Alisandre° he was whan it was wonne;
Full ofte time he had the bord bigonne°
Aboven alle naciouns in Pruce;°
In Lettow° had he reised,° and in Ruce°—
No Christen man so oft of his degree .              55
In Gernade° at the seege eek had he be
Of Algezir, and riden in Belmarye.°
At Lyeis° was he and at Satalye°
Whan they were won, and in the Greete See
At many a noble armee had he be.°                   60
At mortal battails had he been fifteene,
And foughten for our faith at Tramissene
In listes thries,° and ay slain his fo.
This ilke° worthy Knight had been also
Sometime with the lord of Palatye                   65
Again another hethen in Turkye.°

45–46 **chivalrye . . . curteisye** chivalry (the Knight's unwritten code
of conduct): truth (loyalty to one's obligations), honor (a sense of
honorable dealings), courtesy ("courtliness," observance of social
forms). The phrases sum up qualities ideally expected of knights
47 **werre** war   48 **ferre** farther   49 **hethenesse** lands governed by
heathens   51 **Alisandre** Alexandria; it was won in 1365. This and
the other campaigns mentioned had taken place within the past
forty-five years. All were religious campaigns against the infidels.
It is unlikely that Chaucer had an actual knight in mind: the pas-
sage seems rather to present an idealized portrait of a high-minded
adventurer   52 **the bord bigonne** sat at the head of a table, in the
place of honor, presumably with the Teutonic Knights during a
campaign against the pagans in Prussia   53 **Pruce** Prussia   54 **Let-
tow** Lithuania   54 **reised** fought   54 **Ruce** Russia   56 **Gernade**
Grenada. The campaign in 1344 resulted in the capture of the city
Algeciras from the Moors of Spain   57 **Belmarye** in north Africa
near modern Morocco   58 **Lyeis** near Antioch, won from the Turks
in 1367   58 **Satalye** Adalia   59–60 **Greete . . . he be** he had been
on many an armed expedition ("armada") in the Mediterranean
63 **listes thries** three times in single hand-to-hand combats (as a
champion representing his side). This may have been an old-fash-
ioned and romantic practice by Chaucer's time   64 **ilke** same
66 **another hethen in Turkye** the exact battle is not known. The line
may suggest an alliance of Christians with one heathen ruler against
another; but probably "another" means other than the army en-
countered at Tramissene

And evermore he had a sovereign pris;°
And though that he were worthy, he was wis,°
And of his port° as meek as is a maide.
70   He never yet no villainy ne saide
In all his life unto no manner wight.°
He was a veray, parfit gentil knight.°
     But for to tellen you of his array,
His horse were goode but *he* was not gay.°
75   Of fustian he werede a gipoun°
All bismotered with his habergeoun,°
For he was late y-come from his viage,
And wente for to doon his pilgrimage.
     With him there was his son, a yong SQUIER,°
80   A lover and a lusty° bacheler
With lockes crull° as they were laid in presse.°
Of twenty yeer of age he was, I guesse.
Of his stature he was of even° lengthe,
And wonderly deliver,° and of greet strengthe.
85   And he hadde been sometime in chivachye°
In Flandres, in Artois, and Picardye,
And born him well, as of so litel space,°
In hope to standen in his lady° grace.

67 **sovereign pris** distinctive excellence and renown   68 **though . . . wis** though he was valiant, he was prudent   69 **port** bearing   70–71 **He . . . wight** a very emphatic statement with its four negatives: "he never before said anything rude in his whole life to any person of any kind"   72 **veray, parfit gentil** true, perfect. "Gentle" has a broad meaning—the quality of a gentleman   74 **His . . . gay** his horses were good, but he himself was not fancily dressed   75 **gipoun** tunic worn under the coat of mail; "fustian" was cotton and linen   76 **habergeoun** coat of mail. It has stained (bismotered) the tunic underneath   79 **squier** squire—a "bachelor"—i.e., a young noble aspiring to knighthood. Squires were trained in a noble household not necessarily their father's. They learned all the arts pertinent to aristocracy, from the conventions of "courtly" love to the art of carving meat; but warfare was their principal concern   80 **lusty** vigorous   81 **crull** curly   81 **as . . . presse** as if they had been put in a hair-curler   83 **even** medium, average   84 **deliver** agile   85 **chivachye** expedition of cavalry. The places named in the next line suggest a so-called crusade of 1383, not entirely a reputable one because of plundering. This does not reflect on the Squire's character, but may suggest that knightly exploits were not what they used to be. The campaign was recent; the place was close to home and Flanders was somewhat of a joke, being a nation of burgers. In short, he had as yet little experience of great exploits   87 **as . . . space** considering how short a period of time was involved   88 **lady** lady's

Embrouded° was he, as it were a meede,°
All full of freshe flowres, white and rede;          *90*
Singing he was, or floiting,° all the day—
He was as fresh as is the month of May.
Short was his gown, with sleeves long and wide.
Well coud he sit on horse and faire° ride.
He coude songes make, and well endite,°          *95*
Joust, and eek daunce, and well purtray° and write.
So hot he loved that by nightertale°
He slept namore than doth a nightingale.°
Curteis he was, lowly,° and servicable,
And carf biforn his fader at the table.          *100*

  A YEMAN° had he and servants namo°
At that time, for him liste ride so°—
And he was clad in cote and hood of greene.
A sheef of pecock arrwes, bright and keene,°
Under his belt he bare full thriftily.°          *105*
Well coud he dress his tackle° yemanly:
His arrwes drouped not with fetheres lowe,
And in his hand he bare a mighty bowe.
A not-heed° had he with a brown visage.
Of woodecraft well koud° he all the usage.          *110*
Upon his arm he bare a gay bracer,°
And by his side a swerd and a buckler,
And on that other side a gay daggere,
Harneised° well and sharp as point of spere.
A Christophre° on his brest of silver sheene.          *115*

89 **Embrouded** embroidered   89 **as . . . meede** like a meadow.
There is a suggestion that he is dressed in an unusually sumptuous
way   91 **floiting** playing the flute, or perhaps whistling   94 **faire**
beautifully, well   95 **coude . . . endite** could write melodies and
compose words to them   96 **purtray** paint, draw   97 **nightertale**
nighttime   98 **nightingale** nightingales sing all night during the
mating season, hence are traditionally associated with lovers
99 **lowly** modest   101 **yeman** yeoman, a servant to the knight and
his son. He is above the rank of an ordinary servant and acts (see
line 117) as a forester or gamekeeper, perhaps having a small plot
of land for his own   101 **namo** no more   102 **for . . . so** for it
pleased him to ride in this way. *Liste* is an impersonal verb
104 **keene** sharp   105 **thriftily** carefully, properly   106 **dress his
tackle** take care of his arrows; the feathers are trim, which gives
them a clear flight   109 **not-heed** close-cut hair   110 **koud** knew
111 **bracer** leather guard for the forearm to protect it from the
bowstring   114 **Harneised** fastened to a handle   115 **Christophre**
medal of St. Christopher

An horn he bare, the baudrik° was of greene.
A forster° was he soothly, as I guesse.
   There was also a nun, a PRIORESSE,
That of hir smiling was full simple and coy.°
120 Hir greetest ooth was but by Seinte Loy;°
And she was cleped Madame Eglentine.
Full well she song the service divine,
Entuned in hir nose full seemely.
And French she spak full fair and fetisly,°
125 After the scole of Stratford-atte-Bowe—
For French of Paris was to hir unknowe.
At mete° well y-taught was she withalle:
She let no morsel from hir lippes falle,
Ne wet hir fingers in hir sauce deepe;
130 Well coud she carry a morsel, and well keepe°
That no drop ne fill upon hir brest.
In curteisy was set full muchel hir lest.°
Hir overlippe wiped she so clene
That in hir cup there was no ferthing° seene
135 Of grece, whan she drunken had hir draughte.
Full seemely after hir mete she raughte.°
And sikerly° she was of greet disport,°
And full plesaunt, and amiable of port;°
And pained hir to countrefete cheere
140 Of court,° and to been estatlich of mannere,°
And to been holden digne° of reverence.

116 **baudrik** baldric, a belt over one shoulder to hold his hunting-
horn   117 **forster** forester   119 **coy** modest   120 **Seinte Loy** St.
Elegius, called Eloy in French. St. Loy had once refused to swear,
so an oath by him was in effect no oath at all. He was also a fash-
ionable saint in elegant circles of the time. Note that the Prioress's
own name is very elegant (Eglentine means "sweetbriar"), as are
her table manners   124 **fetisly** fastidiously—but she speaks with an
English accent. The English upper class knew French   127 **mete**
meals. The following lines give a notion of medieval table manners
130 **keepe** see to it   132 **In . . . lest** her pleasure was very much set
on courtly conduct   134 **ferthing** tiny spot   136 **after hir mete she
raughte** she reached for her food   137 **sikerly** certainly   137 **dis-
port** affability   138 **amiable of port** pleasant in her conduct
139–40 **pained . . . court** took pains to emulate the manners of the
court   140 **estatlich of mannere** dignified in her behavior   141 **digne**
worthy

But, for to speken of hir conscience,°
She was so charitable and so pitous
She woldę weep if that she saw a mous
Caught in a trap, if it were deed or bleddę.          *145*
Of smallę houndęs° had she that she feddę
With rosted flesh, or milk and wastel breed;°
But sore wept shę if one of hem were deed,
Or if men smote it with a yerdę smertę.°
And all was conscience and tender hertę.          *150*

Full seemęly hir wimpel pinchęd was,°
Hir nose tretis,° hir eyen grey as glass,
Hir mouth full small, and thereto soft and red.
But sikerly she had a fair foreheed—
It was almost a spannę° brood, I trowę;          *155*
For hardily,° she was not undergrowę.
Full fetis° was hir cloke, as I was war.
Of small coral about hir arm she bar
A pair of bedęs, gauded all with greenę,°
And thereon heng a brooch of gold full sheenę,          *160*
On which there was first written a crownęd *A,*
And after, *Amor vincit omnia.*°
Another NUNNE with hir haddę she

---

142 **conscience** sensitivity    146 **Of smalle houndes** some little dogs.
"Of" is sometimes used in this partitive way    147 **wastel breed** a
fine bread; her dogs get nothing but the best    149 **with a yerde
smerte** with a stick sharply    151 **Full . . . was** her wimple (white
headpiece, going down about the face and neck) was pleated very at-
tractively. There is some question whether this was strictly according
to the rules. She wears it off her forehead, has colored beads, keeps
dogs, and owns a curious gold medal, all of which suggests a little
tendency toward self-indulgence. Lowes said she showed "the de-
lightfully imperfect submergence of the woman in the nun"
152 **tretis** graceful—a cliché for ladies' noses. The gray eyes, small
mouth, and wide forehead were also standard equipment for beau-
tiful women in medieval romances    155 **spanne** distance from
thumb to little finger when the hand is outstretched    156 **hardily**
certainly    157 **fetis** neat. Cf. line 124    159 **bedes . . . greene** she
wears a rosary made of small bits of coral; the larger beads are
green    162 **Amor vincit omnia** "Love conquers all." Whether this
meant celestial love or earthly love was probably no clearer to the
Prioress than to us. At any rate, courtly love was aristocratic. The
"crowned A" is likely a royal emblem but otherwise mysterious;
one conjecture is that the brooch was a medallion struck for the
coronation of Queen Anne (1382)

That was hir chapeleyne, and preestes three.°
165   A MONK there was, a fair for the maistrye°—
An outrider, that loved venerye;°
A manly man, to been an abbot able.
Full many a daintee° horse had he in stable,
And whan he rode men might his bridle heere
170   Ginglen in a whistling wind as clere
And eek as loud as doth the chapel belle.
Ther as° this lord was keeper of the celle,°
The rule of Saint Maure or of Saint Beneit,°
By cause that it was old and somedeel strait°—
175   This ilke Monk let olde thinges pace
And held after the newe world the space.°
He yaf not of that text a pulled hen°
That saith that hunters been not holy men,
Ne that a monk, whan he is reccheless,°
180   Is likned til a fish that is waterless
(This is to sayn, a monk out of his cloistre);
But thilke° text held he not worth an oystre.

164 **chapeleyne . . . three** the "chapeleyne" is an assistant accom-
panying her—the "second nun," who tells the legend of St. Cecilia.
One priest is the "Nun's Priest" (or perhaps "Nuns' Priest") who
tells the tale of Chanticleer. The extra two priests would put the
number of pilgrims up to thirty-one (see line 24); however, "preestes
three" could mean the Nun's Priest plus the Monk and Friar, whose
descriptions follow   165 **fair for the maistrye** a fine one, excellent
above all others   166 **outrider . . . venerye** one whose duty was to
ride about tending the property of the abbey; that he loved "venerye"
(hunting) suggests an abuse, for hunting by monks was condemned.
Hunting was an aristocratic sport, and the Monk's love of horses
and fine clothes is altogether questionable. There is also a sexual
suggestion, for "hunting" may hint at hunting women, as "venerye"
may suggest Venus   168 **daintee** splendid, valuable   172 **Ther as**
where   172 **keeper of the celle** prior of a smaller monastery sub-
ordinate to a great abbey   173 **The rule . . . Beneit** St. Benedict,
and St. Maur (his disciple), had written the oldest monastic rules.
The line suggests that the monk is a Benedictine   174 **somedeel
strait** somewhat strict   175–76 **let . . . space** let old things (like the
rule of St. Benedict) pass, and took up with the new world in the
meantime   177 **pulled hen** "he didn't give a plucked hen for that
text which says . . ." Cf. line 182. A plucked hen would be of little
value to him, compared with a fat swan (line 206)   179 **reccheless**
careless (of his duties)   182 **thilke** that

And I said his opinion was good:°
What° shold he study and make himselven wood°
Upon a book in cloistre alway to poure,                    185
Or swinken° with his handes and laboure,
As Austin bit?° How shall the world be served?
Let Austin have his swink to him reserved!
Therefore he was a prickasour° aright.
Greyhounds he had as swift as fowl in flight.              190
Of pricking and of hunting for the hare°
Was all his lust,° for no cost wold he spare.
I saw his sleeves y-purfiled at the hand
With gris,° and that the finest of a land;
And for to festne° his hood under his chin                 195
He had of gold wrought a full curious pin—
A love-knot in the greeter end there was.
His heed was bald, that shone as any glass,
And eek his face, as he had been anoint.
He was a lord full fat and in good point:°                 200
His eyen steep,° and rolling in his heed,
That stemed as a furnais of a leed,°
His bootes souple, his horse in greet estat—
Now certainly he was a fair prelat.
He was not pale as a forpined° ghost;                      205
A fat swan loved he best of any rost.
His palfrey° was as brown as is a berrye.
    A FRERE° there was, a wanton and a merrye,

183 I . . . good here the reader begins to see that Chaucer's role
as a wide-eyed, enthusiastic observer is ironic. Obviously Chaucer
did not approve of these abuses   184 What why   184 wood mad
186 swinken work   187 As Austin bit as St. Augustine commands
189 prickasour hard rider; but doubtless it is a pun   191 pricking
. . . hare pricking was tracking a rabbit by his prints ("pricks");
since rabbits were symbols of lechery and hunting was open to dou-
ble meaning, there is doubtless a pun here as well   192 lust pleasure
193–94 y-purfiled . . . with gris edged with expensive fur   195 festne
fasten   200 in good point in good shape   201 steep sparkling
202 stemed . . . leed sparkled like a fire under a cooking-pot
205 forpined pined away, wasted   207 palfrey riding horse
208 Frere friar. There were four mendicant orders—the Dominicans
("Blackfriars"), Franciscans ("Greyfriars"), Carmelites ("White-
friars"), and Augustinian friars ("Austin" friars, who also wore
black). Unlike monks, who remained in cloisters, the friars went
among the people, begging for their sustenance; all surplus was
given to the poor and sick. The noble idea—that of St. Francis—
easily lent itself to abuse, and by Chaucer's time friars were widely
criticized

A limitour,° a full solempne° man.
210 In all the orders four is none than kan°
So much of daliaunce° and fair langage.
He hadde made full many a marriage
Of yonge women at his owne cost;°
Unto his ordre he was a noble post.
215 Full well beloved and familier was he
With frankelains° over all in his contree,
And with worthy women of the town.
For he had power of confessioun
As said himself, more than a curat,
220 For of his ordre he was licenciat.°
Full sweetly herde he confessioun
And plesant was his absolucioun;
He was an esy man to yive penaunce
There as he wist to have a good pitaunce.°
225 For unto a povre ordre for to yive
Is signe that a man is well y-shrive:°
For if he yaf, he dorste make avaunt,°
He wiste that a man was repentaunt;
For many a man so hard is of his herte
230 He may not weep although him sore smerte:
Therefore, instede of weeping and prayeres,
Men mote° yive silver to the povre freres.
     His tippet was ay farsed° full of knives
And pinnes, for to yiven faire wives.
235 And certainly he had a murry note:°

209 **limitour** friar with the assigned right to beg in a partic-
ular district ("limit")   209 **solempne** impressive   210 **kan** knows
211 **daliaunce** chitchat, usually flirtatious   212–13 **made . . . cost**
arranged many a marriage of young women free of charge; the
line implies that he seduced them first   216 **frankelains** wealthy
landowners   220 **licenciat** his power of hearing confessions; this
license given to friars put them in conflict with parish priests
(curates) because it deprived the latter of some revenue. It is true
that friars had power to absolve certain serious sins which a parish
priest would normally refer to the bishop   224 **There as . . .
pitaunce** where he knew he would get a good donation; hence he
is nice to people when they confess, doesn't scold them, and gives
easy penances   226 **y-shrive** confessed   227 **dorste make avaunt**
dared to state   232 **mote** should   233 **tippet was ay farsed** hood
was always stuffed   235 **murry note** fine singing voice

Well coud he sing and playen on a rote;°
Of yeddings he bare outrely the pris.°
His necke white was as the flowr-de-lis.
Thereto he strong was as a champioun.
He knew the taverns well in every town, 240
And every hostiler and tappestere,°
Bet than a lazar or a beggestere.°
For unto swich a worthy man as he
Accorded not, as by his facultee,°
To have with sike lazars acquaintaunce: 245
It is not honest, it may not avaunce,°
For to deelen with no swich poraille,°
But all with rich, and sellers of vitaille!
And over all there as profit shold arise—
Curteis he was, and lowly of servise.° 250
    There was no man nowhere so vertuous;
He was the beste begger in his hous.
For though a widow hadde not a shoe,
So plèsant was his *In principio*°
Yet wold he have a ferthing ere he wente. 255
His purchase was well better than his rente.°
And rage he coud as it were right a whelpe!°
In love-days° there coud he muchel helpe,
For there he was not like a cloisterer,
With a thredbare cope,° as is a poor scholer, 260
But he was like a maister° or a pope.
Of double worsted was his semicope,
That rounded as a bell out of the presse.

---

236 **rote** stringed instrument played by plucking   237 **Of yeddings
. . . pris** for popular songs he won the prize hands down   241 **hos-
tiler and tappestere** innkeeper and barmaid   242 **Bet . . . beggestere**
better than a leper or a beggar-woman   244 **as by his facultee** for a
man of his position   246 **It . . . avaunce** it isn't respectable, it
won't get you anywhere   247 **poraille** poor people, "rabble"
249–50 **And . . . servise** and in all places where profit would
arise. . . . Note that the last phrase is used of the Squire (line 99)
254 **In principio** first words of the Gospel according to St. John,
a great favorite of friars when entering a house   256 **His . . . rente**
(?) what he got in these questionable ways was much better than
what he got legitimately   257 **And . . . whelp** And he could live
it up just like a puppy   258 **love-days** days for settling disputes out
of court; friars often acted as arbiters   260 **cope** cloak   261 **mais-
ter** the master's degree had enormous prestige then

Somewhat he lipsed for his wantounesse°
265 To make his English sweet upon his tonge.
And in his harping, whan that he had songe,
His eyen twinkled in his heed aright
As doon the sterres in the frosty night.
This worthy limitour was cleped Huberd.

270    A MARCHANT was there with a forked beerd,°
In motlee,° and hy° on horse he sat;
Upon his heed a Flandrish bever hat,°
His bootes clasped fair and fetisly.
His resons° he spak full solempnely,°
275 Souning alway the encrees of his winning.°
He wold the see were kept for any thing°
Bitwixe Middleburgh and Orewelle.
Well coud he in eschaunge sheeldes selle.°
This worthy man full well his wit bisette;°
280 There wiste no wight that he was in dette,°
So estatly was he of his governaunce°
With his bargains and with his chevisaunce.°
Forsooth he was a worthy man withalle.
But, sooth to sayn, I noot° how men him calle.

---

264 lipsed . . . wantounesse lisped as a fetching mannerism. Lisping,
like a white neck (line 238), was thought to suggest lechery
270 forked beerd the "forked" beard was a fashionable shape for
the bourgeoisie. Chaucer himself wore one 271 motlee cloth
woven in a pattern, perhaps a special one denoting the guild of
merchants he belonged to 271 hy high, in a high saddle
272 Flandrish bever hat Flemish hat of beaver fur    274 resons
views   274 solempnely impressively, pompously    275 Souning . . .
winning always touching upon the increase in his profits   276 He
. . . thing he wanted the sea to be kept safe at all costs. . . . The
route was between the Netherlands and Suffolk; the cargo would
have been wool; and the danger was from pirates    278 Well . . .
selle he well knew how to sell Crowns in the money exchanges.
"Shields" were gold coins; the merchant made profit on differences
in the rate of exchange. The practice was illegal    279 his wit bi-
sette used his head    280 There . . . dette no one knew that he was
in debt. (Or, perhaps, "No one knew how much he was in debt")
281 estatly . . . governaunce dignified (i.e., discreet) in doing busi-
ness    282 chevisaunce money-lending    284 noot ne wot, i.e., don't
know

A CLERK° there was of Oxenford also                    285
That unto logic hadde long y-go.°
As leene was his horse as is a rake,
And he was not right fat, I undertake,
But looked hollwe, and thereto sobrely.°
Full thredbare was his overest courtepy°—             290
For he had geten him yet no benefice,
Ne was so worldly for to have office;°
For him was lever have° at his beddes heed
Twenty bookes,° clad in black or red,
Of Aristotle and his philosophye,                      295
Than robes rich, or fithel, or gay sautrye.°
But all be that he was a philosophre°
Yet hadde he but litel gold in coffre;
But all that he might of his freendes hente,°
On bookes and on lerning he it spente,                 300
And bisily gan for the soules praye
Of hem that yaf him wherewith to scholeye.°
Of study° took he most cure and most heede.
Not oo word spak he more than was neede,
And that was said in form and reverence,°             305
And short and quick,° and full of heigh sentence;°
Souning in moral vertu was his speeche;°
And gladly wold he lern and gladly teeche.

A SERGEANT OF THE LAWE,° war° and wis,
310 That often hadde been at the Parvis°
There was also, full rich of excellence.
Discreet he was, and of greet reverence—
He seemed swich, his wordes weren so wise.
Justice he was full often in assise
315 By patent and by plein commissioun.°
For his science° and for his heigh renown
Of fees and robes° had he many oon.
So greet a purchasour was nowhere noon;
All was fee simple to him in effect—
320 His purchasinge might not been infect.°
Nowhere so bisy a man as he there nas;
And yet he seemed bisier than he was.
In termes had he caas and doomes alle°
That from the time of King William were falle.
325 Thereto he coud endite and make a thing,°
There coud no wight pinchen at° his writing;
And every statute koud he plein by rote.°
He rode but homely in a medlee° cote,
Girt with a ceint° of silk, with barres° smalle.
330 Of his array tell I no lenger tale.

309 **Sergeant of the lawe** a very high office. About twenty were
appointed by the King, and from their number were selected the
chief baron of the Exchequer, the judges of the King's court, and
the circuit judges. The portrait is sometimes thought to be a per-
sonal satire of Thomas Pynchbek, Justice of Common Pleas from
1391 to 1396  309 **war** wary, cautious  310 **Parvis** a porch of
St. Paul's Cathedral at which lawyers met for consultation
314–15 **Justice . . . commissioun** the Justices in Assise were cir-
cuit judges who presided in county courts. *By patent* refers to the
"letters patent" from the King making an appointment, and *plein
commissioun* was a statement of full (plein) jurisdiction  316 **sci-
ence** knowledge  317 **robes** robes, often very rich ones, were a
form of payment; the King often granted robes to public servants
319–20 **fee simple . . . infect** he purchased land for himself in "fee
simple"—i.e., having outright ownership which would descend to
all his heirs male or female; with his legal knowledge his purchas-
ing could not be invalidated (*infect*)  323 **In . . . alle** he could reel
off all the cases and decisions . . . (but "terms" may refer to annual
law books which he owned)  325 **Thereto . . . thing** moreover, he
could draft and draw up a legal document  326 **pinchen at** find a
loophole in. The line may be a sly reference to Thomas Pynchbek
327 **koud . . . rote** he knew entirely by memory  328 **medlee** woolen
cloth, dyed first and then woven in a pattern. His would have been
striped in brown and green  329 **ceint** cincture, sash  329 **barres**
metal bars to keep the sash from bunching up

A FRANKELAIN° was in his compaignye.
White was his beerd as is the dayesye;
Of his complexion he was sanguin.°
Well loved he by the morrwe° a sop in win.°
To liven in delit was ever his wone,°                          335
For he was Epicurus' owne sone,
That held opinion that plein delit
Was veray felicitee parfit.°
An householder and that a greet was he—
Saint Julian° he was in his contree.                           340
His breed, his ale, was always after oon°—
A better envined° man was never noon.
Withoute bake mete° was never his hous,
Of fish and flesh, and that so plentevous°
It snowed in his house of mete° and drinke—                    345
Of alle daintees that men coude thinke.
After the sundry sesons of the yeer
So chaunged he his mete° and his supper.
Full many a fat partrich had he in muwe,°
And many a breem, and many a luce in stuwe;°                    350
Woe was his cook but if° his sauce were
Poignant and sharp, and redy all his gere.°
His table dormant in his hall° alway
Stood redy covered all the longe day.

At sessions there was he lord and sire.°                       355
Full ofte time he was knight of the shire.°

331 **Frankelain** Franklins were landowners, the ancestors of "country squires." Their social position was high   333 **sanguin** in medieval medical theory a sanguine complexion, resulting from the dominance of blood over the three other bodily humors, made for a bold, outgoing character   334 **by . . . morrwe** in the morning   334 **sop in wine** (Fr. *soupe*) a cake in wine sauce—a delicacy   335 **wone** habit   336–38 **For . . . parfit** Epicurus was thought, wrongly, to have believed in a life of pleasure   340 **St. Julian** patron saint of hospitality   341 **after oon** of the same high quality   342 **envined** possessing a wine cellar   343 **bake mete** meat baked in pies—another delicacy   344 **plentevous** plentiful   345 **mete** here, "food"   348 **mete** here, "dinner." Changing diet by seasons was considered posh   349 **muwe** cage   350 **breme . . . stuwe** carp and pike in a private fish pond   351 **but if** unless   352 **gere** equipment, such as knives   353 **table dormant** a dining table set up in the main room (hall). Also posh; tables were usually removable   355 **sessions . . . sire** he presided over sessions of the Justices of the Peace   356 **knight of the shire** member of Parliament

An anlaas, and a gipser° all of silk
Heng at his girdle, white as morne milk.
A shireve° had he been, and a contour.°
360 Was nowhere swich a worthy vavasour.°

An HABERDASHER and a CARPENTER,
A WEBBE, a DYER, and a TAPICER°—
And they were clothed all in oo liveree°
Of a solempne and a greet fraternitee.
365 Full fresh and new hir gere apiked° was;
Hir knives were chaped° not with brass
But all with silver; wrought full clene and well
Hir girdles and hir pouches everydeel.
Well seemed ech of hem a fair burgeis
370 To sitten in a yeldhall on a dais.°
Everich, for the wisdom that he kan,
Was shaply for to been an alderman.°
For catel hadde they enough and rente,°
And eek hir wives wold it well assente,
375 And elles certain were they to blame:
It is full fair to been y-cleped "Madame,"
And goon to vigilies all bifore,°
And have a mantel royalich y-bore!

A COOK they hadde with hem for the nones,
380 To boil the chickens with the marybones,°
And powdre-marchant tart, and galingale.°
Well coud he know a draught of London ale.
He coude rost, and seeth,° and broil, and frye,

---

357 **anlaas, and a gipser** dagger and pouch   359 **shireve** shire-
reeve, i.e., sheriff: the King's administrator in a county   359 **con-
tour** (?) auditor; part of a sheriff's duties was to collect taxes
and account for them   360 **vavasour** minor nobleman, or any man
of substance   361–62 **Habadasher . . . tapicer** the "Five Gildsmen"
are of different trades—haberdasher, a dealer in small goods;
webbe, a weaver; tapicer, a rug-maker   363 **oo liveree** one livery:
the costume presumably of a parish trade guild   365 **apiked** fixed
up   366 **chaped** ornamented   369–70 **burgeis . . . dais** a burgess
good enough to preside (as an alderman) in a guildhall   372 **alder-
man** a burgess had to own a certain amount of property to be an
alderman, i.e., head of a guild and member of a town council
373 **catel . . . and rente** property and income   377 **vigilies . . . bi-
fore** religious ceremonies on the eve of a holy day; marching at the
head of a procession was an honor, and their wives are great social
climbers   380 **marybones** ˉ marrow bones   381 **powdre-marchant
tart, galingale** spices   383 **seeth** boil

Maken mortreux,° and well bake a pie.°
But greet harm was it, as it thoughte me,          385
That on his shin a mormal° hadde he.
For blankmanger,° that made he with the beste.
   A SHIPMAN° was there, woning fer by weste°—
For aught I wot, he was of Dertemouthe.
He rode upon a rouncy as he kouthe,°          390
In a gown of falding° to the knee.
A dagger hanging on a laas had he
About his neck, under his arm adown.
The hot summer had made his hew all brown.
And certainly he was a good fellawe!          395
Full many a draught° of wine had he drawe
Fro Bourdeux-ward, while that the chapman sleep.°
Of nice conscience took he no keep.
If that he fought and had the higher hand,
By water he sent hem home to every land.°          400
   But of his craft—to recken well his tides,
His stremes and his daungers him bisides,
His herberwe° and his moon, his lodemenage°—
There nas none swich from Hulle to Cartage.
Hardy he was and wise to undertake.°          405
With many a tempest had his beerd been shake.
He knew alle the havens as they were
Fro Gotland to the Cape of Finistere,
And every crike in Brittain and in Spaine.
His barge y-cleped was the Maudelaine.          410
   With us there was a DOCTOR OF PHYSIC;°
In all this world ne' was there none him lik
To speke of physic and of surgerye.

---

384 **mortreux** a hash or stew    384 **pie** meat pie    386 **mormal** an open sore—unappetizing, but its unsanitary aspects could have been overlooked    387 **blankmanger** a main dish of capon    388 **Shipman** owner and captain of a ship    388 **woning . . . weste** who lived far in the west (Dartmouth was a major port)    390 **rode . . . kouthe** rode on a small horse as best he could    391 **falding** wool    396 **draught** a quantity drawn from the cask, probably for drinking    397 **while . . . sleep** while the merchant slept. The merchant sometimes traveled with the cargo; his sleeping could afford a chance for theft, or at least a drink, from the cargo of wine    400 i.e., he threw his prisoners overboard    403 **herberwe** harbor    403 **lodemenage** navigation    405 **to undertake** in his ventures and risks    411 **physic** medicine

For he was grounded in astronomye;°
415 He kept° his pacient a full greet deel
In houres by his magic naturel;°
Well coud he fortunen the ascendent
Of his images° for his pacient.
He knew the cause of every maladye,
420 Were it of hot or cold, or moist or drye,°
And where engendred and of what humour.
He was a veray parfit practisour.
The cause y-know,° and of his harm the roote,
Anon he yaf the sike man his boote.°
425 Full redy had he his apothecaries
To send him drugges and his letuaries,°
For ech of hem made other for to winne;°
Hir frendship nas not newe to beginne.
Well knew he the old Esculapius,°
430 And Deiscorides and eek Rufus,
Old Ipocras, Hali, and Galien,
Serapion, Razis, and Avicen,
Averrois, Damascien, and Constantin,
Bernard, and Gatesden, and Gilbertin.
435 Of his diete mesurable was he,
For it was of no superfluitee
But of greet norishing and digestible.
His study was but litel on the Bible.
In sanguine and in pers° he clad was all,
440 Lined with taffata and with sendal.°

414 **astronomye** astrology was part of medieval medicine    415 **kept**
watched—waiting for the propitious astrological time for treatment
416 **magic naturel** astrology and related sciences    417–18 **fortunen
. . . images** making projections of constellations, signs of the zodiac,
etc. ("images") which had favorable influences; used in treatment
(See Curry, *Chaucer and the Medieval Sciences*, Chapt. l.)    420 **hot
. . . drye** the basic qualities, found in pairs in the four elements and
the four bodily humors, as well as in planets and diseases. The
balance of bodily humors was a major principle of medical prac-
tice    423 **y-know** known    424 **boote** cure    426 **letuaries** medici-
nal syrups    427 **ech . . . winne** then, as now, doctors and phar-
macists were sometimes in collusion for mutual profit    429 **Escu-
lapius** this and the list following were the great medical authorities
of the ancient world and the Middle Ages; the last three were
Englishmen of the mid-fourteenth century    439 **sanguine, pers**
bright red, blue-gray    440 **taffata, sendal** kinds of silk

And yet he was but esy of dispence.°
He kepte that he won in pestilence;°
For gold in physic is a cordial°—
Therefore he loved gold in special.
 A good WIFE was there OF biside BATHE,°     445
But she was somedeel deef, and that was scathe.°
Of cloth-making she hadde swich an haunt,°
She passed hem of Ypres and of Gaunt.°
In all the parish wife ne was there noon
That to the offring before hir shold goon°—     450
And if there did, certain so wroth° was she
That she was out of alle charitee.
Hir coverchiefs full fine were of ground°—
I dorste swere they weyeden ten pound
That on a Sunday weren upon hir heed!     455
Hir hosen weren of fine scarlet red,
Full strait y-teyd,° and shoes full moist and newe.
Bold was hir face, and fair, and red of hewe.
She was a worthy woman all hir live.
Husbands at chirche door° she hadde five,     460
Withouten° other compaigny in youthe
—But thereof needeth not to speke as nouthe.°
 And thries had she been at Jerusalem.
She hadde passed many a straunge streem—
At Rome she hadde been, and at Bologne,     465
In Galice at Saint Jame, and at Cologne.°

441 esy of dispence cautious in spending     442 pestilence plague
(The Black Plague hit England in 1348, 1362, 1369, and 1376)
443 cordial medicinal stimulant; powdered gold was actually used
as a medicine. It was also sometimes added to prescriptions in
small amounts to raise their price     445 biside Bathe a suburb of
Bath, probably St. Michael's. Chaucer may have passed through
the town often. Some hold that the portrait is based on a living
model because of its minute particularity     446 scathe too bad. The
reason for her deafness is explained in her prologue     447 haunt
skill     448 Ypres, Gaunt Ypres and Ghent were centers of the
Flemish wool trade     450 offring . . . goon a mark of prestige
451 wroth annoyed     453 Hir coverchiefs . . . ground her kerchiefs
were of a very fine texture. They were worn over wire frames
457 strait y-teyd tightly tied     460 chirche door the marriage cere-
mony was performed on the church porch, after which the couple
went to the altar for mass     461 Withouten not to mention     462 as
nouthe right now     462-66 Jerusalem . . . Cologne the great pil-
grimages of the later Middle Ages

She koude° much of wandring by the waye:
Gat-toothed° was she, soothly for to saye.
Upon an ambler° esily she sat,
470  Y-wimpled well, and on hir heed an hat
As brood as is a buckeler or a targe,°
A foot-mantel° about hir hippes large,
And on hir feet a pair of spures sharpe.
In fellawship well coud she laugh and carpe.°
475  Of remedies of love she knew parchaunce,
For she koud of that art the olde daunce.°

   A good man was there of religioun,
And was a povre PERSON° of a town—
But rich he was of holy thought and werk.
480  He was also a lerned man, a clerk,
That Christes gospel trewly wolde preche.
His parishens° devoutly wold he teche.
Benign he was, and wonder diligent,
And in adversitee full pacient,
485  And swich he was y-preved ofte sithes.
Full loth were him to cursen for his tithes,°
But rather wold he yiven, out of doute,
Unto his povre parishens aboute
Of his offring and eek of his substaunce;°
490  He coud in litel thing have suffisaunce.
Wide was his parish, and houses fer asunder,
But he ne lafte nought° for rain ne thunder,
In sickness nor in meschief, to visite
The ferrest° in his parish, much and lite,
495  Upon his feet, and in his hand a staff.

---

467 **koude** knew. The line has an obvious double meaning    468 **gat-
toothed** having a space between the two front teeth; it was thought
a sign of a bold, lascivious character    469 **ambler** horse intended
for "ambling," as opposed to a palfrey for faster riding, a courser
for warfare, etc.    471 **buckeler, targe** kinds of shields    472 **foot-
mantel** outer skirt    474 **carpe** joke    476 **olde daunce** all the
wheeling and dealing of love; a distinctly sexual reference, like
"remedies of love," which suggests Ovid's *Remedia Amoris*
478 **person** parson, parish priest    482 **parishens** parishioners, con-
gregation    486 **Full . . . tithes** it was very disagreeable to him to
excommunicate anyone for nonpayment of tithes    489 **Of . . .
substaunce** what he got from voluntary contributions and from the
income of his benefice    492 **ne lafte nought** did not fail    494 **fer-
rest** farthest

This noble ensample to his sheep he yaf:
That first he wrought, and afterward he taughte.
Out of the Gospel he tho° wordes caughte.
And this figure he added eek thereto:
That "if gold ruste, what shold iren do?"                500
For if a preest be foul, on whom we truste,
No wonder is a lewed° man to ruste!
And shame it is, if a preest take keep—
A shitten° shepherd and a clene sheep!
Well ought a preest ensample for to yive                505
By his clennesse how that his sheep shold live.

He sette not his benefice to hire,
And let his sheep encumbred in the mire,
And ran to London unto Sainte Poules,
To seeken him a chaunterye for soules,                510
Or with a bretherheed to been withholde;°
But dwelt at home and kepte well his folde,
So that the wolf ne made it not miscarrye.
He was a shepherd, and not a mercenarye.
And though he holy were and vertuous,                515
He was to sinful men not despitous,°
Ne of his speeche daungerous ne digne;°
But in his teeching discreet and benigne,
To drawen folk to heven by fairnesse,
By good ensample—this was his bisinesse.                520
But it were any person° obstinat,
What so he were, of heigh or low estat,
Him wold he snibben° sharply for the nones.
A better preest I trow there nowhere none is!
He waited after no pomp and reverence,                525
Ne maked him a spiced conscience,°
But Christes lore and his apostles' twelve
He taught—but first he followed it himselve.

498 **tho** those    502 **lewed** simple    504 **shitten** dirty    507–11 **He . . .**
**withholde** a common practice of the day, much criticized: priests
sublet their landholding and made further money praying for the
soul of a rich patron in an endowed chantry, or being retained
(*withholde*) by a guild as their chaplain    516 **despitous** con-
temptuous    517 **daungerous ne digne** withdrawn or unapproach-
able    521 **it were any person** if any person were    523 **snibben** rep-
rimand    526 **spiced conscience** touchy awareness

With him there was a PLOWMAN,° was his brother,
530 That had y-lad of dung full many a fother.°
A trewe swinker° and a good was he,
Living in pees and parfit charitee.
God loved he best with all his hoole herte
At alle times, though him gamed or smerte,°
535 And than his neighebor right as himselve.
He wolde thresh, and thereto dike and delve,°
For Christes sake, for every povre wight,
Withouten hire, if it lay in his might.
His tithes payde he full fair and well,
540 Both of his propre swink and his catel.°
In a tabard he rode upon a mere.°
    There was also a Reeve and a Millere,
A Somnour and a Pardoner also,
A Manciple and myself; there were namo.
545    The MILLER was a stout carl° for the nones.
Full big he was of brawn and eek of bones:
That proved well, for overall there he cam
At wrastling he wold have alway the ram.°
He was short-shouldred, brood—a thicke knarre.°
550 There was no door that he nold heve off harre,°
Or breke it at a renning with his heed.
His beerd as any sow or fox was red,
And thereto brood, as though it were a spade.
Upon the cop° right of his nose he hadde
555 A wert,° and thereon stood a tuft of heeres,
Red as the bristles of a sowes eres.
His nosethirles° blacke were and wide.

---

529 **Plowman** the plowman was a stock figure for the good simple laborer—*Piers Plowman* is the locus classicus    530 **fother** cartload    531 **trewe swinker** honest worker    534 **though . . . smerte** whether in joy or trouble    536 **dike and delve** dig ditches and dig in general    540 **propre . . . catel** i.e., on his own work and on his possessions    541 **mere** mare, ridden by poor folk    545 **stout carl** thick-set fellow. This and the other details about him are based on the medieval science of physiognomy, a phase of medicine and astrology; they denote a shameless, noisy, lecherous character    547–48 **overall . . . ram** wherever he showed up he would always win the first prize (traditionally a ram) in wrestling matches    549 **knarre** knotty—"a thick, muscular fellow"    550 **heve off harre** pull off its hinges    554 **cop** tip (or, perhaps, bridge)    555 **wert** wart—probably a mole    557 **nosethirles** nostrils

A swerd and buckeler bare he by his side.
His mouth as greet was as a greet furnais.
He was a jangler and a goliardais°—          560
And that was most of sin and harlotries.°
Well coud he stelen corn and tollen thries°—
And yet he had a thumb of gold,° pardee.
A white cote and a blue hood wered he.
A baggepipe° well coud he blow and soune,   565
And therewithal he brought us out of towne.

A gentil MANCIPLE was there of a temple,°
Of which achatours° mighte take exemple
For to be wise in buying of vitaille:
For whether that he paid or took by taille,°  570
Algate he waited so in his achat°
That he was ay biforn° and in good stat!
Now is not that of God a full fair grace
That swich a lewed mannes wit shall pace
The wisdom of an heep of lerned men?        575
Of maistres had he mo than thries ten
That weren of law expert and curious!°—
Of which there were a dozein in that hous
Worthy to been stewards of rent and lond
Of any lord that is in Engelond,            580
To make him live by his propre good
In honour dettless, but if he were wood,°
Or live as scarsly° as him list desire,

---

560 a jangler and a goliardais a loudmouth and a big joker
561 harlotries ribaldry  562 stelen . . . thries steal wheat and
take three times his toll (the portion of the grain which was his
due payment)  563 thumb of gold the proverb "an honest miller
has a thumb of gold" suggests there are no honest millers. The
thumb might turn yellow from sampling grain; but otherwise might
be used to weight down a scale while "tolling"  565 baggepipe
medieval bagpipes, usually having but one pipe, were notably
phallic; Robertson, *Preface to Chaucer*, provides illustrations
567 manciple . . . temple purchasing agent or steward for one of the
Inns of Court (law schools)  568 achatours buyers  570 by taile
on credit  571 Algate . . . achat anyway, he was so careful about a
purchase  572 ay biforn always ahead of the game  577 curious
skillful, the students at the Inns of Court were often young nobles
who might use legal training in looking after their inheri-
tance  581–82 live . . . wood live on his income, honorably debt-
less, unless he were crazy  583 scarsly frugally

And able for to helpen all a shire
585 In any case that mighte fall or happe—
And yet this Manciple set hir aller cappe!°
    The REEVE° was a slender, cholerik° man.
His beerd was shave as neigh as ever he can;
His heer was by his eres full round y-shorn;
590 His top was docked like a preest biforn.°
Full longe were his legges and full lene,
Y-like a staff—there was no calf y-seene.
Well coud he keep a gerner° and a binne—
There was noon auditour coud on him winne!°
595 Well wist he by the drought and by the rain
The yeelding of his seed and of his grain.
His lordes sheep, his neet,° his dayerye,
His swine, his horse, his stoor, and his pultrye
Was holly in this Reeves governinge,
600 And by his covenant yaf the reckeninge.
Sin that his lord was twenty yeer of age,
There coud no man bring him in arrerage.°
There nas bailiff, ne hierd, ne other hine,
That he ne knew his sleight and his covine;°
605 They were adrad of him as of the deeth.°
His woning° was full fair upon an heeth;
With greene trees shadwed was his place.
He coud better than his lord purchace;
Full rich he was astored privly.
610 His lord well coud he plesen subtilly,
To yive and lene him of his owne good,
And have a thank, and yet a cote and hood.°

---

586 set . . . cappe made suckers of them all    587 Reeve the mana-
ger of a farm, chosen from among the serfs    587 cholerik the domi-
nance of choler among his humors would suggest a sly, irritable
character    590 docked . . . biforn snipped short in front like a
priest; short hair suggested servility    593 gerner storehouse for
grain    594 winne get one up on him. He probably kept records by
memory; then once a year an auditor would draw up written rec-
ords. A bit of cheating is suggested    597 neet cattle    602 arrerage
arrears    603–04 There . . . covine there wasn't a bailiff, herdsman,
or other worker that he didn't know their tricks and cheats    605 the
deeth i.e., the plague    606 woning dwelling    611–12 To . . . hood
i.e., he gave or lent things to his lord which he had stolen from
him—and the lord would thank him or give him a gift!

In youth he hadde lerned a good mister:°
He was a well good wright, a carpenter.
This Reeve sat upon a full good stot°                    615
That was all pomely° grey and highte Scot.
A long surcote of pers upon he hadde,
And by his side he bare a rusty blade.
Of Northfolk was this Reeve of which I telle,
Beside a town men clepen Baldeswelle.                    620
Tucked° he was as is a frere aboute,
And ever he rode the hindrest of our route.°
    A SOMNOUR° was there with us in that place
That had a fire-red cherubinnes face—
For saucefleem° he was, with eyen narrwe;                    625
As hot he was and lecherous as a sparrwe,
With scaled° browes black and piled° beerd.
Of his visage children were aferd.
There nas quicksilver, litarge, ne brimstoon,
Boras, ceruce, ne oil of tartre noon,                    630
Ne oinement that wolde clense and bite,
That him might helpen of the whelkes° white,
Nor of the knobbes° sitting on his cheekes.
Well loved he garlek, oinons, and eek leekes,°
And for to drinke strong wine red as blood.                    635
Than wold he speke and cry as he were wood.
And whan that he well drunken had the win,
Than wold he speke no word but Latin—
A fewe termes had he, two or three,

---

613 **mister** trade    615 **stot** farmhorse    616 **pomely** dappled
621 **tucked** his coat tucked up    622 **hindrest . . . route** last of the
company; he is keeping his eye on everyone    623 **Somnour** the
summoner is a minor police officer for the Archdeacon's court,
which had authority over matrimonial matters and moral conduct.
His job is to serve summons for any such offense. Summoners were
given to graft and bribery    625 **saucefleem** infected, inflamed. He
suffers from *alopicia* (perhaps acne, but medieval medical authori-
ties associated it with leprosy); hence his fire-red face—like cheru-
bim, which were conventionally depicted in rosy colors    627 **scaled**
scabby    627 **piled** scraggly    632 **whelkes** pimples    633 **knobbes**
boils, sores    634 **garlek . . . leekes** apart from the smell, and the
contribution they would make to his skin disease, garlic, onions, and
leeks would have been known to the learned as symbols of moral
depravity

640 That he had lernẹd out of some decree;
No wonder is—he herd it all the day,
And eek ye knowen well how that a jay
Can clepen "Watte"° as well as can the Popẹ:
But whoso coud in other thing him gropẹ,°
645 Than had he spent all his philosophyẹ:
Ay *Questio quid juris*° wold he cryẹ.
    He was a gentil harlot° and a kindẹ.
A better fellaw sholdẹ men not findẹ.
He woldẹ suffer, for a quart of win,
650 A good fellaw to have his concubin
A twelfmonth, and excuse him attẹ fullẹ;
Full privẹly a finch eek coud *he* pullẹ.°
And if he fond owhere° a good fellawẹ,
He woldẹ teechen him to have noon awẹ
655 In swich case of the Ercẹdekenes curs,°
But if a mannẹs soul were in his purs°—
For in his purse he shold y-punished be.
"Purse is the Ercẹdekenes hell," said he.
But well I wot he liẹd right in deedẹ:
660 Of cursing ought ech guilty man him dredẹ,
For curse wol slee right as assoiling° savith—
And also ware him of a *significavit*.°
    In daunger° had he at his ownẹ guisẹ
The yongẹ girlẹs of the diocisẹ,
665 And knew hir counseil, and was all hir reed.°
A garland had he set upon his heed
As greet as it were for an alẹ-stakẹ.°
A buckeler had he made him of a cakẹ.

---

643 **"Watte"** jays were then taught to say "Walter" as parrots are
now taught to say "Polly"   644 **grope** challenge   646 **Questio quid
juris** "The question is, what part of the law (applies) . . ." Prob-
ably the usual opening phrase of a legal discussion; the summoner
picks up this but of course understands nothing that follows!
647 **gentil harlot** nice guy   652 **finch . . . pulle** "pulling a finch"
meant seducing a woman   653 **owhere** anywhere   655 **Ercẹdekenes
curs** Archdeacon's power to excommunicate   656 **But . . . purs** un-
less a man's soul were in his purse   661 **assoiling** absolu-
tion   662 **significavit** writ of arrest issued on a Bishop's order—in
effect, "and also don't get arrested"   663 **In daunger** under his
thumb   665 **knew . . . reed** knew their secrets and was their advisor
667 **ale-stake** sign on a tavern, often with a garland hung from it

With him there rode a gentil PARDONER°
Of Rouncival, his freend and his compeer,°                    670
That straight was comen fro the court of Rome.
Full loud he song, "Come hider, love, to me."
This Somnour bare to him a stiff burdoun°—
Was never trump of half so greet a soun.

This Pardoner had heer as yellow as wex,                      675
But smooth it heng as doth a strike of flex:°
By ounces° heng his lockes that he hadde,
And therewith he his shouldres overspradde,
But thin it lay, by colpons oon and oon.°
But hood for jolitee° wered he noon,                          680
For it was trussed up in his wallét:°
Him thought he rode all of the newe jet°—
Dischevelee save his cap he rode all bare.°
Swich glaring eyen had he as an hare.

A vernicle° had he sowed upon his cappe;                      685
His wallét biforn him in his lappe,
Bretful of pardon, comen from Rome all hot.

A voice he had as small as hath a goot.
No beerd had he, ne never sholde have—
As smooth it was as it were late y-shave.                     690

669 **Pardoner** pardoners were in minor orders, or sometimes hired laymen, who sold indulgences from town to town. They were notorious for their abuses and were strictly regulated by prohibitions against false relics, preaching without permission, wearing clerical garb they were not entitled to wear, entering taverns, etc. Some "pardoners" were out-and-out frauds; others, though legitimate, kept more than their share of the proceeds, which were to be used for such causes as crusades or hospitals. Some pardoners forged small written indulgences bearing a fake papal seal. There was a hospital called Our Lady of Rouncivalle, near Charing Cross; and pardoners from it were commonly satirized. But offering alms after a true confession and receiving an indulgence in return was itself legitimate, though it lent itself to abuses  670 **compeer** companion. The pardoner travels with the summoner: Pardoners needed permission from the Archdeacon to enter a diocese  673 **stiff burdoun** strong bass accompaniment  676 **strike of flex** bunch of flax  677 **ounces** strands  679 **by colpons oon and oon** in strips, one by one  680 **for jolitee** to be a sport  681 **trussed . . . wallet** folded up in his saddlebag  682 **newe jet** latest fashion  683 **Dischevelee . . . bare** with hair flying he rode all bareheaded, except for his cap  685 **vernicle** a small replica of St. Veronica's handkerchief, which she gave to Christ on Calvary to wipe His face with. It bore an imprint of the face; the original was preserved in Rome

I trow he were a gelding or a mare.°
   But of his craft, fro Berwik into Ware
Ne was there swich another pardoner!
For in his male he had a pillwebeer°
695 Which that he said was Oure Lady° veil;
He said he had a gobbet° of the sail
That Sainte Peter had whan that he wente
Upon the see, till Jesu Christ him hente;
He had a crois of latoun,° full of stones;
700 And in a glass° he hadde pigges bones.
But with thise "relikes," whan that he fond
A povre person° dwelling upon lond,
Upon a day he gat him more moneye
Than that the person gat in monthes twaye!
705 And thus with feined flattery and japes
He made the person and the peple his apes.°
But trewely to tellen atte laste,
He was in chirch a noble ecclesiaste:°
Well coud he rede a lesson or a storye,
710 But alderbest he song an offertorye,
For well he wiste, whan that song was songe,
He moste preech and well affile° his tonge
To winne silver, as he full well coude—
Therefore he song the murrierly and loude.

\*    \*    \*

715    Now have I told you soothly in a clause°
Th'estate,° th'array, the numbre, and eek the cause
Why that assembled was this compaignye
In Southwerk at this gentil hostelrye

---

691 **gelding or a mare** castrated horse or female horse. The line
suggests that the Pardoner is either a castrated eunuch or a *eunuchus
ex nativitate,* i.e., one born without sexual glands (anorchism). Curry
shows that other details—a small voice, no beard, etc.—would have
suggested this  694 **male . . . pillwebeer** in his pouch he had a
pillowcase  695 **Lady** Lady's  696 **gobbet** piece  699 **crois of latoun**
cross of brass  700 **glass** glass case  702 **person** parson  706 **apes**
he made monkeys of them  708 **ecclesiaste** preacher  712 **affile**
sharpen  715 **clause** few words  716 **estate** rank

That hight the Tabard, faste by the Belle.°
But now is time to you for to telle                    720
How that we baren us that ilke night
Whan we were in that hostelry alight.
And after wol I tell of our viage,°
And all the remnant of our pilgrimage.
    But first I pray you of your curteisye            725
That ye n'arette it not my villainye°
Though that I plainly speke in this mattere
To telle you hir wordes and hir cheere,°
Ne though I speke hir wordes proprely.°
For this ye knowen also well as I:                    730
Whoso shall tell a tale after a man,
He moot reherce° as neigh as ever he can
Everich a word, if it be in his charge°—
Al speke he never so rudelich and large°—
Or elles he moot tell his tale untrewe,              735
Or feine thing, or finde wordes newe;°
He may not spare although he were his brother.
He moot as well say oo word as another.
Christ spak himself full brod in holy writ,
And well ye wot no villainy is it.                     740
Eek Plato saith, whoso can him rede,
The wordes mot be cosin to the deede.
    Also I pray you to foryive it me
Al have I not set folk in hir degree°
Here in this tale as that they sholde stonde:        745
My wit is short, ye may well understonde.


            *       *       *


Greet cheere made our Host us everichoon,
And to the supper set he us anon.
He served us with vitaille at the beste.
Strong was the wine, and well to drink us leste.      750

719 **faste by the Belle** close to the Bell (another inn in Southwark)
723 **viage** trip   726 **that . . . villainye** that you won't chalk it up to
my bad manners   728 **cheere** conduct   729 **proprely** accurately
732 **moot reherce** must report   733 **charge** ability   734 **large** openly
736 **Or . . . newe** or be making something up, or putting words in
someone's mouth   744 **degree** order of social rank

A seemly man our HOSTE° was withalle
For to been a marshall in an halle.°
A large man he was, with eyen steepe;
A fairer burgeis was there none in Chepe—
755  Bold of his speech, and wise, and well y-taught;
And of manhood him lackede right naught.
Eek thereto he was right a mirry man,
And after supper playen° he began,
And spak of mirth amonges other thinges—
760  Whan that we had made our reckeninges°—
And saide thus: "Now, lordings, trewely,
Ye been to me right welcome, hertely!
For by my trouth, if that I shall not lie,
I saw not this yeer so mirry a compaignye
765  At ones in this herberwe° as is now!
Fain wold I doon you mirthe, wist I how.
And of a mirth I am right now bithought,
To doon you ese,° and it shall coste nought:
Ye goon to Canterbury—God you speede;
770  The blissful martyr quite you your meede!°
And well I wot as ye goon by the waye
Ye shapen you to talen° and to playe;
For trewely, comfort ne mirth is noon
To ride by the way dumb as a stoon.
775  And therefore wol I maken you disport
As I said erst, and doon you some comfort:
And if you liketh all, by one assent,
For to standen at my judgement,
And for to werken as I shall you saye,
780  Tomorrwe whan ye riden by the waye—
Now by my fader soule that is deed,
But ye be mirry I wol yive you mine heed.
Hold up your hands withouten more speeche."°

751 **Hoste** his name is given as Harry Bailly in the Cook's Prologue (I, line 4358). There was an actual innkeeper in Southwark of that name during the 1380's. He held various political offices    752 **marshall . . . halle** overseer of service in a palace    758 **playen** to fool around    760 **made our reckeninges** paid our bills    765 **herberwe** inn    768 **doon you ese** amuse you    770 **quite you your meede** grant you your reward    772 **talen** tell tales    783 **Hold up your hands** like a politician, he gets them to make a gesture of agreement before he has said anything

Our conseil was not longe for to seeche—
Us thought it was not worth to make it wis,° 785
And graunted him withouten more avis,
And bade him say his voirdit° as him leste.
"Lordings," quod he, "now herkneth for the beste—
But taketh it not, I pray you, in disdain:
This is the point, to speken short and plain, 790
That ech of you, to shorte with our waye°
In this viage, shall telle tales twaye—
To Canterbury-ward, I mene it so,
And homeward he shall tellen other two,
Of aventures that whilom have bifalle. 795
And which of you that bereth him best of alle—
That is to sayn, that telleth in this cas
Tales of best sentence and most solas°—
Shall have a supper at our aller cost,°
Here in this place, sitting by this post, 800
Whan that we come again fro Canterbury.
And for to make you the more murry
I wol myself goodly with you ride,
Right at mine owne cost, and be your guide.
And whoso wol my judgement withsaye° 805
Shall pay all that we spende by the waye.
And if ye vouchesauf that it be so,
Tell me anon, withouten wordes mo,
And I wol erly shape me° therefore."
   This thing was graunted and our othes swore 810
With full glad hert, and prayden him also
That he wold vouchesauf for to do so,
And that he wolde been our governour,
And of our tales judge and reportour;°
And set a supper at a certain pris, 815
And we wol ruled been at his devis,
In heigh and low.° And thus by one assent

785 Us . . . wis it seemed to us not worth while to quibble
787 voirdit verdict   791 shorte with our waye with which to shorten
our journey   798 sentence . . . solas moral significance and pleasure.
These were the two effects of storytelling in the medieval view
799 at our aller cost at the cost of us all   805 withsaye deny
809 shape me get myself ready   814 reportour reporter of their
merits   817 In . . . low in all respects

We been accorded to his judgement.
And thereupon the wine was fet° anon;
820 We dronken and to reste went echon
Withouten any lenger tarryinge.
    Amorrwe whan that day began to springe
Up rose our Host and was our aller cock,°
And gadred us togidre in a flock;
825 And forth we riden, a litel more than pas,°
Unto the watering° of Saint Thomas.
And there our Host began his horse arreste,
And saide, "Lordings, herkneth if you leste!
Ye wot your forward and it you recorde:°
830 If evensong and morrwesong accorde,
Let see now who shall tell the firste tale.
As ever mote I drinke wine or ale,
Whoso be rebel to my judgement
Shall pay for all that by the way is spent.
835 Now draweth cut° ere that we ferrer twinne:°
He which that hath the shortest shall beginne.
Sir Knight," quod he, "my maister and my lord,
Now draweth cut, for that is mine accord.
Cometh neer," quod he, "my lady Prioresse,
840 And ye, sir Clerk, let be your shamefastnesse—
Ne studieth° not. Lay hand to, every man!"
    Anon to drawen every wight began,
And shortly for to tellen as it was,
Were it by aventure, or sort, or cas,°
845 The sooth is this: the cut fill to the Knight.°
Of which full blithe and glad was every wight,
And tell he most his tale, as was resoun,
By forward and by composicioun,°
As ye han herd. What needeth wordes mo?

819 fet fetched It was a custom to have a drink of wine before
going to bed   823 was . . . cock acted as a rooster for us all (i.e.,
woke us)   825 pas a short walk   826 watering brook. It was two
miles on the road to Canterbury   829 Ye . . . recorde you know
your agreement and you remember it   835 draweth cut draw straws
835 twinne depart   841 studieth think, muse   844 aventure, or sort,
or cas by chance, or luck, or circumstance; essentially they are
synonyms   845 to the Knight this is no surprise; it would be
normal for the one of highest rank to begin   848 composicioun
agreement

And whan this good man saw that it was so,                    *850*
As he that wise was and obedient
To keep his forward by his free assent,
He saide, "Sin I shall begin the game,
What, welcome be the cut, a' Goddes name!
Now let us ride, and herkneth what I saye."                    *855*
And with that word we riden forth our waye,
And he began with right a mirry cheere
His tale anon, and said as ye may heere.

# THE KNIGHT'S TALE

## PART ONE

Whilom,° as olde stories tellen us,
There was a duke that highte Theseus:
Of Athens he was lord and governour,
And in his time swich a conquerour
That greeter was there none under the sunne.          5
Full many a riche contree had he wonne:
What with his wisdom and his chivalrye,
He conquered all the regne of Femenye,°
That whilom was y-cleped° Scythia,
And weddede the queen Ipolyta,                          10
And brought hir home with him in his contree,
With muchel glory and greet solempnitee,°
And eek hir yonge suster° Emelye.
And thus with victory and with melodye
Let I this noble duke to Athens ride,                   15
And all his host in armes him beside.

  And certes, if it nere too long to heere,°
I wold have told you fully the mannere
How wonnen was the regne of Femenye
By Theseus and by his chivalrye,                        20
And of the greet bataille for the nones°
Betwixen Athenes and Amazones,
And how asseged was Ipolyta,

1 **Whilom** once upon a time   8 **Femenye** the country of the Amazons, whose inhabitants were all women   9 **y-cleped** called   12 **solempnitee** ceremony   13 **suster** sister   17 **if . . . heere** if it weren't too long to listen to. The rhetorical device used here, called *occupatio,* permits a writer to summarize a great deal of material by stating what he will not deal with. The Knight's Tale is an adaptation of Boccaccio's *Teseida,* and is much shorter than its original; many omitted passages are treated as this one is   21 **for the nones** in particular

The faire hardy queen of Scythia,
25 And of the feest that was at hir weddinge,
And of the tempest at hir home-cominge.
But all that thing I mot as now forbere.
I have, God wot, a large feeld to ere,°
And waike° been the oxen in my plough;
30 The remnant of the tale is long enough.
I wol not letten° eek none of this route;°
Let every fellaw tell his tale aboute,°
And let see now who shall the supper winne.
And ther I left I wol ayain beginne.

35     This duke of whom I make mencioun,
Whan he was comen almost to the town
In all his wele and in his moste pride,
He was ware as he cast his eye aside
Where that there kneeled in the highe waye
40 A compaigny of ladies, twaye and twaye,
Ech after other, clad in clothes blacke.
But swich a cry and swich a woe they make
That in this world nis creature livinge
That herde swich another waymentinge;°
45 And of this cry they nolde never stenten°
Till they the reines of his bridle henten.°
    "What folk been ye that at mine home-cominge
Perturben so my feeste with cryinge?"
Quod Theseus. "Have ye so greet envye
50 Of mine honour, that thus complain and crye?
Or who hath you misboden° or offended?
And telleth me if it may been amended
And why that ye been clothed thus in black?"
The eldest lady of hem alle spak,
55 Whan she had swouned with a deedly cheere,°
That it was routhe° for to seen and heere.
    She saide, "Lord to whom Fortune hath yiven
Victory, and as a conquerour to liven,
Nought greveth us your glory and your honour,

28 **ere** plow   29 **waike** weak   31 **letten** hinder   31 **route** company
32 **aboute** in his turn   44 **waymentinge** lamenting   45 **stenten** stop
46 **henten** grasped   51 **misboden** harmed   55 **cheere** appearance
56 **routhe** pity

But we biseeken mercy and succour: 60
Have mercy on our woe and our distresse!
Some drop of pitee, thurgh thy gentilesse,
Upon us wretched women let thou falle!
For certes, lord, there is none of us alle
That she ne hath been a duchess or a queene. 65
Now be we caitives,° as it is well seene,
Thanked be Fortune and hir false wheel,°
That none estate assureth to be well.
Now certes, lord, to abiden° your presence,
Here in this temple of the goddess Clemence 70
We have been waiting all this fortenight.
Now help us, lord, sith it is in thy might!
I, wretche, which that weep and waile thus,
Was whilom wife to King Cappaneus
That starf° at Thebes—cursed be that day! 75
And alle we that been in this array°
And maken all this lamentacioun,
We losten all our husbands at that town,
While that the seege thereaboute lay.
And yet now the old Creon, wailaway, 80
That lord is now of Thebes the citee,
Fulfilled of° ire and of iniquitee—
He, for despit and for his tyrannye,
To do the dede bodies villainye
Of all our lordes whiche that been slawe,° 85
Hath all the bodies on an heep y-drawe,
And wol not suffren hem by noon assent
Neither to been y-buried nor y-brent,°
But maketh houndes ete hem in despit!"
And with that word, withouten more respit, 90
They fillen gruf° and criden pitously,
"Have on us wretched women some mercy,
And let our sorrwe sinken in thine herte!"

66 **caitives** captives, or wretches   67 **Fortune . . . wheel** the wheel
of Fortune was the principle of chance in the universe; it showed
that earthly things are transitory and that there is no certain justice
in this wicked world. The theme occurs often in the Knight's Tale
69 **abiden** wait for   75 **starf** died   76 **array** condition   82 **Fulfilled
of** filled with   85 **slawe** slain   88 **y-brent** burnt   91 **gruf** face down

This gentil duke down from his courser° sterte
95  With herte pitous whan he herd hem speke.
Him thoughte° that his herte wolde breke
Whan he saw hem so pitous and so mat,°
That whilom weren of so greet estat.
And in his armes he hem all up hente,
100 And hem comforteth in full good entente,
And swore his ooth, as he was trewe knight,
He wolde doon so ferforthly° his might
Upon the tyrant Creon hem to wreke,°
That all the peple of Greece sholde speke
105 How Creon was of Theseus y-served,
As he that had his deeth full well deserved.
And right anon withouten more abood°
His banner he desplayeth and forth rood
To Thebesward, and all his host beside.
110 No neer° Athenes wold he go° ne ride,
Ne take his ese fully half a day,
But onward on his way that night he lay,
And sent anon Ipolyta the queene,
And Emely hir yonge suster sheene,°
115 Unto the town of Athenes to dwelle,
And forth he rit:° there is namore to telle.
    The red statue of Mars with spere and targe°
So shineth in his white banner large
That all the feeldes glittren up and down.
120 And by his banner born is his penoun°
Of gold full rich, in which there was y-bete
The Minotaur, which that he wan° in Crete.
Thus rit this duke, thus rit this conquerour,
And in his host of chivalry the flowr,
125 Till that he came to Thebes and alighte
Fair in a feeld ther as he thought to fighte.
    But shortly for to speken of this thing,
With Creon which that was of Thebes king

94 **courser** war horse   96 **Him thoughte** it seemed to him (the verb is impersonal)   97 **mat** distracted   102 **so ferforthly** as much as he could   103 **hem to wreke** to avenge them   107 **abood** delay   110 **neer** nearer   110 **go** walk   114 **sheene** fair   116 **rit** rides   117 **targe** shield   120 **penoun** penant   122 **wan** conquered

He faught, and slow° him manly as a knight
In plain° battail, and put the folk to flight.                    130
And by assaut he wan the citee after,
And rent adown both wall and spar° and rafter,
And to the ladies he restored again
The bones of hir freendes that were slain,
To doon obsequies as was tho the guise.°                         135
But it were all too long for to devise
The greete clamour and the waymentinge
That the ladies made at the brenninge
Of the bodies, and the greet honour
That Theseus, the noble conquerour,                              140
Doth to the ladies whan they from him wente;
But shortly for to tell is mine entente.

    Whan that this worthy duke, this Theseus,
Hath Creon slain and wonne Thebes thus,
Still in that feeld he took all night his reste,               145
And did with all the contree as him leste.

    To ransack in the taas° of bodies dede,
Hem for to strep of harneis and of weede,°
The pilours° diden bisiness and cure°
After the battail and disconfiture.                             150
And so bifell that in the taas they founde,
Thurgh-girt° with many a grevous bloody wounde,
Two yonge knightes, ligging by and by,°
Both in one armes° wrought full richely;
Of whiche two, Arcita hight that oon,                           155
And that other knight hight Palamon.
Not fully quick° ne fully deed they were;
But by hir cote-armures° and by hir gere°
The heraudes knew hem best in special
As they that weren of the blood royal                           160
Of Thebes, and of sustren two y-born.
Out of the taas the pilours han hem torn

129 slow slew   130 plain open   132 spar beam   135 guise custom
147 taas pile   148 strep . . . weede strip of armor and clothes   149
pilours pillagers   149 cure care   152 Thurgh-girt pierced through
153 ligging by and by lying near each other   154 in one armes
dressed alike and having the same coat of arms (since they are of the
same family)   157 quick alive   158 cote-armures cloth surcoats
worn over armor, on which was embroidered a coat of arms
158 gere equipment

And han hem carried soft unto the tente
Of Theseus, and he full soon hem sente
165 To Athenes to dwellen in prisoun
Perpetuelly; he nolde no raunsoun.°
And whan this worthy duke hath thus y-doon,
He took his host and home he rit anoon,
With laurer crowned as a conquerour.
170 And there he liveth in joy and in honour
Term of his life. What needeth wordes mo?
And in a tower, in anguish and in wo,
Dwellen this Palamon and eek Arcite
For evermore; there may no gold hem quite.°
175      This passeth yeer by yeer and day by day,
Till it fill ones in a morrwe of May
That Emely, that fairer was to seene
Than is the lily upon his stalke greene,
And fresher than the May with flowres newe
180 (For with the rose colour strof hir hewe—
I noot which was the fairer of hem two)
Ere it were day, as was hir wone° to do,
She was arisen and all redy dight,°
For May wol have no sluggardye anight.
185 The seson pricketh every gentil herte,
And maketh it out of his sleep to sterte,
And saith, "Arise and do thine observaunce."
This maketh Emely have remembraunce
To doon honour to May and for to rise.
190 Y-clothed was she fresh for to devise:
Hir yellow heer was broided in a tresse
Behind hir back a yerde long, I guesse,
And in the garden at the sun upriste°
She walketh up and down, and as hir liste
195 She gadreth flowres party° white and rede
To make a subtil° gerland for hir heede,
And as an angel hevenishly she song.
     The greete tower that was so thick and strong,
Which of the castel was the chief dungeoun,

166 **nolde no raunsoun** did not want a ransom   174 **quite** ransom
182 **wone** habit   183 **dight** dressed   193 **at the sun upriste** at the
sun's rising   195 **party** particolored   196 **subtil** ingenious

Ther as the knightes weren in prisoun                      200
(Of which I tolde you and tellen shall)
Was even joinant° to the garden wall
Ther as this Emely had hir playinge.
Bright was the sun and cleer that morrweninge,
And Palamon, this woeful prisoner,                         205
As was his wone by leve of his jailer,
Was risen and romed in a chambre on heigh,
In which he all the noble citee seigh,°
And eek the garden, full of braunches greene,
Ther as the freshe Emely the sheene                        210
Was in hir walk and romed up and down.
This sorrweful prisoner, this Palamoun,
Goth in the chambre roming to and fro,
And to himself complaining of his wo.
That he was born full oft he said alas!                    215
And so bifell, by aventure or cas,
That thurgh a window thick of many a barre
Of iren greet and square as any sparre,
He caste his eye upon Emelya
And therewithal he bleint° and cride "A!"                  220
As though he stongen were unto the herte.°
And with that cry Arcite anon up sterte
And saide, "Cosin mine, what aileth thee
That art so pale and deedly on to see?
Why cridestou?° Who hath thee done offence?                225
For Goddes love, take all in pacience
Our prison, for it may noon other be.
Fortune hath yiven us this adversitee.
Some wicke aspect or disposicioun
Of Saturn,° by some constellacioun,                        230

202 **even joinant** directly adjacent    208 **seigh** saw    220 **bleint**
blanched, turned white    221 **stongen . . . herte** the "wound" of love,
which enters through the eye and afflicts the heart, is traditional.
Paleness, sighing, and weeping are among its symptoms. Cf. lines
238, 257–58    225 **cridestou** didst thou cry    230 **Saturn** an evil
planet. Arcite blames the stars, working along with Fortune, for
their plight. A "wicke aspect" (evil arrangement of heavenly bodies),
or a "disposicioun" of one planet within the "constellation" of
planets, has affected them from birth. Astrology was legitimately a
science, which helped to explain the element of chance in human
life; it is not inconsistent with the principle of Fortune's wheel

Hath yiven us this, although we had it sworn.°
So stood the heven whan that we were born.
We mot endure it; this is the short and plain."
    This Palamon answered and said again,
235 "Cosin, forsooth, of this opinioun
Thou hast a vain imaginacioun.°
This prison caused me not for to crye,
But I was hurt right now thurghout mine eye
Into mine hert, that wol my bane° be.
240 The fairness of that lady that I see
Yond in the garden romen to and fro
Is cause of all my crying and my wo.
I noot wher° she be woman or goddesse,
But Venus is it soothly, as I guesse."
245 And therewithal on knees down he fill
And saide, "Venus, if it be thy will
You in this garden thus to transfigure
Before me, sorrowful, wretched creature,
Out of this prison help that we may scape.
250 And if so be my destinee be shape
By eterne word to dien in prisoun,
Of our linage have some compassioun,
That is so low y-brought by tyrannye."
    And with that word Arcite gan espye
255 Whereas this lady romed to and fro,
And with that sight hir beautee hurt him so
That if that Palamon was wounded sore,
Arcite is hurt as much as he or more.
And with a sigh he saide pitously,
260 "The freshe beautee sleth me suddenly
Of hir that rometh in the yonder place,
And but I have hir mercy and hir grace,
That I may seen hir at the leste waye,°
I nam but deed:° there nis namore to saye."

231 **although . . . sworn** although we had sworn to the contrary. The point is that man has no power in the face of destinal forces save to accept them patiently  236 **vain imaginacioun** empty fantasy  239 **bane** death  243 **I noot wher** I know not whether. . . . The confusion of women with goddesses is a commonplace of love poetry  263 **I . . . waye** I may at least see her  264 **I nam but deed** I am no better than dead

This Palamon, whan he tho wordes herde,                    265
Despitously he looked and answerde,
"Whether saistou this° in ernest or in play?"
    "Nay," quod Arcite, "in ernest, by my fay.°
God help me so, me list full yvele playe."°
    This Palamon gan knit his browes twaye:                270
"It were to thee," quod he, "no greet honour
For to be false, ne for to be traitour
To me, that am thy cosin, and thy brother,°
Y-sworn full deep, and ech of us til other,
That never, for to dien in the paine,                      275
Till that the deeth departe shall us twaine,
Neither of us in love to hinder other,
Ne in noon other cas,° my leve brother;
But that thou sholdest trewely forthren me
In every cas, as I shall forthre thee.                     280
This was thine ooth, and mine also, certain.
I wot right well thou darst it not withsayn.°
Thus artou of my conseil° out of doute,
And now thou woldest falsely been aboute°
To love my lady whom I love and serve,                     285
And ever shall till that mine herte sterve.°
Now certes, false Arcite, thou shalt not so.
I loved hir first, and tolde thee my wo
As to my conseil and my brother sworn
To forthre me, as I have told biforn.                      290
For which thou art y-bounden as a knight
To helpe me, if it lay in thy might,
Or elles artou false, I dare well sayn."
    This Arcite full proudly spak again:
"Thou shalt," quod he, "be rather false than I;            295
And thou art false, I tell thee outrely°—

267 **Whether saistou this** do you say this    268 **fay** faith    269 **me . . .
playe** it pleases me very little to fool around    273 **brother** "sworn
brotherhood" was an oath of loyalty between friends, sometimes
made by commingling blood (hence the term "blood brothers"). It
was a very sacred relationship: cf. line 275—"even though we die
by torture." From this relationship, more than from their family tie
(as cousins), springs their conflict of love versus honor    278 **cas**
circumstance    282 **withsayn** deny    283 **of my conseil** in on my
secret    284 **been aboute** make ready    286 **sterve** perish, die
296 **outrely** straight out; cf. "utterly"

For *par amour*° I loved hir first ere thou.
What wiltou sayn? Thou woost not yet now
Wheither she be a woman or goddesse:
300 Thine is affeccion of holinesse,
And mine is love as to a creature,
For which I tolde thee mine aventure,
As to my cosin and my brother sworn.
I pose that thou lovedest hir biforn:°
305 Wostou not well the olde clerkes sawe,
That 'Who shall yive a lover any lawe?'
Love is a greeter lawe, by my pan,°
Than may be yive to any erthly man;
And therefore positif law and swich decree
310 Is broke alday for love in ech degree.
A man mot needes love, maugree his heed:
He may not fleen it though he shold be deed,
Al be she maide, widwe, or elles wif.
And eek it is not likely all thy lif
315 To standen in hir grace. Namore shall I,
For well thou wost thyselven, verraily
That thou and I be dampned to prisoun
Perpetuelly; us gaineth no raunsoun.
We strive as did the houndes for the boon:—
320 They fought all day, and yet hir part was noon;
There came a kite, while that they were so wrothe
That bare away the bone bitwix hem bothe.
And therefore, at the kinges court, my brother,
Ech man for himself—there is none other.°
325 Love if thee list, for I love and ay shall—
And soothly, leve brother, this is all:
Here in this prison mote we endure,
And everich of us take his aventure."°

297 **par amour** in the way of love. Arcite's argument is that Palamon
thought she was a goddess and was therefore just having an attack
of religion ("affeccion of holiness"—line 300)    304 **I . . . biforn**
"Suppose *you* loved her first." Arcite raises a hypothetical point:
"Wouldn't *you* agree love has no law?"—a self-defeating argument
if ever there was one; note his previous appeal to legality (lines
297ff.)    307 **pan** skull    324 **none other** no other way. "At the
King's court each man for himself" is a proverb    328 **aventure**
chance

    Greet was the strife and long bitwix hem twaye,
If that I hadde leiser for to saye.                    *330*
But to th'effect: it happed on a day,
To tell it you as shortly as I may,
A worthy duke that hight Perotheus,
That fellaw was unto duke Theseus
Sin thilke day that they were children lite,°     *335*
Was come to Athens his fellaw to visite,
And for to play, as he was wont to do;
For in this world he loved no man so,
And he loved him as tendrely again.°
So well they loved, as olde bookes sayn,     *340*
That whan that one was deed, soothly to telle,
His fellaw went and sought him down in helle—
But of that story list me not to write.°
Duke Perotheus loved well Arcite,
And had him know at Thebes yeer by yeer,     *345*
And finally at request and prayere
Of Perotheus, withouten any raunsoun,
Duke Theseus him let out of prisoun
Freely to goon where that him list overall,
In swich a guise as I you tellen shall.     *350*
This was the forward,° plainly for t'endite,
Bitwixen Theseus and him Arcite:
That if so were that Arcite were y-founde
Ever in his life, by day or night or stounde,°
In any countree of this Theseus,     *355*
And he were caught, it was accorded thus:
That with a swerd he sholde lese his heed.
There was noon other remedy ne reed,
But taketh his leve,° and homeward he him spedde.

335 **lite** little   339 **he . . . again** i.e., Theseus loved him in return
343 **list . . . to write** "It doesn't please me to write." One would ex-
pect the Knight to say "tell," so the line is sometimes considered a
slip on Chaucer's part, or a vestige from an earlier version not in-
tended for *The Canterbury Tales.* But of course everyone knows that
while the Knight is supposedly telling the tale Chaucer is really writ-
ing it: who could tell a rhymed tale on horseback riding through
open country? Here and elsewhere perhaps Chaucer ironically per-
mits his own voice to seep through  351 **forward** agreement
354 **or stounde** or at any time  358–59 **noon . . . leve** no other
remedy or counsel but to take his leave (*lit.* "but takes his leave."
Such ellipses in grammar are not unusual)

360 Let him be ware: his necke lith to wedde.°
    How greet a sorrwe suffreth now Arcite!
The deeth he feeleth thurgh his herte smite.
He weepeth, waileth, crieth pitously;
To sleen himself he waiteth prively.
365 He said, "Alas the day that I was born!
Now is my prison worse than biforn—
Now is me shape eternally to dwelle
Not in purgatory, but in helle!
Alas that ever knew I Perotheus,
370 For elles had I dwelled with Theseus,
Y-fettered in his prison evermo!
Than had I been in bliss and not in wo.
Only the sight of hir whom that I serve,
Though that I never hir grace may deserve,
375 Wold have suffised right enough for me.
O dere cosin Palamon," quod he,
"Thine is the victory of this aventure:
Full blissfully in prison maistou dure°—
In prison?—certes, nay, but in Paradis!
380 Well hath Fortune y-turned thee the dis,°
That hast the sight of hir—and I th'absence.
For possible is, sin thou hast hir presence,
And art a knight, a worthy and an able,
That by some cas, sin Fortune is chaungeable,
385 Thou maist to thy desire some time attaine.
But I, that am exiled, and barreine°
Of alle grace, and in so greet despair
That there nis erthe, water, fire, ne air,°
Ne creature that of hem maked is,
390 That may me help or doon confort in this—
Well ought I sterve in wanhope° and distresse.
Farewell my life, my lust, and my gladnesse!
Alas, why plainen folk so in commune
On purveyance of God,° or of Fortune,

360 **to wedde** under a bond or pledge    378 **dure** remain    380 **dis** dice    386 **barreine** barren    388 **erthe . . . air** these were the four elements of which all things were composed—in short, nothing can help him    391 **sterve in wanhope** die in despair    393–94 **why plainen . . . God** Why do people commonly complain about God's providence?

That yiveth hem full oft in many a guise                    395
Well better than they can hemself devise?
Some man desireth for to have richesse,
That cause is of his murdre or greet sicknesse;
And some man wold out of his prison fain,
That in his house is of his meinee° slain.                  400
Infinite harmes been in this mattere:
We wot not what thing that we prayen here—
We faren as he that drunk is as a mous.°
A drunke man wot well he hath an hous,
But he noot which the righte way is thider,                 405
And to a drunke man the way is slider.°
And certes in this world so faren we:
We seeken fast after felicitee,
But we goon wrong full often, trewely.
Thus may we sayen all, and namelich I,                      410
That wende° and had a greet opinioun
That if I mighte scapen fro prisoun,
Than had I been in joy and parfit hele,°
Ther now I am exiled fro my wele!°
Sin that I may not seen you, Emelye,                         415
I nam but deed! There nis no remedye!"
    Upon that other side Palamon,
Whan that he wist Arcite was agon,
Swich sorrwe he maketh that the greete towr
Resouneth of his yowling and clamour.                       420
The pure fettres of his shinnes greete
Were of his bitter salte teres wete.
"Alas," quod he, "Arcita, cosin min,
Of all our strife, God wot, the fruit is thin!
Thou walkest now in Thebes at thy large,°                   425
And of my woe thou yivest litel charge.°
Thou maist, sin thou hast wisdom and manhede,
Assemblen all the folk of our kinrede,
And make a wer° so sharp on this citee

---

400 **of his meinee** by the people of his own household    403 **drunk
. . . as a mous** proverbial; compare "drunk as a skunk" or "drunk
as a coot"    406 **slider** slithery    411 **wende** imagined    413 **hele** well-
being    414 **wele** good circumstances    425 **at thy large** at large
426 **charge** care    429 **wer** war

430 That by some aventure or some tretee
Thou maist have hir to lady and to wif,
For whom that I most needes lese my lif.
For as by way of possibilitee,
Sith thou art at thy large, of prison free,
435 And art a lord, greet is thine avantage,
More than is mine, that sterve here in a cage.
For I mot weep and waile while I live
With all the woe that prison may me yive,
And eek with pain that love me yiveth also,
440 That doubleth all my torment and my wo!"
Therewith the fire of jalousy up sterte
Within his brest, and hent° him by the herte
So woodly° that he like was to biholde°
The boxtree or the ashen deed and colde.
445 Than said he: "O cruel goddes that governe
This world with binding of your word eterne,
And writen in the table of adamaunt
Your parlement and your eterne graunt,
What is mankinde more unto you holde
450 Than is the sheep that rowketh° in the folde?
For slain is man right as another beest,
And dwelleth eek in prison and arrest,
And hath sickness and greet adversitee,
And ofte times guilteless, pardee.
455 What governance is in this prescience
That guilteless tormenteth innocence?°
And yet encresseth this all my penaunce,
That man is bounden to his observaunce,°
For goddes sake, to letten of his wille,°
460 Ther as a beest may all his lust fulfille.
And whan a beest is deed he hath no paine,
But man after his deeth mot weep and plaine,
Though in this world he have care and wo;

442 **hent** grasped    443 **woodly** madly    443 **he . . . biholde** to look
at him he was like . . . (i.e., he was pale and white)    450 **rowketh**
crouches    455–56 **What . . . innocence** What kind of governance is
there in this foreknowledge which torments innocence but has no
guilt in doing so?    458 **to his observaunce** as a matter of obligation
459 **to letten of his wille** to restrain his own desires

Withouten doute, it may stonden so.°
The answer of this let I to divines,°                                465
But well I wot that in this world greet pine is.
Alas, I see a serpent° or a theef,
That many a trewe man hath done mischeef,
Gone at his large and where him list may turne.°
But I mot been in prison thurgh Saturne,                            470
And eek thurgh Juno, jalous and eek wood,
That hath destroyed well nigh all the blood
Of Thebes, with his waste walles wide!°
And Venus sleth me on that other side
For jalousy and fere of him Arcite!"                                475
    Now wol I stint of Palamon a lite,
And let him in his prison stille dwelle,
And of Arcita forth I wol you telle:
    The summer passeth and the nightes longe
Encreesen double wise the paines stronge                            480
Both of the lover and the prisoner—
I noot which hath the woefuller mister:°
For shortly for to sayn, this Palamoun
Perpetuelly is dampned to prisoun,
In chaines and in fettres to been deed;                             485
And Arcite is exiled upon his heed
For evermo as out of that contree,
Ne nevermo he shall his lady see.
    You lovers ax I now this questioun:°
Who hath the worse, Arcite or Palamoun?                             490
That one may seen his lady day by day,
But in prison mot he dwell alway;
That other where him list may ride or go,
But seen his lady shall he nevermo.
Now deemeth as you liste, ye that can,                              495
For I wol telle forth as I began.


464 **it may stonden so** it is how things are    465 **let I to divines** I
leave to theologians    467 **serpent** scoundrel    469 **Gone . . . turne**
has gone at large and can go where he likes    473 **waste walles wide**
wide walls partly destroyed    482 **mister** situation    489 **questioun**
the Knight poses a typical "*demande d'amour*": stories were often
interrupted or concluded with such questions, which were then de-
bated. Cf. the end of the Franklin's Tale

## PART TWO

Whan that Arcite to Thebes comen was,
Full oft a day he swelt° and said "Alas"—
For seen his lady shall he nevermo.
500 And shortly to concluden all his wo,
So muchel sorrwe had never creature
That is or shall while that the world may dure!
His sleep, his mete, his drink is him biraft,
That lene he wex and dry as is a shaft;
505 His eyen hollow and grisly to biholde,
His hewe fallow,° and pale as ashen colde;
And solitary he was and ever alone,
And wailing all the night, making his mone.
And if he herde song or instrument,
510 Than wold he weep, he mighte not be stent.°
So feeble eek were his spirits and so lowe,
And chaunged so that no man coude knowe
His speeche nor his voice, though men it herde;
And in his gere° for all the world he ferde°
515 Not only like the lover's maladye
Of Hereos,° but rather like manie,
Engendred of humour malencholic,
Biforn his owne celle fantastic.°
And shortly, turned was all up-so-down
520 Both habit and eek disposicioun
Of him, this woeful lover daun Arcite.
    What shold I all day of his woe endite?
Whan he endured had a yeer or two
This cruel torment and this pain and wo
525 At Thebes in his contree, as I saide,

498 **swelt** weakened   506 **fallow** jaundiced   510 **stent** stopped   514
**gere** changeableness   514 **ferde** fared, behaved   516 **lover's malady
of Hereos** i.e., of Eros—a temporary madness induced by love, de-
scribed in medieval medical treatises. The symptoms were sleepless-
ness, depression, paleness, loss of appetite, hysteria. See *Modern
Philology*, XI,491   516–18 **manie . . . fantastic** "mania," brought
about by the humor of melancholy in the front part of the brain
(the "cell fantastic"). The front cell of the brain was thought to
harbor fantasy, the middle one reason, and the back one memory

Upon a night in sleep as he him laide
Him thought how that the winged god Mercurye
Biforn him stood, and bade him to be murrye.
His sleepy yerde° in hand he bare uprighte;
An hat he wered upon his heres brighte—                    *530*
Arrayed was this god, as he took keep,°
As he was whan that Argus took his sleep,
And said him thus: "To Athens shaltou wende.°
There is thee shapen° of thy woe an ende."

    And with that word Arcite woke and sterte:           *535*
"Now trewely, how sore that me smerte,"
Quod he, "to Athens right now wol I fare!
Ne for the drede of deeth shall I not spare
To see my lady that I love and serve.
In hir presence I recche not to sterve."°                  *540*
And with that word he caught a greet mirrour,
And saw that chaunged was all his colour,
And saw his visage all in another kinde;
And right anon it ran him in his minde
That sith his face was so disfigured                       *545*
Of malady the which he had endured,
He mighte well, if that he bare him lowe,°
Live in Athens evermore unknowe,
And seen his lady well nigh day by day.
And right anon he chaunged his array,                      *550*
And clad him as a poore laborer,
And all alone, save only a squier
That knew his privetee and all his cas°—
Which was disguised poorly° as he was—
To Athens is he gone the nexte° way.                       *555*
And to the court he went upon a day,
And at the gate he proffreth his servise,
To drudge and draw what so men wol devise.
And shortly of this matter for to sayn,

---

**529 yerde** Mercury's wand, capable of inducing sleep   **531 as he
took keep** as Arcite noticed   **533 wende** go   **534 There . . . shapen**
there is prepared for you   **540 I recche not to sterve** I don't care
if I die   **547 bare him lowe** acted low-class   **553 privetee . . . cas**
his secret and all his circumstance   **554 poorly** as a poor man
**555 nexte** nearest

560 He fill in office with a chamberlain,°
     The which that dwelling was with Emelye;
     For he was wise, and coude soon espye
     Of every servant which that serveth here.
     Well coud he hewen° wood and water bere,
565 For he was yong and mighty for the nones,
     And thereto he was strong and big of bones,
     To doon what any wight can him devise.
     A yeer or two he was in this servise,
     Page of the chambre of Emely the brighte—
570 And "Philostrate" he saide that he highte.
        But half so well-beloved a man as he
     Ne was there never in court of his degree!°
     He was so gentil of condicioun
     That thurghout all the court was his renown.
575 They saiden that it were a charitee
     That Theseus wold enhauncen his degree,
     And putten him in worshipful servise,
     Ther as he might his vertu° exercise.
     And thus within a while his name is spronge,
580 Both of his deedes and his goode tonge,
     That Theseus hath taken him so neer,
     That of his chambre he made him a squier,
     And gaf him gold to maintene his degree.
     And eek men brought him out of his contree,
585 Fro yeer to yeer, full prively his rente°—
     But honestly and slyly he it spente
     That no man wondred how that he it hadde.
     And three yeer in this wise his life he ladde,
     And bare him so in pees and eek in werre,°
590 There was no man that Theseus hath derre.°
        And in this blisse let° I now Arcite,
     And speke I wol of Palamon a lite:
        In derknesse and horrible and strong prisoun
     This seven yeer hath seten Palamoun,

560 **fill . . . chamberlain** got into the service of a steward   564 **hewen**
chop   572 **degree** social class   578 **vertu** good character and ability
—hence he should have a more honored occupation (worshipful
servise)   585 **rente** income   589 **werre** war   590 **hath derre** liked
better (dearer)   591 **let** leave

Forpined,° what for woe and for distresse!                        595
Who feeleth double sore and hevinesse
But Palamon, that love distraineth so
That wood out of his wit he goth for wo?
And eek thereto he is a prisoner—
Perpetuelly, not only for a yeer.                                 600
Who coude ryme in English proprely
His martyrdom? Forsooth, it am not I.
Therefore I pass as lightly as I may:°
    It fill that in the seventh yeer, of May
The thridde night,° as olde bookes sayn                           605
(That all this story tellen more plain),
Were it by aventure or destinee—
As whan a thing is shapen it shall be°—
That soon after the midnight, Palamoun,
By helping of a freend, brak his prisoun,                         610
And fleeth the citee, fast as he may go,
For he had yive his jailer drinke so
Of a claree, made of a certain win
With nercotics and opie of Thebes fin,°
That all that night, though that men wold him shake,              615
The jailer sleep, he mighte not awake;
And thus he fleeth as fast as ever he may.
The night was short and faste by the day,
That needes cost° he most himselven hide.
And til a grove faste there beside                                620
With dredful° foot than stalketh Palamoun—
For shortly, this was his opinioun,
That in that grove he wold him hide all day,
And in the night than wold he take his way
To Thebesward, his freendes for to praye                          625

595 **Forpined** pined or wasted away   601–03 **Who ... may** again, an
echo of Chaucer's own voice; the Knight is certainly not "ryming."
Notice line 606: Chaucer is here struggling to condense an unwieldy
narrative   604–05 **May ... thridde** May 3 was thought an unlucky
day   608 **As ... be** the phrase explains "destinee": when a thing
is determined, it will happen. "Aventure" is chance   612–14 **drinke
... fin** drink some claree (wine mixed with honey and spices), made
of a special wine with narcotics in it and the fine opium of Thebes.
Such drugs were used to cure love-melancholy; hence Palamon's
possession of them, perhaps   619 **needes cost** by necessity   621 **dred-
ful** timid

On Theseus to help him to werreye.°
And shortly, outher he wold lese his lif,
Or winnen Emely unto his wif—
This is th'effect and his entente plain.
630     Now wol I turn to Arcite again,
That litel wist how neigh that was his care,°
Till that Fortune had brought him in the snare:
The bisy larke, messager of day,
Salueth in hir song the morrwe grey,
635 And firy Phebus riseth up so brighte
That all the orient laugheth of the lighte,
And with his streemes dryeth in the greves°
The silver droppes hanging on the leves.
And Arcita, that in the court royal
640 With Theseus is squier principal,
Is risen and looketh on the murrye day;
And for to doon his observaunce to May,
Remembring on the point° of his desir,
He on a courser startling° as the fir
645 Is riden into the feeldes him to playe,
Out of the court were it a mile or twaye;
And to the grove of which that I you tolde
By aventure his way he gan to holde,
To maken him a garland of the greves,
650 Were it of woodebind or hawthorn leves;
And loud he song ayain the sunne sheene,
"May, with all thy flowres and thy greene,
Welcome be thou, faire freshe May,
In hope that I some greene gete may!"°
655 And from his courser with a lusty herte
Into the grove full hastily he sterte,
And in a path he rometh up and down
Thereas by aventure this Palamoun
Was in a bush, that no man might him see—
660 For sore afered of his deeth was he.
No thing ne knew he that it was Arcite;

626 **werreye** make war    631 **That . . . care** who little knew how
near trouble was    637 **greves** foliage    643 **point** object    644 **star-
tling** leaping    654 **some . . . may** may get something green. His song
may be a wish for love

God wot he wold have trowed° it full lite.
But sooth is said, gon sithen many yeeres,°
That "feeld hath eyen and the wood hath eres":
It is full fair a man to bere him evene,°                          665
For alday meeten men at unset stevene.°
Full litel wot Arcite of his fellawe
That was so neigh to herknen all his sawe,°
For in the bush he sitteth now full stille.
    Whan that Arcite had romed all his fille,                      670
And songen all the roundel lustily,
Into a study he fill suddenly,
As doon thise lovers in hir quaynte geres°—
Now in the crop, now down in the breres,°
Now up, now down, as bucket in a welle.                            675
Right as the Friday, soothly for to telle,
Now it shineth, now it raineth faste,
Right so can gery Venus° overcaste
The hertes of hir folk; right as hir day
Is gereful, right so chaungeth she array—                          680
Seld is the Friday all the wike y-like.°
Whan that Arcite had song, he gan to sike,°
And set him down withouten any more:
"Alas," quod he, "that day that I was bore!
How longe, Juno, thurgh thy crueltee                               685
Woltou werreyen° Thebes the citee?
Alas, y-brought is to confusioun
The blood royal of Cadme and Amphioun—
Of Cadmus, which that was the firste man
That Thebes bilt or° first the town began,                         690
And of the citee first was crowned king.
Of his linage am I and his offspring,
By veray line,° as of the stock royal.

662 **trowed** believed    663 **gon . . . yeeres** since many years ago
665 **It . . . evene** it is very good for a man to conduct himself with
restraint   666 **For . . . stevene** for men constantly meet each other
at unexpected times   668 **so . . . sawe** so close as to hear all he said
673 **quaynte geres** strange moods   674 **crop . . . breres** now in the
treetop, now down in the briars   678 **gery Venus** changeable Venus.
Friday is Venus's day and was said to have different weather from
the rest of the week   681 **all . . . y-like** like the rest of the week
682 **sike** sigh   686 **werreyen** make war upon   690 **or** ere, before
693 **veray line** direct descent

And now I am so caitiff° and so thrall,
695 That he that is my mortal enemy,
I serve him as his squier povrely!°
And yet doth Juno me well more shame,
For I dare not biknow° mine owen name,
But there as I was wont to hight Arcite,
700 Now hight I Philostrate, not worth a mite!
Alas, thou felle Mars! Alas, Juno!
Thus hath your ire our linage all fordo,
Save only me and wretched Palamoun,
That Theseus martyreth in prisoun!
705 And over all this, to sleen me outrely,
Love hath his firy dart so brenningly
Y-sticked thurgh my trewe careful herte,
That shapen was my deeth erst than my sherte!°
Ye sleen me with your eyen, Emelye!
710 Ye been the cause wherefore that I die!
Of all the remnant of mine other care
Ne set I nought the mountance of a tare,°
So that I coud doon ought to your plesaunce!"
And with that word he fill down in a traunce
715 A longe time. And after he up sterte.
    This Palamon, that thought that thurgh his herte
He felt a cold swerd suddenliche glide,
For ire he quoke, no longer wold he bide.°
And whan that he had herd Arcite's tale,
720 As he were wood, with face deed and pale,
He stert him up out of the bushes thicke
And said, "Arcite, false traitour wicke,
Now artou hent, that lovest my lady so,
For whom that I have all this pain and wo—
725 And art my blood, and to my conseil sworn,
As I full oft have told thee herebiforn,
And hast bijaped° here duke Theseus,
And falsely chaunged hast thy name thus.

---

694 **caitiff** wretched   696 **povrely** in a humble capacity   698 **biknow**
reveal   708 **shapen . . . sherte** my death was predestined before my
shirt, i.e., before my first garment was made. A commonplace
712 **mountance . . . tare** value of a weed   718 **bide** wait   727 **bijaped**
duped

I wol be deed or elles thou shalt die!
Thou shalt not love my lady Emelye, 730
But I wol love hir only and namo!
For I am Palamon, thy mortal fo,
And though that I no wepne have in this place,
But out of prison am astert° by grace,
I drede not that outher thou shalt die, 735
Or thou ne shalt not loven Emelye.
Chees which thou wolt, or thou shalt not asterte."

   This Arcite with full despitous herte,
Whan he him knew and had his tale herd,
As fierce as leon pulled out his swerd, 740
And saide thus: "By God that sit above,
Nere it that thou art sick and wood for love,
And eek that thou no wepne hast in this place,
Thou sholdest never out of this grove pace,
That thou ne sholdest dien of my hond! 745
For I defy the suretee and the bond
Which that thou saist that I have made to thee.
What, veray fool, think well that love is free,
And I wol love hir, maugree° all thy might!
But for as much thou art a worthy knight, 750
And wilnest to darrein° hir by battaile,
Have here my trouth, tomorrwe I wol not faile,
Withouten witing of any other wight,
That here I wol be founden as a knight,
And bringen harneis° right enough for thee— 755
And chees the best, and leeve the worst for me.
And mete and drinke this night wol I bringe
Enough for thee, and clothes for thy beddinge.
And if so be that thou my lady winne
And slee me in this wood ther I am inne, 760
Thou maist well have thy lady as for me."°
This Palamon answered, "I graunt it thee."
And thus they been departed till amorrwe,
Whan ech of hem had laid his faith to borrwe.° 765

   O Cupid, out of alle charitee! 765

734 astert escaped   749 maugree in spite of   751 wilnest to darrein
wish to decide (your claim to) her   755 harneis armor   761 as for
me as far as I am concerned   764 to borrwe as a pledge

O regne,° that wold no fellaw° have with thee!
Full sooth is said that love ne lordshipe
Wol not, his thankes, have no fellawshipe;°
Well finden that Arcite and Palamoun!

770    Arcite is riden anon unto the town,
And on the morrwe ere it were dayes light,
Full prively two harneis hath he dight,
Both suffisant and meete to darreine
The battaile in the feeld bitwix hem twaine;

775    And on his horse, alone as he was born,
He carrieth all this harneis him biforn;
And in the grove at time and place y-set
This Arcite and this Palamon been met.

To chaungen gan the colour in hir face,°
780    Right as the hunters in the regne of Trace,
That standeth at the gappe° with a spere,
Whan hunted is the leon or the bere,
And hereth him come rushing in the greves,
And breketh bothe boughes and the leves,

785    And thinketh, "Here cometh my mortal enemy!
Withoute fail he moot be deed or I,
For outher I mot sleen him at the gappe,
Or he mot slee me if that me mishappe."
So ferden they in chaunging of hir hewe.

790    As fer as everich of hem other knewe,
There nas no "Good day" ne no saluinge,
But straight, withouten word or rehersinge,
Everich of hem help for to armen other,
As freendly as he were his owne brother.

795    And after that with sharpe speres stronge
They foinen ech at other° wonder longe—
Thou mightest weene that this Palamoun
In his fighting were a wood leoun,
And as a cruel tiger was Arcite:

800    As wilde bores gonnen they to smite,
That frothen white as foom, for ire wood—

766 regne rule    766 fellaw companion    768 his . . . fellawshipe
willingly have any companionship    779 face faces    781 gappe the
space between hunters and game    796 foinen . . . other thrust out
at each other

Up to the ankle fought they in hir blood.
And in this wise I let hem fighting dwelle,°
And forth I wol of Theseus you telle.
   The destinee, ministre general,        805
That executeth in the world overall
The purveyance° that God hath seen biforn,
So strong it is that, though the world had sworn
The contrary of a thing by ye or nay,
Yet sometime it shall fallen on a day        810
That° falleth not eft° within a thousand yeer.
For certainly, our appetites heer,
Be it of wer, or pees, or hate, or love,
All is this ruled by the sight above.
This mene I now by mighty Theseus,        815
That for to hunten is so desirous,
And namely at the greete hert in May,
That in his bed there daweth him° no day
That he nis clad and redy for to ride
With hunt and horn and houndes him beside;        820
For in his hunting hath he swich delit
That it is all his joy and appetit
To been himself the greete hertes bane;°
For after Mars he serveth now Diane.°
   Cleer was the day, as I have told ere this,        825
And Theseus, with alle joy and bliss,
With his Ipolyta the faire queene,
And Emelye clothed all in greene,
On hunting been they riden royally,
And to the grove that stood full faste by,        830
In which there was an hert, as men him tolde,
Duke Theseus the straighte way hath holde,
And to this land he rideth him full right.
For thider was the hert wont have his flight,
And over a brook, and so forth on his waye.        835
This Duke wol han a course° at him or twaye,
With houndes swich as that him list commande.
And whan this Duke was come unto the lande,

---

803 **dwelle** continue  807 **purveyance** foreknowledge  811 **That** what
811 **eft** again  818 **daweth him** dawns for him  823 **bane** death
824 **Diane** goddess of hunting  836 **course** charge, run

Under the sun° he looketh, and anon
840 He was ware of Arcite and Palamon,
That foughten breme° as it were boles° two!
The brighte swerdes wenten to and fro
So hidously that with the leste strook
It seemed as it wolde fell an ook!
845 But what they were no thing he ne wot.
This Duke his courser with the spores smot,
And at a stert he was bitwix hem two,
And pulled out a swerd, and cried, "Ho!
Namore, up° pain of lesing of your heed!
850 By mighty Mars, he shall anon be deed
That smiteth any stroke that I may seen!
But telleth me what mister° men ye been,
That been so hardy for to fighten heer,
Withouten judge or other officer,
855 As it were in a listes royally?"
        This Palamon answerde hastily
And saide, "Sir, what needeth wordes mo?
We have the deeth deserved bothe two.
Two woeful wretches been we, two caitives,
860 That been encumbred of° our owne lives;
And as thou art a rightful lord and judge,
Ne yive us neither mercy ne refuge;
But slee me first, for sainte charitee,
But slee my fellow eek as well as me;
865 Or slee him first, for though thou knowest it lite,
This is thy mortal foe, this is Arcite,
That fro thy land is banished on his heed,°
For which he hath deserved to be deed;
For this is he that came unto thy gate,
870 And saide that he highte Philostrate.
Thus hath he japed thee full many a yeer,
And thou hast maked him thy chief squier;
And this is he that loveth Emelye.
For sith the day is come that I shall die,

---

839 **Under the sun** in a low sun (?); or, perhaps, shielding his eyes
841 **breme** furiously    841 **boles** bulls    849 **up** on    852 **mister** kind
of    860 **encumbred of** burdened by, tired of    867 **on his heed** on
pain of losing his head

I make plainly my confessioun                                   875
That I am thilke woeful Palamoun,
That hath thy prison broken wickedly.
I am thy mortal foe, and it am I
That loveth so hot Emely the brighte,
That I wol die present in hir sighte;                           880
Wherefore I axe deeth and my juwise.°
But slee my fellow in the same wise,
For both have we deserved to be slain."
    This worthy Duke answered anon again
And said, "This is a short conclusioun.                         885
Your owne mouth by your confessioun
Hath dampned you, and I wol it recorde:
It needeth not to pine you with the corde°—
Ye shull be deed, by mighty Mars the rede!"°
    The queen anon for veray womanheede                         890
Gan for to weep, and so did Emelye,
And all the ladies in the compaignye.
Greet pitee was it, as it thought hem alle,
That ever swich a chaunce sholde falle;
For gentilmen they were of greet estat,                         895
And nothing but for love was this debat;
And saw hir bloody woundes wide and sore,
And alle criden, bothe lass and more,
"Have mercy, lord, upon us women alle!"
And on hir bare knees adown they falle,                         900
And wold have kist his feet ther as he stood;
Till at the last aslacked was his mood°—
For pitee renneth soon in gentil herte°—
And though he first for ire quoke and sterte,
He hath considered shortly, in a clause,                        905
The trespass of hem both, and eek the cause;
And although that his ire hir guilt accused,
Yet in his reson he hem both excused,
As thus: He thoughte well that every man
Wol help himself in love if that he can,                        910
And eek deliver himself out of prisoun.

881 **juwise** sentence   888 **pine . . . corde** torture   889 **rede** red is
associated with Mars   902 **aslacked . . . mood** his anger was assuaged
903 **For . . . herte** the line is a great favorite of Chaucer's

And eek his herte had compassioun
Of women, for they wepten ever in oon.
And in his gentil hert he thought anon,
915 And soft unto himself he saide, "Fy
Upon a lord that wol have no mercy,
But be a leon both in word and deede
To hem that been in repentance and drede,
As well as to a proud despitous man
920 That wol maintene that he first began.°
That lord hath litel of discrecioun
That in swich case kan no divisioun,°
But weyeth pride and humbless after oon."°
And shortly, whan his ire is thus agoon,
925 He gan to looken up with eyen lighte,
And spak thise same wordes all on highte:°
"The God of Love, ah, *benedicite!*
How mighty and how greet a lord is he!
Agains his might there gaineth none obstacles.
930 He may be cleped a god for his miracles!
For he can maken at his owen guise°
Of everich hert as that him list devise.
Lo, here this Arcite and this Palamoun,
That quitly° weren out of my prisoun,
935 And might have lived in Thebes royally,
And witen° I am hir mortal enemy,
And that hir deeth lith in my might also—
And yet hath Love, maugree hir eyen two,
Brought hem hider bothe for to die.
940 Now looketh, is not that an heigh follye?
     Who may been a fool, but if he love?
Behold, for Goddes sake that sit above,
See how they bleed! Be they not well arrayed?
Thus hath hir lord the God of Love y-payed
945 Hir wages and hir fees for hir servise.
And yet they weenen for to be full wise,
That serven Love, for aught that may bifalle.

920 **maintene . . . began** keep up what he first started (i.e., stubbornly)
922 **kan no divisioun** sees no distinction     923 **weyeth . . . oon** weighs
pride and humility equally     926 **on highte** aloud     931 **at . . . guise**
at will     934 **quitly** freely     936 **witen** know

But this is yet the beste game° of alle,
That she for whom they have this jolitee
Can hem therefore as muche thank as me!°        950
She wot namore of all this hote fare,
By God, than wot a cockoo of an hare.°
But all mot been assayed,° hot and cold—
A man mot been a fool, or yong or old.
I wot it by myself full yore agoon,        955
For in my time a servant° was I oon.
And therefore, sin I know of Love's paine,
And wot how sore it can a man distraine,°
As he that hath been caught oft in his las,°
I you foryive all holly this trespass,        960
At request of the queen that kneeleth here,
And eek of Emely my suster dere;
And ye shall both anon unto me swere
That never mo ye shall my contree dere,°
Ne make wer upon me, night nor day,        965
But been my freendes in all that ye may.
I you foryive this trespass everydeel."
      And they him sworen his axing° fair and well,
And him of lordship and of mercy prayde;
And he hem graunteth grace, and thus he saide:        970
      "To speke of royal linage and richesse,
Though that she were a queen or a princesse,
Ech of you both is worthy, douteless,
To wedden whan time is. But, natheless—
I speke as for my suster Emelye        975
For whom ye have this strife and jalousye—
Ye wot yourself she may not wedden two
At ones, though ye fighten evermo.
That one of you, al be him loth or lief,°
He mot go pipen in an ivy leef°—        980
This is to sayn, she may not now have bothe,

948 game joke    950 Can . . . me is as much obliged to them for
it as to me    952 than . . . hare than a cuckoo knows about a hare.
(Some editors give the reading "or an hare.")    953 assayed tried
out    956 servant i.e., of Love    958 distraine afflict    959 las snare
964 dere harm    968 axing what he asked    979 al . . . lief whether
it be disagreeable or agreeable to him    980 pipen . . . leef whistle
(for consolation) using an ivy leaf as a reed

Al be ye never so jalous ne so wrothe.
And forthy I you put in this degree,°
That ech of you shall have his destinee
985 As him is shape, and herkneth in what wise—
Lo, here your end of that I shall devise:
　　My will is this, for plat° conclusioun,
Withouten any replicacioun°—
If that you liketh, take it for the beste:
990 That everich of you shall goon where him leste,
Freely, withouten raunson or daunger,
And this day fifty wikes, fer ne neer,°
Everich of you shall bring an hundred knightes,
Armed for listes up° at alle rightes,°
995 All redy to darrein hir by battaile.
And this bihote° I you withouten faile,
Upon my trouth and as I am a knight,
That whether of you bothe that hath might—
This is to sayn, that whether he or thou
1000 May with his hundred as I spak of now
Sleen his contrary, or out of listes drive—
Than shall I yive Emely to wive
To whom that Fortune yiveth so fair a grace.
The listes shall I maken in this place,
1005 And God so wisly on my soule rewe,°
As I shall even judge been and trewe.
Ye shall none other ende with me maken,
That one of you ne shall be deed or taken.
And if you thinketh this is well y-said,
1010 Say your avis,° and holdeth you apaid.°
This is your end and your conclusioun."
　　Who looketh lightly now but Palamoun?
Who springeth up for joye but Arcite?
Who coude tell or who coud it endite
1015 The joye that is maked in the place,
Whan Theseus hath done so fair a grace?
But down on knees went every manner wight,

---

983 **degree** state   987 **plat** plain, flat   988 **replicacioun** protest
992 **fer ne neer** more or less   994 **Armed . . . up** cf. "dressed up"
994 **at alle rightes** in all respects   996 **bihote** promise   1005 **rewe**
pity   1010 **avis** opinion   1010 **apaid** satisfied

And thanken him with all hir hert and might,
And namely the Thebans ofte sithe.°
And thus with good hope and with herte blithe          *1020*
They take hir leeve, and homeward gonne they ride
To Thebes, with his olde walles wide.

## PART THREE

I trow men wolde deem it necligence
If I foryet to tellen the dispence°
Of Theseus, that goth so bisily                        *1025*
To maken up the listes royally,
That swich a noble theatre° as it was
I dare well sayen in this world there nas.
The circuit a mile was aboute,
Walled of stone and ditched all withoute.              *1030*
Round was the shape in manner of compass,
Full of degrees, the height of sixty pas,°
That whan a man was set on oo degree°
He letted not his fellaw for to see.°

Eestward there stood a gate of marble whit,            *1035*
Westward right swich another in th'opposit;
And shortly to concluden, swich a place
Was none in erth as in so litel space.°
For in the land there was no crafty man
That geometry or ars-metrik kan,°                       *1040*
Ne purtrayour, ne kerver of images,
That Theseus ne yaf him mete and wages,
The theatre for to maken and devise.
And for to doon his rite and sacrifise,
He eestward hath, upon the gate above,                 *1045*
In worship of Venus, goddess of love,
Doon make an auter° and an oratorye.
And on the gate westward, in memorye
Of Mars, he maked hath right swich another,

---

1019 **ofte sithe** many times   1024 **dispence** expenditure   1027 **theatre**
arena   1032 **Full . . . pas** constructed fully in steps, sixty yards high
1033 **on oo degree** on one step   1034 **letted . . . see** did not keep
someone else from seeing   1038 **as . . . space** of comparable size
1040 **ars-metrik kan** knows arithmetic   1047 **auter** altar

1050 That coste largely of gold a fother.°
And northward in a touret on the wall,
Of alabastre white and red coral,
An oratory riche for to see,
In worship of Diane of chastitee,
1055 Hath Theseus doon wrought° in noble wise.
      But yet had I forgeten to devise
The noble kerving and the portraitures,
The shape, the countenance, and the figures,
That weren in thise oratories three.

\*    \*    \*

1060     First, in the temple of Venus maistou see,
Wrought on the wall, full pitous to beholde,
The broken sleepes and the sikes° colde,
The sacred teres and the waymentinge,
The firy strokes of the desiringe
1065 That Love's servants in this life enduren,
The othes that hir covenants assuren,
Plesance and Hope, Desire, Foolhardinesse,
Beautee and Youthe, Bawdery, Richesse,
Charmes and Force, Lesinges,° Flatterye,
1070 Dispence, Bisiness, and Jalousye,
That wered of yellow goldes° a garland,
And a cockoo sitting on hir hand;
Feestes, instruments, caroles, daunces,
Lust and array,° and all the circumstances
1075 Of love, which that I° reckened and recken shall,
By order weren painted on the wall,
And mo than I can make of mencioun.
For soothly all the Mount of Citheroun,°
Ther Venus hath hir principal dwellinge,

1050 **fother** cartload   1055 **doon wrought** had made. The kind of
symbolical scenes which follow occur often in medieval literature
1062 **sikes** sighs   1069 **Lesinges** lies   1071 **goldes** marigolds. Yellow
is the color of jealousy; the cuckoo in the next line is associated
with cuckoldry   1074 **Lust and array** pleasure and dress   1075 **I**
conventional device in descriptions; the knight speaks as if he had
been there   1078 **Citheroun** Cythera, where Venus rose from the
sea

Was shewed on the wall in portrayinge,                    *1080*
With all the garden and the lustinesse.
Not was foryeten the porter Idelnesse,
Ne Narcissus the fair of yore agoon,
Ne yet the folly of king Salomon,
Ne yet the greete strength of Ercules,                    *1085*
Th'enchantments of Medea and Circes,
Ne of Turnus with the hardy fierce corage,
The riche Cresus, caitiff in servage.
Thus may ye seen that wisdom ne richesse,
Beautee ne sleighte,° strengthe, hardinesse,              *1090*
Ne may with Venus holde champartye,°
For as hir list, the world than may she gie.°
Lo, all thise folk so caught were in hir las°
Till they for woe full ofte said alas.
Suffiseth here ensamples one or two,                      *1095*
And though I coude recken a thousand mo.
    The statue of Venus, glorious for to see,
Was naked, fleting° in the large see,
And fro the navel down all covered was
With wawes° green and bright as any glass.                *1100*
A citole° in hir right hand hadde she,
And on hir heed, full seemly for to see,
A rose garland fresh and well smellinge,
Above hir heed hir douves° flickeringe.
Biforn hir stood hir sone Cupido;                         *1105*
Upon hir shouldres winges had he two,
And blind he was, as it is ofte seene;
A bow he bare, and arrwes bright and keene.


                *    *    *


    Why shold I not as well eek tell you all
The portraiture that was upon the wall                    *1110*
Within the temple of mighty Mars the rede?
All painted was the wall in length and brede

1090 **sleighte** trickery   1091 **champartye** rivalry   1092 **gie** govern
1093 **las** snare   1098 **fleting** floating   1100 **wawes** waves   1101 **citole**
stringed instrument   1104 **douves** doves were thought to be "max-
ime in coitu fervidae"

Like to the estres° of the grisly place
That hight the greete temple of Mars in Trace,
1115 In thilke colde frosty regioun
Ther as Mars hath his sovereign mansioun.
　　First on the wall was painted a forest,
In which there dwelleth neither man ne beest,
With knotty, knarry, barrein trees olde,
1120 Of stubbes sharp and hidous to beholde,
In which there ran a rumble in a swough,°
As though a storm shold bresten every bough.
And downward on an hill under a bente°
There stood the temple of Mars armipotente,°
1125 Wrought all of burned steel, of which th'entree
Was long and strait and ghastly for to see,
And thereout came a rage and swich a veze°
That it made all the gate for to reze.°
The northren light in at the doores shoon,
1130 For window on the wall ne was there noon
Thurgh which men mighten any light discerne.
The door was all of adamant eterne,
Y-clenched overthwart and endelong°
With iren tough; and for to make it strong
1135 Every piler the temple to sustene
Was tonne-greet,° of iren bright and sheene.
There saw I first the derk imagininge
Of Felony, and all the compassinge,°
The cruel Ire, red as any gleede,°
1140 The pike-purse, and eek the pale Drede,
The smiler with the knife under the cloke,
The shepne° brenning with the blacke smoke,
The treson of the murdring in the bed,
The open Wer with woundes all bibled,°
1145 Contek° with bloody knife and sharp menace;
All full of chirking° was that sorry place!

1113 **estres** interior parts    1121 **in a swough** in the form of a great
wind    1123 **bente** hillside    1124 **armipotente** powerful in arms
1127 **veze** blast (of wind)    1128 **reze** shake    1133 **overthwart and
endelong** crosswise and lengthwise    1136 **tonne-greet** as thick as
a tun (barrel)    1138 **compassinge** scheming    1139 **gleede** live coal
1142 **shepne** stable    1144 **bibled** covered wtih blood    1145 **Contek**
strife    1146 **chirking** creaking or scraping sound

The sleer° of himself yet saw I ther—
His herte blood hath bathed all his heer;
The nail y-driven in the shode° anight;
The colde Deeth with mouth gaping upright.                    *1150*
Amiddes of the temple sat Meschaunce,
With disconfort and sorry countenaunce.
Yet saw I Woodness,° laughing in his rage;
Armed Complaint, Outhees,° and fierce Outrage;
The caroine° in the bush with throt y-corve,°                    *1155*
A thousand slain and nought of qualm y-storve,°
The tyrant with the prey by force y-raft,
The town destroyed—there was nothing laft.
Yet saw I brent the shippes hoppesteres,°
The hunte° strangled with the wilde beres,                    *1160*
The sow freten° the child right in the cradel,
The cook y-scalded for all his longe ladel.
Nought was forgetten by the infortune of Marte
The carter overriden with his carte—
Under the wheel full low he lay adown.                    *1165*
There were also of Martes divisioun°
The barbour and the butcher and the smith
That forgeth sharpe swerdes on his stith.°
And all above depainted in a towr
Saw I Conquest, sitting in greet honour,                    *1170*
With the sharpe swerd over his heed
Hanging by a subtil twines threed.
Depainted was the slaughtre of Julius,
Of grete Nero, and of Antonius—
Al be that thilke time they were unborn,                    *1175*
Yet was hir deeth depainted therebiforn,
By menacing of Mars, right by figure!°
So was it showed in that portraiture,
As is depainted in the sters above
Who shall be slain, or elles deed for love.                    *1180*

1147 **sleer** slayer   1149 **shode** skull   1153 **Woodness** madness   1154
**Outhees** outcry   1155 **caroine** corpse   1155 **y-corve** cut   1156 **of
qualm y-storve** killed by pestilence (which would have come under
the influence of Saturn)   1159 **shippes hoppesteres** dancing ships
1160 **hunte** hunter   1161 **freten** finished devouring   1166 **of . . .
divisioun** in Mars' jurisdiction   1168 **stith** anvil   1177 **menacing
. . . figure** the threat of Mars figured in the stars

Suffiseth one ensample in stories olde:
I may not recken hem alle, though I wolde.
　　The statue of Mars upon a carte stood
Armed, and looked grim as he were wood.
1185 And over his heed there shinen two figures
Of sterres, that been cleped in scriptures
That one Puella, that other Rubeus.°
This god of armes was arrayed thus:
A wolf there stood before him at his feet,
1190 With eyen red, and of a man he eet—
With subtil pencil depainted was this storye
In redouting° of Mars and of his glorye.

*　　*　　*

　　Now to the temple of Diane the chaste
As shortly as I can I wol me haste,
1195 To telle you all the descripsioun.
Depainted been the walles up and down
Of hunting and of shamefast° chastitee.
There saw I how woeful Calistopee,°
Whan that Diane agreved was with here,
1200 Was turned fro a woman til a bere,
And after was she made the Lode-Sterre—
Thus was it painted, I can say you no ferre.°
Hir son is eek a ster, as men may see.
There saw I Dane° y-turned til° a tree—
1205 I mene not the goddesse Diane,
But Penneus' daughter, which that highte Dane.
There saw I Atheon° an hert y-maked,
For vengeance that he saw Diane all naked—
I saw how that his houndes have him caught
1210 And freten° him, for that they knew him nought.

1187 **Puella . . . Rubeus** these were figures in geomancy, the art of
interpreting dots hurriedly made on paper. Both are devoted to
Mars    1192 **redouting** reverence    1197 **shamefast** modest    1198
**Calistopee** Callisto. Jove lay with her, and Diana was angry because
she was no longer a virgin. Juno changed her into a bear, and Jove
put her in the heavens (as Ursa Major). The connection of mythology
and astrology seemed natural to the medievals    1202 **ferre** farther
1204 **Dane** Daphne    1204 **til** into    1207 **Atheon** Actaeon    1210 **freten**
devoured

Yet painted was a litel further moor
How Athalante° hunted the wilde boor,
And Meleagre, and many another mo,
For which Diane wrought him care and wo.
There saw I many another wonder storye,     1215
The which me list not drawen to memorye.
    This goddess on an hert° full hye seet,
With smalle houndes all about hir feet,
And underneth hir feet she had a moone—
Waxing it was, and sholde wanie soone.     1220
In gaudee° green hir statue clothed was,
With bow in hand and arrwes in a cas;
Hir eyen caste she full low adown
Ther Pluto hath his derke regioun.
A woman travailing° was hir biforn,     1225
But for hir child so longe was unborn,
Full pitously Lucina° gan she calle,
And saide, "Help, for thou maist best of alle."
Well coud he painte lifly that it wroughte;
With many a florin he the hewes boughte.     1230

\*     \*     \*

    Now been thise listes made, and Theseus,
That at his greete cost arrayed thus
The temples and the theatre everydeel,
Whan it was done him liked wonder well.
But stinte I wol of Theseus a lite,     1235
And speke of Palamon and of Arcite.
    The day approcheth of hir returninge,
That everich shold an hundred knightes bringe
The battaile to darrein, as I you tolde.
And til Athens, hir covenant for to holde,     1240
Hath everich of hem brought an hundred knightes,
Well armed for the wer at alle rightes;
And sikerly there trowed many a man
That never sithen that the world bigan,

1212 **Athalante** Atalanta   1217 **hert** harts were associated with
chastity   1221 **gaudee** yellowish   1225 **travailing** in labor   1227 **Lucina** goddess of childbirth

1245 As for to speke of knighthood of hir hand,
     As fer as God hath maked see and land,
     Nas of so few so noble a compaignye.
     For every wight that loved chivalrye,
     And wold, his thankes, han a passant name,°
1250 Hath prayed that he might been of that game—
     And well was him° that thereto chosen was;
     For if there fill tomorrwe swich a cas,
     Ye knowen well that every lusty knight
     That loveth paramours° and hath his might,
1255 Were it in Engelond or elleswhere,
     They wold, hir thankes, wilnen to be there.
     To fighten for a lady, *ben'dic'te*
     It were a lusty sighte for to see!
         And right so ferden they with Palamon.
1260 With him there wenten knightes many oon;
     Some wol been armed in an habergeoun,°
     And in a brestplate and in a light gipoun;°
     And some wol have a paire plates° large;
     And some wol have a Pruce° sheeld or a targe;°
1265 Some wol be armed on his legges well,
     And have an ax, and some a mace of steel—
     There nis no newe guise that it nas old.°
     Armed were they as I have you told,
     Everich after his opinioun.
1270     There maistou seen coming with Palamon
     Lygurge° himself, the grete king of Trace.
     Black was his beerd and manly was his face;
     The cercles of his eyen in his heed,
     They gloweden bitwixen yellow and red,

1249 **wold . . . name** would willingly have an outstanding reputation
1251 **well was him** (there was) happiness for him    1254 **paramours**
with knightly devotion    1261 **habergeoun** coat of mail    1262 **gipoun**
tunic    1263 **paire plates** set of plate-armor    1264 **Pruce** Prussian
1264 **targe** round shield    1267 **nis . . . old** is no new (Fourteenth-
century) fashion that was not found among the ancients. The line
implies that there is nothing new under the sun    1271 **Lygurge**
Lycurgus is described, according to Curry (*Chaucer and the Medie-
val Sciences*) as a "Saturnalian" type, i.e., under the influence of
Saturn in astrology. Saturn has favored Palamon. The figure of
Emetrius, described below in Arcite's throng, is a Martian type.
Chaucer thus employs the medieval science of astrology to give
consistency to the armies

And like a griffon looked he aboute,                    1275
With kempe heres° on his browes stoute.
His limes greet, his brawnes hard and stronge,
His shouldres brod, his armes round and longe,
And as the guise was in his contree,
Full hye upon a chaar° of gold stood he,                1280
With foure white boles in the trais.°
Insted of cote-armure° over his harneis,
With nailes yellow and bright as any gold
He had a beres skin, col-black for old.°
His longe heer was kembed behind his back—            1285
As any raven's fether it shone for black.
A wreth of gold, arm-greet,° of huge wighte,°
Upon his heed, set full of stones brighte,
Of fine rubies and of diamaunts;
About his chaar there wente white alaunts,°             1290
Twenty and mo, as greet as any steer,
To hunten at the leon or the deer,
And followed him with mosel° fast y-bounde,
Collared of gold, and tourettes filed rounde.°
An hundred lordes had he in his route,                  1295
Armed full well, with hertes stern and stoute.

     With Arcita, in stories as men finde,
The greet Emetrius, the king of Inde,
Upon a steede bay trapped in steel,
Covered in cloth of gold, diapred° well,                1300
Came riding like the god of armes, Mars.
His cote-armure was of cloth of Tars,°
Couched with perles white and round and greete;
His saddle was of brend° gold new y-bete.
A mantlet upon his shoulder hanginge,                   1305
Bretful of rubies red as fire sparklinge;
His crispe heer like ringes was y-runne,°

1276 **kempe heres** shaggy hairs   1280 **chaar** chariot   1281 **boles in the trais** bulls in the traces (i.e., attached to his chariot)   1282 **cote-armure** tunic worn over armor   1284 **for old** black because of age; the bearskin has gilded claws   1287 **arm-greet** thick as an arm   1287 **wighte** weight   1290 **alaunts** hunting dogs   1293 **mosel** muzzle   1294 **tourettes filed rounde** rings for attaching a leash, filed into roundness (?)   1300 **diapred** patterned, decorated   1302 **cloth of Tars** silk   1304 **brend** refined   1307 **crispe . . . y-runne** curly hair flowed in rings

And that was yellow and glittred as the sunne;
His nose was heigh, his eyen bright citrin,°
1310 His beerd was well begunne for to springe;
A fewe fraknes° in his face y-spreind,°
Bitwixen yellow and somdeel black y-meind;°
And as a leon he his looking caste.
Of five and twenty yeer his age I caste;
1315 His beerd was well begunne for to springe;
His voice was a trumpe thunderinge;
Upon his heed he wered of laurer greene
A garland fresh and lusty for to seene;
Upon his hand he bare for his deduit°
1320 An egle tame, as any lily whit.
An hundred lordes had he with him there,
All armed, save hir heedes, in all hir gere,
Full richely in alle manner thinges;
For trusteth well that dukes, erles, kinges,
1325 Were gadred in this noble compaignye,
For love and for encrees of chivalrye.
About this king there ran on every part
Full many a tame leon and leopart.
    And in this wise thise lordes all and some
1330 Been on the Sunday to the citee come
Aboute prime,° and in the town alight.
This Theseus, this Duke, this worthy knight,
Whan he had brought hem into his citee,
And inned hem, everich at his degree,°
1335 He feesteth hem and doth so greet labour
To esen hem and doon hem all honour,
That yet men weenen that no mannes wit,
Of noon estate, ne coud amenden it.
The minstralcy, the service at the feeste,
1340 The grete yiftes to the mest° and leste,
The rich array of Theseus' palais,
Ne who sat first or last upon the dais,
What ladies fairest been and best dauncinge,

1309 citrin yellow (probably hazel or light brown), consistent with
his Martian characteristics   1311 fraknes freckles; also Martian
1311 y-spreind scattered   1312 y-meind mixed   1319 deduit amuse-
ment   1331 prime nine a.m.   1334 inned . . . degree lodged them,
each one by his rank   1340 mest most (in rank)

Or which of hem can dauncen best and singe,
Ne who most feelingly speketh of love,                    1345
What hawkes sitten on the perch above,
What houndes liggen on the floor adown—
Of all this make I now no mencioun,
But all th'effect; that thinketh me the beste.
Now cometh the point,° and herkneth if you leste:        1350

\*　　\*　　\*

The Sunday night, ere day bigan to springe,
Whan Palamon the larke herde singe—
Although it nere not day by houres two
Yet song the lark; and Palamon right tho,
With holy hert and with an heigh corage,                  1355
He rose to wenden on his pilgrimage,
Unto the blissful Cytherea benigne—
I mene Venus honourable and digne.
And in hir hour° he walketh forth a pas
Unto the listes ther hir temple was,                      1360
And down he kneeleth, and with humble cheere
And herte sore, he said as ye shall heere:
"Fairest of fair, O lady mine Venus,
Daughter of Jove and spouse to Vulcanus,
Thou gladder° of the Mount of Citheron:                   1365
For thilke love thou haddest to Adon,°
Have pitee of my bitter teres smerte,
And take mine humble prayer at thine herte!
Alas, I ne have no langage to telle
Th'effect ne the torments of mine helle.                  1370
Mine herte may mine harmes not biwraye°;
I am so confus that I can not saye

1350 the point very much the point indeed: note how in their pray-
ers which follow each prays for what he really wants, in accordance
with his character   1359 hir hour each day is named for a planet,
and each successive hour belongs to a planet—beginning with the
one for which the day is named and proceeding in rotation with
this sequence: Sun, Venus, Mercury, Moon, Saturn, Jupiter, Mars.
Thus on "Sunday night" the twenty-third hour comes around to
Venus; this is when Palamon prays to his goddess   1365 gladder
gladdener   1366 Adon Adonis   1371 biwraye show

But mercy, lady bright, that knowest welle
My thought, and seest what harmes that I feele.
1375 Consider all this, and rew upon my sore,
As wisly as I shall for evermore,
Emforth° my might, thy trewe servant be,
And holden wer° alway with chastitee.
That make I mine avow, so ye me helpe.
1380 I keepe nought of armes for to yelpe,°
Ne I n'axe not tomorrwe to have victorye,
Ne renown in this cas, ne vaine glorye
Of pris of armes blowen up and down:
But I wold have fully possessioun
1385 Of Emely, and die in thy servise.
Find thou the manner how and in what wise—
I recche not but it may better be
To have victory of hem, or they of me,
So that I have my lady in mine armes!
1390 For though so be that Mars is god of armes,
Your vertu is so greet in heven above
That, if you list, I shall well have my love.
Thy temple wol I worship evermo,
And on thine auter, wher° I ride or go,°
1395 I wol doon sacrifice and fires bete.°
And if ye wol not so, my lady sweete,
Than pray I thee tomorrwe with a spere
That Arcita me thurgh the herte bere;
Than rekke I not, whan I have lost my lif,
1400 Though that Arcita win hir to his wif.
This is th'effect and end of my prayere:
Yif me my love, thou blissful lady dere!"
      Whan the orison was done of Palamon,
His sacrifice he did, and that anoon,
1405 Full pitously, with alle circumstaunces°—
Al° tell I not as now his observaunces.
But at the last the statue of Venus shook,
And made a signe whereby that he took
That his prayer accepted was that day;

1377 **Emforth** according to    1378 **holden wer** be at odds    1380 **yelpe**
boast    1394 **wher** whether    1394 **go** walk    1395 **bete** light    1405 **circumstaunces** ceremonies    1406 **Al** although

For though the signe shewed a delay,                    1410
Yet wist he well that graunted was his boone,
And with glad hert he went him home full soone.

\*          \*          \*

The thrid hour inequal° that Palamon
Began to Venus' temple for to goon,
Up rose the sun, and up rose Emelye—                    1415
And to the temple of Diane gan hie.
Hir maidens that she thider with hir ladde,
Full redily with hem the fire they hadde,
Th'encens, the clothes, and the remnant all°
That to the sacrifice longen° shall—                    1420
The hornes full of meeth,° as was the guise.
There lacked nought to doon hir sacrifise.
Smoking the temple, full of clothes faire,
This Emely with herte debonaire
Hir body wesh with water of a welle.                    1425
(But how she did hir rite I dare not telle,
But it be any thing in general—
And yet it were a game° to heeren all.
To him that meneth well it were no charge;
But it is good a man be at his large.°)                    1430
Hir brighte heer was kembed untressed all;
A corown of a green ook cerial°
Upon hir heed was set, full fair and meete.
Two fires on the auter gan she bete,
And did hir thinges as men may beholde                    1435
In Stace of Thebes° and thise bookes olde.
Whan kindled was the fire, with pitous cheere
Unto Diane she spak as ye may heere:
"O chaste goddess of the woodes greene,
To whom both heven and erth and see is seene;                    1440

1413 hour inequal daylight hour (one-twelfth the time between sun-
rise and sunset despite the length of the day). The sunrise hour of
Monday (Moon's day) is Diana's    1419 encens . . . all the incense,
the cloth hangings, and all the rest    1420 longen belong    1421 meeth
mead    1428 game joy    1429–30 no charge . . . large no matter,
but it is good for a man to be free    1432 ook cerial a kind of oak;
the crown is of its leaves    1436 Stace of Thebes Statius' *Thebaid*

Queen of the regne of Pluto, derk and lowe,
Goddess of maidens, that mine hert hast knowe
Full many a yeer, and wost what I desire,
As keep me fro thy vengeance and thine ire,
1445 That Atheon aboughte cruelly:
Chaste goddess, well wostou that I
Desire to been a maiden° all my lif,
Ne never wol I be no love ne wif.
I am, thou wost, yet of thy compaignye,
1450 A maid, and love hunting and venerye,
And for to walken in the woodes wilde,
And not to been a wife and be with childe.
Not wol I knowe compaigny of man.
Now help me, lady, sith ye may and can,
1455 For tho three formes° that thou hast in thee.
And Palamon, that hath swich love to me,
And eek Arcite, that loveth me so sore,
This grace I praye thee withoute more,
As sende love and pees bitwix hem two,
1460 And fro me turn away hir hertes so
That all hir hote love and hir desir,
And all hir bisy torment and hir fir,
Be queint° or turned in another place.
And if so be thou wolt not do me grace,
1465 Or if my destinee be shapen so
That I shall needes have one of hem two,
As send me him that most desireth me.
Behold, goddess of clene chastitee,
The bitter teers that on my cheekes falle!
1470 Sin thou art maid and keeper of us alle,
My maidenhood thou keep and well conserve,
And while I live, a maid I wol thee serve."
    The fires bren upon the auter clere,
While Emely was thus in hir prayere,
1475 But suddenly she saw a sighte quainte°:
For right anon one of the fires queinte,°
And quicked again, and after that anon

1447 **maiden** virgin   1455 **three formes** the Moon (in heaven),
Diana (on earth), Proserpina (in hell)   1463 **queint** quenched
1475 **quainte** strange   1476 **queinte** was quenched

The other fire was queint and all agon,
And as it queint it made a whistelinge,
As doon thise wete bronds in hir brenninge,          *1480*
And at the brondes' end out ran anon
As it were bloody droppes many oon.
For which so sore aghast was Emelye
That she was well nigh mad, and gan to crye—
For she ne wiste what it signified;                  *1485*
But only for the fere° thus hath she cried,
And weep that it was pitee for to heere.
And therewithal Diane gan appere,
With bow in hand, right as an hunteresse,
And saide, "Daughter, stint thine hevinesse.         *1490*
Among the goddes hye it is affermed,
And by eterne word written and confermed,
Thou shalt be wedded unto one of tho
That han for thee so muche care and wo—
But unto which of hem I may not telle.               *1495*
Farewell, for I ne may no lenger dwelle.
The fires which that on mine auter brenne
Shull thee declaren ere that thou go henne
Thine aventure of love as in this caas."
And with that word the arrwes in the caas°           *1500*
Of the goddess clatteren fast and ringe,
And forth she went, and made a vanishinge.
For which this Emely astoned was,
And saide, "What amounteth this, alas?
I putte me in thy proteccioun,                       *1505*
Diane, and in thy disposicioun!"
And home she goth anon the nexte° waye;
This is th'effect—there is namore to saye.

\*       \*       \*

The nexte hour of Mars follwinge this,
Arcite unto the temple walked is                     *1510*
Of fierce Mars, to doon his sacrifise,
With all the rites of his payen° wise.

1486 for the fere out of fear    1500 caas quiver    1507 nexte nearest
1512 payen pagan

With pitous hert and high devocioun,
Right thus to Mars he said his orisoun:
1513  "O stronge god, that in the regnes colde
Of Trace honoured art and lord y-holde,
And hast in every regne and every land
Of armes all the bridle in thine hand,
And hem fortunest° as thee list devise:
1520  Accept of me my pitous sacrifise!
If so be that my youthe may deserve,
And that my might be worthy for to serve
Thy godheed, that I may be one of thine,
Than pray I thee to rew upon my pine,
1525  For thilke pain and thilke hote fir
In which thou whilom brendest for desir
Whan that thou usedest° the beautee
Of faire, yonge, freshe Venus free,
And haddest hir in armes at thy wille—
1530  Although thee ones on a time misfille,°
Whan Vulcanus had caught thee in his las,
And foond thee ligging° by his wife, alas!
For thilke sorrwe that was in thine herte,
Have routh° as well upon my paines smerte!
1535  I am yong and unkonning, as thou woost,
And as I trow, with love offended most
That ever was any lives creature.°
For she that doth me all this woe endure
Ne reccheth never wher I sink or flete;°
1540  And well I wot ere she me mercy hete,°
I mot with strengthe win hir in the place°—
And well I wot withouten help or grace
Of thee ne may my strengthe not availe.
Than help me, lord, tomorrwe in my battaile,
1545  For thilke fire that whilom brente thee,
As well as thilke fire now brenneth me,
And do that I tomorrwe have victorye.

---

1519 **fortunest** give them (good or bad) fortunes   1527 **usedest**
exploited   1530 **misfille** it went wrong   1532 **ligging** lying   1534 **routh**
pity   1537 **lives creature** living creature   1539 **wher . . . flete**
whether I sink or float   1540 **ere . . . hete** before she promises me
mercy   1541 **place** lists

Mine be the travaille, and thine be the glorye!
Thy sovereign temple wol I most honouren
Of any place, and alway most labouren
In thy plesance and in thy craftes stronge.                    1550
And in thy temple I wol my banner honge,
And all the armes of my compaignye,
And evermo until that day I die
Eterne fire I wol before thee finde.°
And eek to this avow I wol me binde:                    1555
My beerd, mine heer, that hangeth long adown,
That never yet ne felt offensioun
Of rasour ne of shere, I wol thee yive;
And been thy trewe servant while I live.
Now lord, have routh upon my sorrwes sore!                    1560
Yif me the victory—I axe namore."
    The prayer stint of Arcita the stronge,
The ringes on the temple door that honge
And eek the doores clattereden full faste,                    1565
Of which Arcita somewhat him aghaste.
The fires brenden upon the auter brighte
That it gan all the temple for to lighte.
A sweete smell anon the ground up yaf.
And Arcita anon his hand up haf,°                    1570
And more encens into the fire he caste,
With other rites mo, and at the laste
The statue of Mars began his hauberk ringe,
And with that soun he herd a murmuringe,
Full low and dim, and saide thus: "Victorye!"                    1575
For which he yaf to Mars honour and glorye.
And thus with joy and hope well to fare
Arcite anon unto his inn is fare,
As fain° as fowl is of the brighte sunne.

\* \* \*

    And right anon swich strife there is begunne                    1580
For thilke graunting in the heven above
Bitwixe Venus, the goddess of love,
And Mars, the sterne god armipotente,

1555 finde provide for   1570 haf raised   1579 fain glad

That Jupiter was bisy it to stente°—
1585 Till that the pale Saturnus the colde,
That knew so many of aventures olde,
Foond in his old experience an art
That he full soon hath plesed every part.°
As sooth is said, eld hath greet avantage:
1590 In eld is bothe wisdom and usage;
Men may the old atrenne and not atrede.°
Saturn anon, to stinten strife and drede,
Al be it that it is again his kinde,°
Of all this strife he can remedy finde.
1595    "My dere daughter Venus," quod Saturne,
"My course,° that hath so wide for to turne,
Hath more power than woot any man.
Mine is the drenching° in the see so wan;°
Mine is the prison in the derke cote;°
1600 Mine is the strangling and hanging by the throte,
The murmur and the cherles' rebelling,
The groining° and the privee empoisoning.
I do vengeance and plain correccioun
While I dwell in the sign of the leoun.
1605 Mine is the ruin of the hye halles,
The falling of the towers and of the walles
Upon the miner or the carpenter.
I slow Sampson, shaking the piller;
And mine be the maladies colde,
1610 The derke tresons, and the castes° olde;
My looking° is the fader of pestilence.
Now weep namore, I shall doon diligence
That Palamon, that is thine owen knight,
Shall have his lady as thou hast him hight.
1615 Though Mars shall help his knight, yet natheless,
Bitwixe you there moot be some time pees,
Al be ye not of oo complexioun°—
That causeth alday swich divisioun.

1584 was . . . stente had trouble stopping it    1588 part side, party
1591 Men . . . atrede one can outrun the old, but not outwit them
1593 kinde nature    1596 course i.e., as a planet    1598 drenching
drowning. These disasters were normally ascribed to Saturn
1598 wan dark    1599 cote dungeon    1602 groining groaning    1610
castes deceits    1611 looking gaze    1617 oo complexioun one tem-
perament

I am thine aiel,° redy at thy wille.
Weep now namore; I wol thy lust° fulfille."            1620
    Now wol I stinten of the gods above,
Of Mars and of Venus, goddess of love,
And telle you as plainly as I can
The greet effect for which that I began.

## PART FOUR

    Greet was the feest in Athenes that day,          1625
And eek the lusty seson of that May
Made every wight to been in swich plesaunce
That all that Monday jousten they and daunce,
And spenden it in Venus' high servise.
But by the cause that they sholde rise              1630
Erly for to seen the greete fight,
Unto hir reste wenten they at night.
And on the morrwe whan the day gan springe,
Of horse and harneis noise and clatteringe
There was in hostelries all aboute;                 1635
And to the palais rode there many a route°
Of lordes upon steedes and palfreys.
There maistou seen devising° of harneis,
So uncouth° and so rich, and wrought so well
Of goldsmithry, of brouding,° and of steel;         1640
The sheeldes brighte, testers, and trappures,°
Gold-hewen helmes, hauberks, cote-armures,
Lordes in parements° on hir courseres,
Knightes of retenue and eek squieres
Nailing the speres° and helmes bockelinge;          1645
Gigging° of sheeldes, with lainers lacinge°—
There as need was they were no thing idel;
The fomy steedes on the golden bridel
Gnawing; and fast the armurers also
With file and hammer pricking° to and fro;          1650

1619 **aiel** forefather   1620 **lust** desire   1636 **route** band   1638 **de-
vising** preparing   1639 **uncouth** wondrous   1640 **brouding** orna-
mentation   1641 **testers, and trappures** headpieces, and horse-cover-
ings   1643 **parements** rich clothing   1645 **Nailing the speres** fasten-
ing the points onto shafts   1646 **Gigging** fastening straps   1646 **lain-
ers lacinge** lacing (them) with thongs   1650 **pricking** spurring their
horses

Yemen on foot and communes many oon,
With shorte staves, thick as they may goon;
Pipes, trumpes, nakers,° clariouns,
That in the battaile blowen bloody souns;
1655 The palais full of peple up and down—
Here three, there ten, holding hir questioun,
Divining of° thise Theban knightes two.
Some saiden thus, some said it shall be so;
Some helden with him with the blacke beerd,
1660 Some with the bald, some with the thicke-herd.°
Some said he looked grim, and he wold fighte°—
"He hath a sparth° of twenty pound of wighte."
Thus was the halle full of divininge
Long after that the sunne gan to springe.
1665     The greete Theseus, that of his sleep awaked
With minstralcy and noise that was maked,
Held yet the chambres of his palais riche,
Till that the Theban knightes, both y-liche°
Honoured, weren into the palais fet.°
1670 Duke Theseus is at a window set,
Arrayed right as he were a god in trone;
The peple presseth thiderward full soone,
Him for to seen and doon heigh reverence,
And eek to herkne his hest° and his sentence.
1675 An heraud on a scaffold made an "O!"
Till all the noise of peple was y-do.°
And whan he saw the peple of noise all stille,
Thus shewed he the mighty dukes wille:
"The lord hath of his high discrecioun
1680 Considered that it were destruccioun
To gentil blood to fighten in the guise
Of mortal battaile now in this emprise;°
Wherefore, to shapen that they shall not die,
He wol his firste purpose modifye:
1685 No man, therefore, up° pain of loss of lif,

1653 **nakers** horns (?); the word more often means drums    1657 **Di-
vining of** speculating about    1660 **herd** haired    1661 **he . . . fighte**
they are pointing at different warriors    1662 **sparth** battle-axe
1668 **y-liche** alike, equally    1669 **fet** brought    1674 **hest** command
1676 **y-do** done, finished    1682 **emprise** undertaking    1685 **up** upon

No manner shot,° ne pole-ax, ne short knif,
Into the listes send or thider bringe.
Ne short-swerd for to stoke° with point bitinge,
No man ne draw ne bere it by his side.
Ne no man shall unto his fellaw ride                    1690
But oo course with sharp y-grounde spere—
Foine, if him list, on foot, himself to were.°
And he that is at meschief° shall be take,
And not slain, but be brought unto the stake
That shall been ordained on either side;                1695
But thider he shall by force,° and there abide.
And if so falle the chieftain be take,
On either side, or elles sleen his make,°
No lenger shall the tourneyinge laste.
God speede you: go forth and lay on faste.              1700
With long swerd and with maces fighteth your fille.
Go now your way. This is the lordes wille."

    The voice of peple touchede the hevene,
So loude cride they with merry stevene,°
"God save swich a lord that is so good:                 1705
He wilneth no destruccion of blood!"

    Up goon the trumpes and the melodye,
And to the listes rit° the compaignye,
By ordinance, thurghout the citee large,
Hanged with cloth of gold and not with sarge.°          1710
Full like a lord this noble Duke gan ride,
Thise two Thebans upon either side.
And after rode the Queen and Emelye,
And after that another compaignye
Of one and other after hir degree.                      1715
And thus they passen thurghout the citee,
And to the listes come they bitime—
It was not of the day yet fully prime.

    Whan set was Theseus full rich and hye,
Ipolyta the queen and Emelye,
And other ladies in degrees aboute,                     1720

1686 **shot** arrows   1688 **stoke** stab   1692 **Foine . . . were** let him
parry, if he likes, on foot, to defend himself   1693 **at meschief** in
trouble   1696 **thider . . . force** he shall go thither of necessity
1698 **sleen his make** slay his opponent   1704 **stevene** voice   1708 **rit**
rides   1710 **sarge** serge

Unto the setes presseth all the route,
And westward thurgh the gates under Marte
Arcite and eek the hundred of his parte,
1725 With banner red, is entred right anon.
And in that selve° moment Palamon
Is under Venus eestward in the place,
With banner white and hardy cheer and face.
In all the world, to seeken up and down,
1730 So even withouten variacioun
There nere swiche compaignies twaye;
For there was none so wise that coude saye
That any had of other avantage,
Of worthiness, ne of estate ne age,
1735 So even were they chosen for to guesse;
And in two renges° faire they hem dresse.
    Whan that hir names rad° were everichon,
That in hir numbre guile was there non,
Tho were the gates shet and cried was loude:
1740 "Do now your devoir,° yonge knightes proude!"
    The heraudes left hir pricking up and down.
Now ringen trumpes loud and clarioun.
There is namore to sayn, but west and eest
In goon the speres full sadly in th'arest,°
1745 In goth the sharpe spur into the side—
There seen men who can joust and who can ride:
There shiveren shaftes upon sheeldes thicke—
He° feeleth thurgh the herte-spoon° the pricke.
Up springen speres twenty foot on highte;
1750 Out goon the swerdes as the silver brighte;
The helmes they to-hewen and to-shrede;
Out brest the blood with sterne° streemes rede.
With mighty maces the bones they to-breste;
He thurgh the thickest of the throng gan threste;

1726 selve self-same   1736 renges ranks   1737 rad read   1740 devoir duty   1744 sadly in th'arest firmly into their rests (a device on the armor for holding the spear aimed)   1748 He one (cf. line 1661). "He" is used in this impersonal way throughout the passage   1748 herte-spoon the hollow just below the breastbone   1752 sterne dreadful

There stumblen steedes strong, and down goth all!° 1755
He rolleth under foot as doth a ball;
He foineth on his feet with his trunchoun;°
And he him hurtleth with his horse adown;
He thurgh the body is hurt and sithen y-take,
Maugree his heed, and brought unto the stake— 1760
As forward° was, right there he most abide;
Another lad° is on that other side.
　　And some time doth hem Theseus to reste,°
Hem to refresh and drinken if hem leste.
Full oft aday have thise Thebans two 1765
Togidre y-met and wrought his fellaw wo:
Unhorsed hath ech other of hem tweye.
There is no tigre in Vale of Galgopheye,°
Whan that hir whelp is stole whan it is lite,
So cruel on the hunt as is Arcite, 1770
For jalous hert, upon this Palamoun.
Ne in Belmarye° there nis no fell leoun,
That hunted is or for his hunger wood,
Ne of his prey desireth so the blood,
As Palamon to sleen his foe Arcite. 1775
The jalous strokes on hir helmes bite—
Out renneth blood on both hir sides rede.
　　Some time an end there is of every deede:
For ere the sun unto the reste wente,
The stronge king Emetrius gan hente 1780
This Palamon as he fought with Arcite,
And made his swerd deep in his flesh to bite,
And by the force of twenty is he take,
Unyolden, and y-drawen to the stake.
And in the rescous° of this Palamoun, 1785

1741–55 **The heraudes . . . all!** in this passage Chaucer imitates the clash of arms by lapsing into alliterative verse. Without dropping the rime, of course, or the blank verse either, he simulates the old native English poetry, chiefly heroic in its tradition, which relied upon the repetition of a single initial sound three or more times in a line. This goes on until the climactic line "and down goth all!" 1757 **foineth . . . trunchoun** parries with the shaft of his spear 1761 **forward** agreement 1762 **lad** lead (to the stake) 1763 **doth . . . reste** Theseus causes them to rest 1768 **Galgopheye** Gargaphie, mentioned in Ovid, *Metamorphoses* III, 155 1772 **Belmarye** See General Prologue, line 57 1785 **rescous** rescue

The stronge king Lygurge is born adown,
And King Emetrius, for all his strengthe,
Is born out of his saddle a swerdes lengthe,
So hit him Palamon ere he were take.
1790 But all for nought: he was brought to the stake.
His hardy herte might him helpe naught;
He most abide whan that he was caught,
By force and eek by composicioun.°
　　Who sorrweth now but woeful Palamoun,
1795 That mot namore goon again to fighte?
And whan that Theseus had seen this sighte,
Unto the folk that foughten thus echon
He cride, "Ho, namore, for it is don!
I wol be trewe judge and not partye.°
1800 Arcite of Thebes shall have Emelye,
That by his fortune hath hir fair y-wonne."
Anon there is a noise of peple begunne,
For joy of this, so loud and heigh withalle,
It seemed that the listes sholde falle.
1805 　　What can now faire Venus doon above?
What saith she now? What doth this queen of love?—
But weepeth so for wanting of hir wille,
Till that hir teres in the listes fille.
She said, "I am ashamed,° douteless."
1810 Saturnus saide: "Daughter, hold thy pees!
Mars hath his will—his knight hath all his boone.°
And, by mine heed, thou shalt been esed soone."
　　The trumpours with the loude minstralcye,
The heraudes that full loude yell and crye,
1815 Been in hir wele for joy of daun Arcite.
But herkneth me, and stinteth noise a lite,°
Which a miracle there befell anon—
　　This fierce Arcite hath off his helm y-don,°
And on a courser for to shew his face,
1820 He pricketh endelong the large place,
Looking upward upon this Emelye;

1793 **By . . . composicioun** out of necessity and also according to
their agreement   1799 **partye** partisan   1809 **ashamed** shamed   1811
**boone** petition   1816 **But herkneth . . . lite** note how the Knight
speaks here as to an audience   1818 **off . . . y-don** taken off his
helmet

And she again him cast a freendly eye—
For women, as to speken in commune,°
They follwen all the favour of Fortune—
And she was all his cheer as in his herte.°
Out of the ground a Fury infernal° sterte,                    1825
From Pluto sent at request of Saturne,
For which his horse for fere gan to turne
And leep aside, and foundred as he leep.
And ere that Arcite may taken keep,                          1830
He pight him on the pommel of his heed,°
That in the place he lay as he were deed,
His brest to-brosten with his saddle-bowe.°
As black he lay as any cole or crowe,
So was the blood y-runnen in his face.                        1835
Anon he was y-born out of the place,
With herte sore, to Theseus' palais.
Tho was he corven° out of his harneis,
And in a bed y-brought full fair and blive,°
For he was yet in memory° and alive,                          1840
And alway crying after Emelye.

Duke Theseus with all his compaignye
Is comen home to Athens his citee
With alle bliss and greet solempnitee.
Al be it that this aventure was falle,                         1845
He nolde not discomforten hem alle.

Men said eek that Arcite shall not die—
"He shall been heeled of his maladye."
And of another thing they were as fain:
That of hem alle was there none y-slain,                       1850
Al were they sore y-hurt, and namely oon,
That with a spere was thirled his brest-boon.°
To other woundes and to broken armes
Some hadden salves and some hadden charmes;

1823 **in commune** in general   1825 **she . . . herte** she was all his
joy, in his heart   1826 **Fury infernal** the Fury, which Boccaccio
took from Statius, was a hellish monster   1831 **pight . . . heed**
pitched him (so that he fell) on the top of his head   1833 **to-brosten**
**. . . bowe** shattered by the front edge of the saddle   1838 **corven** cut
1839 **blive** quickly   1840 **in memory** conscious   1852 **That . . .**
**boon** "that his breastbone was pierced with a spear"—i.e., "*whose*
breastbone was . . .*"

1855 Fermacies° of herbes and eek save°
      They drunken, for they wold hir limes have.
      For which this noble Duke, as he well can,
      Comforteth and honoureth every man,
      And made revel all the longe night
1860 Unto the straunge° lordes, as was right.
      Ne there was holden no disconfitinge,°
      But as a joustes or a tourneyinge,
      For soothly there was no disconfiture—
      For falling nis not but an aventure,
1865 Ne to be lad by force unto the stake,
      Unyolden, and with twenty knightes take,
      Oo person alone, withouten mo,
      And harried° forth by arme, foot, and to,°
      And eek his steede driven forth with staves,
1870 With footmen, bothe yeman and eek knaves—
      It nas aretted him no villainye;°
      There may no man clepe it cowardye.
          For which anon Duke Theseus let crye,°
      To stinten° alle rancour and envye,
1875 The gree° as well of oo side as of other,
      And either side y-like as other's brother;
      And yaf hem yiftes after hir degree,
      And fully held a feeste dayes three,
      And conveyed the kinges worthily
1880 Out of his town a journee largely.°
      And home went every man the righte way—
      There was namore but "Farewell, have good day."
      Of this battaile I wol namore endite,
      But speke of Palamon and of Arcite.
1885      Swelleth the brest of Arcite, and the sore
      Encresseth at his herte more and more;
      The clothered° blood, for any leechecraft,°

---

1855 **Fermacies** medicines    1855 **save**    an    herb    1860 **straunge**
foreign    1861 **disconfitinge** defeat    1868 **harried** dragged    1868 **to**
toe    1871 **It . . . villainye** it was not put down against him as a
disgrace    1873 **let crye** caused to be announced    1874 **To stinten**
in order to stop    1875 **gree** good will    1880 **a journee largely** fully
a day's journey    1887 **clothered** clotted    1887 **for . . . leechecraft**
in spite of any medical skill

Corrupteth, and is in his bouk y-laft,°
That neither veine-blood, ne ventusinge,°
Ne drink of herbes may been his helpinge.          1890
The vertu expulsif or animal
Fro thilke vertu cleped natural
Ne may the venim voiden ne expelle;°
The pipes of his lunges gan to swelle,
And every lacert° in his brest adown          1895
Is shent with venim and corrupcioun.°
Him gaineth neither, for to get his lif,
Vomit upward, ne downward laxatif.°
All is to-brosten thilke regioun;°
Nature hath now no dominacioun;          1900
And certainly, ther Nature wol not werche,°
Farewell, physic—go bere the man to cherche.
This all and sum: that Arcita moot die.
For which he sendeth after Emelye,
And Palamon that was his cosin dere.          1905
Than said he thus, as ye shall after heere:
    "Not may the woeful spirit in mine herte
Declare a point° of all my sorrwes smerte
To you, my lady, that I love most;
But I biquethe the service of my gost°          1910
To you aboven every creature
Sin that my life may no lenger dure.
Alas the woe, alas the paines stronge
That I for you have suffered, and so longe!
Alas the deeth, alas, mine Emelye!          1915

1888 in . . . y-laft left in the trunk of his body   1889 veine . . .
ventusinge drawing blood from a vein or from the skin (by "cup-
ping," i.e., by a partial vacuum)   1891–93 The vertu . . . expelle
in medieval medicine there were three "virtues"—natural, vital, and
animal (associated with the liver, heart, and brain respectively).
Here, the animal virtue is unable to expel the poison from the
natural virtue   1895 lacert muscle   1896 shent . . . corrupcioun
damaged by poison and decomposition; as a result he cannot cough
to expel congestion from his lungs   1897–98 Him . . . laxatif be-
cause his expulsive virtue is impaired, emetics and laxatives given
him fail to purge the unnatural humor   1899 to-brosten . . . regioun
that region (his breast) is completely afflicted   1901 ther Nature
. . . werche where Nature will not work; his natural virtue is poisoned
(see lines 1892–93)   1908 point even a small detail   1910 gost soul,
i.e., after death

Alas, departing of our compaignye!
Alas, mine hertes queen, alas, my wif,
Mine hertes lady, ender of my lif!
What is this world? What asketh men to have?
1920 Now with his love, now in his colde grave—
Alone, withouten any compaignye.
    Farewell, my sweete foe, mine Emelye,
And softe take me in your armes twaye,
For love of God, and herkneth what I saye:
1925 I have here with my cosin Palamon
Had strife and rancour many a day agon
For love of you, and for my jalousye.
And Jupiter so wis my soule gie°
To speken of a servant proprely
1930 With circumstances alle trewely—
That is to sayn, truth, honour, knighthede,
Wisdom, humbless, estate, and heigh kinrede,
Freedom, and all that longeth to that art—
So Jupiter have of my soule part,
1935 As in this world right now ne know I non
So worthy to been loved as Palamon,
That serveth you and wol doon all his lif.
And if that ever ye shall been a wif,
Foryet not Palamon, the gentil man."
1940 And with that word his speeche faile gan;
For from his feet up to his brest was come
The cold of deeth that had him overcome.
And yet more over,° for in his armes two
The vital strength is lost and all ago;
1945 Only, the intellect° withoute more,
That dwelled in his herte sick and sore,
Gan failen whan the herte felte deeth.
Dusked° his eyen two and failed breeth—
But on his lady yet cast he his eye.
1950 His laste word was: *"Mercy, Emelye!"*

---

1928 so . . . gie guide my soul surely    1943 yet more over still more
than that    1945 intellect the intellect was thought to reside in the
heart; it is the last faculty to go—"the intellect began to fail only
when . . ."    1948 Dusked dimmed

His spirit chaunged house and wente ther
As *I* came never,° I can not tellen wher;
Therefore I stint—I nam no divinistre:°
Of soules find I not in this registre,°
Ne me ne list thilke opinions to telle                    1955
Of hem, though that they writen where they dwelle.
Arcite is cold, ther Mars his soule gie.°
Now wol I speken forth of Emelye.

 Shright° Emely and howleth Palamon,
And Theseus his suster took anon                          1960
Swouning, and bare hir fro the corpse away.
What helpeth it to tarrien forth the day
To tellen how she weep both eve and morrwe?
For in swich cas women have swich sorrwe,
Whan that hir husbonds been from hem ago,                 1965
That for the more part they sorrwen so,
Or elles fallen in swich a maladye,
That at the laste certainly they die.

 Infinite been the sorrwes and the teres
Of olde folk and folk of tendre yeeres                    1970
In all the town for deeth of this Theban;
For him there weepeth bothe child and man.
So greet weeping was there noon, certain,
Whan Ector was y-brought all fresh y-slain
To Troy. Alas, the pitee that was ther—                   1975
Cratching° of cheekes, renting eek of heer—
"Why woldestou be deed," thise women crye,
"And haddest gold enough, and Emelye?"

 No man mighte gladden Theseus
Saving his olde fader Egeus,                              1980
That knew this worldes transmutacioun,
As he had seen it chaungen, up and down,
Joy after woe, and woe after gladnesse,
And shewed hem ensample and likenesse:

1951–52 **His . . . never** "His vital spirit changed its abode (i.e.,
perhaps from body to immortal soul) and went to a place where *I*
never came . . ." Chaucer breaks the tragic feeling of the passage
with a characteristic bit of self-humor   1953 **divinistre** theologian
1954 **Of . . . registre** I'm not providing anything about souls for this
table of contents   1957 **ther . . . gie** wherefore may Mars guide
his soul   1959 **Shright** shrieked   1976 **Cratching** scratching

1985 "Right as there died never man," quod he,
     "That he ne lived in erth in some degree,
     Right so there lived never man," he saide,
     "In all this world that some time he ne deide.
     This world nis but a thurghfare full of wo,
1990 And we been pilgrims passing to and fro:
     Deeth is an end of every worldly sore."
         And overall this yet said he muchel more
     To this effect, full wisely to enhorte°
     The peple that they shold hem reconforte.°
1995     Duke Theseus with all his bisy cure°
     Caste now where that the sepulture
     Of good Arcite may best y-maked be,
     And eek most honourable in his degree.
     And at the last he took conclusioun
2000 That there as first Arcite and Palamoun
     Hadden for love the battaile hem betweene,
     That in the selve° grove, swoot and greene,
     There as he had his amorous desires,
     His complaint, and for love his hote fires,
2005 He wolde make a fire in which th'office
     Funeral he might all accomplice—
     And let anon command to hack and hewe
     The okes old, and layen hem on a rewe,
     In colpons° well arrayed for to brenne.
2010 His officers with swifte feet they renne
     And ride anon at his commandement,
     And after this Theseus hath y-sent
     After a beer,° and it all overspradde
     With cloth of gold, the richest that he hadde.
2015 And of the same suite° he clad Arcite—
     Upon his handes two his gloves white,
     Eek on his heed a crown of laurer greene,
     And in his hand a swerd full bright and keene;
     He laid him, bare the visage,° on the beere.

1993 **enhorte** exhort   1994 **hem reconforte** console themselves
1995 **cure** care   2002 **selve** self-same   2008–09 **on . . . colpons** in
a row, in pieces   2013 **beer** bier   2015 **of . . . suite** in the same
array; the white gloves in the next line were traditional mourning
for the unmarried   2019 **bare the visage** his face uncovered

Therewith he weep that pitee was to heere!—          2020
And for the peple sholde seen him alle,
Whan it was day he brought him to the halle,
That roreth of the crying and the soun.
Tho came this woeful Theban Palamoun,
With fluttery beerd and ruggy ashy heres,°          2025
In clothes black, y-dropped all with teres;
And passing other of weeping, Emelye,
The rewfullest of all the compaignye.
In as much as the service sholde be
The more noble and rich in his degree,              2030
Duke Theseus let forth three steedes bringe
That trapped were in steel all glitteringe,
And covered with the arms of daun Arcite.
Upon thise steedes fair, so huge and white,
There seten folk of which one bare his sheeld;      2035
Another his spere upon his handes held;
The thridde bare with him his bow Turkeis—
Of brend gold was the case and eek th' harneis—
And riden forth a pas with sorrweful cheere
Toward the grove, as ye shall after heere.          2040
    The noblest of the Greekes that there were
Upon hir shouldres carrieden the beere,
With slacke pas,° and eyen red and wete,
Thurghout the citee by the maister streete,
That sprad was all with black. And wonder hye       2045
Right of the same is the street y-wrye.°
Upon the right hand went old Egeus,
And on that other side Duke Theseus,
With vessels in hir hand of gold full fin,
All full of honey, milk, and blood, and win;        2050
Eek Palamon with full greet compaignye;
And after that came woeful Emelye,
With fire in hand, as was that time the guise,
To do the office of funeral servise.
    High labour and full greet apparailinge°         2055
Was at the service and the fire-makinge,

2025 **ruggy . . . heres** unkempt hair covered with ashes—symbolic
of mourning   2043 **slacke pas** slow steps   2046 **y-wrye** hung
2055 **apparailinge** preparation

That with his greene top the heven raughte,°
And twenty fadme of brede the armes straughte—
This is to sayn, the boughes were so brode.
2060 Of stree° first there was laid many a lode;
But how the fire was maked upon highte,°
Ne eek the names how the trees highte
(As ook, fir, birch, asp, alder, holm, popler,
Willow, elm, plane, ash, box, chestain, linde, laurer,
2065 Maple, thorn, beech, hasel, ew, whippletree)
How they were feld shall not been told for me;
Ne how the goddes runnen up and down,
Disherited of hir habitacioun
In which they woneden in rest and pees—
2070 Nymphes, faunes, and hamadryades;
Ne how the beestes and the briddes alle
Fledden for fere whan the wood was falle;
Ne how the ground aghast was of the light,
That was not wont to seen the sunne bright;
2075 Ne how the fire was couched first with stree,
And than with drye stickes cloven a-three,
And than with greene wood and spicerye,
And than with cloth of gold and with perrye,°
And garlands hanging with full many a flowr—
2080 The myrrh, th'incense with all so greet odour:
Ne how Arcite lay among all this,
Ne what richess about the body is,
Ne how that Emely, as was the guise,
Put in the fire of funeral servise,
2085 Ne how she swouned whan men made the fir,
Ne what she spak, ne what was hir desir,
Ne what jewels men in the fire caste
Whan that the fire was greet and brente faste;
Ne how some cast hir sheeld and some hir spere,
2090 And of hir vestiments which that they were,
And cuppes full of milk and wine and blood

2057 **with . . . raughte** with its green top (i.e., piled with boughs)
reached toward heaven   2060 **stree** straw   2061 **how . . . highte**
how high the fire was made. From here to line 2108 is a protracted
*occupatio* in which Chaucer condenses Boccaccio's elaborate epic
funeral rites   2078 **perrye** jewels

Into the fire that brent as it were wood;
Ne how the Greekes with an huge route
Thries riden all the fire aboute,
Upon the left hand, with a loud shoutinge,        2095
And thries with his speres clatteringe,
And thries how the ladies gonne crye,
And how that lad was homeward Emelye;
Ne how Arcite is brent to ashen colde;
Ne how that liche-wake° was y-holde             2100
All thilke night; ne how the Greekes playe
The wake-playes,° ne keep° I nought to saye;
Who wrastleth best naked with oil anoint,
Ne who that bare him best in no disjoint.°
I wol not tellen alle how they goon             2105
Home til Athens whan the play° is doon,
But shortly to the point than wol I wende,
And maken of my longe tale an ende.

*    *    *

By process° and by length of certain yeeres,
All stinted is the mourning and the teres       2110
Of Greekes by one general assent.
Than seemed me there was a parlement
At Athens, upon a certain point and cas;
Among the whiche points y-spoken was
To have with certain contrees alliaunce,        2115
And have fully of Thebans obeisaunce;
For which this noble Theseus anon
Let senden after gentil Palamon,
Unwist of him what was the cause and why.
But in his blacke clothes sorrwefully            2120
He came at his commandement in hie.°
Tho sente Theseus for Emelye.
    Whan they were set, and hust° was all the place,
And Theseus abiden hath a space

2100 **liche-wake** wake (a medieval Christian term)  2102 **wake-playes** funeral games (an epic convention)  2102 **keep** bother  2104 **in no disjoint** in any difficulty  2106 **play** event  2109 **By process** in due course  2121 **in hie** in a hurry  2123 **hust** hushed

2125 Ere any word came from his wise brest,
    His eyen set he ther as was his lest,
    And with a sad visage he siked stille,°
    And after that right thus he said his wille:
    "The Firste Mover of the cause above,
2130 Whan he first made the faire Chain of Love,
    Greet was th'effect, and high was his entente;
    Well wist he why and what thereof he mente.
    For with that faire Chain of Love he bond
    The fire, the air, the water, and the lond
2135 In certain boundes that they may nat flee.
    That same Prince and that Mover," quod he,
    "Hath stablissed in this wretched world adown
    Certaine dayes and duracioun
    To all that is engendred in this place,
2140 Over the whiche day they may not pace,
    Al mow they yet tho dayes well abregge.°
    There needeth noon auctoritee to allegge,
    For it is proved by experience,
    But that me list declaren my sentence.
2145 Than may men by this order well discerne
    That thilke Mover stable is and eterne.
    Well may men knowe, but it be a fool,
    That every part deriveth from his hool.
    For Nature hath not taken his beginning
2150 Of no party or cantel° of a thing,
    But of a thing that parfit is and stable,
    Descending so till it be corrumpable.
    And therefore for his wise purveyaunce
    He hath so well biset his ordinaunce
2155 That speces of thinges and progressiouns
    Shullen enduren by successiouns,
    And not eterne, withouten any lie.
    This maistou understand and seen at eye.°
        Lo, th' ook that hath so long a norishinge

2127 **siked stille** sighed quietly   2141 **abregge** shorten   2150 **party
or cantel** part or portion   2129–58 **The Firste . . . eye** this passage,
based on Boethius, sets forth an idea as old at least as Plato, that all
things in the universe are bound together by love, in a hierarchy
(chain). The idea that all things have a limited time on earth and
must pass away is of course very medieval

Fro time that it first beginneth springe,                    2160
And hath so long a life, as ye may see,
Yet at the laste wasted is the tree.
Considereth eek how that the harde ston
Under our foot on which we tred and gon,
Yet wasteth it as it lith by the waye.                        2165
The brode river some time wexeth dreye.
The greete townes see we wane and wende.
    Than ye see that all this thing hath ende.
Of man and woman see we well also
That needes in one of thise termes two—                      2170
This is to sayn, in youth or elles age—
He mot be deed, the king as shall a page:
Some in his bed, some in the deepe see,
Some in the large feeld, as ye may see.
There helpeth nought—all goth that ilke waye.                2175
Than may I sayn that all this thing mot deye.
What maketh this but Jupiter the king,
That is Prince and cause of alle thing,
Converting all unto his propre welle°
From which it is derived, sooth to telle?                     2180
And here agains no creature on live,
Of no degree, availeth for to strive.
    Than is it wisdom, as it thinketh me,
To maken vertu of necessitee,
And take it well that we may not eschue—°                     2185
And namelich that° to us all is due.
And whoso grucheth aught,° he doth follye,
And rebel is to Him that all may gie.°
And certainly a man hath most honour
To dien in his excellence and flower,                        2190
Whan he is siker° of his goode name,
Than hath he done his freend ne him° no shame;
And gladder ought his freend been of his deeth

2179 propre welle own will   2185 that . . . eschue what we cannot
avoid   2186 that what   2187 grucheth aught complains at all
2188 to . . . gie to Him who guides all   2191 siker certain. The idea
that it is best to die at the height of one's glory is a very chivalric
notion of the kind a Knight would have believed; from a Christian
viewpoint, one should die in a state of grace   2192 him himself

Whan with honour up yolden° is his breeth,
2195 Than whan his name appalled° is for age,
For all forgetten is his vasselage.°
Than is it best, as for a worthy fame,
To dien whan that he is best of name.
    The contrary of all this is wilfulnesse.
2200 Why gruchen we, why have we hevinesse,
That good Arcite, of chivalry the flowr,
Departed is with duetee° and honour
Out of this foule prison of this lif?
Why gruchen here his cosin and his wif
2205 Of his welfare that loveth hem so well?
Can he hem thank?—Nay, God wot, neveradeel—
That both his soul and eek hemself offende.
And yet they mow hir lustes not amende.°
    What may I conclude of this longe serie,°
2210 But after woe I rede° us to be merrye,
And thanken Jupiter of all his grace;
And, ere we departen from this place,
I rede that we make of sorrwes two
Oo parfit joye, lasting evermo.
2215 And looketh now where most sorrwe is herinne,
There wol I first amenden and beginne.
Suster," quod he, "this is my full assent,
With all th'avis here of my parlement:
That gentil Palamon, your owne knight,
2220 That serveth you with will and hert and might
And ever hath done sin ye first him knewe,
That ye shall of your grace upon him rewe,
And taken him for husbond and for lord.
Lene me your hand, for this is our accord:
2225 Let see now of your womanly pitee.
He is a kinges brother son,° pardee,
And though he were a povre bacheler,
Sin he hath served you so many a yeer

---

2194 **yolden** yielded  2195 **appalled** faded  2196 **vasselage** knightly
prowess  2202 **duetee** dignity  2208 **mow** ... **amende** cannot im-
prove upon their happiness. The idea in the passage is that too much
mourning is a disservice to the dead  2209 **serie** argument  2210 **rede**
advise  2226 **kinges** ... **son** King's brother's son

And had for you so greet adversitee,
It moste been considered, leveth° me;                    2230
For gentil mercy oughte passen right."°
    Than said he thus to Palamon the knight:
"I trow there needeth litel sermoning
To make you assente to this thing.
Come neer and taketh your lady by the hond."        2235
Bitwixen hem was made anon the bond
That highte matrimoigne or marriage,
By all the conseil and the baronage.
And thus with alle bliss and melodye
Hath Palamon y-wedded Emelye.                          2240
And God, that all this wide world hath wrought,
Send him his love that hath it dere abought;
For now is Palamon in alle wele,
Living in bliss, in richess, and in hele,
And Emely him loveth so tenderly,                      2245
And he hir serveth also gentilly,
That never was there no word hem betweene
Of jalousy or any other teene.°
    Thus endeth Palamon and Emelye,
And God save all this faire compaignye.                2250
                    Amen

---

**2230 leveth** believe   **2231 passen right** prevail over justice   **2248 teene**
trouble

# THE MILLER'S PROLOGUE

Whan that the Knight had thus his tale y-told,
In all the route nas there yong ne old
That he ne said it was a noble storye
And worthy for to drawen to memorye—
5   And namely° the gentils everichoon.

Our Hoste lough and swore, "So mote I goon,
This goth aright! Unbuckeled is the male!°
Let see now who shall tell another tale,
For trewely the game is well begunne!
10   Now telleth ye, sir Monk, if that ye conne,
Somewhat to quite with the Knightes tale."°

The Miller, that for drunken° was all pale
So that unnethe° upon his horse he sat,
He nolde avalen° neither hood ne hat,
15   N'abiden no man for his curteisye,
But in Pilate's voice° he gan to crye,
And swore, "By armes and by blood and bones!°
I kan a noble tale for the nones,
With which I wol now quit the Knightes tale!"
20   Our Host saw that he was drunk of ale,
And said, "Abide, Robin, leve brother,
Some better man shall tell us first another.
Abide, and let us werken thriftily."°

"By Goddes soul," quod he, "that wol not I!
25   For I wol speke or elles go my way."

Our Host answered, "Tell on, a devil way!
Thou art a fool—thy wit is overcome."

"Now herkneth," quod the Miller, "all and some. . .
But first I make a protestacioun

5 namely in particular   7 Unbuckeled . . . male the bag is un-
fastened   11 to quite . . . tale to match the Knight's tale with
12 for drunken because of being drunk (and it is still morning!)
13 unnethe hardly   14 avalen remove (i.e., out of respect)   16 Pi-
late's voice in the mystery plays Pilate ranted and shrieked
17 armes . . . bones the arms, blood, and bones of Christ; such
inventiveness in swearing was not unusual   23 thriftily profitably

That I am drunk. I know it by my soun.°                          30
And therefore if that I misspeke or saye,°
Wite it° the ale of Southwerk, I you praye.
For I wol tell a legend and a lif
Both of a carpenter and of his wif,
How that a clerk hath set the wrightes cappe."°               35
    The Reeve answered and saide, "Stint thy clappe.°
Let be thy lewed drunken harlotrye.°
It is a sin and eek a greet follye
T'apairen° any man, or him defame,
And eek to bringen wives in swich fame.                        40
Thou maist enough of other thinges sayn."
    This drunken Miller spak full soon again,
And saide, "Leve brother Osewold,
Who hath no wife, he is no cockewold°—
But I say not therefore that thou art oon.                     45
There been full goode wives many oon,
And ever a thousand good ayains one badde.
That knowestou well thyself, but if thou madde.°
Why artou angry with my tale now?
I have a wife, pardee, as well as thou,                        50
Yet nolde I, for the oxen in my plough,
Take upon me more than enough
As deemen of myself that I were oon;°
I wol bileve well that I am noon.
An husbond shall not been inquisitif                           55
Of Goddes privetee—nor of his wif.
So he may finde Goddes foison there,°
Of the remnant needeth nought enquere."

        *     *     *

    What shold I more sayn but this Millere
He nold his wordes for no man forbere,                         60

30 **soun** sound of my voice   31 **misspeke or saye** misspeak or
missay   32 **Wite it** blame it on   35 **set . . . cappe** made a fool of the
craftsman   36 **Stint thy clappe** shut your mouth. The Reeve, who
is a carpenter, assumes that the miller is going to satirize him
personally. Reeves (managers of farms) and millers had dealings
with each other, of course, and doubtless tried to cheat each other;
hence they are natural enemies   37 **harlotrye** ribaldry   39 **apairen**
injure   44 **cockewold** cuckold—note the miller's logic here   48 **but
. . . madde** unless you're crazy   52–53 **Take . . . oon** go so far
beyond evidence as to decide that I'm one (ie., a cuckold)   57 **So
. . . there** So long as he finds God's plenty there (in his wife)

But told his cherles tale in his mannere.
M'athinketh° that I shall reherse it here.
And therefore every gentil wight, I praye,
Deemeth not, for God's love, that I saye
65 Of yvel entent, but for I mot reherse
Hir tales alle, be they bet or werse,
Or elles falsen some of my mattere.
And therefore, whoso list it not y-heere
Turn over the leef and chese another tale.
70 For he shall find enoughe, greet and smalle,
Of storial° thing that toucheth gentilesse
And eek moralitee and holinesse.
Blameth not me if that ye chese amiss.
The Miller is a cherl, ye know well this—
75 So was the Reeve eek, and other mo;
And harlotry they tolden bothe two.
Aviseth you, and put me out of blame—
And eek men shall not make ernest of game.°

# THE MILLER'S TALE°

Whilom there was dwelling at Oxenford
A riche gnof that guestes held to bord,°
And of his craft he was a carpenter.
With him there was dwelling a poor scholer,

---

62 **M'athinketh** I regret to say   71 **storial** historical   78 **ernest of game** something serious out of a joke   0 **The Miller's Tale** this tale is a "fabliau"—a comic tale reflecting the life of common people. Such tales were told orally and passed by word of mouth, but some —a good many all told—were written down. In writers like Sercambi, Boccaccio, and Chaucer they gain literary status. Chaucer's art in the Miller's Tale lies in his combining *two* tales, that of the "second flood" and that (as it is politely called) of the "misdirected kiss." He combines them in such a way that the climax of both occurs at once—with the cry of "Water!" And he adds to the fun by making the whole a parody of the Knight's Tale   2 **riche . . . bord** a rich lout that took in boarders; "gnof" suggests a common fellow and a cheat

Had lerned art;° but all his fantasye°                                5
Was turned for to lerne astrologye—
And koud a certain of conclusiouns,
To deemen by interrogaciouns,°
If that men asked him in certain houres
Whan that men shold have drought or elles showres;        10
Or if men asked him what shold befalle
Of everything—I may not recken hem alle.
    This clerk was cleped hende° Nicholas.
Of derne love he koud,° and of solas;
And thereto he was sly and full privee,                              15
And like a maiden meeke for to see.
A chambre had he in that hostelrye°—
Alone, withouten any compaignye—
Full fetisly y-dight with herbes swoote;°
And he himself as sweet as is the roote                              20
Of licoris or any setewale.
His *Almageste*° and bookes greet and smalle,
His astrelaby, longing for his art,°
His augrim stones,° layen fair apart
On shelves couched at his beddes heed,                               25
His press y-covered with a falding red;°
And all above there lay a gay sautrye,°
On which he made a-nightes melodye
So sweetely that all the chambre rung—

5 art i.e., had completed the first part of a liberal arts education,
the "trivium"   5 fantasye fascination, real interest (note that astrol-
ogy loomed large in the Knight's Tale)   7–8 koud . . . interroga-
ciouns (he) knew a certain number of astrological procedures, to
answer questions (by determining the position of heavenly bodies
at the hour the question was asked)   13 hende a fine old word
which combines the meaning of "handy," "clever" with "pleasant,"
"gentle"   14 Of . . . koud he knew all about secret love affairs; but
his kind of love is very different from that depicted in the Knight's
Tale. Chaucer hints at this contrast in line 18 (cf. Knight's Tale,
line 1921)   17 hostelrye lodging. The fact that he has a private
room would have been very unusual   19 fetisly . . . swoote nicely
fixed up with sweet-smelling plants   22 Almageste a textbook of
astrology   23 His . . . art his astrelabe pertaining to his art (an
astronomical instrument, ancestor of the sextant; Chaucer himself
wrote a treatise on the astrolabe)   24 augrim stones instrument for
mathematical calculations   26 press . . . red his clothes closet (or
chest) covered with a red cloth   27 sautrye psaltery, a string instru-
ment played by plucking

30 And *Angelus ad Virginem* he sung,
    And after that he sung the *Kinges Note*.
    Full often blessed was his murry throte!
    And thus this sweete clerk his time spente,
    After his freendes' finding and his rente.°

35    This carpenter had wedded new a wif
    Which that he loved more than his lif.
    Of eigheteene yeer she was of age.
    Jalous he was, and held hir narrwe in cage:
    For she was wild and yong, and he was old,
40 And deemed himself been like a cokewold.
    He knew not Caton, for his wit was rude,
    That bade man shold wed his similitude:
    "Men sholde wedden after hir estat,
    For youth and eld is often at debat."
45 But sith that he was fallen in the snare,
    He most endure, as other folk, his care.
       Fair was this yonge wife, and therewithal
    As any wesel° hir body gent and small.
    A ceint° she wered, barred all of silk,
50 A barmecloth° as white as morne milk
    Upon hir lendes,° full of many a gore.°
    White was hir smock,° and broiden° all before
    And eek behind, on hir coller aboute,
    Of col-black silk, within and eek withoute.
55 The tapes of hir white voluper°
    Were of the same suite of° hir coller,
    Hir fillet° brod of silk and set full hye.
    And sikerly she had a likerous° eye.
    Full small y-pulled° were hir browes two,
60 And tho were bent, and black as any slo.
    She was full more blissful on to see
    Than is the newe perejonette tree,

---

**34 After . . . rente** living on money his friends gave him plus his own income. The whole passage suggests a well-to-do student with a taste for the good life   **48 wesel** weasel. Notice the large amount of animal imagery in the description of her   **49 ceint** belt, girdle   **50 barmecloth** apron   **51 lendes** hips   **51 gore** pleat   **52 smock** petticoat   **52 broiden** embroidered   **55 tapes . . . voluper** ribbons of her white cap   **56 suite** of color (or cloth) as   **57 fillet** hair-band   **58 likerous** frisky   **59 small y-pulled** thinly plucked

And softer than the wool is of a wether.°
And by hir girdle heng a purse of lether,
Tasseled with silk and perled with latoun.°          65
In all this world, to seeken up and down,
There nis no man so wise that coude thenche
So gay a popelote° or swich a wenche!
Full brighter was the shining of hir hewe
Than in the Tower the noble y-forged newe.°         70
But of hir song, it was as loud and yerne°
As any swallow sitting on a berne;°
Thereto she coude skip and make game
As any kid or calf follwing his dame.
Hir mouth was sweet as bragot or the meeth,°       75
Or hoord of apples laid in hay or heeth.
Winsing° she was as is a jolly colt,
Long as a mast, and upright as a bolt.
A brooch she bare upon hir low coller
As brood as is the boss of a buckeler.              80
Hir shoes were laced on hir legges hye.
She was a primerole, a piggesnye,°
For any lord to leggen° in his bedde,
Or yet for any good yeman to wedde.

   Now, sir, and eft, sir, so bifell the cas          85
That on a day this hende Nicholas
Fill with this yonge wife to rage and playe,
While that hir husbond was at Oseneye°
—As clerkes been full subtil and full queinte°—
And prively he caught hir by the queinte,°          90
And said, "Ywis, but if ich° have my wille,
For derne love of thee, lemman,° I spille,"°

63 **wether** sheep   65 **perled with latoun** beaded with brass beads
67–68 **thenche . . . popelote** imagine such a good-looking doll   70 **in
. . . newe** the newly minted gold coin in the Tower of London
71 **yerne** peppy   72 **berne** barn   75 **bragot . . . meeth** ales made with
honey   77 **Winsing** skittish   82 **primerole, piggesnye** names of
flowers   83 **leggen** lay   88 **Oseneye** an island in the Thames, just
west of Oxford   89 **queinte** clever   90 **queinte** genitals; the gesture
is illustrated, from a fourteenth-century book of hours, in Robertson,
*Preface to Chaucer*, plate 5   91 **ich** I   92 **lemman** sweetheart
92 **spille** perish; waste time; with a possible bawdy sense as well,
which would make it a triple pun

And held hir harde by the haunche-bones,
And saide, "Lemman, love me all atones,°
95 Or I wol dien, also God me save."
And she sprong as a colt doth in the trave,°
And with hir heed she wried° fast away.
She said, "I wol not kiss thee, by my fay.
Why, let be!" quod she, "let be, Nicholas,
100 Or I wol cry 'Out! Harrow! and Alas!'
Do way your handes—for your curteisye."
   This Nicholas gan "mercy" for to crye,°
And spak so fair, and proffred him so faste,
That she hir love him graunted atte laste;
105 And swore hir ooth, by Saint Thomas of Kent,
That she wold been at his commandement,
Whan that she may hir leiser well espye.°
"Mine husbond is so full of jalousye
That but ye waite well and been privee,
110 I wot right well I nam but deed," quod she—
"Ye moste been full derne° as in this cas."
   "Nay, thereof care thee nought," quod Nicholas.
"A clerk had litherly biset his while°
But if he coud a carpenter beguile."
115 And thus they been accorded and y-sworn
To wait a time, as I have told biforn.
Whan Nicholas had done this everydeel,
And thakked hir about the lendes° well,
He kist hir sweet, and taketh his sautrye,
120 And playeth fast and maketh melodye.
   Than fill it thus, that to the parish chirche,
Christes owne werkes for to wirche,°
This goode wife went on an holiday:
Hir foreheed shone as bright as any day,
125 So was it washen whan she let hir werk.

94 **atones** at once   96 **trave** a device for holding horses still while
being shod   97 **wried** turned   102 **"mercy" . . . crye** compare
Arcite's dying words, Knight's Tale, line 1950   107 **hir leiser . . .
espye** find her chance   111 **derne** secret. Secrecy was one of the
requirements in courtly love   113 **had . . . while** would have used
his time badly   118 **thakked . . . lendes** patted her on the behind
122 **wirche** perform

Now was there of that chirch a parish clerk,°
The which that was y-cleped Absolon.
Crul° was his heer, and as the gold it shoon,
And strouted° as a fanne large and brode:
Full straight and even lay his jolly shode.°          130
His rode° was red, his eyen grey as goos.
With Poules window° corven on his shoes,
In hoses red he wente fetisly.
Y-clad he was full small and properly,°
All in a kirtel of a light waget°—          135
Full fair and thicke been the pointes° set—
And thereupon he had a gay surplis,
As white as is the blossme upon the ris.°
A merry child he was, so God me save!
Well coud he laten blood, and clip, and shave,          140
And maken a chartre of land, or acquitaunce.°
In twenty manner coud he trip and daunce
After the scole of Oxenforde tho,°
And with his legges casten to and fro,
And playen songes on a small rubible.°          145
Thereto he song sometime a loud quinible,°
And as well coud he play on a giterne.°
In all the town nas brewhouse ne taverne
That he ne visited with his solas,
Ther any gaillard tappestere° was.          150
But, sooth to sayn, he was somedeel squaimous°
Of farting; and of speeche daungerous.°
    This Absolon, that jolly was and gay,

---

126 **clerk** in Absolon's case, a clerk in minor orders who is the
handyman about the church and jack-of-all-trades; see lines 140–41.
128 **Crul** curly    129 **strouted** spread out    130 **shode** part in his
hair    131 **rode** complexion    132 **Poules window** design cut in his
shoes resembling in shape the windows of St. Paul's Cathedral
134 **small and properly** discreetly and splendidly    135 **kirtel . . .
waget** coat of light blue    136 **pointes** laces    138 **ris** twig    140–41
**laten . . . acquitaunce** let blood, cut hair, shave, write a charter for
the sale of land or a deed of release    143 **scole . . . tho** manner of
Oxford then    145 **rubible** the rebeck, a two-stringed instrument
played with a bow    146 **quinible** high-pitched voice, perhaps counter
tenor or falsetto    147 **giterne** guitar    150 **gaillard tappestere** merry
barmaid    151 **squaimous** squeamish    152 **daungerous** delicate

Goth with a sencer° on the holiday,
155 Sencing the wives of the parish faste,
And many a lovely look on hem he caste,
And namely on this carpenteres wif.
To look on hir him thought a merry lif!
She was so propre and sweet and likerous,
160 I dare well sayn, if she had been a mous
And he a cat—he wold hir hent° anon!
This parish clerk, this jolly Absolon,
Hath in his herte swich a love-longinge
That of no wife took he noon offringe—
165 For curteisy he said he wolde noon.
The moon, whan it was night, full brighte shoon,
And Absolon his giterne hath y-take,
For paramours, he thoughte for to wake;°
And forth he goth, jolif and amorous,
170 Till he came to the carpenteres hous,
A litel after cockes had y-crowe,
And dressed him up by a shot-windowe°
That was upon the carpenteres wall.
He singeth in his voice gentil and small,
175 *Now, dere lady, if thy wille be,*
*I praye you that ye wol rew on me*—
Full well accordant to his giterninge.
This carpenter awoke, and herd him singe,
And spak unto his wife and said anon,
180 "What, Alison, heerestou not Absolon
That chaunteth thus under our bowre's wall?"
And she answered hir husbond therewithal,
"Yis, God wot, John, I heer it everydeel."
    This passeth forth—what wol ye bet than well?
185 Fro day to day this jolly Absolon
So woweth° hir that him is woe-bigon.
He waketh all the night and all the day;
He kembeth his lockes brod and made him gay.
He woweth hir by menes and brocage,°

154 **sencer** censer, incense-burner; he censes the church or their
homes, a form of blessing   161 **hent** catch   168 **For . . . wake** for
the sake of love he planned to stay up   172 **shot-windowe** casement
window   186 **woweth** woos   189 **menes and brocage** go-betweens
and agents

And swore he wolde been hir owne page.                          190
He singeth, brokking° as a nightingale.
He sent hir piment, meeth,° and spiced ale,
And wafers piping hot out of the gleede,°
And—for she was of town—he proffred meede:°
For some folk wol be wonnen for richesse,                       195
And some for strokes, and some for gentilesse.
Sometime to shew his lightness and maistrye,
He playeth Herodes upon a scaffold hye.°
But what availeth him, as in this cas?
She loveth so this hende Nicholas                               200
That Absolon may blow the buckes horn;°
He n'hadde for his labour but a scorn!
And thus she maketh Absolon hir ape,°
And all his ernest turneth til a jape.
Full sooth is this proverb, it is no lie,                       205
Men saith right thus: *Alway the nye slye*
*Maketh the ferre leve to be loth.*°
For though that Absolom be wood or wroth,
By cause that he fer was from hir sighte,
This nye Nicholas stood in his lighte.                          210
Now beer thee well, thou hende Nicholas!
For Absolon may wail and sing "alas!"

                    *    *    *

    And so befell it on a Saterday
This carpenter was gone til Oseney,
And hende Nicholas and Alisoun                                  215
Accorded been to this conclusioun,
That Nicholas shall shapen him a wile°
This sely° jalous husbond to beguile;
And if so be the game went aright,

---

191 **brokking** in a breaking voice   192 **piment, meeth** honeyed wine,
mead   193 **gleede** iron (like a waffle iron)   194 **meede** cash
198 **Herodes . . . hye** i.e., he played Herod in a mystery play; the
scaffold would be a temporary stage   201 **blow . . . horn** i.e., he
is wasting his time   203 **ape** Cf. General Prologue, line 706
206–07 **Alway . . . loth** always the sly fellow nearby causes the
loved one far off to be despised   217 **wile** trick   218 **sely** poor, silly,
foolish

220 She sholde sleepen in his arm all night—
For this was hir desire, and his also.
And right anon, withouten wordes mo,
This Nicholas no lenger wolde tarrye,
But doth full soft unto his chambre carrye
225 Both mete and drinke for a day or twaye,
And to hir husbond bade hir for to saye—
If that he asked after Nicholas—
She sholde say she niste where he was,
Of all that day she saw him nought with eye;
230 She trowed that he was in maladye,
For, for no cry hir maide coud him calle,
He nold answer for no thing that might falle.
    This passeth forth all thilke Saterday
That Nicholas still in his chambre lay,
235 And eet, and sleep, or dide what him leste,
Till Sunday that the sunne goth to reste.
This sely carpenter hath greet mervaile
Of Nicholas, or what thing might him aile,
And said, "I am adrad, by Saint Thomas,
240 It stondeth not aright with Nicholas.
God shilde° that he deide suddenly!
This world is now full tikel,° sikerly!
I saw today a corpse y-born to chirche
That now on Monday last I saw him wirche.
245 Go up," quod he unto his knave° anon,
"Clepe° at his door or knocke with a ston.
Look how it is and tell me boldely."
    This knave goth him up full sturdily,
And at the chambre door while that he stood
250 He cried and knocked as that he were wood,
"What! How! What do ye, maister Nicholay?
How may ye sleepen all the longe day?"
But all for nought: he herde not a word.
An hole he foond full low upon a boord,
255 Ther as the cat was wont in for to creepe,
And at that hole he looked in full deepe,
And atte last he had of him a sighte:

241 **shilde** forbid   242 **tikel** unstable   245 **knave** servant   246 **Clepe**
call

This Nicholas sat gaping ever uprighte
As he had kiked° on the newe moone.
   Adown he goth and told his maister soone     *260*
In what array he saw this ilke man.
This carpenter to blessen him° began,
And saide, "Help us, Sainte Frideswide!°
A man wot litel what him shall bitide!
This man is falle, with his astromye,°     *265*
In some woodness or in some agonye.°
I thought ay well how that it sholde be°—
Men shold not know of Goddes privetee.
Ye, blessed be alway a lewed° man
That nought but only his bileve kan!°     *270*
So ferde another clerk with astromye:
He walked in the feeldes for to prye
Upon the sterres, what there shold bifalle,
Till he was in a marle-pit y-falle—
He saw not *that!* But yet, by Saint Thomas,     *275*
Me reweth sore for hende Nicholas—
He shall be rated of his studying,°
If that I may, by Jesus, heven king.
Get me a staff that I may underspore°
While that thou, Robin, hevest up the doore.     *280*
He shall out of his studying, as I guesse"—
And to the chambre door he gan him dresse.
His knave was a strong carl for the nones,
And by the hasp he haf it up° atones—
Into the floor the doore fill anon.     *285*
This Nicholas sat ay as still as ston,
And ever gaped up into the air.
This carpenter wend he were in despair,°
And hent him by the shoulders mightily,
And shook him hard, and cride spitously,°     *290*

259 As . . . kiked as if he were staring (i.e., as if moon-struck)
262 blessen him cross himself   263 Sainte Frideswide patron saint
of Oxford   265 astromye the carpenter mispronounces "astronomy"
266 woodness . . . agonye madness or fit   267 I . . . be I always
thought it would be this way   269 lewed ignorant   270 That . . .
kan who knows nothing but his creed   277 rated . . . studying
scolded for his musing   279 underspore pry   284 haf it up pulled
it off   288 wend . . . despair supposed he was in some desperate
plight   290 spitously harshly

"What, Nicholay! what, how! What! Look adown!
Awake, and thenk on Christes passioun!
I crouche thee from elves and fro wightes!"°
Therewith the nightspell said he anonrightes°
295 On foure halves° of the house aboute,
And on the threshfold on the door withoute:
"Jesu Christ and Saïnt Benedict,
Bless this house from every wicked wight!
For nightes verye, the white Pater Noster!
300 Where wentestou, Saïnt Petres soster?"°
And at the last this hende Nicholas
Gan for to sike sore°—and said, "Alas!
Shall all the world be lost eftsoones now?"
    This carpenter answerde, "What saistou?
305 What! think on God, as *we* doon, men that swinke!"°
    This Nicholas answerde, "Fetch me drinke!
And after wol I speke in privetee
Of certain thing that toucheth me and thee.
I wol tell it noon other man, certain."
310     This carpenter goth down and cometh again,
And brought of mighty ale a large quart,
And whan that ech of hem had drunk his part,
This Nicholas his doore faste shette,
And down the carpenter by him he sette,
315 And saide, "John, mine hoste lief and dere,
Thou shalt upon thy trouthe swere me here
That to no wight thou shalt this conseil wraye;°
For it is Christes conseil that I saye,
And if thou tell it man, thou art forlore;°
320 For this vengeance thou shalt have therefore,
That if thou wraye me, thou shalt be wood."°
    "Nay, Christ forbede it, for his holy blood!"

---

293 **crouche ... wightes** defend with the sign of the cross from
elves and living creatures   294 **nightspell ... anonrightes** he said
the night spell right away (a charm against evil spirits)   295 **halves**
sides   299–300 **For ... soster** like most charms this is chiefly non-
sense. The white Pater Noster was a prayer against evil spirits in
the night; where St. Peter's sister went remains unanswered   302 **sike
sore** sigh deeply   305 **swinke** work   317 **this ... wraye** betray this
secret   319 **forlore** utterly lost   321 **if ... wood** if you betray me
you will go mad

Quod tho this sely man, "I nam no labbe,°
And, though I say,° I nam not lief to gabbe.
Say what thou wolt, I shall it never telle                             325
To child ne wife, by Him that harrwed helle."°
    "Now John," quod Nicholas, "I wol not lie:
I have y-found in mine astrologye,
As I have looked in the moone bright,
That now a-Monday next, at quarter night,                             330
Shall fall a rain, and that so wild and wood,
That half so greet was never Noeh's flood.
This world," he said, "in lasse than an hour
Shall all be dreint,° so hidous is the shower.
Thus shall mankinde drench° and lese hir lif."                         335
    This carpenter answered, "Alas, my wif!
And shall *she* drench? Alas, mine Alisoun!"
For sorrow of this he fill almost adown,
And said, "Is there no remedy in this cas?"
    "Why, yis,° for God," quod hende Nicholas,                        340
"If thou wolt werken after lore and reed;°
Thou maist not werken after thine own heed.
For thus saith Salomon that was full trewe:
*Werk all by conseil and thou shalt nought rewe.*°
And if thou werken wolt by good conseil,                              345
I undertake, withouten mast or sail,
Yet shall I save hir, and thee, and me.
Hastou not herd how saved was Noeh
Whan that Our Lord had warned him biforn
That all the world with water shold be lorn?"                         350
    "Yis," quod this carpenter, "full yore ago."
    "Hastou not herd," quod Nicholas, "also
The sorrow of Noeh with his fellawshipe?°
Ere that he mighte get his wife to shipe,

323 labbe blabbermouth   324 though I say if I do say so myself
326 Him . . . helle Christ descended into Hell to save virtuous souls
born before the Incarnation; the incident was depicted in mystery
plays   334 dreint drowned   335 drench drown   340 yis the emphatic
form (as opposed to "ye"): "why, yes—for *sure*"   341 lore and reed
learning and advice   344 rewe be sorry   353 sorrow . . . fellawshipe
In the mystery play Noah's wife will not get on the boat, scolds
him, and so on; the Noah play was sponsored by the carpenter's
guild, and old John, doubtless having seen it, has a clear idea of
Noah's troubles in escaping the flood

355 Him had lever, I dare well undertake,
      At thilke time than all his wetheres° blacke
      That she hadde had a ship hirself alone.
      And therefore wostou what is best to doone?
      This asketh haste, and of an hastif thing
360 Men may not preche or maken tarrying.
      Anon go get us fast into this inn°
      A kneeding-trough or elles a kimelin°
      For ech of us—but look that they be large—
      In which we mowen swim as in a barge,
365 And han therein vitaille suffisaunt
      But for a day—fy on the remenaunt!
      The water shall aslake and goon away
      Aboute prime upon the nexte day.
      But Robin may not wite of this, thy knave,
370 Ne eek thy maide Gille I may not save.
      Axe not why, for though thou axe me,
      I wol not tellen Goddes privetee.
      Suffiseth thee, but if thy wittes madde,°
      To han as greet a grace as Noeh hadde.
375 Thy wife shall I well saven, out of doute.
      Go now thy way, and speed thee hereaboute.
      But whan thou hast for hir and thee and me
      Y-geten us thise kneeding-tubbes three,
      Than shaltou hang hem in the roof full hye,
380 That no man of our purveyance° espye.
      And whan thou thus hast done as I have said,
      And hast our vitaille fair in hem y-laid,
      And eek an ax to smite the cord atwo
      Whan that the water cometh, that we may go,
385 And breke an hole on high upon the gable
      Unto the gardenward, over the stable,
      That we may freely passen forth our way,
      Whan that the grete shower is gone away—
      Than shaltou swim as murry, I undertake,
390 As doth the white duck after hir drake!
      Than wol I clepe, 'How, Alison? How, John?

---

356 **wetheres** sheep   361 **inn** house   362 **kimelin** brewing-tub   373 **but
. . . madde** unless your wits have gone mad   380 **purveyance** prepa-
ration

Be murry, for the flood wol pass anon!'
And thou wolt sayn, 'Hail, maister Nicholay!
Good morrwe, I see thee well, for it is day!'
And than shall we be lordes all our lif                              395
Of all the world, as Noeh and his wif.
But of oo thing I warne thee full right:
Be well avised on that ilke night
That we been entred into shippes boord
That none of us ne speke not a word,                                 400
Ne clepe, ne cry, but been in his prayere,
For it is Goddes owne heste dere.°
Thy wife and thou mot hange fer atwinne,°
For that bitwixe you shall be no sinne—
Namore in looking than there shall in deede.                         405
This ordinance is said. Go, God thee speede.
Tomorrwe at night whan men been all asleepe,
Into our kneeding-tubbes wol we creepe,
And sitten there, abiding° Goddes grace.
Go now thy way, I have no lenger space                               410
To make of this no lenger sermoning.
Men sayn thus, *Send the wise and say no thing.*
Thou art so wise it needeth thee not teche.
Go save our life, and that I thee biseeche."

　　This sely carpenter goth forth his way.                         415
Full oft he said "Alas!" and "Weilaway!"
And to his wife he told his privetee—
And she was ware, and knew it bet than he,
What all this quainte cast was for to saye.°
But natheless she ferd as she wold deye,°                            420
And said, "Alas! go forth thy way anon!
Help us to scape, or we been dede echon!
I am thy trewe veray wedded wif:
Go, dere spouse, and help to save our lif."
—Lo, which a greet thing is affeccioun!°                             425
Men may die of imaginacioun,
So deepe may impression be take!

402 **Goddes . . . dere** God's own dear command    403 **fer atwinne**
far apart, 409 **abiding** waiting for    419 **What . . . saye** what all
this weird plan was about    420 **ferd . . . deye** acted as if she were
about to die 425 **affeccioun** love—but it also means "state of
mind"

This sely carpenter beginneth quake;
Him thinketh verailich that he may see°
430  Noeh's flood come wallowing as the see
To drenchen Alison, his honey dere.
He weepeth, waileth, maketh sorry cheere;
He siketh with full many a sorry swough,°
And goth and geteth him a kneeding-trough,
435  And after, a tubbe and a kimelin,
And prively he sent hem to his inn,
And heng hem in the roof in privetee.
His owne hand° he made ladders three,
To climben by the runges and the stalkes
440  Unto the tubbes hanging in the balkes,°
And hem vitailled, bothe trough and tubbe,
With breed and cheese and good ale in a jubbe,°
Suffising right enough as for a day.
But ere that he had made all this array,°
445  He sent his knave, and eek his wench also,
Upon his need to London for to go.
    And on the Monday whan it drow to night,
He shet his door withouten candle-light,
And dressed alle thing as it shold be,
450  And shortly up they clomben alle three.
They seten stille well a furlong way.°
"Now, *Pater Noster, clum*,"° said Nicholay,
And *"Clum"* quod John, and *"Clum"* said Alisoun.
This carpenter said his devocioun,
455  And still he sit and biddeth his prayere,
Awaiting on the rain, if he it heere.
    The dede sleep, for wery bisinesse,
Fill on this carpenter right as I guesse
Aboute curfew time, or litel more.
460  For travail of his gost° he groneth sore,
And eft he routeth,° for his heed mislay.

---

429 Him . . . see it really seems to him that he can see    433 swough
a loud sigh    438 His owne hand with his own hand    440 balkes
beams between the rafters    442 jubbe jug    444 array preparation
451 furlong way the time it takes to walk two hundred twenty yards
452 Pater Noster, clum "say a Pater Noster, and then mum"
460 travail . . . gost i.e., his troubled spirit    461 routeth snores

Down off the ladder stalketh Nicholay,
And Alison full soft adown she spedde:
Withouten wordes mo they goon to bedde
Ther as the carpenter is wont to lie.                            465
There was the revel and the melodye,
And thus lith Alison and Nicholas
In bisiness of mirth and in solas,
Till that the bell of laudes° gan to ringe,
And freres in the chauncel gonne singe.                          470

*        *        *

This parish clerk, this amorous Absolon,
That is for love alway so woe-bigon,
Upon the Monday was at Oseneye,
With compaigny him to disport and playe,
And asked upon a cas° a cloisterer                               475
Full prively after John the carpenter.
And he drow him apart out of the cherche,
And said, "I noot; I saw him here not werche
Sith Saterday. I trowe that he be went
For timber ther our abbot hath him sent;                         480
For he is wont for timber for to go,
And dwellen at the grange a day or two;
Or elles he is at his house, certain.
Where that he be I can not soothly sayn."
This Absolon full jolly was and light,                           485
And thoughte, "Now is time to wake all night,
For sikerly I saw him not stirringe
About his door sin day began to springe.
So mot I thrive, I shall at cockes crowe
Full prively knocken at his windowe                              490
That stant full low upon his bowres wall.°
To Alison now wol I tellen all
My love-longing, for yet I shall not misse
That at the leste way I shall hir kisse.
Some manner comfort shall I have, parfay.                        495

---

**469 laudes** about four-thirty a.m.   **475 upon a cas** by chance
**491 low . . . wall** just how low on the wall of his house is to be an
important detail; cf. line 510

My mouth hath itched all this longe day—
That is a sign of kissing, at the leeste.
All night me mette° eek I was at a feeste.
Therefore I wol go sleep an hour or twaye,
500 And all the night than wol I wake and playe."
        Whan that the firste cock hath crow, anon
Up rist this jolly lover Absolon,
And him arrayeth gay at point devis.°
But first he cheweth grain° and licoris
505 To smellen sweet, ere he had kembd his heer.
Under his tonge a trewe-love° he beer,
For thereby wende he to be gracious.°
He rometh to the carpenteres hous,
And still he stant under the shot-windowe
510 (Unto his brest it raught, it was so lowe)
And soft he cougheth with a semy° soun.
"What do ye, honey-comb, sweet Alisoun,
My faire brid,° my sweete cinnamome?
Awaketh, lemman° mine, and speketh to me.
515 Well litel thinken ye upon my wo
That for your love I swete ther I go.°
No wonder is though that I swelt° and swete:
I morne as doth a lamb after the tete.°
Ywis, lemman, I have swich love-longinge,
520 That like a turtle trew is my morninge;°
I may not ete namore than a maide."
        "Go fro the window, Jacke fool!" she saide.
"As help me God, it wol not be *com-pa-me!*°
I love another, and elles I were to blame,
525 Well bet than thee, by Jesu, Absolon.
Go forth thy way, or I wol cast a ston,
And let me sleep, a twenty devil way!"

498 me mette I dreamed (*lit.* it dreamed to me)   503 gay . . . devis
fancily to the last detail   504 grain a spice   506 trewe-love an herb-
leaf, perhaps thought to give luck—or sweeten the breath
507 wende . . . gracious he imagined he'd be irresistible   511 semy
delicate   513 brid bird   514 lemman sweetheart   516 swete . . . go
sweat wherever I go. Sweating was hardly conventional for courtly
lovers; the whole passage is in fact a bumpkin's idea of love-longing
517 swelt get faint from the heat   518 tete teat   520 like . . . morn-
inge my suffering is true as the turtledove's   523 com-pa-me come
kiss me

"Alas," quod Absolon, "and weilaway,
That trewe love was ever so yvel biset.
Than kiss me, sin that it may be no bet,     530
For Jesus' love, and for the love of me."
    "Woltou than go thy way therewith?" quod she.
"Ye, certes, lemman," quod this Absolon.
"Than make thee redy," quod she. "I come anon."
And unto Nicholas she saide stille,     535
"Now hust, and thou shalt laughen all thy fille."
    This Absolon down set him on his knees
And said, "I am a lord at all degrees!°
For after this I hope there cometh more.
Lemman, thy grace! and sweete brid, thine ore!"°     540
    The window she undoth, and that in haste.
"Have do," quod she, "come off° and speed thee faste,
Lest that our neighebores thee espye."
    This Absolon gan wipe his mouth full drye.
Derk was the night as pitch or as the cole;     545
And at the window out she put hir hole.
And Absolon, him fill no bet ne wers,
But with his mouth he kist hir naked ers—
Full savourly—ere he were ware of this.
Aback he stert, and thought it was amiss,     550
For well he wist a woman hath no beerd.
He felt a thing all rough and long y-herd,°
And saide, "Fy, alas! what have I do?"
    "*Teehee,*" quod she, and clapt the window to.
And Absolon goth forth a sorry pas.     555
    "A beerd! a beerd!"° quod hende Nicholas,
"By Goddes corpus, this goth fair and well!"
    This sely Absolon herd everydeel,
And on his lip he gan for anger bite,
And to himself he said—"I shall thee quite."°     560
Who rubbeth now, who froteth° now his lippes
With dust, with sand, with straw, with cloth, with
      chippes,

538 **at all degrees** in all respects—love has ennobled him already!
540 **ore** grace    542 **Have . . . off** "let's get it over with, come on"
552 **y-herd** haired    556 **beerd** beard (the word was also slang for a
trick)    560 **quite** get even with. Note how fast his artificiality disap-
pears    561 **froteth** scrapes

But Absolon, that saith full oft "alas"?
"My soul bitake I unto Sathanas,
565 But me were lever than all this town," quod he,
"Of this despite awroken° for to be.
Alas," quod he, "Alas I n'had y-bleint!"°
His hote love was cold and all y-queint,°
For fro that time that he had kist hir ers
570 Of paramours he sette not a kers°—
For he was heled° of his maladye.
Full ofte paramours he gan defye,
And weep as doth a child that is y-bete.
    A softe pas he went over the streete
575 Until a smith men clepen daun Gervais,
That in his forge smithed plough-harneis:
He sharpeth shar and cultour bisily.
This Absolon knocketh all esily,
And said, "Undo, Gervais, and that anon!"
580 "What, who artou?" "It am I, Absolon."
"What, Absolon? What, Christes sweete tree!°
Why rise ye so rathe?° Ey, *ben'dic'te*,
What aileth you? Some gay girl, God it wot,
Hath brought you thus upon the veritoot.°
585 By Sainte Note, ye wot well what I mene."
    This Absolon ne roughte° not a bene
Of all his play; no word again he yaf.
He hadde more tow on his distaff
Than Gervais knew, and saide, "Freend so dere,
590 This hote cultour in the chimnee here,
As, lene° it me; I have therewith to doone.
I wol bring it thee again full soone."
    Gervais answerde, "Certes, were it gold,
Or in a poke nobles all untold,°
595 Thou sholdest have, as I am trewe smith.
Ey, Christes foe, what wol ye do therewith?"

---

566 awroken avenged    567 I . . . y-bleint if only I had held back
568 y-queint put out    570 Of . . . kers he didn't give a damn about
love affairs    571 heled healed. Healing the lover's malady, a tradi-
tional phrase, was usually done by the lady's favor    581 tree cross
582 rathe early    584 veritoot "on the move"    586 roughte cared
591 lene lend    594 in . . . untold countless gold coins in a sack

"Thereof," quod Absolon, "be as be may.
I shall well tell it thee tomorrwe day"—
And caught the cultour by the colde steele.
Full soft out at the door he gan to stele,          600
And went unto the carpenteres wall.
He cougheth first, and knocketh therewithal
Upon the window, right as he did er.
 This Alison answerde, "Who is ther
That knocketh so? I warrant it a thief."          605
 "Why, nay!" quod he, "God wot, my sweete lief,
I am thine Absolon, my dereling!°
Of gold," quod he, "I have thee brought a ring;
My moder yaf it me, so God me save.
Full fine it is and thereto well y-grave.          610
This wol I yiven thee, if thou me kisse."
 This Nicholas was risen for to pisse,
And thought he wold amenden all the jape°—
He sholde kiss *his* ers ere that he scape.
And up the window did he hastily,          615
And out his ers he putteth prively,
Over the buttock to the haunche-bon.
And therewith spak this clerk, this Absolon:
"Spek, sweete brid, I noot not where thou art."
This Nicholas anon let flee a fart          620
As greet as it had been a thunder-dent,
That with the stroke he was almost y-blent;°
And he was redy with his iren hot,
And Nicholas amid the ers he smoot.
Off goth the skin an hande-brede aboute;          625
The hote cultour brende so his toute
That for the smert he wende for to die;
As he were wood, for woe he gan to crye,
"Help! Water! *Water!* Help, for Goddes herte!"
 This carpenter out of his slumber sterte,          630
And herd one cryen *"Water!"* as he were wood,
And thought, "Alas, now cometh Noweles flood!"
He set him up withoute wordes mo,
And with his ax he smote the cord atwo,

607 **dereling** darling 613 **amenden . . . jape** improve upon the joke
622 **y-blent** blinded

635   *And down goth all!* He fond neither to selle
     Ne breed ne ale till he came to the celle°
     Upon the floor—and there aswoun he lay.
       Up stirt hir Alison and Nicholay,
     And criden "Out!" and "Harrow!" in the streete.
640  The neighebores, bothe small and greete,
     In runnen for to gauren° on this man
     That aswoun lay bothe pale and wan—
     For with the fall he brosten° had his arm.
     But stond he most unto his owne harm,°
645  For whan he spak he was anon bore down
     With° hende Nicholas and Alisoun.
     They tolden every man that he was wood:
     He was so aghast of Noweles flood,
     Thurgh fantasy, that of his vanitee°
650  He had y-bought him kneeding-tubbes three
     And had hem hanged in the roof above,
     And that he prayed hem, for Goddes love,
     To sitten in the roof, *par compaignye.*
     The folk gan laughen at his fantasye.
655  Into the roof they kiken° and they gape,
     And turned all his harm unto a jape;
     For what so that this carpenter answerde
     It was for nought—no man his reson herde.
     With othes greet he was so sworn adown
660  That he was holden wood in all the town,
     For every clerk anonright held with other:
     They said, "The man was wood, my leve brother,"
     And every wight gan laughen at this strif.
     Thus swived° was the carpenteres wif
665  For all his keeping and his jalousye;
     And Absolon hath kist hir nether eye;
     And Nicholas is scalded in the toute.
     This tale is done and God save all the route!°

---

635–36 **He fond . . . celle** he didn't stop to sell bread or ale till he hit
the floor   641 **gauren** gape   643 **brosten** broken   644 **stond . . .
harm** accept the blame   645–46 **anon bore down with** immediately
put down by   649 **vanitee** silliness   655 **kiken** gawk   664 **swived**
layed   669 **route** crowd, bunch

# THE REEVE'S PROLOGUE

Whan folk had laughen at this nice cas
Of Absolon and hende Nicholas,
Diverse folk diversely they saide,
But for the more part they laugh and playde;°
Ne at this tale I saw no man him greve                    5
But it were only Osewold the Reeve:
Because he was of carpenteres craft
A litel ire is in his hert y-laft°—
He gan to grucche° and blamed it a lite:
    "So thee'k,"° quod he, "full well coud I thee quite    10
With blering of a proud milleres eye,°
If that me liste speke of ribaudye.°
But ik° am old; me list not play for age.
Grass time is done, my fodder is now forage;
This white top writeth mine olde yeeres.                  15
Mine hert is also mouled° as mine heeres,
But if° ik fare as doth an open-ers°—
That ilke fruit is ever lenger the wers°
Till it be rotten in mullok or in stree.°
We olde men, I drede, so fare we—                         20
Till we be rotten can we not be ripe;
We hoppen ay, while that the world wol pipe,°
For in our will there sticketh ever a nail

---

4 **playde** joked   8 **y-laft** left   9 **grucche** grumble   10 **So thee'k** (so thee ik) so may I prosper; heaven help me   11 **blering . . . eye** deceiving   12 **ribaudye** ribaldry   13 **ik** I. The Reeve speaks in the dialect of East Anglia, a region influenced by northern speech forms. His dialect falls somewhere between the dialect of the two northern clerks (see line 95) and the London dialect of Chaucer's audience   16 also **mouled** as decayed, aged   17 **But if** unless   17 **open-ers** the fruit of the medlar tree, edible only after it has partially decayed   18 **ever lenger the wers** always worse and worse   19 **in mullok . . . stree** in refuse or in straw   22 **We hoppen . . . pipe** we hop behind always while the world calls the tune

To have an hoor hed and a greene tail,
25 As hath a leek; for though our might be goon,
Our will desireth folly ever in oon:°
For whan we may nought doon, than wol we speke.
Yet in our ashen old is fire y-reke.°
Four gleedes° have we which I shall devise:
30 Avaunting,° lying, anger, coveitise—
Thise foure sparkles longen unto elde.°
Our olde limes° mowe well been unwelde,°
But will ne shall not failen, that is sooth.
And yet ik have alway a coltes tooth,°
35 As many a yeer as it is passed henne°
Sin that my tap of life began to renne°—
For sikerly, whan ik was bore, anon
Deeth drow° the tap of life and let it gon,
And ever sith hath so the tap y-ronne
40 Till that almost all empty is the tonne:°
The streem of life now droppeth on the chimbe.°
The sely tonge may well ring and chimbe°
Of wretchedness that passed is full yore—
With olde folk save dotage is namore."°
45     Whan that our Host had herd this sermoning,
He gan to speke as lordly as a king:
He saide, "What amounteth all this wit?
What shall° we speke alday of holy writ?
The devil made a reeve for to preche,
50 Or of a soutere° a shipman or a leeche!°
Say forth thy tale, and tarry not the time:
Lo, Depford,° and it is halfway prime!°
Lo, Greenwich, ther many a shrew° is inne!
It were all time thy tale to beginne."

26 **ever in oon** all the same   28 **y-reke** raked up   29 **gleedes** burning
coals   30 **Avaunting** boasting   31 **longen unto elde** belong to old
age   32 **limes** limbs   32 **unwelde** unwieldy, weak   34 **coltes tooth**
young lusts, lecherous streak   35 **henne** from now   36 **renne** run
38 **drow** pulled out   40 **tonne** cask, barrel   41 **chimbe** rim of the
barrel   42 **chimbe** chime   44 **save dotage is namore** there is noth-
ing but dotage   48 **What shall** why must   50 **soutere** cobbler
50 **leeche** physician   52 **Depford** Deptford, about four miles out-
side of Southwark   52 **halfway prime** seven-thirty a.m.   53 **shrew**
scoundrel

"Now, sires," quod this Osewold the Reeve, 55
"I pray you alle that ye nought you greve
Though I answer and somedeel set his houve,°
For leveful is with force force off-shouve.°
This dronken Miller hath y-told us heer
How that beguiled was a carpenter— 60
Paraventure in scorn, for I am oon;
And by your leve, I shall him quite anoon:
Right in his cherles° termes wol I speke.
I pray to God his necke mot tobreke—
He can well in mine eye seen a stalke, 65
But in his own he can not seen a balke."°

# THE REEVE'S TALE

At Trumpington, not fer fro Cantebridge,°
There goth a brook, and over that a bridge,
Upon the whiche brook there stant a melle°—
And this is veray sooth that I you telle.
A miller was there dwelling many a day; 5
As any pecock he was proud and gay;
Pipen° he coud, and fish, and nettes beete,°
And turne coppes° and well wrastle and sheete.°
And by his belt he bare a long panade,°
And of a swerd full trenchant° was the blade; 10

57 set his houve arrange his hood, i.e., make him look silly   58 leve-
ful . . . shouve it is lawful to repel force with force   63 cherles
peasant's   66 balke beam   1 Cantebridge Cambridge   3 melle mill
7 Pipen play the bagpipe (see General Prologue, lines 565–66)
7 nettes beete mend nets   8 turne coppes drink heavily   8 sheete
shoot   9 panade cutlass   10 trenchant sharp

A jolly poppere° bare he in his pouche—
There was no man for peril dorst him touche;
A Sheffeld thwitel° bare he in his hose,
Round was his face, and camuse° was his nose;
15  As piled° as an ape was his skulle.
He was a market-beter° atte fulle.
There dorste no wight hand upon him lege°
That he ne swore he shold anon abege.°
A thief he was forsooth of corn and mele,
20  And that a sly, and usant° for to stele.
His name was hoten deinous° Simekin.

A wife he hadde, comen of noble kin:
The person° of the town hir fader was.
With hir he yaf full many a pan° of brass,
25  For that Simekin shold in his blood allye;°
She was y-fostred in a nonnerye,
For Simekin wolde no wife, as he saide,
But she were well y-norished and a maide,°
To saven his estate of yemanrye.°
30  And she was proud and pert as is a pie.°
A full fair sight was it upon hem two—
On holidays biforn hir wold he go
With his tippet° wound about his heed,
And she came after in a gite° of red,
35  And Simekin hadde hosen of the same.
There dorste no wight clepen° hir but "dame."
Was none so hardy that went by the waye
That with hir dorste rage or ones playe,°
But if he wold be slain of Simekin,
40  With panade, or with knife or boidekin;°

11 poppere dagger   13 thwitel knife   14 camuse flat   15 piled bald
16 market-beter loafer in a market, bully   17 lege lay   18 abege be
punished   20 usant accustomed   21 hoten deinous called haughty
23 person parson   24 pan penny; or perhaps "pan," i.e., panfuls of
money. The point is that the priest's daughter is illegitimate and the
priest has had to put up a good dowry to marry her off   25 For . . .
allye to get Simkin to make a blood alliance with her   28 well
y-norished . . . maide well brought up and a virgin   29 saven . . .
yemanrye to preserve his status as a freeman (which carried with it
certain exemptions from obligations and hence a certain prestige)
30 pie magpie   33 tippet scarf   34 gite gown   36 clepen call
38 dorste . . . playe dared to fool around or make one joke   40
boidekin dagger

For jalous folk been perilous° everemo—
Algate they wold hir wives wenden so.°
And eek, for she was somedeel smoterlich,°
She was as digne as water in a ditch,°
And full of hoker and of bisemare.°                          45
Hir thoughte that a lady shold hir spare,°
What for hir kinred, and hir nortelrye°
That she had lerned in the nonnerye.

A doughter hadde they bitwix hem two
Of twenty yeer, withouten any mo,                            50
Saving a child that was of half yeer age:
In cradle it lay and was a proper page.°
This wenche thick and well y-growen was,
With camuse nose, and eyen grey as glass,
With buttocks brod, and brestes round and hye,              55
But right fair was hir heer, I wol nat lie.
The person of the town, for she was fair,
In purpose was° to maken hir his heir
Both of his catel and his mesuage,°
And straunge he made it of° hir marriage.                   60
His purpose was for to bistow hir hye
Into some worthy blood of auncetrye,
For holy chirches good moot been dispended
On holy chirches blood that is descended;°
Therefore he wold his holy blood honoure,                   65
Though that he holy chirche shold devoure.

Greet soken° hath this miller out of doute
With whete and malt of all the land aboute;
And namelich there was a greet college,
Men clepth the Soler Hall° of Cantebrege;                   70

---

**41 perilous** dangerous    **42 Algate . . . so** anyway, they would have
their wives think so    **43 smoterlich** sullied, stained because of her
illegitimacy    **44 digne . . . ditch** i.e., as unapproachable as stagnant
ditch water    **45 hoker . . . bisemare** scorn . . . contempt    **46 hir**
**spare** be aloof, reserved    **47 What . . . nortelrye** what with her back-
ground and good breeding    **52 proper page** sturdy lad    **58 In pur-**
**pose was** intended    **59 catel . . . mesuage** possessions and household
**60 straunge . . . of** was particular about    **63–64 dispended . . . de-**
**scended** spent on those who spring from holy church's blood    **67**
**soken** power, monopoly    **70 Soler Hall** King's Hall, Cambridge, for
thirty-two scholars

There was hir whete and eek hir malt y-grounde.
And on a day it happed in a stounde°
Sick lay the manciple° on a maladye;
Men wenden wisly° that he sholde die,
75 For which this miller stal° both mele and corn
An hundred time more than biforn—
For therebiforn he stal but curteisly,
But now he was a thief outrageously.
For which the wardein chidde and made fare;°
80 But thereof set the miller not a tare—
He cracked boost,° and swore it was not so.
   Than were there yonge povre° scholers two
That dwelten in the hall of which I saye.
Testif° they were and lusty for to playe,
85 And only for hir mirth and revelrye
Upon the wardein bisily they crye
To yive hem leve but a litel stounde
To go to mill and seen hir corn y-grounde,
And hardily they dorste lay hir necke
90 The miller shold not stele hem° half a pecke
Of corn by sleighte, ne by force hem reve;°
And atte last the wardein yaf hem leve.
John hight that one, and Alain hight that other;
Of one town were they born that highte Strother,
95 Fer in the north°—I can not telle where.

72 in a stounde at one time  73 manciple steward, purchaser
74 wisly surely  75 stal stole  79 made fare made a to-do
81 cracked boost talked loudly, sounded off  82 povre poor
84 Testif headstrong  90 stele hem steal from them  91 hem reve
take away from them  95 Fer in the north The East Anglian Reeve
(Pro. line 13) identifies Aleyn and John as northerners. In Chaucer's
day the southern universities were invaded from the north by young
clerks interested in university education and university life in the
south. The clerks' speech in the tale contains a number of northern
words but no northern forms with which a Londoner would have
been unfamiliar. Chaucer gives to their speech what would have
seemed a rustic peasant sound. The most important dialect form is
the use of ā for Chaucer's usual ō (na, no; banes, bones; haam,
hoom; bathe, bothe). Also note the 3rd sing. pres. ind. -s, -es for
-eth (how fares thy faire doughter); the third plural pres. ind. -s, -es
for -en; and til (to), I is (I am), gif (if), sall (shall), and swa (so).
Dialect words will be marked (dial.) in the text

This Alain maketh redy all his gere,
And on a horse the sack he cast anon;
Forth goth Alain the clerk and also John,
With good swerd and with buckler by his side.
John knew the way—him needede no guide;                    *100*
And at the mill the sack adown he laith.
  Alain spak first: "All hail, Simond, in faith.
How fares° thy faire doughter and thy wif?"
  "Alain, welcome!" quod Simekin, "by my lif!
And John also! How now, what do ye heer?"                    *105*
  "By God," quod John, "Simond, need has na peer;°
Him boes° serve himself that has na swain,°
Or elles he is a fool, as clerkes sayn.
Our manciple, I hope° he will be deed,
Swa werkes ay the wanges° in his heed.                    *110*
And therefore is° I come, and eek Alain,
To grind our corn and carry it haam° again.
I pray you, speed us heithen° that ye may."
  "It shall be done," quod Simekin, "by my fay.°
What wol ye doon while that it is in hande?"°                    *115*
  "By God, right by the hopper will I stande,"
Quod Johan, "and see how the corn gaas° in.
Yet saw I never, by my fader° kin,
How that the hopper wagges til and fra."°
  Alain answered, "Johan, and wiltou swa?°                    *120*
Than will I be binethe, by my crown,
And see how that the mele falles down
Into the trough—that sall° be my desport.
For John, in faith, I may been of your sort:
I is as ill a miller as are° ye."                    *125*
  This miller smiled of hir nicetee,°
And thought, "All this nis done but for a wile.°

---

103 **fares** (dial.) Chaucer's dialect would have had *faren*    106 **need**
**. . . peer** (dial.) necessity has no equal    107 **Him boes** (dial.) one
should    107 **na swain** no servant    109 **hope** fear    110 **Swa . . .**
**wanges** (dial.) so ache always the molars    111 **is** (dial.) am
112 **haam** (dial.) home    113 **heithen** (dial.) from here    114 **fay** faith
115 **in hande** in the making    117 **gaas** goes    118 **fader** father's
119 **til and fra** (dial.) to and fro    120 **wiltou swa** (dial.) will you do
that    123 **sall** (dial.) shall    125 **are** (dial.) Chaucer's dialect had
"ye ben"    126 **nicetee** naïveté    127 **wile** subterfuge

They wene that no man may hem beguile
But by my thrift, yet shall I blere hir eye,°
130 For all the sleight in hir philosophye.°
The more quainte crekes° that they make,
The more wol I stele whan I take—
In stede of flour yet wol I yive hem bren.°
The grettest clerks been not the wisest men,
135 As whilom to the wolf thus spak the mare.
Of all hir art count I not a tare."°
Out at the door he goth full prively,
Whan that he saw his time softely:
He looketh up and down till he hath founde
140 The clerkes' horse there as it stood y-bounde
Behind the mille, under a leefsel,°
And to the horse he goth him fair and well.
He strepeth off the bridel right anoon,
And whan the horse was laus,° he ginneth goon°
145 Toward the fen ther wilde mares renne,°
And forth with "Weehee," thurgh thick and thenne.
The miller goth ayain°—no word he saide—
But doth his note° and with the clerkes playde,
Till that hir corn was fair and well y-grounde.
150 And whan the mele is sacked and y-bounde,
This John goth out and fint° his horse away,
And gan to cry "Harrow and weilaway!
Our horse is lost! Alain, for Goddes banes,°
Step on thy feet! Come off, man, all atanes!°
155 Alas, our wardein has his palfrey° lorn!"
    This Alain all forgat both mele and corn—
All was out of his mind his housbondrye.°
"What, whilk way is he gaan?"° he gan to crye.
    The wife came leping inward with a ren;
160 She said, "Alas, your horse goth to the fen

129 blere hir eye fool them    130 sleight . . . philosophye cleverness
in their logic-chopping    131 quainte crekes clever tricks    133 bren
bran    136 tare weed    141 leefsel leafy arbor    144 laus loose
144 ginneth goon began to go    145 renne run    147 goth ayain re-
turns    148 note work    151 fint finds    153 banes (dial.) bones
154 atanes (dial.) at once    155 palfrey riding-horse    157 housbond-
rye alert management    158 whilk . . . gaan (dial.) which way is he
gone

With wilde mares, as fast as he may go.
Unthank° come on his hand that bond him so,
And he that better shold have knit° the reine!"

"Alas," quod John, "Alain, for Christes paine,
Lay down thy swerd, and I will mine alswa.°          165
I is full wight, God waat, as is a raa.°
By Goddes herte, he sal nat scape us bathe.°
Why n'had thou pit the capil in the lathe?°
Illhail,° by God, Alain, thou is a fonne."°

Thise sely clerkes han full fast y-ronne               170
Toward the fen, both Alain and eek John;
And whan the miller saw that they were goon,
He half a bushel of hir flour hath take
And bade his wife go kneed it in a cake.
He said, "I trowe the clerkes were aferd.              175
Yet can a miller make a clerkes beerd°
For all his art. Ye, let hem gon hir waye.
Lo, where he goth! Ye, let the children playe.
They get him not so lightly, by my crown."

Thise sely clerkes rennen up and down                  180
With "Keep! Keep! Stand! Stand! Jossa! Warderere!
Gaa° whistle thou, and I sall keep him here."
But shortly, till that it was veray night,
They coude not, though they did all hir might,
Hir capil catch, he ran alway so faste,                185
Till in a ditch they caught him at the laste.

Wery and wet as beest is in the rain,
Comth sely John, and with him comth Alain.
"Alas," quod John, "the day that I was born!
Now are we driven til hething° and til scorn—          190
Our corn is stoln, men will us fooles calle,
Bath the wardein and our fellawes° alle,
And namely the miller, wailaway . . ."
Thus plaineth John as he goth by the way

162 **Unthank** misfortune   163 **knit** tied   165 **alswa** (dial.) also
166 **wight . . . raa** (dial.) fast, God knows, as a roe   167 **bathe** (dial.)
both   168 **pit . . . lathe** (dial.) put the horse in the barn   169 **Illhail**
a curse on you   169 **fonne** fool   176 **make . . . beerd** get the better
of a clerk   182 **Gaa** (dial.) go   190 **til hething** into derision
192 **fellawes** fellow clerks

195 Toward the mill, and Bayard in his hond.
The miller sitting by the fire he foond,
For it was night, and ferther might they nought;
But for the love of God they him bisought
Of herberwe° and of ese, as for hir peny.°
200    The miller said again, "If there be eny,
Swich as it is yet shal ye have your part.
Mine house is strait,° but *ye* han lerned *art*°—
Ye can by argumentes make a place
A mile brood of twenty feet of space!
205 Let see now if this place may suffise,
Or make it room° with speech, as is your guise."°
    "Now Simond," said this John, "by Saint Cutberd,
Ay is thou mirye,° and that is fair answered.
I have herd say men sal taa of twa thinges,°
210 Swilk° as he findes, or taa swilk as he bringes;
But specially I pray thee, hoste dere,
Get us some mete and drink and make us cheere,
And we wol payen trewely atte fulle—
With empty hand men may na hawkes tulle.°
215 Lo, here our silver, redy for to spende."
This miller into town his doughter sende
For ale and breed, and rosted hem a goos,
And bond hir horse, it shold namore go loos.
And in his owen chambre hem made a bed
220 With sheetes and with chalons° fair y-spred,
Not from his owen bed ten foot or twelve.
His doughter had a bed all by hirselve
Right in the same chambre by and by.
It mighte be no bet, and cause why?—
225 There was no roumer herberwe° in the place.
They soupen and they speken hem to solace,
And drinken ever strong ale at the beste.
Aboute midnight wente they to reste.

199 **herberwe** lodging   199 **as** . . . **peny** for their money   202 **strait** small   202 **lerned art** learned dialectic; he maliciously taunts the debating and logic of medieval universities   206 **roum** spacious 206 **guise** custom   208 **mirye** merry   209 **sal** . . . **thinges** (dial.) shall get either of two things   210 **Swilk** (dial.) such   214 **tulle** lure 220 **chalons** blankets   225 **roumer herberwe** more spacious lodging

Well hath this miller vernished his heed;°
Full pale he was for dronke, and nought red.                    230
He yexeth° and he speketh thurgh the nose
As he were on the quake or on the pose.°
    To bed he goth, and with him goth his wif.
As any jay she light° was and jolif,
So was hir jolly whistle well y-wet.                            235
The cradle at hir beddes feet is set
To rocken, and to yive the child to souke.°
    And whan that dronken all was in the crouke,°
To bedde went the doughter right anon.
To bedde goth Alain and also John.                             240
There nas namore—hem needede no dwale.°
This miller hath so wisly bibbed ale°
That as an horse he fnorteth° in his sleep;
Ne of his tail behind he took no keep.°
His wife bare him a burdon,° a full strong—                    245
Men might hir routing° heeren a furlong.
The wenche routeth eek, *par compaignye.*°
    Alain the clerk, that herd this melodye,
He poked John and saide, "Sleepestou?
Herdstou ever slik° a sang ere now?                            250
Lo, swilk a coupling is ymel hem alle°—
A wilde fire upon their bodies falle!
Wha herkned ever swilk a ferly thing?°
Ye, they sal have the flower of ill ending!
This lange night there tides me na reste.°                     255
But yit, na fors,° all sal be for the beste;
For John," said he, "als ever mote I thrive,
If that I may, yon wenche will I swive.°
Some esement° has lawe shapen us;

229 **vernished his heed** got himself thoroughly drunk    231 **yexeth**
hiccups    232 **were . . . pose** were hoarse or had a cold    234 **light**
frivolous    237 **yive . . . souke** to give suck    238 **crouke** crock
241 **dwale** sedative    242 **wisly bibbed ale** stoutly drunk ale
243 **fnorteth** snores    244 **took no keep** paid no attention    245 **bur-
don** accompaniment    246 **routing** snoring    247 **par compaignye**
together with them    250 **slik** (dial.) such    251 **swilk . . . alle** (dial.)
such a collaboration is among them    253 **Wha . . . thing** who ever
heard such a weird thing    255 **there . . . reste** no rest is in store for
me    256 **na fors** no matter    258 **swive** lay    259 **esement** recourse,
benefit

260    For John, there is a lawe that says thus,
       That gif° a man in a point be agreved,
       That in another he sal be releved.
       Our corn is stolen soothly, it is na nay,
       And we han had an ille fit° today,
265    And sin I sal have naan° amendement
       Again my loss, I will have esement.
       By Goddes saule, it sal naan other be."
           This John answered, "Alain, avise thee!°
       The miller is a perilous man," he saide,
270    "And if that he out of his sleep abraide,°
       He mighte doon us bath a villainye."
       Alain answered, "I count him nought a flye,"
       And up he rist, and by the wench he crepte.
       This wenche lay upright and faste slepte,
275    Till he so neigh was ere she might espye
       That it had been too late for to crye;
       And shortly for to sayn, they were at oon.°
       Now play, Alain, for I wol speke of John.
           This John lith still a furlong way or two,
280    And to himself he maketh routh° and wo.
       "Alas," quod he, "this is a wicked jape.°
       Now may I sayn that I is but an ape.
       Yet has my fellaw somewhat° for his harm—
       He has the miller's doughter in his arm.
285    He auntred him,° and has his needes sped,°
       And I lie as a draf-sack° in my bed.
       And whan this jape is tald another day,
       I sal be halden a daff, a cokenay.°
       I will arise and auntre it, by my faith!
290    Unhardy is unsely,° thus men saith."
       And up he rose, and softely he wente
       Unto the cradle, and in his hand it hente,
       And bare it soft unto his beddes feet.

---

261 **gif** (dial.) if    264 **ille fit** (dial.) bad time    265 **naan** (dial.) no
268 **avise thee** think it over    270 **abraide** should wake    277 **at oon**
together    280 **routh** lamentation    281 **jape** joke    283 **somewhat**
something    285 **auntred him** took a risk    285 **sped** accomplished
286 **draf-sack** junk-sack    288 **daff, cokenay** jerk, sissy    290 **Un-
hardy is unsely** i.e., nothing ventured nothing gained

Soon after this the wife hir routing leet,°
And gan awake, and went hir out to pisse,                    295
And came again, and gan hir cradle misse,
And groped here and there, but she foond noon.
"Alas," quod she, "I had almost misgoon;
I had almost gone to the clerkes bed—
Ey, *ben'dic'te*, than had I foul y-sped!"                    300
And forth she goth till she the cradle foond.
She gropeth alway ferther with hir hond,
And foond the bed, and thoughte nought but good,
Bicause that the cradle by it stood;
And niste where she was, for it was derk,                    305
But fair and well she creep into the clerk,
And lith full still, and wold have caught a sleep.°

Within a while this John the clerk up leep,
And on this goode wife he laith on sore.°
So murry a fit ne had she not full yore:                    310
He pricketh hard and deep as he were mad.
This jolly life han thise two clerkes lad
Till that the thridde cock began to singe.

Alain wex° wery in the daweninge,
For he had swonken° all the longe night,                    315
And saide, "Farewell, Malin, sweete wight.
The day is come, I may no lenger bide.
But everemo, whereso I go or ride,
I is thyn awen° clerk, swa have I seel."°

"Now dere lemman"° quod she, "go, farewell.                    320
But ere thou go, oo thing I wol thee telle:
Whan that thou wendest homeward by the melle,
Right at the entree of the door behinde
Thou shalt a cake of half a bushel finde,
That was y-maked of thine owne mele,                    325
Which that I help my sire for to stele.
And goode lemman, God thee save and keepe."
And with that word almost she gan to weepe.

Alain up rist and thought, "Ere that it dawe,

---

294 **leet** stopped   307 **caught a sleep** gone to sleep   309 **sore** hard
314 **wex** grew   315 **swonken** labored   319 **awen** (dial.) own
319 **swa . . . seel** as I may have bliss   320 **lemman** lover

330 I will go creepen in by my fellawe,
      And foond the cradle with his hand anon.
      "By God," thought he, "all wrang I have misgon.
      Mine heed is toty° of my swink tonight;
      That maketh me that I go nought aright.
335 I wot well by the cradle I have misgo;
      Here lith the miller and his wife also."
      And forth he goth a twenty devil way°
      Unto the bed ther as the miller lay.
      He wende have cropen by his fellaw John,
340 And by the miller in he creep anon,
      And caught him by the neck and soft he spak.
      He said, "Thou John, thou swines-heed, awak,
      For Cristes saul, and heer a noble game:
      For by that lord that called is Saint Jame,
345 As I have thries in this shorte night
      Swived the miller's doughter bolt upright,°
      While thou hast as a coward been aghast."
      "Ye, false harlot," quod the miller, "hast?
      Ah, false traitour, false clerk," quod he,
350 "Thou shalt be deed, by Goddes dignitee—
      Who dorste be so bold to disparage°
      My doughter, that is come of swich linage?"
      And by the throte-boll° he caught Alain,
      And he hent him despitously° again,
355 And on the nose he smote him with his fest—
      Down ran the bloody streem upon his brest.
      And on the floor, with nose and mouth to-broke,
      They walwen° as doon two pigs in a poke,°
      And up they goon and down again anoon,
360 Till that the miller sporned at° a stoon,
      And down he fill backward upon his wif
      That wiste nothing of this nice strif,
      For she was fall asleep a lite wight°
      With John the clerk that waked had all night—

---

333 **toty** dizzy    337 **twenty devil way** way of twenty devils, i.e., an
unfortunate path    346 **bolt upright** flat on her back    351 **disparage**
dishonor    353 **throte-boll** Adam's apple    354 **despitously** spitefully
358 **walwen** wallow, grovel    358 **poke** sack    360 **sporned at** tripped
on    363 **lite wight** short while

And with the fall out of hir sleep she braide.°          365
"Help, holy crois of Bromeholm!" she saide.
*"In manus tuas,*° Lord, to thee I calle!
Awake, Simond, the feend is on me falle!
Mine hert is broken. Help! I nam but deed!
There lith one upon my womb and on mine heed!          370
Help, Simekin, for the false clerkes fighte!"
This John stert up as fast as ever he mighte,
And graspeth by the walles to and fro
To find a staff; and she stert up also,
And knew the estres° bet than did this John,          375
And by the wall a staff she foond anoon,
And saw a litel shimmering of a light—
For at an hole in shone the moone bright—
And by that light she saw hem bothe two,
But sikerly she niste who was who,          380
But as she saw a white thing in her eye,
And whan she gan this white thing espye,
She wende the clerk had wered a voluper,°
And with the staff she drow ay neer and neer,
And wende han hit this Alain atte fulle—          385
And smote the miller on the piled° skulle
That down he goth and cried, "Harrow, I die!"
Thise clerkes bete him well and let him lie,
And greithen hem,° and took hir horse anon
And eek hir mele, and on hir way they goon,          390
And at the mille yet they took hir cake,
Of half a bushel flour full well y-bake.
Thus is this proude miller well y-bete,
And hath y-lost the grinding of the whete,
And payed for the supper everydeel          395
Of Alain and of John, that bete him well;
His wife is swived and his doughter als.
Lo, swich it is a miller° to be fals!

---

365 **braide** woke    367 **In manus tuas** "Into Thy hands . . ."
375 **estres** layout of the room    383 **voluper** nightcap    386 **piled**
bald    389 **greithen hem** ready themselves    398 **swich . . . miller** it is
that way for a miller

And therefore this proverb is said full sooth:
400 Him thar nat weene well° that yvele doth;
A gilour° shall himself biguiled be.
And God, that sitteth heigh in majestee,
Save all this compaignye, greet and smalle:
Thus have I quit the Miller in my tale.

# THE SHIPMAN'S TALE

A marchant whilom° dwelled at Saint Denis°
That riche was, for which men held him wis.
A wife he had of excellent beautee,
And compaignable and revelous° was she—
Which is a thing that causeth more dispence°      *5*
Than worth is all the cheer° and reverence
That men hem doon at feestes and at daunces;
Swich salutacions and countenances
Passen as doth a shadwe upon the wall.
But woe is him that payen mot for all:      *10*
"The sely° husbond algate° he mot paye!
He mot us clothe and he mot us arraye,
All for his owne worship, richely—
In which array we dauncen jollily!
And if that he not may, paraventure,      *15*
Or elles list no swich dispence endure,
But thinketh it is wasted and y-lost,
Than mot another payen for our cost
Or lene° us gold—and that is perilous!"°
    This noble marchant held a worthy hous,      *20*
For which he had alday so greet repair°
For his largesse,° and for his wife was fair,
That wonder is. But herkneth to my tale:
Amonges all his guestes greet and smalle
There was a monk, a fair man and a bold—      *25*

1 **whilom** once upon a time  1 **Saint Denis** near Paris  4 **revelous**
pleasure loving  5 **dispence** spending  6 **cheer** friendly greeting
11 **sely** unfortunate  11 **algate** at any rate. In lines 11–19 the Ship-
man mimics women's attitudes; but perhaps these lines show that
Chaucer originally meant this tale to be told by the Wife of Bath
and forgot to cancel them when he assigned it to the Shipman
19 **lene** lend  19 **perilous** dangerous  21 **so . . . repair** such frequent
visitation  22 **For . . . largesse** because of his liberality. Largesse
was considered an aristocratic virtue

I trowe° a thrity winter he was old—
That ever in one° was drawing to that place.
This yonge monk, that was so fair of face,
Acquainted was so with the goode man
30 Sith that hir firste knowliche° began
That in his house as familier was he
As it is possible any freend to be.
And for as muchel as this goode man,
And eek this monk of which that I began,
35 Were bothe two y-born in oo village,
The monk him claimeth as for cosinage°—
And he again, he saith not ones nay,
But was as glad thereof as fowl of day,
For to his hert it was a greet plesaunce.
40 Thus been they knit with eterne alliaunce,
And ech of hem gan other for t'assure
Of bretherhede° while that hir life may dure.
      Free was Daun° John—and namely of dispence,
As in that house, and full of diligence
45 To doon plesance and also greet costage.°
He not forgat to yive the leeste page
In all that house; but after hir degree
He yaf the lord and sithen all his meinee,°
Whan that he came, some manner honest thing.°
50 For which they were as glad of his coming
As fowl is fain° whan that the sun up riseth.
Namore of this as now, for it suffiseth.
      But so bifell,° this marchant on a day
Shop him° to make redy his array°
55 Toward the town of Bruges° for to fare
To byen there a portion of ware;
For which he hath to Paris sent anon
A messenger, and prayed hath Daun John
That he shold come to Saint Denis and playe

---

26 trowe believe    27 ever . . . one continually    30 knowliche ac-
quaintance    36 for cosinage as a relative    42 bretherhede sworn
friendship—a very sacred relationship    43 Daun lord, master
45 costage spending    48 meinee household    49 some . . . thing i.e.,
something appropriate    51 fain glad    53 so bifell it so happened
54 Shop him prepared    54 array gear    55 Bruges a great Flemish
mercantile center

With him and with his wife a day or twaye,                60
Ere he to Bruges went, in alle wise.°
This noble monk of which I you devise
Hath of his abbot as him list licence,°
Because he was a man of high prudence
And eek an officer, out for to ride                       65
To seen hir granges and hir bernes wide.°
And unto Saint Denis he comth anon.
Who was so welcome as my lord Daun John,
Our dere cosin, full of curteisye?
With him brought he a jubbe of malvesye°                  70
And eek another, full of fine vernage,°
And volatil,° as ay was his usage.
And thus I let hem ete and drink and playe,
This marchant and this monk, a day or twaye.

    The thridde day this marchant up ariseth,            75
And on his needes sadly him aviseth,°
And up into his countour-house° goth he
To recken with himself, as well may be,
Of thilke yeer how that it with him stood,
And how that he dispended had his good,°                  80
And if that he encresed were° or noon.
His bookes and his bagges many oon
He laith biforn him on his counting-boord:
Full riche was his tresor and his hoord,
For which full fast his countour-door he shette,°         85
And eek he nold that no man shold him lette
Of his accountes° for the mene time.
And thus he sit° till it was passed prime.°
    Daun John was risen in the morrwe also
And in the garden walketh to and fro,                     90
And hath his thinges° said full curteisly.

61 **in alle wise** in all respects   63 **licence** Daun John had permission
to travel outside the boundaries of his abbey in order to inspect the
landholdings of his order   66 **hir . . . wide** their farms and barns
far off   70 **jubbe . . . malvesye** jug of Malmsey   71 **vernage** Italian
sweet wine   72 **volatil** game fowls   76 **on . . . aviseth** seriously goes
over his business affairs   77 **countour-house** office   80 **good** wealth
81 **encresed were** had profited   85 **shette** shut   86–87 **lette . . . ac-
countes** keep from his accounts   88 **sit** sits   88 **prime** nine a.m.
91 **thinges** devotions

This goode wife came walking prively°
Into the garden ther he walketh softe
And him salueth, as she hath done ofte.
95  A maide child came in hir compaignye,
Which as hir list she may govern and gie,°
For yet under the yerde° was the maide.
"O dere cosin mine, Daun John," she saide,
"What aileth you so rathe° for to rise?"
100     "Nece," quod he, "it ought enough suffise
Five houres for to sleep upon a night,
But it were for an old appalled wight,°
As been thise wedded men that lie and dare°
As in a fourme° sit a wery hare
105  Were all forstraught° with houndes greet and smalle.
But dere nece, why be ye so pale?
I trowe° certes that our goode man
Hath you laboured sith the night began,
That you were need to resten hastily."
110  And with that word he lough full murrily,
And of his owne thought he wex° all red.
        This faire wife gan for to shake hir heed
And saide thus, "Ye, God wot° all," quod she.
"Nay, cosin mine, it stant not so with me.
115  For by that God that yaf me soul and lif,
In all the reaume° of France is there no wif
That lasse lust hath to that sorry play.
For I may sing 'alas' and 'weilaway
That I was born'—but to no wight," quod she,
120  "Dare I not tell how that it stant with me;°
Wherefore I think out of this land to wende,
Or elles of myself to make an ende,
So full am I of drede and eek of care."
        This monk began upon this wife to stare
125  And said, "Alas, my nece, God forbede
That ye for any sorrwe or any drede

92 **prively** alone   96 **gie** guide   97 **under . . . yerde** under the rod,
i.e., subject to discipline   99 **rathe** early   102 **appalled wight**
palsied man   103 **dare** wait motionless   104 **fourme** rabbit mound
105 **Were . . . forstraught** which was distraught, harried   107 **trowe**
think   111 **wex** grew   113 **wot** knows   116 **reaume** realm   120 **it
. . . me** what my situation is

Fordo° yourself! But telleth me your grief.
Paraventure I may in your meschief°
Conseil or help. And therefore telleth me
All your annoy, for it shall been secree.                    130
For on my porthors° I make an ooth
That never in my life, for lief ne loth,°
Ne shall I of no conseil you biwraye."°
  "The same again to you," quod she, "I saye.
By God and by this porthors I you swere,                     135
Though men me wold all into pieces tere,
Ne shall I never, for to goon° to helle,
Biwray a word of thing that ye me telle—
Not for no cosinage ne alliance,
But veraily for love and affiance."°                         140
Thus been they sworn, and hereupon they kiste,
And ech of hem told other what hem liste.
  "Cosin," quod she, "if that I hadde space,
As I have none, and namely in this place,
Than wold I tell a legend° of my lif—                        145
What I have suffered sith I was a wif
With mine husbond, al be he° your cosin."
  "Nay," quod this monk, "by God and Saint Martin,
He is namore cosin unto me
Than is the leef that hangeth on the tree!                   150
I clepe him so, by Saint Denis of France,
To han the more cause of acquaintance
Of *you,* which I have loved specially
Aboven alle women, sikerly.
This swere I you on my professioun.°                         155
Telleth your grief, lest that he come adown,
And hasteth you,° and goth away anon."
  "My dere love," quod she, "O my Daun John,
Full lief were me this conseil for to hide!°

127 **Fordo** destroy   128 **meschief** distress   131 **porthors** breviary,
containing the daily canonical prayers   132 **for . . . loth** i.e., for love
or hate   133 **biwraye** give away, betray   137 **for . . . goon** though I
go   140 **affiance** trust   145 **legend** moral story of suffering   147 **al
. . . he** even though he is   155 **professioun** monastic vow of poverty,
chastity, and obedience   157 **hasteth you** be quick about it
159 **Full . . . hide** I would be much happier to conceal this matter

160 But out it mot°—I may namore abide:
Mine husbond is to me the worste man
That ever was sith that the world began!
But sith I am a wife it sit not me°
To tellen no wight of our privetee—
165 Neither abed ne in noon other place.
God shilde° I shold it tellen, for his grace!
A wife ne shall not sayn of hir husbonde
But all honour, as I can understonde.
Save unto you this much I tellen shall:
170 As help me God, he is not worth at all
In no degree the value of a flye!
But yet me greveth most his niggardye.°
And well ye wot that women naturelly
Desiren thinges six as well as I:
175 They wolde that hir husbonds sholde be
Hardy and wise and rich, and thereto free,
And buxom° unto his wife, and fresh abedde.
And by that ilke Lord that for us bledde,
For his honour myself for to arraye
180 A° Sunday next I moste needes paye
An hundred frankes, or elles I am lorn.°
Yet were me lever° that I were unborn
Than me were done a slaundre° or villainye.
And if mine husbond eek might it espye,
185 I nere but lost. And therefore I you praye
Lene me this sum, or elles mot I deye!
Daun John—I say lene me thise hundred frankes!
Pardee,° I wol not faile you my thankes
If that you list to doon that I you praye;
190 For at a certain day I wol you paye,
And doon to you what plesance and servise
That I may doon, right as you list devise.
And but I do,° God take on me vengeance
As foul as ever had Genelon of France."°

160 But . . . mot but it must be divulged   163 it . . . me it is not my
place   166 shilde forbid   172 niggardye miserliness   177 buxom
obedient   180 A on   181 lorn undone   182 were . . . lever I had
rather   183 slaundre slander   188 Pardee par dieu, by God
193 but . . . do if I do not   194 Genelon Ganelon, Roland's enemy,
who was torn apart by wild horses

This gentil monk answered in this mannere:                     *195*
"Now trewely, mine owne lady dere,
I have," quod he, "on you so greet a routhe°
That I you swere and plighte you my trouthe
That whan your husbond is to Flandres fare°
I wol deliver you out of this care,°                           *200*
For I wol bringe you an hundred frankes."
And with that word he caught hir by the flankes
And hir embraceth hard, and kist hir ofte.
"Goth now your way," quod he, "all still and softe,
And let us dine as soon as that ye may,                        *205*
For by my chilindre° it is prime of day.
Goth now, and beth as trew as I shall be."
     "Now elles God forbede, sir," quod she—
And forth she goth as jolif as a pie,°
And bade the cookes that they shold hem hie°                   *210*
So that men mighte dine—and that anon.
Up to hir husbond is this wife y-gon
And knocketh at his countour boldely.
*"Qui la?"*° quod he. "Peter!° it am I,"
Quod she. "What, sir! How longe wol ye faste?                  *215*
How longe time wol ye recken and caste
Your summes° and your bookes and your thinges?
The devil have part on° all swich reckeninges!
Ye have enough, pardee, of Goddes sonde!°
Come down today, and let your bagges stonde.                   *220*
Ne be ye not ashamed that Daun John
Shall fasting all this day alenge° gon!
What, let us heer a mass and go we dine."
     "Wife," quod this man, "litel canstou divine
The curious° bisinesse that we have.                           *225*
For of us chapmen,° also God me save,
And by that lord that cleped is Saint Ive,
Scarsely, amonges twelve, twain° shall thrive

197 **so . . . routhe** such great pity   199 **fare** gone   200 **care** trouble
206 **chilindre** portable sundial   209 **jolif . . . pie** jolly as a magpie
210 **hie** hurry   214 **Qui la** (*qui est la,* Fr.) who's there?   214 **Peter**
by St. Peter   216–17 **caste . . . summes** compute your figures
218 **The . . . on** the devil take   219 **sonde** gift   222 **alenge** miserable
225 **curious** involved, elaborate   226 **chapmen** merchants   228
**twain** two

Continuelly, lasting unto our age.
230 We may well make cheer and good visage
And drive forth° the world as it may be
And keepen our estate in privetee°
Till we be deed, or elles that we playe°
A pilgrimage, or goon out of the waye.°
235 And therefore have I greet necessitee
Upon this quainte° world t'avise me,
For evermore we mote stond in drede
Of hap° and Fortune in our chapmanhede.°
To Flandres wol I go tomorrwe at day
240 And come again as soon as ever I may.
For which, my dere wife, I thee biseeke°
As be to every wight buxom and meeke.
And for to keep our good be curious,°
And honestly° governe well our hous.
245 Thou hast enough in every manner wise°
That to a thrifty household may suffise—
Thee lacketh noon array ne no vitaille;°
Of silver in thy purse shaltou not faile."
And with that word his countour-door he shette,
250 And down he goth, no lenger wold he lette;°
But hastily a masse was there said,
And speedily the tables were y-laid
And to the dinner faste they hem spedde,
And richely this monk the chapman fedde.
255     At after-dinner Daun John sobrely°
This chapman took apart, and prively
He said him thus: "Cosin, it standeth so
That well I see to Bruges wol ye go.
God and Saint Austin° speede you and guide.
260 I pray you, cosin, wisely that ye ride.
Governeth you also of your diete
Attemprely,° and namely in this hete.

231 **drive forth** pass through   232 **keepen . . . privetee** go about our
affairs quietly   233 **playe** make   234 **goon . . . waye** run off some-
where (to avoid debts)   236 **quainte** strange   238 **hap** chance
238 **chapmanhede** business   241 **biseeke** beg   243 **curious** careful
244 **honestly** honorably   245 **in . . . wise** in every way possible
247 **vitaille** foodstuffs   250 **lette** delay   255 **sobrely** seriously
259 **Saint Austin** St. Augustine   262 **Attemprely** moderately

Bitwix us two needeth no strange fare.°
Farewell, cosin, God shilde you fro care.°
And if that any thing by day or night,                                 265
If it lay in my power and my might,
That ye me wol command in any wise,
It shall be done, right as ye wol devise.
Oo thing ere that ye goon, if it may be:
I wolde pray you for to lene me                                        270
An hundred frankes for a wike or twaye,
For certain beestes that I moste beye
To store with a place° that is oures.
God help me so, I wold it were youres!
I shall not faile surely of my day,                                    275
Not for a thousand franks, a mile way.°
But let this thing be secree,° I you praye:
For yet tonight thise beestes mot I beye.
And fare now well, mine owne cosin dere;
Graunt mercy of your cost° and of your cheere."                        280
    This noble marchant gentilly° anon
Answered and said, "O cosin mine, Daun John,
Now sikerly this is a small requeste.
My gold is youres whan that it you leste—
And not only my gold, but my chaffare;°                                285
Take what you list, God shilde that ye spare.°
But oo thing is, ye know it well enow,
Of chapmen°—that hir money is hir plow.
We may creance° while we han a name
But goldless for to been, it is no game.                               290
Pay it again whan it lith° in your ese;
After my might full fain wold I you plese."
Thise hundred franks he fette° forth anon,
And prively he took hem to Daun John.
No wight in all this world wist of this lone,                          295
Saving this marchant and Daun John alone.

263 **strange fare** formality    264 **shilde . . . care** keep you from harm
273 **To . . . place** with which to stock a plot of land    276 **a . . . way**
by a mile's distance    277 **secree** secret    280 **Graunt . . . cost** thank
you for your generosity    281 **gentilly** courteously    285 **chaffare**
possessions    286 **spare** refrain    287–88 **But . . . chapmen** but there
is one thing . . . about businessmen    289 **creance** borrow on credit
291 **lith** lies    293 **fette** brought

They drink, and speke, and rome a while and playe,
Till that Daun John rideth to his abbeye.
      The morrow came, and forth this marchant rideth
300 To Flandresward; his prentis° well him gideth
Till he came into Bruges murrily.°
Now goth this marchant fast and bisily
About his need, and byeth and creaunceth°—
He neither playeth at the dees,° ne daunceth,
305 But as a marchant, shortly for to telle,
He let his life.° And there I let him dwelle.

          *        *        *

      The Sunday next the marchant was agon,
To Saint Denis y-comen is Daun John
With crown and beerd all fresh and new y-shave.
310 In all the house there nas so litel a knave,
Ne no wight elles, that he nas full fain°
That my lord Daun John was come again.
And shortly to the point right for to goon,
This faire wife accorded° with Daun John
315 That for thise hundred franks he shold all night
Have hire in his armes bolt upright.°
And this accord parfourned° was in deede:
In mirth all night a bisy life they lede
Till it was day, that Daun John went his way,
320 And bade the meinee° "Farewell, have good day"—
For none of hem, ne no wight in the town,
Hath of Daun John right no suspecioun.°
And forth he rideth home to his abbeye,
Or where him list. Namore of him I saye.
325      This marchant whan that ended was the faire
To Saint Denis he gan for to repaire,
And with his wife he maketh feest and cheere
And telleth hir that chaffare is so dere

---

300 **prentis** apprentice   301 **murrily** pleasantly   303 **creaunceth**
borrows   304 **dees** dice   306 **He . . . life** conducted himself   311
**fain** glad   314 **accorded** agreed   316 **bolt upright** flat on her back
317 **parfourned** performed   320 **meinee** household, i.e., servants
322 **right . . . suspecioun** no suspicions at all

That needes most he make a chevissaunce°—
For he was bounden in a reconissaunce°                    330
To paye twenty thousand sheeld° anon.
For which this marchant is to Paris gon
To borrwe of certain freendes that he hadde
A certain franks,° and some with him he ladde.°
And whan that he was come into the town,                    335
For greet cheertee° and greet affeccioun
Unto Daun John he first goth, him to playe—
Not for to ask or borrwe of him moneye,
But for to wite° and seen of his welfare,
And for to tellen him of his chaffare,                    340
As freendes doon whan they been met yfere.°
Daun John him maketh feest and murry cheere,
And he him told again full specially
How he had well y-bought and graciously,
Thanked be God, all whole his marchandise—                    345
Save that he most, in alle manner wise,°
Maken a chevissance as for the beste,°
And than he sholde been in joy and reste.

Daun John answerde, "Certes, I am fain
That ye in hele° are comen home again!                    350
And if that I were rich, as have I blisse,°
Of twenty thousand sheeld shold ye not misse,
For ye so kindely this other day
Lente me gold. And as I can and may
I thanke you, by God and by Saint Jame!                    355
But natheless, I took unto our dame—
Your wife at home—the same gold again
Upon your bench. She wot it well, certain,
By certain tokens° that I can you telle.
Now by your leve, I may no lenger dwelle—                    360
Our abbot wol out of this town anon,
And in his compaignye mot I gon.

329 make . . . chevissaunce get a loan  330 reconissaunce promissory note  331 sheeld gold coins  334 A . . . franks an amount of francs  334 ladde took along  336 cheertee fondness  339 wite know  341 yfere together  346 in . . . wise in any event  347 as . . . beste in the best manner  350 hele health  351 as . . . blisse as I may have bliss  359 tokens signs, evidence

Greet well our dame, mine owne nece sweete;
And farewell, dere cosin, till we meete."
365    This marchant which that was full ware° and wis
Creanced hath° and paid eek in Paris
To certain Lumbards,° redy in hir hond,
The sum of gold, and gat of hem his bond;
And home he goth, murry as a papinjay.°
370    For well he knew he stood in swich array°
That needes most he win in that viage°
A thousand franks aboven his costage.°
His wife full redy met him at the gate,
As she was wont of old usage algate.°
375    And all that night in mirthe they bisette°
For he was rich and cleerly out of dette.
Whan it was day this marchant gan embrace
His wife all new, and kist hir on hir face;
And up he goth and maketh it full tough.°
380    "Namore," quod she, "by God, ye have enough!"
And wantounly again with him she playde
Till at the laste thus this marchant saide,
"By God," quod he, "I am a litel wroth
With you, my wife, although it be me loth.°
385    And wot ye why? By God, as that I guesse
That ye han made a manner straungenesse°
Bitwixen me and my cosin Daun John.
Ye shold han warned me ere I had gon
That he you had an hundred frankes paid
390    By redy token.° And held him yvel apaid°
For that I to him spak of chevissaunce—
Me seemed so as° by his countenaunce.
But natheless, by God our hevene king,
I thoughte not to ask of him no thing.

365 **full ware** very prudent    366 **Creanced hath** got credit    367
**Lumbards** Lombards of northern Italy, who were noted bankers and
money-lenders    369 **papinjay** parrot    370 **stood . . . array** was in
such a position    371 **viage** enterprise    372 **costage** expenses    374
**algate** always    375 **bisette** applied themselves    379 **maketh . . .
tough** shows great energy    384 **it . . . loth** I don't like to be    386
**straungenesse** disaffection    390 **By . . . token** in ready money, i.e.,
in ready exchange (a double entendre)    390 **held . . . apaid** he
took offense    392 **Me . . . as** it seemed so to me

I pray thee, wife, ne do namore so!                              395
Tell me alway ere that I fro thee go
If any dettour hath in mine absence
Y-payed° thee, lest thurgh thy necligence
I might him ask a thing that he hath paid."

   This wife was not afered ne afraid,                      400
But boldely she said, and that anon,
"Marie!° I defy the false monk Daun John!
I keep not° of his 'tokens' neveradele!
He took me certain gold, this wot I well!
What, yvel thedam° on his monkes snoute!               405
For God it wot, I wend° withouten doute
That he had yive it me because of you
To doon therewith mine honour and my prow,
For cosinage and eek for *belle cheere*°
That he hath had full ofte times here.                          410
But sith I see I stand in this disjoint°
I wol answer you shortly to the point:
Ye han mo slacker° dettours than am I!
For I wol pay you well and redily
Fro day to day, and if so be I faile,                            415
I am your wife—score it upon my taile!°
And I shall pay as soon as ever I may;
For by my truth I have on mine array,°
And not in waste, bistowed every deel.°
And for I have bistowed it so well                               420
For your honour, for Goddes sake, I saye
As be not wroth, but let us laugh and playe:
Ye shall my jolly body have to wedde.
By God, I wol nought pay you but abedde!
Forgive it me, mine owne spouse dere—                       425
Turn hiderward° and maketh better cheere . . ."

   This marchant saw there was no remedye,
And for to chide it nere but follye.

---

398 **Y-payed** paid. "Pay" has a double meaning    402 **Marie** by St.
Mary    403 **keep not** care not    405 **yvel thedam** misfortune
406 **wend** understood    409 **belle cheere** good times    411 **disjoint**
predicament    413 **mo slacker** more delinquent    416 **score . . . taile**
i.e., put it on my bill (with a pun on "tail")    418 **array** clothing
419 **bistowed . . . deel** spent everything    426 **hiderward** toward me

"Sith that the thing may not amended be,
430  Now wife," he said, "and I foryive it thee.
But by thy life, ne be namore so large.°
Keep bet my good, this yive I thee in charge."°
Thus endeth now my tale; and God us sende
Tailing enough unto our lives ende!

431 large generous    432 Keep . . . charge I charge you to take bet-
ter care of what belongs to me

# THE SHIPMAN-PRIORESS LINK

"Well said, by *corpus dominus*," quod our Host.
"Now longe mote thou saile by the coost,
Sir gentil maister, gentil mariner.
God yive the monk a thousand last quad yeer!°
Aha, fellaws! beth ware of swich a jape!      *5*
The monk put in the mannes hood an ape,°
And in his wives eek, by Saint Austin!
Draweth no monkes more into your inn!
    But now pass over, and let us seek aboute . . .
Who shall now telle first of all this route      *10*
Another tale?"—and with that word he saide,
As curteisly as it had been a maide,°
"My Lady Prioresse: by your leve,
So that° I wist I sholde you not greve,
I wolde deemen that ye tellen sholde      *15*
A tale next, if so were that ye wolde.
Now wol ye vouche sauf, my lady dere?"
"Gladly," quod she, and said as ye shall heere:

---

4 **thousand . . . yeer** a thousand cartloads of bad years   6 **in . . . ape** i.e., made a monkey out of him (who would then wear his hood)   12 **as . . . maide** as if it were a young girl he was addressing. The speech that follows is indeed delicately put   14 **So that** so long as

# THE PRIORESS' PROLOGUE

*Domine Dominus noster . . .*°

O Lord, Our Lord, thy name how merveilous
Is in this large world y-sprad (quod she),
For not only thy laude° precious
Performed is by men of dignitee,
5  But by the mouth of children thy bountee
Performed is: for on the brest suckinge
Sometime shewen they thine heryinge.°

Wherefore in laud, as I best can or may,
Of thee and of the white lily-flower°
10  Which that thee bare, and is a maid alway,
To tell a story I wol do my labour;
Not that I may encreesen hir honour,
For she hirself is honour and the roote
Of bountee, next hir son, and soules boote.°

15  O moder maid, O maide moder free!
O bush unbrent, brenning in Moises' sighte,°
That ravisedest° down fro the deitee,
Thurgh thine humbless, the Ghost that in thee alighte,
Of whose vertu, whan He thine herte lighte,
20  Conceived was the Fadre's Sapience—
Help me to tell it in thy reverence.

**Domine Dominus noster . . .** the opening verse of Psalm 8, which
occurs in the *Little Office of the Blessed Virgin*, recited in nun-
neries; the following lines translate it. The Prioress' Prologue is
thus in effect a hymn to the Blessed Virgin, as her Tale is a
miracle of the Virgin. Both are in the seven-line rhyming stanza
(later to be called rhyme royal), which suggests a hymn in the
prologue and a ballad in the tale. (See note on line 197.)  3 **laude**
praise  7 **heryinge** praise. The reference is to St. Nicholas, who
in infancy fasted on Wednesdays and Fridays by sucking only
once. Cf. lines 27–28 of her tale  9 **white lily-flower** symbol of the
Virgin  14 **boote** salvation  16 **bush . . . sighte** the burning bush
of *Exodus* 3:2–4 was another symbol of the Virgin: the bush re-
mained uninjured, as the Mother of God remained undefiled
17 **ravisedest** drew

Lady, thy bountee, thy magnificence,
Thy vertu and thy greet humilitee
There may no tonge express in no science.
For sometime, lady, ere men pray to thee,                    25
Thou gost biforn of thy benignitee,
And gettest us the light, of° thy prayere,
To guiden us unto thy Son so dere.

My konning is so waik,° O blissful Queene,
For to declare thy grete worthinesse,                         30
That I ne may the weighte not sustene;
But as a child of twelfmonth old or lesse,
That can unnethe° any word expresse,
Right so fare I. And therefore, I you praye,
Guideth my song that I shall of you saye.                     35


# THE PRIORESS' TALE°


There was in Asie° in a greet citee,
Amonges Christen folk, a Jewerye,°
Sustened by a lord of that contree
For foul usure and lucre of villainye°


27 of through   29 waik weak   33 unnethe hardly   0 The Prioress'
Tale the tale the Prioress tells is a "miracle of the Virgin," a
characteristic kind of story found in Latin as well as in the ver-
nacular languages. This particular tale—of a Christian child mur-
dered by Jews—had a long history before Chaucer's time and ac-
counted for a long and bloody chapter in medieval anti-Semitic per-
secution. Chaucer seems to present her tale as an example of
naïve and thoughtless cruelty submerged under sentimental piety
1 Asie Asia Minor. No other version places the incident so far
away. Possibly Chaucer's motive was to emphasize at the end (lines
197ff.) the nearness and actuality of similar incidents   2 Jewerye
colony of Jews, ghetto   4 foul . . . villainye wicked usury and
evil kinds of money-making. Usury was forbidden by the Church,
as was excessive profit

5   Hateful to Christ and to his compaignye.
    And thurgh the streete men might ride and wende,
    For it was free and open at either ende.

    A litel scole of Christen folk there stood
    Down at the ferther end, in which there were
10  Children an heep, y-comen of Christen blood,
    That lerned in that scole yeer by yeere
    Swich manner doctrine° as men used there;
    This is to sayn, to singen and to rede,
    As smalle children doon in her childhede.

15  Among thise children was a widow's sone,
    A litel clergeon° seven yeer of age,
    That day by day to scole was his wone;°
    And eek also, where as he saw th'image
    Of Christes moder, had he in usage,
20  As him was taught, to kneel adown and saye
    His *Ave Marie* as he goth by the waye.

    Thus hath this widwe hir litel son y-taught
    Our blissful Lady, Christes moder dere,
    To worship ay; and he forgat it naught,
25  For sely child wol alday soone lere.°
    But ay whan I remembre on this mattere,
    Saint Nicholas stant ever in my presence,
    For he so yong to Christ did reverence.

    This litel child his litel book lerninge,
30  As he sat in the scole at his primer,°
    He *Alma redemptoris°* herde singe,
    As children lerned hir antiphoner;°
    And as he dorst, he drow him neer and neer,
    And herkned ay the wordes and the note,
35  Till he the firste verse koud all by rote.

    12 **manner doctrine** such kind of subjects   16 **clergeon** schoolboy
    17 **to . . . wone** was accustomed to go to school   25 **For . . . lere** for
    the innocent child will always learn fast   30 **primer** an elementary
    schoolbook primarily of prayers, the creed, etc.   31 **Alma redemp-
    toris** a hymn to the Virgin   32 **antiphoner** hymnbook

Nought wist he what this Latin was to saye,
For he so yong and tender was of age;
But on a day his fellaw° gan he praye
T'expounden him this song in his langage,
Or tell him why this song was in usage—                          40
This prayed he him to construen and declare,
Full ofte time upon his knowes° bare.

His fellaw, which that elder was than he,
Answered him thus: "This song, I have herd saye,
Was maked of° our blissful Lady free,                            45
Hir to salue,° and eek hir for to praye
To been our help and succour whan we deye.
I can namore expound in this mattere.
I lerne song; I kan but small° grammere."

"And is this song maked in reverence                             50
Of Christes moder?" said this innocent.
"Now certes I wol do my diligence
To kon it all ere Christemas is went.
Though that I for my primer shall be shent°
And shall be beten thries in an houre,                           55
I wol it kon Our Lady for t'honoure."

His fellaw taught him homeward prively,
Fro day to day, till he koud it by rote.
And than he song it well and boldely,
Fro word to word, according with the note.                      60
Twies a day it passed thurgh his throte—
To scoleward and homeward whan he wente;
On Christes moder set was his entente.

As I have said, thurghout the Jewerye
This litel child, as he came to and fro,                         65
Full murrily wolde he sing and crye
O alma redemptoris evere mo.
The sweetness hath his herte perced so

Of Christes moder, that to hir to praye
70 He can not stint of singing by the waye.

Our firste foe, the serpent Sathanas,
That hath in Jewes' hert his waspes nest,
Up swal,° and said: "O Hebraic peple, alas!
Is this to you a thing that is honest,°
75 That swich a boy shall walken as him lest
In your despite, and sing of swich sentence,
Which is agains our lawes° reverence?"

Fro thennes forth the Jewes han conspired
This innocent out of the world to chase.
80 An homicide thereto han they hired
That in an alley had a privee place.
And as the child gan forby for to pace,°
This cursed Jew him hent and held him faste,
And kit° his throt, and in a pit him caste.

85 I say that in a wardrobe° they him threwe,
Where as thise Jewes purgen hir entraile.
O cursed folk of Herodes all newe,°
What may your yvel entente you availe?
Murder wol out, certain it wol not faile!
90 And namely ther th'honour of God shall sprede,
The blood out cryeth on your cursed deede!

O martyr souded to° virginitee,
Now maistou singen, follwing ever in oon
The White Lamb celestial (quod she)
95 Of which the greet evangelist Saint John
In Pathmos° wrote—which saith that they that gon

73 **Up swal** swelled up    74 **honest** honorable    77 **our lawes** due to
our law. Satan identifies himself with the Jews. But some manu-
scripts read "your"    82 **forby . . . pace** pass by    84 **kit** cut
85 **wardrobe** privy    87 **folk . . . newe** people composed of new
Herods    92 **souded to** confirmed in    96 **Pathmos** Patmos, an island
in the Aegean, where St. John was thought to have written the
Apocalypse. The vision of the 144,000 virgins (*Revelations* 14:1–4)
was thought to involve "innocents"—baptized children who died

Biforn this Lamb and sing a song all newe,
That never fleshly° women they ne knewe.

This poore widwe awaiteth all that night
After hir litel child, but he came nought.          *100*
For which, as soon as it was dayes light,
With face pale of drede and bisy thought
She hath at scole and elleswhere him sought;
Till finally she gan so fer espye,°
That he last seen was in the Jewerye.          *105*

With modres pitee in hir brest enclosed
She goth, as she were half out of hir minde,
To every place where she hath supposed
By likliheed hir litel child to finde.
And ever on Christes moder, meek and kinde,          *110*
She cried—and at the laste thus she wroughte:
Among the cursed Jewes she him soughte.

She fraineth° and she prayeth pitously
To every Jew that dwelt in thilke place
To tell hir if hir child went ought forby.          *115*
They saide nay; but Jesu of his grace
Yaf in hir thought, inwith a litel space,°
That in that place after hir son she cride
Where he was casten in a pit beside.

O grete God, that parfourmest thy laude          *120*
By mouth of innocents, lo, here thy might!
This gem of chastitee, this emeraude,°
And eek of martyrdom the ruby° bright,
Ther he with throt y-corven lay upright
He *Alma redemptoris* gan to singe          *125*
So loud that all the place gan to ringe!

The Christen folk that thurgh the streete wente
In comen for to wonder upon this thing,

98 **fleshly** in a carnal way   104 **gan . . . espye** found out this much
113 **fraineth** asks   117 **inwith . . . space** in a short time   122 **emeraude** symbolic of chastity   123 **ruby** symbolic of martyrdom

And hastily they for the Provost° sente.
130 He came anon, withouten tarrying,
And herieth° Christ, that is of hevene king,
And eek his moder, honour of mankinde,
And after that the Jewes let he binde.°

This child with pitous lamentacioun
135 Up taken was, singing his song alway;
And with honour of greet processioun
They carryen him unto the next° abbay.
His moder swouning by his beere lay:
Unnethe° might the peple that was there
140 This newe Rachel° bringen fro his beere.

With torment and with shameful deeth echon
The Provost doth thise Jewes for to sterve°
That of this murder wist, and that anon.
He nolde no swich cursedness observe:°
145 "Yvel shall have that yvel wol deserve!"
Therefore with wilde horse he did hem drawe;°
And after that he heng hem by the lawe.

Upon his beer ay lith this innocent
Biforn the chief auter,° while the mass laste;
150 And after that the abbot with his covent
Han sped hem° for to buryen him full faste;
And whan they holy water on him caste
Yet spak this child when spreind° was holy water
And song O alma redemptoris mater.

155 This abbot which that was an holy man,
As monkes been—or elles oughten be°—

129 Provost chief magistrate  131 herieth praises  133 the Jewes
. . . binde he had the Jews bound. Note the abruptness of the Magis-
trate's judgment and the lack of an inquiry  137 next nearby
139 Unnethe hardly  140 newe Rachel Rachel stood for the
mothers of the slaughtered Innocents (*Matthew* 2:18)  142 doth . . .
sterve has these Jews killed  144 observe put up with  146 with
. . . drawe he had them drawn by wild horses  149 auter altar
150–51 abbot . . . sped hem the abbot and his convent (of monks)
hastened  153 spreind sprinkled  156 or . . . be the Prioress is
perhaps thinking here of the evil monk in the Shipman's Tale

This yonge child to conjure° he began,
And said, "O dere child, I halse° thee,
In vertu of the Holy Trinitee,
Tell me what is thy cause for to singe,     *160*
Sith that thy throt is cut, to my seeminge."

"My throt is cut unto my necke-bon,"
Saide this child, "and as by way of kinde°
I shold have died, ye, long time agon.
But Jesu Christ, as ye in bookes finde,     *165*
Will that his glory last and be in minde;
And for the worship of his moder dere
Yet may I° sing *O alma* loud and clere.

This well of mercy, Christes moder sweete,
I loved alway as after my konninge;     *170*
And whan that I my life sholde forlete°
To me she came, and bade me for to singe
This anthem veraily in my deyinge,
As ye han herd. And whan that I had songe,
Me thought she laid a grain° upon my tonge.     *175*

Wherefore I sing and singe mot, certain,
In honour of that blissful maiden free,
Till fro my tonge off taken is the grain;
And after that thus saide she to me,
'My litel child, now will I fetche thee     *180*
Whan that the grain is fro thy tonge y-take.
Be not aghast, I wol thee not forsake.'

This holy monk, this abbot, him mene I,
His tonge out caught, and took away the grain;
And he yaf up the ghost full softely.     *185*
And whan this abbot had this wonder seen,
His salte teres trickled down as rain

---

157 **conjure** entreat   158 **halse** beseech   163 **as . . . kinde** according to nature   168 **Yet may I** I can still   171 **sholde forlete** was about to give up   175 **grain** probably a seed, the "grain of paradise" (*cardamon*); but in other versions the "grain" is a precious stone—notably a pearl, which symbolized chastity

And gruf he fill all plat° upon the grounde,
And still he lay as he had been y-bounde.

190 The covent eek lay on the pavement
Weeping, and herying° Christes moder dere.
And after that they rise and forth been went,
And took away this martyr from his beere.
And in a tomb of marblestones cleere
195 Enclosen they his litel body sweete,
Ther he is now—God leve us for to meete!

O yonge Hugh of Lincoln, slain also
With cursed Jewes,° as it is notable
(For it is but a litel while ago)
200 Pray eek for us, we sinful folk unstable,
That of his mercy God so merciable
On us his greete mercy multiplye,
For reverence of his moder Marie. Amen.

---

188 gruf . . . plat he fell on his face all flat    191 herying praising
197–98 O . . . Jewes O young Hugh of Lincoln, also slain by cursed
Jews . . . The eight-year-old Hugh was supposed to have been
murdered by Jews at Lincoln in 1255. The story became the subject
of a ballad, "Sir Hugh" or "The Jew's Daughter"—see F. J. Child,
English and Scottish Ballads, III, 233ff. He is sometimes confused
with St. Hugh, Bishop of Lincoln (d. 1200). The Jews were expelled
from England in 1290, and the persecution of them for "ritual mur-
ders" was not known in England during Chaucer's time; but such
legends remained, and such persecutions continued on the continent,
for example in the cremation of the Strasburg Jewry in 1349

# PROLOGUE TO SIR THOPAS

Whan said was all this miracle, every man
As sober was that wonder was to see;
Till that our Hoste japen he began,
And than at erst he looked upon me,
And saide thus: "What man artou?" quod he.      *5*
"Thou lookest as thou woldest find an hare,
For ever upon the ground I see thee stare.

Approche neer and look up murrily!
Now, ware you, sirs, and let this man have place.
He in the waast is shape as well as I:      *10*
This were a puppet in an arm t'enbrace,
For any woman, small and fair of face!
He seemeth elvish° by his contenaunce,
For unto no wight doth he dalliaunce.°

Say now somewhat, sin other folk han said:      *15*
Tell us a tale of mirth, and that anon."
"Host," quod I, "ne beth not yvel apaid,°
For other tale, certes, kan° I non,
But of a ryme I lerned long agon."
"Ye, that is good," quod he. "Now shull we heere      *20*
Some daintee° thing, me thinketh by his cheere."

---

13 **elvish** mysterious, withdrawn   14 **unto . . . dalliaunce** is not
sociable with anyone   17 **ne . . . apaid** don't be displeased   18 **kan**
know   21 **daintee** worthy

# THE TALE OF SIR THOPAS°

## *THE FIRST FIT*

Listeth, lords, in good entent,°
And I wol telle verayment°
    Of mirth and of solas;
All of a knight was fair and gent
5   In battail and in tournament—
    His name was Sir Thopas.°

Y-born he was in fer contree,
In Flandres° all beyond the see,
    At Popering in the place;
10  His fader was a man full free,
And lord he was of that contree,
    As it was Goddes grace.

0 **The Tale of Sir Thopas** this tale is a burlesque of the metrical
romances. Romance itself had an aristocratic heritage, and in this
Chaucer was well schooled: the Knight's Tale is a high-minded
romance, and *Troilus and Criseyde* is often called the greatest of
romances. By the fourteenth century, however, the form and
subject of romance had become sadly debased. Stories of heroic
knights, set in a sing-song rhyme scheme, were recited by minstrels
for audiences of middle-class burghers. Hence the idealism of ro-
mance came to be tailored for a middle-class mentality, and the form
itself became tedious and cliché. The best way to see the humor of
*Sir Thopas* is to read one of its prototypes—*Guy of Warwick*, for
example. But it should be understood that there were good metrical
romances as well—*Sir Gawain and the Green Knight* being the
greatest. Chaucer's burlesque takes an effeminate and cowardly hero,
attributes to him decidedly middle-class characteristics, sets him off
looking for an elf-queen (it was supposed to be the other way
around, the elf-queen finding *him*). And he tells the whole in a
deadly singsong filled with clichés. *Sir Thopas* is often compared
with *Don Quixote*, but Cervantes' work comments profoundly upon
the nature of human life itself; Chaucer is content to have his fun
briefly at the expense of middle-class romances and be done—hence
the Host's interruption   **1 Listeth . . . entent** a characteristic stock
opening line   **2 verayment** truly; used here for a desperate rhyme
**6 Thopas** i.e., topaz. The topaz was a charm worn by young girls
against luxury. It may have been used as a feminine name as well
**8 Flanders** Flanders was generally thought a nation of burghers; it
was scarcely "in a far country"

Sir Thopas wax a doughty swain°—
White was his face as paindemain,°
　　His lippes red as rose;　　　　　　　　　　*15*
His rode is like scarlet in grain,°
And I you tell in good certain
　　He had a seemly nose.

His heer, his beerd, was like saffroun,
That to his girdle raught adown,
　　His shoon of Cordewane;　　　　　　　　　*20*
Of Brugges were his hosen brown,
His robe was of siklatoun,°
　　That coste many a jane.°

He koude hunt at wilde deer,°　　　　　　　*25*
And ride on-hawking for river,°
　　With grey goshawk° on hande;
Thereto he was a good archer,°
Of wrastling° was there none his peer,
　　Ther any ram shall stande.　　　　　　　　*30*

Full many a maide bright in bower
They moorne for him paramour,
　　Whan hem were bet to sleepe;
But he was chaste and no lechour,
And sweet as is the bramble flower　　　　*35*
　　That bereth the rede hepe.°

And so bifell upon a day,
Forsooth as I you telle may,
　　Sir Thopas wold out ride;
He worth° upon his steede grey,　　　　　　*40*

13 **wax . . . swain** grew into a brave young fellow—a romance tag;
but the description which follows is that of an effeminate burgher
14 **paindemain** fine white bread  16 **rode . . . grain** complexion is
like cloth dyed in grain  23 **siklatoun** costly material  24 **jane** small
silver coin  25 **deer** animals  26 **for river** by the river  27 **goshawk**
a hawk used by yeomen, not Knights  28 **archer** archery was not
appropriate to Knights  29 **wrastling** wrestling was low class; on
the ram as a prize in wrestling matches, cf. the description of the
miller in the General Prologue, line 548  36 **hepe** fruit of wild
rose  40 **worth** got up

And in his hand a launcegay,°
A long swerd by his side.

He pricketh° thurgh a fair forest,
Therein is many a wilde beest—
45        Ye, bothe buck and hare;
And as he pricketh north and est,
I tell it you, him had almest
        Bitide° a sorry care.

There springen herbes greet and smalle—
50    The licoris and setewale,
        And many a clowe-gilofre;°
And nutemeg to put in ale,
Whether it be moist or stale,
        Or for to lay in coffre.

55    The briddes sing, it is no nay,
The sparhawk and the popinjay,
        That joy it was to heere;
The thrustlecock made eek his lay,
The woodedove upon the spray,
60        She sang full loud and clere.

Sir Thopas fill in love-longinge
All whan he herd the thrustle singe,
        And pricked as he were wood;
His faire steed in his prickinge
65    So swatte° that men might him wringe—
        His sides were all blood.

Sir Thopas eek so wery was
For pricking on the softe grass,°
        So fierce was his corage—
70    That down he laid him in the plas,

**41 launcegay** short lance, not a very serious weapon   **43 pricketh**
spurs his horse   **47–48 him . . . Bitide** there almost happened to
him. "Almost" is the key word   **51 clowe-gilofre** clove. Such lists
are common in romances. But spices would be of more interest to
a tradesman than a knight-errant   **65 swatte** sweated   **68 grass** he
is supposed to be pricking through wild forest

To make his steede some solas,
   And yaf him good forage.°


"O Sainte Mary, *ben'dic'te,*
What aileth this love at me
   To binde me so sore?                                    75
Me dreemed all this night, pardee,
An elf-queen shall my lemman° be
   And sleep under my gore.°


An elf-queen wol I love, ywis,
For in this world no woman is                              80
   Worthy to be my make°
      In towne.
All other women I forsake,
And to an elf-queen I me take,
   By dale and eek by downe."                            85


Into his saddle he clomb° anon,
And pricketh over stile and ston,°
   An elf-queen for t'espye;
Till he so long hath riden and goon
That he fond in a privee woon°                             90
   The contree of Fairye
      So wilde:
For in that contree was there noon
That to him dorste ride or goon:
   Neither wife ne childe.                                95


Till that there came a greet geaunt:
His name was Sir Oliphaunt,°
   A perilous man of deede.
He saide, "Child, by Termagaunt,°
But if thou prick out of mine haunt,                       100


72 **forage** dry fodder, normally found in a barn    77 **lemman** sweet-
heart    78 **gore** garment    81 **make** mate    86 **clomb** Cf. line 40. He
should leap or vault into the saddle    87 **stile and ston** he should
jump the horse over stone walls rather than walking it over a stile
(a set of steps)    90 **woon** dwelling-place    97 **Oliphaunt** Elephant
99 **Termagaunt** a Mohammedan god, supposedly

Anon I slee thy steede
    With mace.
Here is the Queen of Faïrye,
With harp and pipe and symphonye,
105    Dwelling in this place!"


The child said, "Also mote I thee,°
Tomorrwe will I meete thee,
    Whan I have mine armoure.°
And yet I hope, *par ma fay,*
110 That thou shalt with this launcegay
    Abyen it full sore.
        Thy mawe°
Shall I percen, if I may,
Ere it be fully prime of day—
115    For here thou shalt be slawe!"°


—Sir Thopas drow aback full faste.
This geaunt at him stones caste,
    Out of a fell staff-slinge.°
But fair escapeth child° Thopas,
120 And all it was thurgh Goddes gras,
    And thurgh his fair beringe.°


Yet, listeth, lordes, to my tale,
Murrier than the nightingale,
    For now I wol you roune°
125 How Sir Thopas with sides smalle,°
Pricking over hill and dale,
    Is come again to towne.


His murry men commanded he
To make him bothe game and glee,
130    For needes most he fighte
With a geaunt with hevedes° three,

---

106 **Also . . . thee** so may I thrive; another tag    108 **armoure of
course** he is supposed to ride in his armor    112 **mawe** belly
115 **slawe** slain    118 **fell staff-slinge** dread slingshot    119 **child** com-
monly used of young knights    121 **fair beringe** i.e., he ran fast
124 **roune** whisper, tell a secret    125 **sides smalle** a detail normally
used of ladies    131 **hevedes** heads

For paramour and jolitee
  Of one that shone full brighte.


"Do come," he saide, "my minstrales
And gestours° for to tellen tales,               135
  Anon in mine arminge,
Of romances that been royales,
Of popes and of cardinales,
  And eek of love-likinge."


They fette him first the sweete win,          140
And meed eek in a maselin,°
  And royal spicerye,
And gingerbreed that was full fin,
And licoris, and eek comin,
  With sugre that is trye.°             145


He dide next his white leere,
Of cloth of lake° fine and cleere,
  A breech and eek a sherte:
And next his shert an aketoun,°
And over that an haubergeoun          150
  For° percing of his herte:


And over that a fine hauberk,°
Was all y-wrought of Jewes werk,°
  Full strong it was of plate:
And over that his cote-armour,          155
As white as is a lily-flower,
  In which he wol debate.°


His sheeld was all of gold so red,
And therein was a bores heed,
  A charbocle° by his side;         160

---

134–35 **Do . . . gestours** have my minstrels and storytellers come
141 **maselin** wooden bowl    145 **trye** choice    146–47 **dide . . . lake** put
on next to his white skin (breech and shirt) of linen    149 **aketoun**
padded vest    151 **For** to prevent    152 **hauberk** plate-armor, worn
over the habergeon (mail)    153 **Jewes werk** Jews were famed as
metal workers    157 **debate** fight    160 **charbocle** i.e., his shield has
a carbuncle and boar's head painted on it as an emblem

And there he swore on ale and breed°
How that the geaunt shall be deed,
   Bitide what bitide.


His jambeux were of quirboily,°
165 His swerdes sheeth of ivory,
   His helm of latoun bright;
His saddle was of rewel bon,°
His bridle as the sunne shon,
   Or as the moone light.


170 His spere was of fine cypress,°
That bodeth wer and nothing pees°—
   The heed full sharp y-grounde.
His steede was all dapple grey:
It goth an amble in the way,
175    Full softely and rounde,
      In londe.
Lo, lordes mine, here is a fit!
If ye wol any more of it,
   To tell it wol I fonde° . . .


## THE SECOND FIT


180 —Now hold your mouth, *par charitee,*
Bothe knight and lady free,
   And herkneth to my spelle:°
Of battail, and of chivalry,
And of ladies' love-drury,°
185    Anon I wol you telle.


Men speken of romances of pris,°
Of Horn Child and of Ypotis,


161 **ale and breed** knights in romances swore on aristocratic fare
like peacocks  164 **jambeux . . . quirboily** shin-guards were of
leather (which had been boiled, shaped, and let dry)  167 **rewel
bon** whalebone  170 **cypress** unusual for lances, but traditionally
associated with death  171 **bodeth . . . pees** signifies war and not
peace  179 **fonde** attempt; note the desperate appeal for si-
lence in the next line, which suggests the audience's reaction
182 **spelle** tale (typical romance usage)  184 **love-drury** love-making
186 **pris** value

Of Beves and Sir Guy,
Of Sir Libeux and Pleindamour;
But Sir Thopas he bereth the flower          190
  Of royal chivalry.


His goode steed all he bistrood,
And forth upon his way he glood,
  As sparkle out of the bronde.°
Upon his crest he bare a tower,             195
And therein sticked a lily-flower—
  God shild his corse fro shonde!°


And for he was a knight auntrous°
He nolde sleepen in noon hous,
  But liggen in his hoode.°                    200
His brighte helm was his wonger,°
And by him baiteth his destrer,°
  Of herbes fine and goode.


Himself drank water of the well,
As did the knight Sir Percivell,            205
  So worthy under weede;
      Till on a day . . .


"Namore of this, for Goddes dignitee!"
Quod oure Hoste, "for thou makest me
So wery of thy veray lewednesse°           210
That, also wisly God my soule blesse,
Mine eres aken of thy drasty speeche!°
Now swich a ryme the devil I biteche!°
This may well be ryme doggerel," quod he.
  "Why so?" quod I. "Why wiltou lette° me   215
More of my tale than another man,
Sin that it is the beste ryme I kan?"


193–94 glood . . . bronde glided like a spark from a firebrand
197 shild . . . shonde keep his body from harm   198 auntrous adven-
turous   200 liggen . . . hoode lie (wrapped in) his hood   201 wonger
pillow   202 baiteth . . . destrer his steed grazes   210 lewednesse
stupidity   212 eres . . . drasty speeche ears ache with your worthless
chatter   213 biteche give to   215 lette cut short

"By God," quod he, "For plainly at oo word—
Thy drasty ryming is not worth a turd!
220 Thou dost nought elles but dispendest° time:
Sir, at oo word, thou shalt no lenger ryme.
Let see wher° thou canst tellen ought in geste,°
Or tell in prose somewhat, at the leste,
In which there be some mirth or some doctrine."
225    "Gladly," quod I. "By Goddes sweete pine,
I wol you tell a litel thing in prose
That oughte liken you, as I suppose,
Or elles certes ye be too daungerous.°
It is a moral tale vertuous,
230 Al be it told sometime in sundry wise,
Of sundry folk, as I shall you devise.
As thus:° Ye wot that every evangelist
That telleth us the pain of Jesu Christ
Ne saith not all thing as his fellaw dooth;
235 But, natheless, hir sentence° is all sooth,
And all accorden, as in hir sentence,
Al be there in hir telling difference.
For some of hem sayn more and some sayn lesse
Whan they his pitous passion expresse—
240 I mene of Mark and Matthew, Luke, and John;
But douteless hir sentence is all oon.
Therefore, lordinges all, I you biseeche,
If that ye think I vary as in my speeche—
As thus, though that I telle somewhat more
245 Of proverbes than ye han herd before
Comprehended in this litel tretise here,°
To enforcen with the effect of my mattere,
And though I not the same wordes saye

220 dispendest waste    222 wher whether    222 ought in geste any-
thing in the way of a good story    228 daungerous finicky    232 thus
what follows is Chaucer's typical self-satire: he has himself speak
in a long-winded, vague, apologetic way, using repetitious and
awkward expressions and bumbling language    235 hir sentence their
meaning    246 litel tretise here he refers to the *Melibee*, a trans-
lation of a French allegorical treatise in prose addressed to aristo-
crats. This is Chaucer's other tale, omitted here. It is entirely serious,
dealing with such problems as when to declare war, how to choose
advisors, how to use temporal goods, how to do justice

As ye han herd—yet to you all I praye
Blameth me not, for as in my sentence                    250
Shull ye nowhere finden difference
Fro the sentence of this tretise lite
After the which this mirye tale I write.
And, therefore, herkneth what that I shall saye,
And let me tellen *all* my tale, I praye."               255

# THE MONK'S PROLOGUE

Whan ended was my tale of Melibee
And of Prudence and hir benignitee,
Our Hoste said, "As I am faithful man!
And by that precious corpus Madrian,
5  I hadde lever than a barrel ale
That Goodelief my wife had herd this tale!
For she nis nothing of swich pacience
As was this Melibeus' wife Prudence!
By Goddes bones, whan I bete my knaves,°
10 She bringeth me the greete clobbed° staves,
And cryeth—'Slee the dogges everichon,
And breke hem bothe back and every bon!'
And if that any neighebor of mine
Wol not in chirche to my wife encline,°
15 Or be so hardy to hir to trespace,
Whan see cometh home she rampeth in my face
And cryeth—'False coward, wreek thy wif!
By corpus' bones, I wol have thy knif
And thou shalt have my distaff and go spinne!'
20 Fro day to night right thus she wol beginne:
'Alas,' she saith, 'that ever that I was shape
To wedden a milksop or a coward ape,
That wol been overlad of every wight!
Thou darst not stonden by thy wives right!'
25 This is my life, but if that I wol fighte.
And out at door anon I mot me dighte,
Or elles I am but lost, but if that I
Be like a wilde leon foolhardy.

9 **bete my knaves** hit my servants   10 **clobbed** clublike   14 **encline** bow. Cf. General Prologue, lines 449–52

I wot well she wol do me slee° someday
Some neighebor and thanne go my way;°                 30
For I am perilous with knife in hande,
Al be it that I dare not *hir* withstande,
For she is big in armes, by my faith—
That shall he find that hir misdoth or saith.
But let us pass away fro this mattere.               35
—My lord the Monk," quod he, "be merry of cheere,
For ye shall tell a tale trewely.
Lo, Rochester stant here faste by!
Ride forth, mine owne lord, breke not our game!
But by my truth, I knowe not your name—              40
Wher shall I calle you my lord Daun John?°—
Or Daun Thomas or elles Daun Albon?
Of what house° be ye, by your fader kin?
I vow to God, thou hast a full fair skin:
It is a gentil pasture ther *thou* goost!             45
*Thou* art not like a penant° or a ghost!
Upon my faith, thou art some officer,
Some worthy sextein, or some celerer°—
For by my fader soul, as to my doom,°
Thou art a maister whan thou art at hoom,             50
No poore cloisterer, ne no novis,
But a governour, wiley° and wis,
And therewithal of brawnes and of bones
A well-faring persone for the nones!
I praye God yive him confusioun                        55
That first thee brought unto religioun:°
Thou woldest han been a tredefowl° aright.
Haddestou as greet a leve as thou hast might
To perform all thy lust in engendrure,
Thou haddest begetten many a creature!                 60

29 **do me slee** make me slay   30 **go my way** i.e., be hanged, or flee
41 **Daun John** the name of the evil monk in the Shipman's Tale
43 **house** monastery   46 **penant** penitent   48 **sextein . . . celerer**
officers of a monastery, in charge respectively of the buildings,
altar, vestments, etc., and of the food and drink   49 **doom** judgment
52 **wiley** clever   56 **unto religioun** into the monastic life   57 **trede-**
**fowl** a rooster who keep his hens satisfied. Cf. lines 66–67

Alas, why werestou so wide a cope?°
God yive me sorrwe but, and I were Pope,
Not only thou, but every mighty man,
Though he were shorn full high upon his pan,°
65    Shold have a wife—for all the world is lorn:
Religious hath take up all the corn
Of treding; and we burel men been shrimpes!°
Of fieble trees there comen wretched impes;°
This maketh that our heires been so slendre
70    And fieble that they may not well engendre;
This maketh that our wives wol assaye
Religious folk, for they mowe better paye
Of Venus' payements than may we.
God wot, no Lusheburghes° payen ye!
75    But be not wroth, my lord, though that I playe:
Full oft in game a sooth I have herd saye."
    This worthy Monk took all in pacience,
And said, "I wol doon all my diligence,
As fer as souneth into honestee,°
80    To telle you a tale or two or three.
And if you list to herkne hiderward,
I wol you sayn the life of Saint Edward.
Or elles, first, tragedies wol I telle,
Of which I have an hundred in my celle.
85        Tragedy is to sayn a certain storye
(As olde bookes maken us memorye)
Of him that stood in greet prosperitee
And is y-fallen out of high degree
Into misery—and endeth wretchedly.
90    And they been versified communely
Of six feet, which men clepe hexametron.
In prose eek been endited many oon,
And eek in metre in many a sundry wise.
Lo, this declaring ought enough suffise.

---

61 **cope** cloak   64 **shorn . . . pan** shaved on the top of his skull
(i.e., had the monk's tonsure)   66–67 **Religioun . . . shrimpes** the
monasteries have taken off the wheat with respect to sexual relations,
and we laymen are shrimps (i.e., weaklings)   68 **impes** shoots
74 **Lusheburghes** the bad coin of Luxembourg   79 **souneth . . .
honestee** accords with morality

Now herkneth if you liketh for to heere.     95
But first I you beseek in this mattere,
Though I by ordre telle not thise thinges,
Be it of popes, emperours, or kinges,
After hir ages° as men written finde,
But tell hem some before and some behinde,     100
As it now cometh unto my remembraunce;
Have me excused of mine ignoraunce."

*[The Monk's "tale" which follows, omitted in the present
edition, is a collection of "tragedies"—stories that de-
scribe the capricious turning of Fortune's wheel in the
lives of various figures, from Satan and Adam to Chaucer's
contemporary Bernabò Visconti, whom Chaucer might
actually have met on his Italian voyage of 1378. Why the
self-indulgent monk (as he is described in the General
Prologue) begins with such a pedantic prologue, and tells
so serious and dull a tale, is somewhat of a puzzle. It is
perhaps an effort to keep up a solemn facade. At all
events, the Knight interrupts him and saves the pilgrims
from further boredom—Ed.]*

**99 After hir ages** chronologically

# THE NUN'S PRIEST'S PROLOGUE°

"Ho!" quod the Knight. "Good sir, namore of this!
That ye han said is right enough, ywis,
And muchel more; for litel hevinesse
Is right enough to muche folk, I guesse.
5   I say for me it is a greet disese,°
Where as men han been in greet welth and ese
To heeren of hir suddein fall—alas.
And the contrary is joy and greet solas,
As whan a man hath been in poor estat,
10   And climbeth up and wexeth fortunat,
And there abideth in prosperitee:
Swich thing is gladsome, as it thinketh me,
And of swich thing were goodly for to telle."
   "Ye," quod our Host, "by Sainte Poules belle,
15   Ye say right sooth—this Monk he clappeth° loude!
He spak how Fortune 'covered with a cloude'
I noot never what! And als° of a tragedye
Right now ye herd, and pardee, no remedye

0 **Prologue to the Nun's Priest's Tale** this is a beast fable, embody-
ing a literary device of which Donald Duck or Snoopy are modern
examples. Chaucer's barnyard animals behave with all kinds of
human pretensions—they act like courtly lovers, intellectuals, theo-
logians; hence they delightfully satirize human follies. Much of the
humor depends on Chaucer's periodically reminding us that they
are a rooster and a hen: just as we get involved with their high
seriousness we hear them make a barnyard noise or "fly down from
the beams." The chase of the fox was a set scene in medieval litera-
ture. And the "morality" drawn at the end (lines 611–15) is so
simple that most readers miss it: keep your eyes open and your
mouth shut.
  Part of the effect relies on the incongruity between a high style
and humdrum events. The widow and her little barnyard are de-
scribed according to the rules of medieval rhetoric, with formal
"dilations" or descriptions, "apostrophes" in which the author nobly
comments and moralizes, and much name-dropping of authoritative
writers   **5 disese** displeasure   **15 clappeth** chatters   **17 als** also

It is for to biwaile ne complaine
That that is done; and als it is a paine,                     20
As ye han said, to heere of hevinesse.
Sir Monk, namore of this, so God you blesse—
Your tale annoyeth all this compaignye!
Swich talking is not worth a butterflye,
For therein is there no disport ne game!                     25
Wherefore, sir Monk—or Daun Piers, by your name—
I pray you hertely tell us somewhat elles.
For sikerly, nere° clinking of your belles,
That on your bridle hang on every side,
By hevene King° that for us alle dyde                         30
I shold ere this have fallen down for sleep,
Although the slough° had never been so deep!
Than had your tale all be told in vain—
For certainly, as that thise clerkes sayn,
Where as a man may have noon audience                        35
Nought helpeth it to tellen his sentence.
And well I wot the substance° is in me,
If any thing shall well reported be.
Sir, say somewhat of *hunting,* I you praye."
   "Nay," quod this Monk, "I have no lust to playe.    40
Now let another tell, as I have told."
   Than spak our Host with rude speech and bold
And said unto the Nonnes Preest anon:
"Come neer, thou Preest! Come hider, thou sir John!
Tell us swich thing as may our hertes glade.                 45
Be blithe, though thou ride upon a jade!
What though thine horse be bothe foul and lene?
If he wol serve thee, rekke not a bene.
Look that thine hert be murry evermo."
   "Yis, sir," quod he, "yis, Host, so mote I go,           50
But I be murry, ywis, I wol be blamed."
And right anon his tale he hath attamed,°
And thus he said unto us everichon,
This sweete preest, this goodly man sir John:

28 **nere** were it not for the   30 **hevene King** Heaven's King   32 **slough** mire   37 **substance** capacity to understand   52 **attamed** started

# THE NUN'S PRIEST'S TALE

A povre° widow, somedeel stape° in age
Was whilom dwelling in a narrwe° cottage,
Beside a grove, standing in a dale.
This widwe, of which I telle you my tale,
5 Sin thilke day that she was last a wif,
In pacience lad a full simple lif;
For litel was hir catel and hir rente:°
By husbondry° of swich as God hir sente
She fond° hirself and eek hir daughtren two.
10 Three large sowes had she, and namo,
Three kin,° and eek a sheep that highte Malle.
Full sooty was hir bower and eek hir halle,°
In which she eet full many a slendre meel:
Of poignant sauce hir needed neveradeel;
15 No daintee morsel passed thurgh hir throte—
Hir diet was accordant to hir cote.°
Repleccioun° ne made hir never sick:
Attempre° diet was all hir physik,
And exercise, and hertes suffisaunce;°
20 The goute let° hir nothing for to daunce,
N'apoplexye shente° not hir heed.
No wine ne drank she, neither white ne red:
Hir boord was served most with white and black—
Milk and brown breed, in which she fond no lack;
25 Seind° bacon, and sometime an ey or twaye,°
For she was as it were a manner daye.°
A yerd she had, enclosed all aboute
With stickes, and a drye ditch withoute,
In which she had a cock heet° Chauntecleer.

1 povre poor   1 stape advanced   2 narrwe small   7 catel . . . rente
possessions . . . income   8 husbondry thrifty management   9 fond
provided for   11 kin cows   12 bower . . . halle inner apartment . . .
main hall (the words exaggeratedly suggest a castle; they are likely
one room divided by a curtain, and sooty from the fireplace)
16 cote hut   17 Repleccioun overindulgence   18 Attempre temper-
ate   19 suffisaunce contentment   20 let hindered   21 shente in-
jured   25 Seind singed, broiled   25 ey or twaye egg or two   26 a
manner daye a kind of dairy farmer   29 heet named

In all the land, of crowing nas his peer:°                    30
His voice was murrier than the murrye orgon°
On massedayes that in the chirche gon;
Well sikerer° was his crowing in his lodge
Than is a clock or an abbey orlogge;°
By nature he knew ech ascensioun                              35
Of th'equinoxial in thilke town—
For whan degrees fifteene weren ascended,°
Than crew he that it might not been amended.°
His comb was redder than the fine coral,
And battailed as it were a castel wall;                       40
His bill was black, and as the jet it shoon;
Like azure were his legges and his toon,°
His nailes whiter than the lily-flower,
And like the burned° gold was his colour.

    This gentil cock had in his governaunce             45
Seven hennes for to doon all his plesaunce,
Which were his sustres and his paramours—
And wonder like to him as of colours.
Of which the fairest hewed on hir throte
Was cleped fair damoiselle° Pertelote:                        50
Curteis she was, discreet, and debonaire,
And compaignable, and bare hirself so faire
Sin thilke day that she was seven night old
That trewely she hath the hert in hold
Of Chauntecleer, locken in every lith.°                       55
He loved hir so that well was him therewith.
But swich a joy was it to heer hem singe,
Whan that the brighte sunne gan to springe,
In sweet accord—*"My lief is faren in lande . . ."*
For thilke time, as I have understande,                       60
Beestes and briddes coude speke and singe.

30 **of . . . peer** in crowing there was none his peer   31 **orgon** organ
pipes   33 **sikerer** more accurate   34 **orlogge** chiming steeple clock;
very fashionable in Chaucer's time, they indicated phases of the
moon, struck the hours, etc.   37 **degrees . . . ascended** i.e., one hour
38 **amended** improved upon   42 **toon** toes   44 **burned** burnished
50 **damoiselle** a very aristocratic word—a noble young lady. The ad-
jectives which follow are similarly aristocratic, up to the reminder
"seven night old"   55 **locken . . . lith** locked in every limb

And so bifell that in a daweninge,
As Chauntecleer, among his wives alle,
Sat on his perche that was in the halle—
65 And next him sat this faire Pertelote—
This Chauntecleer gan gronen in his throte,
As man that in his dreem is drecched sore.°
And whan that Pertelote thus herd him rore
She was aghast and saide, "Herte dere!°
70 What aileth you to grone in this mannere?
Ye been a veray sleeper°—fy, for shame!"
    And he answered and saide thus: "Madame,
I pray you that ye take it not agrief.
By God, me mette° I was in swich meschief
75 Right now, that yet mine hert is sore afright.
Now God," quod he, "my sweven recche aright°
And keep my body out of foul prisoun!
Me mette how that I romed up and down
Within our yerd, wher as I saw a beest°
80 Was like an hound, and wold han made arrest
Upon my body, and han had me deed.
His colour was bitwix yellow and red,
And tipped was his tail and both his eres
With black, unlike the remnant of his heres;
85 His snoute small, with glowing eyen twaye.
Yet of his look for fere almost I deye!
This caused me my groning, douteless."
    "Avoi!" quod she, "fy on you, herteless!°
Alas," quod she, "for by that God above
90 Now han ye lost mine hert and all my love!
I can not love a coward, by my faith.
For certes, what so any woman saith,
We all desiren, if it mighte be,°

67 drecched sore deeply troubled   69 Herte dere dear heart—a
courtly phrase; but note that, pronounced with the final e's, it sounds
exactly like a hen's clucking. Cf. "Avoi" (line 88) and "chuk" (line
354)   71 a veray sleeper a fine sleeper   74 me mette i.e., I dreamed
76 my . . . aright make my dream turn out favorably   79 beest he
goes on to describe a fox, which in the old idea of "animal mag-
netism" would have been the natural enemy of all roosters. See lines
459–61   88 herteless coward   93 We . . . be she describes the
qualities expected of the ideal courtly lover

To han husbondes hardy, wise, and free,
And secree, and no niggard, ne no fool,                    95
Ne him that is aghast of every tool,°
Ne noon avauntour°—by that God above.
How dorst ye sayn, for shame, unto your love
That any thing might make you aferd!—
Have ye no mannes hert, and han a beerd?                  100
Alas! and can ye been aghast of swevenes!°
Nothing, God wot, but vanitee in sweven is!
Swevenes engendren of replexions,
And oft of fume, and of complexions,°
Whan humours been too abundant in a wight.               105
Certes, this dreem which ye han mette tonight
Comth of the grete superfluitee
Of youre rede cholera,° pardee,
Which causeth folk to dreden in hir dreemes
Of arrwes, and of fire with rede lemes,°                 110
Of rede beestes that they wol hem bite,
Of contek,° and of whelpes greet and lite;
Right as the humour of malencolye
Causeth full many a man in sleep to crye
For fere of blacke beres, or boles° blacke,              115
Or elles blacke devils wol hem take.
Of other humours coud I tell also
That werken many a man in sleep full wo;
But I wol pass as lightly as I can.
Lo, Caton, which that was so wise a man                   120
Said he not thus: 'Ne do no fors of dreemes'?°
Now, sir," quod she, "whan we flee fro the beemes,
For Goddes love, as take some laxatif.
Up° peril of my soul and of my lif
I conseil you the best, I wol not lie,                    125
That both of choler and of malencolye
Ye purge you. And for ye shall not tarrye,

---

**96 tool** weapon **97 avauntour** boaster **101 swevenes** dreams
**103–04 engendren . . . complexions** come from overeating, and often
from vapors rising to the head (after drinking), and from im-
balance of bodily humors. She goes on to describe the theory of
the physical ("natural") origin of dreams **108 rede cholera** red
choler (bile) **110 lemes** flames **112 contek** strife **115 boles** bulls
**121 "Ne . . . dreemes."** pay no attention to dreams **124 Up** upon

Though in this town is noon apothecarye,
I shall myself to herbes techen° you
130 That shall been for your hele and for your prow;°
And in our yerd tho herbes shall I finde
The which han of hir propretee by kinde°
To purge you binethe and eek above.
Foryet not this, for Goddes owne love:
135 Ye been full cholerik of complexioun.
Ware the sun in his ascencioun
Ne find you not replete of humours hote.
And if it do, I dare well lay a grote°
That ye shull have a fever terciane,°
140 Or an ague that may be youre bane.°
A day or two ye shull have digestives°
Of wormes, ere ye take your laxatives
Of lauriol, centaure, and fumetere,
Or elles of ellebor that groweth there,
145 Of catapuce or of gaitrys berries,
Of herb-ive growing in our yerd, ther merry is.°
Peck hem up right as they grow and ete hem in.
Be merry, husbond, for your fader kin;
Dredeth no dreem! I can say you namore."
150     "Madame," quod he, "graunt mercy of your lore.°
But, natheless, as touching Daun Catoun,
That hath of wisdom swich a greet renown,
Though that he bade no dreemes for to drede,
By God, men may in olde bookes rede
155 Of many a man more of auctoritee
Than ever Caton was—so mote I thee°—
That all the reverse sayn of his sentence—
And han well founden by experience

129 techen direct    130 hele ... prow health ... benefit    132 kinde
nature    138 lay a grote bet a groat (small silver coin)    139 fever
terciane fever recurring within three days, i.e., every other day
140 youre bane the death of you    141 digestives medicines to ab-
sorb the humors before purging. Her remedy is an accurate account
of medieval treatment; worms were actually used for tertian fever,
and the medicines which follow were in fact laxatives or emetics
146 ther merry is where it's nice    150 graunt ... lore thank
you for your instruction (the French phrase was very toney)
156 so ... thee so may I prosper

That dreemes been significacious°
As well of joy as tribulaciouns                                    160
That folk enduren in this life present.
There needeth make of this noon argument—
The veray preve° sheweth it in deede.
    One of the greetest auctour that men rede
Saith thus: that whilom two fellawes wente          165
On pilgrimage, in a full good entente,
And happed so they comen in a town
Where as there was swich congregacioun
Of peple, and eek so strait of herbergage,°
That they ne found as much as oo cottage            170
In which they bothe might y-lodged be.
Wherefore they mosten of necessitee
As for that night departe compaignye.
And ech of hem goth to his hostelrye
And took his lodging as it wolde falle.              175
That one of hem was lodged in a stalle
Fer in a yerd, with oxen of the plow.
That other man was lodged well enow
As was his aventure or his fortune
—That us governeth all as in commune.°              180
And so bifell that long ere it were day
This man mette in his bed, ther as he lay,
How that his fellaw gan upon him calle
And said, 'Alas! for in an oxes stalle
This night I shall be murdred ther I lie!           185
Now help me, dere brother, or I die!
In alle haste come to me!' he saide.
This man out of his sleep for fere abraide,°
But whan that he was wakened of his sleep
He turned him and took of this no keep—             190

---

159 **significaciouns** forewarnings. Chauntecleer proceeds to argue
the notion that his dream was a *somnium celeste,* a warning from on
high—which would make him a heroic figure. His citing of authori-
ties and *exempla* is very learned  163 **veray preve** real occurrence
(of such dreams)  169 **so . . . herbergage** such a shortage of lodg-
ings  180 **That . . . commune** the Nun's Priest throws in a refer-
ence to the Monk's Tale which has preceded, a collection of various
men's "falls" on Fortune's wheel  188 **abraide** started

Him thought his dreem nas but a vanitee.
Thus twies in his sleeping dreemed he,
And atte thridde time yet his fellawe
Came, as him thought, and said, 'I am now slawe:°
195  Behold my bloody woundes deep and wide.
Arise up erly in the morrwe tide
And at the west gate of the town,' quod he,
'A carte full of dung there shaltou see,
In which my body is hid full prively:
200  Do thilke cart arresten° boldely.
My gold caused my murdre, sooth to sayn'
—And told him every point how he was slain,
With a full pitous face, pale of hewe.
And truste well, his dreem he fond full trewe,
205  For on the morrwe, as soon as it was day,
To his fellawes inn he took the way.
And whan that he came to this oxes stalle,
After his fellaw he began to calle.
The hostiler answerde him anon
210  And saide, 'Sir, your fellaw is agon;
As soon as day he went out of the town.'
This man gan fallen in suspecioun
Remembring on his dreemes that he mette,
And forth he goth, no lenger wold he lette,°
215  Unto the west gate of the town, and fond
A dung-cart, went, as it were, to dunge-lond—
That was arrayed in that same wise
As ye han herd the dede man devise.
And with an hardy hert he gan to crye,
220  'Vengeance and justice of this fellonye!
My fellaw murdred is this same night
And in this cart he lith gaping upright!°
I cry out on the ministres,'° quod he,
'That sholden keep and rulen this citee!
225  Harrow! Alas, here lith my fellaw slain!'
What shold I more unto this tale sayn?
The peple out stert and cast the cart to grounde,

194 slawe slain   200 Do . . . arresten have that cart stopped
214 lette delay   222 lith gaping upright lies with mouth open,
face up   223 ministres magistrates

And in the middle of the dung they founde
The dede man that murdred was all newe.
  O blissful God that art so just and trewe,        230
Lo, how that thou biwrayest° murdre alway!
Murdre wol out—that see we day by day:
Murdre is so wlatsome° and abhominable
To God, that is so just and resonable,
That He ne wol not suffre it heled° be        235
Though it abide a yeer or two or three.
*Murdre wol out*—this my conclusioun.°
And right anon ministres of that town
Han hent the carter, and so sore him pined,°
And eek the hostiler so sore engined,°        240
That they biknew hir wickedness anon—
And were anhanged by the necke-bon.
Here may men seen that dreemes been to drede!
  And, certes, in the same book I rede
Right in the next chapitre after this        245
(I gabbe° not, so have I joy or bliss)
Two men that wold han passed over see
For certain cause into a fer contree,
If that the wind ne hadde been contrarye,
That made hem in a citee for to tarrye,        250
That stood full mirry upon an haven side:
But on a day again the even tide°
The wind gan chaunge, and blew right as hem leste.
Jolif and glad they went unto his reste,
And casten hem° full erly for to saile.        255
But to that oo man fill a greet mervaile:
That one of hem, in sleeping as he lay,
Him mette a wonder dreem again the day.°
Him thought a man stood by his beddes side
And him commanded that he shold abide        260
And said him thus: 'If thou tomorrwe wende,°
Thou shalt be dreint:° my tale is at an ende.'

231 **biwrayest** reveal  233 **wlatsome** loathsome  235 **heled** concealed  230–37 **O . . . conclusioun** a rhetorical "apostrophe" in which the narrator comments emotionally and moralizes  239 **pined** tortured  240 **engined** put to the rack  246 **gabbe** lie  252 **again . . . tide** toward evening  255 **casten hem** planned  258 **again the day** toward dawn  261 **wende** leave  262 **dreint** drowned

He woke and told his fellaw what he mette,
And prayed him his viage to lette°—
265 As for that day he prayed him to abide.
His fellaw that lay by his beddes side
Gan for to laugh, and scorned him full faste:
'No dreem,' quod he, 'may so mine hert aghaste°
That I wol lette for to do my thinges.
270 I sette not a straw by thy dreeminges,
For swevenes been but vanitees and japes.°
Men dreem alday of owles and of apes
And eek of many a maze° therewithal;
Men dreem of thing that never was, ne shall.
275 But sith I see that thou wolt here abide
And thus forsleuthen° willfully thy tide,°
God wot it reweth me,° and have good day.'
And thus he took his leve and went his way.
But ere that he had half his course y-sailed—
280 Noot I not why, ne what meschaunce it ailed—
But, casuelly,° the shippes bottme rente,
And ship and man under the water wente
In sight of other shippes it beside°
That with hem sailed at the same tide.
285 And therefore, faire Pertelote so dere,
By swich ensaumples olde maistou lere
That no man sholde been too reccheless°
Of dreemes. For I say thee douteless
That many a dreem full sore is for to drede!
290    Lo, in the life of Saint Kenelm I rede
(That was Kenulphus' son, the noble King
Of Mercenrike) how Kenelm mette a thing
A lite ere he was murdred on a day.
His murdre in his avision he sey.°
295 His norice him expounded everydeel
His sweven, and bade him for to keep him well
For° traison. But he nas but seven yeer old,

---

264 **viage to lette** delay his voyage   268 **aghaste** frighten   271 **japes**
deceits   273 **maze** fantasy   276 **forsleuthen** idle away   276 **tide**
time   277 **God . . . me** God knows I'm sorry   281 **casuelly** by
chance   283 **it beside** near it   287 **reccheless** unheedful   294 **sey**
saw   296–97 **keep . . . For** guard himself against

And therefore litel tale hath he told
Of any dreem, so holy was his herte.
By God, I hadde lever than my sherte                    300
That ye had rad his legend, as have I.
    Dame Pertelote, I say you trewely,
Macrobeus,° that writ th'*Avisioun
In Afrik of the Worthy Scipioun*
Affermeth° dreemes, and saith that they been            305
Warning of thinges that men after seen.
And furthermore I pray you looketh well
In th'Olde Testament of Daniel,
If he held dreemes any vanitee.
Rede eek of Joseph and there shull ye see               310
Where dreemes be sometime (I say not alle)
Warning of thinges that shull after falle.
Look of Egypte the king Daun Pharao,
His baker and his botteler° also,
Wher° they ne felte noon effect in dreemes.             315
Whoso wol seek actes of sundry remes°
May rede of dreemes many a wonder thing!
    Lo Cresus, which that was of Lyde king,
Mette he not that he sat upon a tree,
Which signified he shold anhanged be?                   320
Lo here Andromacha, Ectores° wif,
That day that Ector sholde lese his lif,
She dreemed on the same night biforn
How that the life of Ector shold be lorn
If thilke day he went into battaile.                    325
She warned him, but it might not availe:
He wente for to fighte natheless,
But he was slain anon of Achilles
—But thilke tale is all too long to telle,
And eek it is nigh day, I may not dwelle.               330
Shortly I say, as for conclusioun,
That I shall han of this avisioun
Adversitee. And I say furthermoor

303 **Macrobeus** author of a commentary on Cicero's *Somnium Scipionis;* the work was one of the great medieval authorities on dreams
305 **Affermeth** acknowledges      314 **botteler** butler      315 **Wher**
whether      316 **actes . . . remes** histories of various realms      321 **Ectores** Hector's

That I ne tell of laxatives no stoor.
335 For they been venimous, I wot it well—
I hem defy! I love hem neveradeel!
Now let us speke of mirth and stint all this:
Madame Pertelote, so have I bliss,
Of oo thing God hath sent me large grace:
340 For whan I see the beautee of your face—
Ye been so scarlet red about your eyen—
It maketh all my drede for to dien.
For also siker as *in principio*,°
'*Mulier est hominis confusio*'°—
345 Madame, the sentence of this Latin is
'Woman is mannes joy and all his bliss.'
For whan I feel anight your softe side—
Al be it that I may not on you ride,
For that our perch is made so narrwe, alas—
350 I am so full of joy and of solas
That I defye bothe sweven and dreem."
And with that word he fley° down fro the beem,
For it was day, and eek his hennes alle,
And with a *"chuk"* he gan hem for to calle,
355 For he had found a corn lay in the yerd.
Real° he was! *He* was namore aferd—
He fethered° Pertelote twenty time,
And trad° hir eek as oft ere it was prime.
He looketh as it were a grim leoun;
360 And on his toes he rometh up and down—
Him deigned not to set his foot to grounde.
He *chuk*eth whan he hath a corn y-founde
And to him rennen than his wives alle.
Thus royal as a prince is in his halle
365 Leve I this Chauntecleer in his pasture;
And after wol I tell his aventure.

\*     \*     \*

343 **also . . . in principio** as sure as *in principio* (first words of Gospel
according to John, used as a charm; see General Prologue, line 254)
344 **'Mulier . . . confusio'** 'Woman is man's confusion.' Probably in
line 346 Chauntecleer mistranslates it purposely; though he might
misunderstand it himself   352 **fley** flew   356 **Real** regal   357 **feth-
ered** covered with his wings   358 **trad** laid

Whan that the month in which the world began,
That highte March, whan God first maked man,
Was complet, and passed were also,
Sin March began, thirty days and two,                    370
Bifell that Chauntecleer in all his pride,
His seven wives walking him beside,
Cast up his eyen to the brighte sunne
(That in the signe of Taurus had y-runne
Twenty degrees and one, and somewhat more),             375
And knew by kind,° and by noon other lore,
That it was prime;° and crew with blissful stevene.°
"The sun," he said, "is clomben up on hevene
Fourty degrees and one and more, ywis.
Madame Pertelote, my worldes bliss,                     380
Herkneth thise blissful briddes how they singe,
And see the freshe flowres how they springe!
Full is mine hert of revel and solas!"
But suddenly him fill a sorrweful cas:°
For ever the latter end of joy is wo—                   385
God wot that "worldly joy is soon ago,"°
And if a rethor° coude fair endite
He in a chronicle saufly might it write,
As for a sovereign notabilitee.
Now every wise man, let him herkne me:                  390
This story is also trew, I undertake,
As is the book of Launcelot de Lake,°
That women hold in full greet reverence.
Now wol I turn again to my sentence:
A colfox°—full of sly iniquitee—                        395
That in the grove had woned° yeres three

376 kind nature   377 prime the astrological references accurately
make it nine a.m. of May 3, the same date as the battle in the
Knight's Tale   377 stevene voice   384 him . . . cas a sorrowful
chance befell him   386 ago gone. The Monk's "tragedies" illus-
trated this point   387 rethor rhetorician   392 Launcelot de Lake a
romance, scarcely notable for truthfulness; it was this book which
Paolo and Francesca were reading when they fell in love (Dante,
Inferno V)   395 colfox coal-fox, having black feet, ears, and tail.
Cf. lines 82–85   396 woned lived

By high imaginacion forncast,°
The same night thurghout the hedges brast
Into the yerd ther Chauntecleer the faire
400 Was wont, and eek his wives, to repaire.
And in a bed of wortes° still he lay
Till it was passed undren of the day,°
Waiting his time on Chauntecleer to falle
As gladly doon thise homicides alle
405 That in await liggen° to murdre men.
O false murdrour, lurking in thy den!
O newe Scariot! Newe Geniloun!°
False dissimilour! O Greek Sinoun°—
That broughtest Troy all outrely° to sorrwe!
410 O, Chauntecleer! Accursed be that morrwe
That thou into the yerd flaugh fro the beemes!
Thou were full well y-warned by thy dreemes
That thilke day was perilous to thee—
But what that God forwot° mot needes be,
415 After th'opinion of certain clerkes:
Witness on him that any parfit clerk is
That in scole° is greet altercacioun
In this matter, and greet disputisoun,°
And hath been of an hundred thousand men;
420 But I ne can not bult it to the bren,°
As can the holy doctour Augustin,
Or Boece,° or the bishop Bradwardin,°
Wheither that Goddes worthy forwiting

397 By . . . forncast foreseen by the noble imagination (i.e., in
Chauntecleer's "celestial" dream); the imaginative faculty of the
mind was thought to mediate between the senses and the intellect,
producing pictures, ideas, and dreams   401 wortes herbs   402 un-
dren . . . day midmorning   405 liggen lie   407 Scariot . . . Geniloun
Judas Iscariot, betrayer of Jesus, and Genilon, betrayer of Roland
in the *Chanson de Roland*   408 Sinoun Sinon, who deceived the
Trojans by the wooden horse   409 outrely utterly   414 forwot
foreknows   417 scole the universities   418 disputisoun the dispu-
tation over predestination and free will was indeed heated in the
fourteenth century, and the three positions outlined below were held
by various parties   420 bult . . . bren sift it down to the bran
422 Boece Boethius   422 Bradwardin Bp. Thomas Bradwardine
(d. 1349) had lectured at Oxford against free will. St. Augustine be-
lieved that God granted free will to man. Boethius believed that God
knew what any man would choose but His foreknowledge did not
cause man's choice ("conditional necessity")

Straineth° me needly for to doon a thing
—"Needly" clepe I "simple necessitee";                                    425
Or elles if free choice be graunted me
To do that same thing, or do it nought
Though God forwot it ere that it was wrought;
Or, if his witing straineth neveradeel
But by "necessitee condicionel"—                                         430
I wol not han to do of swich mattere:
My tale is of a cock, as ye may heere,
That took his conseil of his wife, with sorrwe,
To walken in the yerd upon that morrwe
That he had mette the dreem that I you tolde.                            435
Women's conseils been full ofte colde!°
Woman's conseil brought us first to wo,
And made Adam fro paradise to go,
Ther as he was full mirrye and well at ese!
—But, for I noot to whom it might displese,                              440
If I conseil of women wolde blame,
Pass over, for I said it in my game:°
Rede auctours where they trete of swich mattere,
And what they sayn of women ye may heere—
Thise been the cockes wordes and not mine;                               445
I can noon harm of no woman divine.°
  Fair in the sond° to bath hir mirrily
Lith Pertelote, and all hir sustres by,
Again the sun; and Chauntecleer so free
Song mirrier than the mermaid in the see                                 450
—For Physiologus° saith sikerly
How that they singen well and mirrily.
And so bifell that as he cast his eye,
Among the wortes,° on a butterflye,
He was ware of this fox that lay full lowe.                              455
No thing ne list him thanne for to crowe,
But cried anon "*Cok cok!*" and up he sterte

---

424 **Straineth** constrains   436 **colde** fatal. The Nun's Priest
launches into a typical expression of medieval antifeminism; then
presumably remembers that the Prioress is present, backs down,
and claims the idea was Chauntecleer's   442 **in my game** for fun
446 **divine** imagine   447 **sond** sand   451 **Physiologus** the "natu-
ralist," i.e., the Bestiary, a collection of fanciful facts about different
kinds of creatures   454 **wortes** herbs

As man that was affrayed° in his herte
—For, naturelly, a beest desireth flee
460 Fro his contrary, if he may it see
Though he never erst had seen it with his eye.
This Chauntecleer, whan he gan him espye,
He wold han fled, but that the fox anon
Said: "Gentil sir! Alas, where wol ye gon?
465 Be ye afraid of *me,* that am your freend?
Now, certes, I were worse than a feend
If I to *you* wold harm or villainye.
I am not come your conseil for t'espye,°
But trewely, the cause of my cominge
470 Was only for to herkne how that ye singe.
For trewely, ye han as mirry a stevene
As any angel hath that is in hevene.
Therewith ye han in music more feelinge
Than had Boece,° or any that can singe.
475 My lord your fader—God his soule blesse!—
And eek your moder, of hir gentilesse,
Han in mine house y-been—to my greet ese.°
And certes, sir, full fain wold I *you* plese.
    But for men speke of singing, I wol saye—
480 So mote I brouke° well mine eyen twaye!—
Save ye, I herde never man so singe
As did your fader in the morrweninge.
Certes, it was of hert all that he song!
And for to make his voice the more strong
485 He wold so pain him that with both his eyen
He moste *wink°*—so loud he wolde cryen,
And standen on his tiptoon therewithal,
And stretche forth his necke long and small!
And eek he was of swich discrecioun
490 That there nas no man in no regioun
That him in song or wisdom mighte passe.
I have well rad in *Daun Burnel the Asse*
Among his verse how that there was a cock,

---

458 **affrayed** frightened   468 **your . . . espye** butt into your private
business   474 **Boece** Boethius had written a treatise on music
477 **ese** pleasure   480 **brouke** use   486 **wink** close his eyes

For a preestes son yaf him a knock
Upon his leg while he was yong and nice,                    495
He made him for to lese his benefice.°
But certain, there nis no comparisoun
Bitwix the wisdom and discrecioun
Of youre fader and of his subtiltee.
Now singeth, sir, for sainte charitee!                      500
Let see, can ye your fader countrefete?"°
    This Chauntecleer his winges gan to beete,
As man that coud his traison not espye
So was he ravished° with his flatterye.
—Alas, ye lordes! Many a false flattour°                    505
Is in your court, and many a losengeour,°
That plesen you well more, by my faith,
Than he that soothfastness unto you saith!
Redeth Ecclesiaste of flatterye.
Beth ware, ye lordes, of hir trecherye!                     510
    This Chauntecleer stood hye upon his tos,
Stretching his neck, and held his eyen clos,
And gan to crowe loude for the nones.
And Daun Russell the fox stert up atones
And by the gargat° hente Chauntecleer                       515
And on his back toward the wood him beer,
For yet ne was there no man that him sued.°
—O Destinee, that maist not been eschued!
Alas that Chauntecleer fleigh fro the beemes!
Alas his wife ne roughte not of dreemes!                    520
And on a Friday fill all this meschaunce!°
O Venus, that art goddess of plesaunce,
Sin that thy servant was this Chauntecleer,
And in thy service did all his power—
More for delit than world to multiplye—                     525
Why woldestou suffre him on thy day to die?

496 lese his benefice the young man in Nigel Wireker's story
did not get to his ordination as priest because the cock did
not wake him; so he could not take possession of a priest's benefice
501 countrefete imitate   504 ravished overcome   505 flattour flat-
terer   506 losengeour liar   515 gargat throat   517 sued pursued
521 Friday . . . meschaunce Friday, Venus' day, was also associated
with misfortune

O Gaufred,° dere maister sovereign,
That whan thy worthy King Richard was slain
With shot, complainedest his deeth so sore,
530  Why n'had I now thy sentence and thy lore,
The Friday for to chide, as diden ye?
For on a Friday soothly slain was he!
Than wold I shew you how that I coud plaine
For Chauntecleeres drede and for his paine!
535      Certes swich cry ne lamentacioun
Was never of ladies made whan Ilioun°
Was won, and Pyrrus with his straite swerd,
Whan he had hent King Priam by the beerd
And slain him (as saith us *Eneidos*),
540  As maden all the hennes in the cloos,
Whan they had seen of Chauntecleer the sighte.
But sovereignly Dame Pertelote shrighte
Full louder than did Hasdrubales wif
Whan that hir husbond hadde lost his lif,
545  And that the Romains hadden brend Cartage
(She was so full of torment and of rage
That willfully into the fire she sterte,
And brend hirselven with a stedefast herte).
O woeful hennes, right so criden ye
550  As, whan that Nero brende the citee
Of Rome, criden senatoures wives
For that hir husbonds losten all hir lives—
Withouten guilt this Nero hath hem slain.
Now wol I turne to my tale again.
555      The sely widwe and eek hir daughtres two
Herden thise hennes cry and maken wo,
And out at doores sterten they anon
And sien° the fox toward the grove gon
And bare upon his back the cock away,
560  And criden—"Out, harrow, and weilaway!

527 **Gaufred** Geoffrey of Vinsauf, author of the standard textbook
of rhetoric used in medieval schools. It gives rules and examples.
His example of a lamentation treats the death of Richard I, slain
on a Friday; he was hit by an arrow ("shot," line 529)—a somewhat
unromantic death for a king. The Nun's Priest's "apostrophe" in the
next paragraph follows Geoffrey's rules  536 **Ilioun** Troy  558 **sien**
saw

Ha, ha—the fox!" and after him they ran,
And eek with staves many another man—
Ran Colle our dog and Talbot and Gerland,°
And Malkin with a distaff in hir hand,
Ran cow and calf and eek the veray hogges,    565
So afered for barking of the dogges
And shouting of the men and women eke!
They runne so hem thought hir herte breke!
They yelleden as feendes doon in helle:
The duckes criden as men wold hem quelle,    570
The geese for fere flowen over the trees,
Out of the hive came the swarm of bees:
So hidous was the noise, ah, *ben'dic'te,*
Certes, he Jacke Straw and his meinee°
Ne made never shoutes half so shrille    575
Whan that they wolden any Fleming kille,
As thilke day was made upon the fox.
Of brass they broughten bemes,° and of box,°
Of horn, of bone, in which they blew and pouped,
And therewithal they skriked and they houped    580
—It seemed as that heven sholde falle!
    Now, goode men, I pray you, herkneth alle:
Lo, how Fortune turneth suddeinly
The hope and pride eek of hir enemy.
    This cock that lay upon the fox's back,    585
In all his drede unto the fox he spak
And saide, "Sir: if that I were as ye,
Yet shold I sayn, as wise God helpe me,
'Turneth again, ye proude cherles alle!
A veray pestilence upon you falle!    590
Now am I come unto this woodes side,
Maugree° your heed, the cock shall here abide!
I wol him ete, in faith, and that anon!' "
    The fox answered, "In faith, it shall be don!"—
And as he spak that word, all suddeinly    595

---

563 **Talbot and Gerland** stock names of dogs, like Fido and Rover
574 **Jacke . . . meinee** Jack Straw was one of the leaders of the
Peasant's Revolt (1381). The Flemings were their competition in
labor, and the "meinee" killed many of them    578 **bemes** trumpets
578 **box** boxwood    592 **Maugree** in spite of

The cok brak from his mouth deliverly,°
And hye upon a tree he fley anon!
And whan the fox saw that the cock was gon,
"Alas!" quod he, "O, Chauntecleer! Alas!
600 I have to you," quod he, "y-done trespass—
In as much as I maked you aferd,
Whan I you hent and brought out of the yerd.
But, sir, I did it in no wicke entente.
Come down! and I shall tell you what I mente.
605 I shall say sooth to you, God help me so."
      "Nay than," quod he, "I shrew° us bothe two,
And first I shrew myself both blood and bones,
If thou beguile me ofter than ones!
Thou shalt namore thurgh thy flatterye
610 Do me to sing and winken with mine eye.
For he that winketh whan he sholde see,
All willfully, God let him never thee."°
      "Nay," quod the fox, "but, God yive him mes-
            chaunce
That is so undiscreet of governaunce
615 That jangleth° whan he sholde hold his pees."
      Lo, swich it is for to be reccheless°
And necligent and trust on flatterye!
But ye that holden this tale a follye
As of a fox, or of a cock and hen,
620 Taketh the moralitee, good men.
For Saint Paul saith that all that written is
To our doctrine° it is y-writ, ywis:
Taketh the fruit and let the chaff be stille.°
Now goode God, if that it be thy wille,
625 As saith my Lord, so make us all good men,
And bring us to His heighe bliss.   Amen.

---

596 **deliverly** nimbly   606 **shrew** beshrew   612 **thee** prosper   615
**jangleth** chatters   616 **reccheless** careless   622 **To our doctrine** for
our learning   623 **fruit . . . stille** the "fruit" is the grain of wheat
extracted from the "chaff"—i.e., the kernel of moral truth in a
story

# THE WIFE OF BATH'S PROLOGUE

Experience, though noon auctoritee°
Were in this world, is right enough for me
To speke of woe that is in marriage.
For lordings, sith I twelve yeer was of age,
Thanked be God that is eterne on live,                          5
Husbands at chirche door° I have had five
(If I so ofte might han wedded be).°
And all were worthy men in hir degree.
But me was told, certain, not long agon is,
That sith that Christ ne went never but ones                   10
To wedding in the Cane of Galilee,
That by the same ensample taught he me
That I ne sholde wedded be but ones.
Herk eek, lo, which a sharp word for the nones,
Beside a welle, Jesus, God and man,                            15
Spak in repreve of the Samaritan:°
"Thou hast y-had five husbandes," quod he,
"And that ilke man that now hath thee
Is not thine husband." Thus he said certain;

1 **Experience . . . auctoritee** the wife claims to use experience in
presenting her views on marriage. She is right that to the Middle
Ages experience was not generally viewed as having validity for es-
tablishing truth. Truth was usually claimed by citing "authorities"—
the Bible, or "authors" generally—a habit of mind satirized in the
Nun's Priest's Tale. It will be seen that the Wife herself cites a good
many authorities, no doubt picked up from her fifth husband the
clerk   6 **at chirche door** Cf. General Prologue, line 460   7 **If . . . be**
if I may have been validly married that many times. She raises an
important point in moral theology. Chastity was considered the
highest grade of perfection; monogamous marriage was a lesser
grade, but still righteous. Some felt, however, that "monogamy"
meant one could not remarry after the death of one's spouse. This
opinion is what troubles her   16 **Samaritan** see *John* 4:6–26

20  What that he *ment* thereby I can not sayn—
    But that I ask why that the fifthe man
    Was noon husband to the Samaritan?
    How many might she have in marriage?
    Yet herd I never tellen in mine age
25  Upon this number diffinicioun.
    Men may divine and glossen° up and down,
    But well I wot, express° withouten lie,
    God bade us for to wex and multiplye.
    That gentil text can I well understande.
30  Eek well I wot he said that mine husbande
    Shold lete fader and moder and take to me.
    But of no number mencioun made he
    Of bigamy, or of octogamye:
    Why shold men than speke of it villainye?
35      Lo, here the wise king daun Salomon,
    I trow he hadde wives mo than oon—
    As wolde God it leveful were to me
    To be refreshed half so oft as he!
    Which° yift of God had he for all his wives!
40  No man hath swich that in this world alive is!
    God wot this noble king, as to my wit,
    The firste night had many a merry fit
    With ech of hem, so well was him on live.
    Blessed be God that I have wedded five,
45  Of which I have picked out the beste,
    Both of hir nether purse and of hir cheste.°
    Diverse scoles maken parfit clerkes,
    And diverse practik in many sundry werkes
    Maken the werkman parfit sikerly:
50  Of five husbands' scoleying° am I—
    Welcome the sixte whan that ever he shall!
    For sith I wol not keep me chaste in all,°
    Whan mine husband is fro the world y-gon
    Some Christen man shall wedde me anon.

---

26 **divine and glossen** conjecture and write commentaries    27 **express** explicitly    39 **Which** what a (he had seven hundred wives and three hundred concubines according to *I Kings* 11)    46 **nether . . . cheste** lower purse and of their coffer (with a pun on each no doubt)    50 **scoleying** studying    52 **in all** entirely

For than th'apostle saith that I am free            55
To wed, a Goddes half, where it liketh me—
He saith that to be wedded is no sinne:
"Bet is to be wedded than to brinne."°
What rekketh me though folk say villainye
Of shrewed Lameth and his bigamye?                  60
I wot well Abraham was an holy man,
And Jacob eek, as fer as ever I kan,
And ech of hem had wives mo than two,
And many another holy man also.

Where can ye say in any manner age                  65
That heighe God defended° marriage
By express word? I pray you telleth me.
Or where commanded he virginitee?
I wot as well as ye, it is no drede,
Th'apostle, whan he speketh of maidenhede,°         70
He said that precept° thereof had he noon:
Men may *conseil* a woman to be oon,°
But conseiling is no commandement.
He put it in our owne judgement.
For hadde God commanded maidenhede,                 75
Than had he dampned wedding with the deede;°
And certes, if there were no seed y-sowe,
Virginitee than whereof shold it growe?°
Paul dorste not commanden at the leeste
A thing of which his maister yaf noon heeste.°      80
The dart° is set up for virginitee:
Catch° whoso may, who renneth best let see.
But this word is not take of every wight,°
But there as God list yive it of his might.
I wot well that th'apostle was a maide;             85
But natheless, though that he wrote and saide

58 Bet . . . brinne it is better to be married than to burn (*I Corinthians* 7:9); but St. Paul meant to imply that it was best not to burn (with lust). The Wife shifts the emphasis   66 defended forbade   70 maidenhede virginity   71 precept commandment   72 oon single. *Conseil* refers to the "counsels of perfection"—desirable rules for a virtuous life but not commandments all must follow   76 with the deede in the act (of commanding)   77–78 And . . . growe the argument was used by St. Jerome   80 heeste command   81 dart prize (in a race)   82 Catch win   83 take . . . wight applicable to everyone

He wold that every wight were swich as he,
All nis but *conseil* to virginitee:
And for to been a wife he yaf me leve
90 Of indulgence. So is it no repreve
To wedde me if that my make° die,
Without excepcioun of bigamye.°
Al were it° good no woman for to touche,
He ment as in *his* bed or in *his* couche:
95 For peril is both fire and tow t'assemble°—
Ye know what this ensample may resemble.
This all and some, he held virginitee
More parfit than wedding in freletee°—
Freletee clepe I but if that he and she
100 Wold leden all hir life in chastitee.
I graunt it well—I have noon envye
Though maidenhede preferre bigamye:°
It liketh hem to be clene in body and gost.
Of mine estate° ne wol I make no boost;
105 For well ye know, a lord in his household
Ne hath not every vessel all of gold—
Some been of tree,° and doon hir lord servise.
God clepeth folk to him in sundry wise,
And everich hath of God a proper yifte.
110 Some this, some that, as Him liketh shifte.°
Virginitee is greet perfeccioun,
And continence eek with devocioun;
But Christ, that of perfeccioun is welle,
Bade not every wight he shold go selle
115 All that he had and yive it to the poore,
And in swich wise follwe him and his foore;°
He spak to hem that wold live parfitly—
And lordings, by your leve, that am not I.

91 make mate    92 **Without . . . bigamye** without being charged with
bigamy    93 **Al were it** although it is    95 **fire . . . assemble** to put
fire and flax together    98 **freletee** frailty, imperfection    102 **pre-
ferre bigamye** is better than remarrying    104 **estate** state    107 **tree**
wood    110 **as . . . shifte** as it pleases Him to ordain. She is arguing
that the state of virginity is one to which some are especially called;
a legitimate view    116 **foore** footsteps. She refers to *Matthew* 19:21,
a text applied to the monastic life

I wol bestow the flower of all mine age°
In th'actes and in fruit° of marriage.
   Tell me also, to what conclusioun°                    *120*
Were members made of generacioun
And of so parfit wise a Wright y-wrought?°
Trusteth right well, they were not made for nought!
Gloss whoso wol, and say both up and down          *125*
That they were made for purgacioun
Of urine, and our both thinges smalle
Was eek to know a female from a male
And for noon other cause—say ye no?
Th'experience wot well it is not so!               *130*
So that the clerkes be not with me wrothe,
I say this, that they maked been for bothe—
That is to say, for office° and for ese
Of engendrure, there we not God displese.
Why shold men elles in hir bookes sette            *135*
That man shall yelde to his wife hir dette?°
Now wherewith shold he make his payement
If he ne used his sely instrument?
Than were they made upon a creature
To purge urine, and eek for engendrure.            *140*
   But I say not that *every* wight is holde°
That hath swich harneis° as I to you tolde
To goon and usen hem in engendrure;
Than shold men take of chastitee no cure.
Christ was a maid and shapen as a man,             *145*
And many a saint sith that the world began,
Yet lived they ever in parfit chastitee.
I nil envye no virginitee.
Let hem be breed of pured whete seed,
And let us wives hote° barly breed—                *150*

---

**119 flower ... age** best years of my life   **120 fruit** i.e., childbearing; but there is no suggestion that she has children   **121 to what conclusioun** for what purpose   **123 And of ... y-wrought** and made by so perfectly wise a Creator (or, "Wright" may be "wight" and the line may mean "and a creature made in such a perfect way")   **133 office** their obvious function   **136 dette** the "marriage debt" is the necessity incumbent upon both partners to encourage fidelity by satisfying the other sexually. See *I Corinthians* 7:3   **141 holde** obliged   **142 harneis** equipment   **150 hote** be called

And yet with barly breed, Mark telle can,
Our Lord Jesu refreshed many a man.
In swich estate as God hath cleped us
I wol persevere: I nam not precious.°
155 In wifehood wol I use mine instrument
As freely as my Maker hath it sent;
If I be daungerous,° God yeve me sorrwe.
Mine husband shall it have both eve and morrwe,
Whan that him list come forth and pay his dette.
160 An husband wol I have, I wol not lette,°
Which shall be both my dettour and my thrall,
And have his tribulacioun withal
Upon his flesh, while that I am his wif.
I have the power during all my lif
165 Upon his proper body, and not he.
Right thus th'apostle told it unto me,
And bade our husbands for to love us well.
All this sentence me liketh everydeel . . .

\*      \*      \*

Up stirt the Pardoner and that anon:
170 "Now dame," quod he, "by God and by Saint John,
Ye been a noble prechour in this cas.
I was about to wed a wife! alas,
What shold I bye it on my flesh so dere?°
Yet had I levere wed no wife to-yere."°
175      "Abide," quod she, "my tale is not begunne.
Nay, thou shalt drinken of another tonne,°
Ere that I go, shall savour worse than ale.
And whan that I have told thee forth my tale
Of tribulacioun in marriage,
180 Of which I am expert in all mine age—
This is to say, myself hath been the whippe—
Than maistou chese° whether thou wolt sippe
Of thilke tonne that I shall abroche.°

154 **precious** overly particular  157 **daungerous** sparing, unap-
proachable  160 **lette** conceal it; or, hesitate, desist  173 **What . . .
dere?** Why should I pay such a price?  174 **to-yere** this year
176 **tonne** barrel  182 **chese** decide  183 **abroche** open

Be ware of it, ere thou too neigh approche,
For I shall tell ensamples mo than ten.      *185*
'Whoso that nil be ware by other men,
By him shall other men corrected be.'°
Thise same wordes writeth Ptolomee—
Rede in his *Almageste* and take it there."
    "Dame, I wold pray you if your will it were,"      *190*
Saide this Pardoner, "as ye began,
Tell forth your tale. Spareth for no man,
And teeche us yonge men of your practike."°
    "Gladly," quod she, "sith it may you like;
But that I pray to all this compaignye,      *195*
If that I speke after my fantasye,°
As taketh not agrief° of that I saye:
For mine entente nis but for to playe."

*     *     *

Now sire, than wol I tell you forth my tale.
As ever mot I drinke wine or ale,      *200*
I shall say sooth: tho husbands that I hadde,
As, three of hem were good and two were badde.
The three men were good, and rich, and olde:
Unnethe° mighte they the statute holde
In which that they were bounden unto me—      *205*
Ye wot well what I mene of° this, pardee.
As help me God, I laughe whan I thinke
How pitously anight I made hem swinke!°
And by my fay, I told of it no stoor:°
They had me yeven hir land and hir tresor—      *210*
Me needed not do lenger diligence
To win hir love or doon hem reverence.
They loved me so well, by God above,
That I ne told no daintee of° hir love.
A wise woman wol bisy hir ever in oon°      *215*

186–87 Whoso . . . be he who will not take warning from others,
by him others will be reproved 193 practike experience 196 after
my fantasye according to my fancy, as I please 197 As . . . agrief
don't take offense 204 Unnethe hardly 206 of by 208 swinke
work 209 told . . . stoor didn't care anything about it 214 told
no daintee of put any value on 215 ever in oon always

To get hir love, ye, there as she hath noon.
But sith I had hem holly in mine hand,
And sith that they had yeven me all hir land,
What shold I take keep hem for to plese,
220 But it were for my profit and mine ese?
I set hem so awerke, by my fay,
That many a night they songen "weilaway."
The bacon was not fet for hem, I trowe,
That some men han in Essex at Dunmowe.°
225 I governed hem so well after my lawe
That ech of hem full blissful was and fawe°
To bring me gaye thinges fro the faire.
They were full glad whan I spak to hem faire,
For God it wot, I chid° hem spitously.
230     Now herkneth how I bare me properly,°
Ye wise wives that can understande:
Thus shold ye speke and bere hem wrong on hande;°
For half so boldely can there no man
Swere and lien as a woman can.
235 I say not this by wives that been wise,
But if it be whan they hem misavise.°
A wise wife, if that she kan hir good,°
Shall beren him on hond the cow is wood,°
And take witness of hir owne maide
240 Of hir assent.° But herkneth how I saide:
    "Sir olde cainard,° is this thine array?°
Why is my neighebores wife so gay?°
She is honoured overal ther she gooth;
I sit at home, I have no thrifty cloth . . .
245     "What dostou at my neighebores hous?
Is she so fair? Artou so amorous? . . .

223–24 bacon . . . Dunmowe the bacon was offered as a prize to
any married couple who lived a year without quarreling or regret-
ting their marriage   226 fawe willing   229 chid chided   230 prop-
erly well   232 bere . . . hande talk them down, accuse them   236 But
. . . misavise except when they act inadvisedly   237 can hir good
knows what's good for her   238 beren . . . wood deceive him into
believing that the chough is crazy; referring to a folk tale in which
a bird (a chough) tells a cuckold of his wife's infidelity but the wife
convinces him the chough is crazy   239–40 take . . . assent call her
maid to testify that she agrees   241 cainard dotard   241 thine ar-
ray how you are   242 gay well-dressed

"What roune° ye with our maide, *ben'dic'te?*
Sir olde lechour, let thy japes be!
And if I have a gossib° or a freend,
Withouten guilt ye chiden as a feend,                                    250
If that *I* walk or play unto *his* hous! . . .
      "Thou comest home as dronken as a mous,
And prechest on thy bench, with yvel preef.°
Thou saist° to me, it is a greet meschief
To wed a povre woman for costage.°                                       255
And if that she be rich, of heigh parage,°
Than saistou that it is a tormentrye
To suffre hir pride and hir malencolye.
And if that she be fair, thou veray knave,
Thou saist that every holour° wol hir have—                             260
She may no while in chastitee abide
That is assailed upon ech a side.
      "Thou saist some folk desire us for richesse,
Some for our shape, and some for our fairnesse,
And some for she can either sing or daunce,                             265
And some for gentilesse and daliaunce,
Some for hir handes and hir armes smalle—
Thus goth all to the devil by thy tale!
      "Thou saist men may not keep a castel wall,
It may so long assailed been overal.°                                    270
And if that she be foul, thou saist that she
Coveiteth every man that she may see;
For as a spaniel she wol on him lepe,
Till that she finde some man hir to chepe.°
Ne none so grey goose goth there in the lake                            275
As, saistou, wol be withoute make;
And saist it is an hard thing for to welde
A thing that no man wol, his thankes, helde.°
      "Thus saistou, lorel,° whan thou gost to bedde,
And that no wise man needeth for to wedde,                              280
Ne no man that entendeth unto hevene—

247 **roune** whisper   249 **gossib** acquaintance   253 **with yvel preef**
bad luck to you   254 **Thou saist** . . . There follows a long com-
pendium of antifeminist clichés   255 **for costage** because of the ex-
pense   256 **heigh parage** good family   260 **holour** lecher   270 **It**
. . . **overal** if it is attacked a long time everywhere   274 **chepe** take
277–78 **welde** . . . **helde** control a thing which no one will willingly
hold on to   279 **lorel** wretch

With wilde thunder-dint and firy levene
Mote thy welked° necke be to-broke!
   "Thou saist that dropping houses, and eek smoke,
285 And chiding wives maken men to flee
Out of hir owne houses—a, *ben'dic'tee,*
What aileth swich an old man for to chide?
   "Thou saist we wives will our vices hide
Till we be fast,° and than we wol hem shewe—
290 Well may that be a proverb of a shrewe!
   "Thou saist that oxen, asses, horse, and houndes,
They been assayed° at diverse stoundes;°
Basins, lavours,° ere that men hem bye,
Spoones, stooles, and all swich husbondrye,°
295 And so be pottes, clothes, and array;
But folk of wives maken noon assay
Till they be wedded—olde dotard shrewe—
And than, saistou, we will our vices shewe.
   "Thou saist also that it displeseth me
300 But if that thou wolt praise my beautee,
And but thou pour alway upon my face,
And clepe me 'faire dame' in every place,
And but thou make a feest on thilke day
That I was born, and make me fresh and gay,
305 And but thou do to my norice° honour,
And to my chamberere° within my bower,
And to my fadres folk, and his allies
—Thus saistou, olde barrel-ful of lies!
   "And yet of our apprentice Janekin,
310 For his crisp heer shining as gold so fin,
And for he squiereth me both up and down,
Yet hastou caught a false suspecioun:
I will him not,° though thou were deed tomorrwe.
   "But tell me this, why hidestou with sorrwe
315 The keyes of thy chest away fro me?
It is my good as well as thine, pardee.

---

**283 welked** wrinkled    **289 fast** safely married    **292 assayed** tried
out    **292 stoundes** times    **293 lavours** washbasins    **294 husbondrye**
household equipment    **305 norice** nurse    **306 chamberere** cham-
bermaid    **313 I will him not** I don't want him

What, weenestou make an idiot of our dame?°
Now by that lord that called is Saint Jame,
Thou shalt not bothe, though that thou were wood,
Be maister of my body and of my good:                    320
That one thou shalt forgo, maugree thine eyen.
What helpeth it of me enquere and spyen?
I trow thou woldest lock me in thy chiste.
Thou sholdest saye, 'Wife, go where thee liste.
Take your disport. I nil leve no talis:°                 325
I know you for a trewe wife, dame Alis.'
We love no man that taketh keep or charge
Where that we goon—we wol been at our large.°
Of alle men y-blessed mote he be
The wise astrologen daun Ptolomee,                       330
That saith this proverb in his *Almageste*:
'Of alle men his wisdom is hyeste
That rekketh not who hath the world in hande.'
By this proverbe thou shalt understande,
Have thou enough, what thar thee rekke° or care         335
How mirrily that other folkes fare?
For certes, olde dotard, by your leve,
Ye shall han queinte° right enough at eve!
He is too greet a niggard that will werne°
A man to light a candle at his lanterne;                 340
He shall han never the lasse light, pardee.
Have thou enough, thee thar not plaine thee!°
    "Thou saist also that if we make us gay
With clothing and with precious array,
That it is peril of our chastitee;                       345
And yet with sorrwe thou most enforce thee,°
And say thise wordes in th'apostle's name:
'In habit made with chastitee and shame
Ye women shall apparail you,' quod he,
'And not in tressed heer and gay perree,°               350
As perles ne with gold ne clothes riche.'

---

317 **our dame** me—i.e., "the lady of the house"   325 **leve no talis**
believe any tales   328 **large** liberty   335 **thar . . . rekke** do you
need to worry   338 **queinte** sex (*lit.* female genitals)   339 **werne**
forbid   342 **thar . . . thee** needn't complain   346 **enforce thee** back
yourself up   350 **perree** jewelry

After thy text, ne after thy rubriche,
I wol not werk as muchel as a gnat.
Thou saidest this, that I was like a cat:
355 For whoso wolde senge° a cattes skin,
Than wold the cat well dwellen in his inn;
And if the cattes skin be slick and gay,
She wol not dwell in house half a day,
But forth she wol, ere any day be dawed,
360 To shew her skin and goon a-caterwawed.°
This is to say, if I be gay, sir shrewe,
I wol ren out, my borel° for to shewe.
Sir olde fool, what helpeth thee t'espyen?
Though thou pray Argus with his hundred eyen
365 To be my wardecorse,° as he can best,
In faith, he shall not keep me but me lest°—
Yet coud I make his berd,° so mote I thee!
    "Thou saidest eek that there been thinges three,
The whiche thinges troublen all this erthe,
370 And that no wight may endure the ferthe.°
O leve sir shrewe, Jesu short thy lif!
Yet prechestou and saist an hateful wif
Y-rekened° is for one of thise mischaunces.
Been there not none other resemblaunces
375 That ye may liken your parables to,
But if a sely wife be one of tho?
    "Thou liknest eek womanes love to helle,
To barren land ther water may not dwelle;
Thou liknest it also to wilde fir—
380 The more it brenneth, the more it hath desir
To consume everything that brent wol be.
Thou saist, right as wormes shend° a tree,
Right so a wife destroyeth hir husbonde—
This knowen they that been to wives bonde . . ."
385     Lordinges, right thus, as ye han understande,
Bare I stiffly mine old husbands on hande°

355 **senge** singe (to make it shine)   360 **a-caterwawed** prowling
about howling for a mate   362 **borel** clothes   365 **wardecorse**
guardian   366 **but me lest** unless I please   367 **make his berd** pull
the wool over his eyes   370 **ferthe** fourth   373 **Y-rekened** named
382 **shend** ruin   386 **Bare . . . on hande** accused

That thus they saiden in hir dronkenesse—
And all was false; but that I took witnesse
On Janekin and on my nece also.
O Lord, the pain I did hem, and the wo!     *390*
Full guilteless, by Goddes sweete pine!°
For as an horse I coude bite and whine;
I coude plaine°—and I was in the guilt—
Or elles often time I had been spilt.°
Whoso that first to mille comth first grint.     *395*
I plained first; so was our werre stint.°
They were full glad t'excusen hem full blive°
Of thing of which they never agilt hir live.°
Of wenches wold I beren hem on hande°
Whan that for sick they might unnethe° stande;     *400*
Yet tickled I his herte for that he
Wende that I had of him so greet cheertee.°
I swore that all my walking out by nighte
Was for t'espye wenches that he dighte.°
Under that colour had I many a mirthe.     *405*
For all swich wit is yiven us in our birthe:
Deceite, weeping, spinning God hath yive
To women kindely° while they may live.
And thus of oo thing I avaunte me:°
At end I had the bet in ech degree     *410*
By sleight or force, or by some manner thing,
As by continuel murmur or grucching:°
Namely,° abedde hadden they meschaunce.
There wold I chide and do hem no plesaunce;
I wold no lenger in the bed abide     *415*
If that I felt his arm over my side,
Till he had made his raunceon° unto me;
Than wold I suffre° him do his nicetee.
And therefore every man this tale I telle:

391 **pine** suffering   393 **plaine** accuse   394 **spilt** ruined   396 **werre stint** warfare stopped   397 **blive** hastily   398 **agilt hir live** were guilty in their lives   399 **Of . . . hande** I would accuse them of seducing girls   400 **might unnethe** could hardly   402 **cheertee** affection   404 **dighte** lay with   408 **kindely** by nature   409 **avaunte me** boast   412 **grucching** grumbling   413 **Namely** especially   417 **raunceon** penalty, ransom   418 **suffre** let

420 Win whoso may, for all is for to selle.°
With empty hand men may no hawkes lure.
For winning° wold I all his lust endure
And make me a feined appetit—
And yet in bacoun° had I never delit!
425 That made me that ever I wold hem chide—
For though the pope had seten hem beside,
I wold not spare hem at hir owne boord.°
For by my truth, I quit° hem word for word.
As help me veray God omnipotent,
430 Though I right now shold make my testament,
I n'owe hem not a word that it nis quit!
I brought it so aboute by my wit
That they most yeve it up as for the beste,
Or elles had we never been in reste.
435 For though he looked as a wood leoun,
Yet shold he fail of his conclusioun.
        Than wold I saye, "Goode lief,° take keep
How meekly looketh Wilkin, oure sheep!
Come neer, my spouse, let me ba° thy cheeke—
440 Ye sholden be all pacient and meeke,
And han a sweete-spiced conscience,
Sith ye so prech of Jobes pacience.
Suffreth alway, sin ye so well can preeche;
And but ye do, certain, we shall you teeche
445 That it is fair to han a wife in pees.
One of us two most bowen, douteless,
And sith a man is more resonable
Than woman is, ye mosten been suffrable.°
What aileth you to grucche thus and grone?
450 Is it for ye wold have my queint alone?
Why, take it all—lo, have it everydeel!
Peter, I shrew you but ye love it well!
For if I wolde sell my *belle chose*
I coude walk as fresh as is a rose;
455 But I wol keep it for your owne tooth.

420 **all . . . selle** everything has its price    422 **winning** my own advantage    424 **bacoun** i.e., preserved meat, not fresh    427 **boord**
table    428 **quit** got even with    437 **Goode lief** dearest    439 **ba** kiss
448 **suffrable** patient

Ye be to blame, by God, I say you sooth!"
—Swich manner wordes hadde we on hande.
Now wol I speke of my ferthe husbande.

\*          \*          \*

My ferthe husband was a revelour:
This is to sayn, he had a paramour.°          460
And I was yong and full of ragerye,°
Stibourn° and strong and jolly as a pie!°
How coud I daunce to an harpe smalle,
And sing, ywis, as any nightingale,
Whan I had drunk a draught of sweete win.          465
Metellius, the foule cherl, the swin,
That with a staff biraft his wife hir lif
For she drank wine, though *I* hadde been his wif,
Ne sholde not han daunted *me* fro drinke.
And after wine on Venus most I thinke.          470
For also siker as° cold engendreth hail,
A likerous mouth most han a likerous tail:
In women vinolent is no defence°—
This knowen lechours by experience.
    But Lord Christ, whan that it remembreth me          475
Upon my youth and on my jolitee,
It tickleth me about mine herte roote!
Unto this day it doth mine herte boote°
That I have had my world° as in my time!
But age, alas, that all wol envenime,          480
Hath me biraft my beautee and my pith°—
Let go, farewell, the devil go therewith!
The flower is gone, there is namore to telle;
The bren° as I best can now most I selle.
But yet to be right murry wol I fonde.°          485
Now wol I tellen of my ferth husbonde.
    I say I had in herte greet despit
That he of any other had delit,

460 **paramour** mistress  461 **ragerye** passion  462 **Stilbourn** stub-
born  462 **pie** magpie  471 **also siker as** as sure as  473 **In . . .
defence** in women who drink wine, there's no refusing  478 **boote**
good  479 **world** fun  481 **pith** vigor  484 **bren** bran  485 **fonde**
try

But he was quit, by God and by Saint Joce:
490 I made him of the same wood a croce°—
Not of my body in no foul mannere—
But, certainly, I made folk swich cheere°
That in his owne grece I made him frye,
For anger and for veray jalousye.
495 By God, in erth I was his purgatorye—
For which I hope his soule be in glorye.
For God it wot, he sat full oft and sung
Whan that his shoe full bitterly him wrung.°
There was no wight save God and he that wiste
500 In many wise how sore I him twiste.°
He deide whan I came fro Jerusalem;
And lith y-grave under the roode-beem.°
Al is his tombe not so curious°
As was the sepulcre of him Darius,
505 Which that Appelles wroughte subtilly.
It nis but waste to bury him preciously.
Let him fare well, God give his soule reste;
He is now in his grave and in his cheste.

*    *    *

Now of my fifthe husband wol I telle—
510 God let his soule never come in helle!
And yet was he to me the moste shrewe!°
That feel I on my ribbes all by rewe°
And ever shall unto mine ending day.
But in our bed he was so fresh and gay,
515 And therewithal so well coud he me glose°
Whan that he wolde han my *belle chose,*
That though he had me beet on every bon,
He coude win again my love anon.
I trow I loved him best for that he
520 Was of his love daungerous° to me.

490 **croce** cross   492 **made . . . cheere** treated people so   498 **shoe
. . . wrung** shoe pinched him   500 **twiste** tortured   502 **lith . . .
beem** lies buried in the church under the entrance to the choir
503 **curious** elaborate   511 **moste shrewe** biggest rascal   512 **all by
rewe** one after another   515 **glose** cajole, please   520 **daungerous**
sparing

We women han, if that I shall not lie,
In this matter a quainte fantasye:°
Waite what° thing we may not lightly have,
Thereafter wol we cry all day and crave.
Forbid us thing, and that desiren we;                         525
Press on us fast, and thanne wol we flee.
With daunger oute we all our chaffare:°
Greet press at market maketh dere ware,°
And too greet chepe° is holden at litel pris.
This knoweth every woman that is wis.                         530
    My fifthe husband—God his soule blesse!—
Which that I took for love and no richesse,
He sometime was a clerk of Oxenford,
And had left scole and went at home to bord
With my gossib,° dwelling in our town—                        535
God have hir soul!—hir name was Alisoun;
She knew mine hert and eek my privetee°
Bet than our parish preest, so mote I thee.
To hir biwrayed I my conseil all;°
For had mine husband pissed on a wall,                        540
Or done a thing that shold have cost his lif,
To hir, and to another worthy wif,
And to my nece which that I loved well,
I wold han told his conseil everydeel—
And so I did full often, God it woot,                         545
That made his face often red and hot
For veray shame, and blamed himself for he
Had told to me so greet a privetee.
And so bifell that ones in a Lente,
So often times I to my gossib wente—                          550
For ever yet I loved to be gay,
And for to walk in March, April, and May,
From house to house, to heere sundry tales—
That Jankin clerk and my gossib dame Alis
And I myself into the feeldes wente.                          555

522 **quainte fantasye** curious fancy   523 **Waite what** whatever
527 **With . . . chaffare** sparingly we give out our wares   528 **Greet
. . . ware** a big crowd in the market makes the merchandise expen-
sive   529 **too greet chepe** too much of a bargain   535 **gossib** friend
537 **privetee** secrets   539 **biwrayed . . . all** told all my secrets

Mine husband was at London all that Lente.
I had the better leiser for to playe,
And for to see, and eek for to be seye°
Of lusty folk—what wist I where my grace
560 Was shapen° for to be, or in what place?
Therefore I made my visitacions
To vigilies and to processions,°
To preeching eek, and to thise pilgrimages,
To plays of miracles and to marriages,
565 And wered upon my gaye scarlet gites;°
Thise wormes ne thise mothes ne thise mites,
Upon my peril, fret° hem neveradeel—
And wostou why? For they were used well.
    Now wol I tellen forth what happed me.
570 I say that in the feeldes walked we,
Till trewely we had swich daliaunce,°
This clerk and I, that of my purveyaunce°
I spak to him and said him how that he,
If I were widow, sholde wedde me.
575 For certainly, I say for no bobaunce,°
Yet was I never withouten purveyaunce
Of marriage n'of other thinges eek.
I hold a mouse's hert not worth a leek
That hath but one hole for to sterte to,
580 And if that faile than is all y-do.
I bare him on hand° he had enchaunted me
(My dame° taughte me that subtiltee).
And eek I said I mette° of him all night:
He wold han slain me as I lay upright
585 And all my bed was full of veray blood—
"But yet I hope that ye shall do me good;
For blood bitokeneth gold, as me was taught."
And all was false—I dreemed of it right naught;
But as I followed ay my dames lore
590 As well of that as other thinges more.

558 **seye** seen    559–60 **what . . . shapen** how did I know where my
good luck was destined    562 **vigilies . . . processions** religious cere-
monies and processions    565 **wered . . . gites** wore my fine red cloaks
567 **fret** ate    571 **daliaunce** chitchat, flirtation, intimacy    572 **pur-
veyunce** foresight    575 **bobaunce** pride    581 **bare . . . hand** made
him think    582 **dame** mother    583 **mette** dreamed

But now sir—let me see, what shall I sayn? . . .
Aha! by God, I have my tale again—
　Whan that my fourthe husband was on beere,°
I weep algate, and made sorry cheere,
As wives moten, for it is usage,                                   595
And with my coverchief covered my visage:
But for that I was purveyed of a make,°
I wept but small, and that I undertake.
To chirche was mine husband born a-morrwe
With neighebors that for him maden sorrwe,              600
And Jankin oure clerk was one of tho.
As help me God, whan that I saw him go°
After the beer, me thought he had a paire
Of legges and of feet so clene and faire
That all mine hert I yaf unto his hold.                         605
　He was, I trowe, twenty winter old,
And I was forty, if I shall say sooth.
But yet I had alway a coltes tooth:°
Gat-toothed° I was, and that became me well;
I had the prent of Sainte Venus seel.°                        610
As help me God, I was a lusty oon,
And fair and rich and yong and well-bigon,°
And trewly, as mine husbands tolde me,
I had the beste *quoniam*° mighte be.
For certes I am all Venerien                                       615
In feeling, and mine hert is Marcien:
Venus me yaf my lust, my likerousnesse,
And Mars yaf me my sturdy hardinesse;
Mine ascendent was Taur and Mars thereinne—
Alas, alas, that ever love was sinne!                           620
I followed ay mine inclinacioun
By vertu of my constellacioun;
That made me I coude not withdrawe

593 **on beere** on his bier    597 **for . . . make** since I was provided
with a mate    602 **go** walk    608 **coltes tooth** youthful appetite
609 **Gat-toothed** see General Prologue, line 468    610 **seel** birth-
mark. Medieval physiognomists believed that everyone had certain
marks imparted at birth through the influence of the stars. The Wife
goes on to argue that because of these influences she cannot help
being as she is    612 **well-bigon** having a good disposition
614 **quoniam** genitalia

My chambre of Venus from a good fellawe.
625 Yet have I Martes mark upon my face,
And also in another privee place.
For God so wis be my savacioun,
I loved never by no discrecioun,
But ever followede mine appetit.
630 Al were he short or long or black or whit,
I took no keep, so that he liked me,
How poor he was, ne eek of what degree.
    What shold I say but at the monthes ende
This jolly clerk, Jankin, that was so hende,°
635 Hath wedded me with greet solempnitee.°
And to him yaf I all the land and fee
That ever was me yeven therebefore.
But afterward repented me full sore:
He nolde suffer no thing of my list.°
640 By God, he smote me ones on the list°
For that I rent out of his book a leef,
That of the stroke mine ere wex all deef.
Stibourn I was as is a leonesse,
And of my tong a veray jangleresse,
645 And walk I wold, as I had done biforn,
From house to house, although he had it sworn;°
For which he often times wolde preeche,
And me of olde Romain gestes° teeche,
How he Simplicius Gallus left his wif,
650 And hir forsook for term of all his lif,
Nought but for open-heveded he hir say°
Looking out at his door upon a day.
Another Romain told he me by name
That, for his wife was at a summer's game°
655 Withouten his witing, he forsook hir eke;
And than wold he upon his Bible seeke
That ilke proverb of Ecclesiaste
Where he commandeth and forbedeth faste
Man shall not suffre his wife go roule° aboute;

634 **hende** pleasant, clever    635 **greet solempnitee** much ceremony
639 **suffer . . . list** permit any of my desire    640 **list** ear    646 **sworn**
forbidden    648 **gestes** tales    651 **open . . . say** he saw her bare-
headed    654 **game** midsummer revels, which included plays    659
**roule** roam

Than wold he say right thus withouten doute:    660
"Whoso that buildeth his house all of salwes,°
And pricketh his blinde horse over the falwes,°
And suffreth his wife to go seeken halwes,°
Is worthy to be hanged on the galwes."
But all for nought—I sette not an hawe°    665
Of his proverbes n'of his olde sawe.°
Ne I wold not of him corrected be;
I hate him that my vices telleth me,
And so do mo, God wot, of us than I.
This made him with me wood all outrely:°    670
I nolde not forbere° him in no cas.
    Now wol I say you sooth, by Saint Thomas,
Why that I rent out of his book a leef,
For which he smote me so that I was deef.
He had a book that gladly night and day    675
For his disport he wolde rede alway.
He cleped it Valerie and Theofraste,°
At whiche book he lough alway full faste.
And eek there was sometime a clerk at Rome,
A cardinal, that highte Saint Jerome,    680
That made a book again Jovinian.
In which book eek there was Tertulan,°
Crysippus, Trotula, and Hélois
(That was abbesse not fer fro Paris),
And eek the *Parables of Salomon,*    685
Ovides *Art,* and bookes many oon—
And alle thise were bounden in oo volume.
And every night and day was his custume
Whan he had leiser and vacacioun
From other worldly occupacioun,    690
To reden in this book of wicked wives.
He knew of hem mo legendes and lives

---

661 **salwes** willow branches   662 **falwes** fallow ground, i.e., plowed
fields   663 **halwes** shrines, i.e., on pilgrimages   665 **hawe** hawthorn
berry   666 **sawe** saws   670 **wood . . . outrely** utterly furious   671
**forbere** put up with   677 **Valerie and Theofraste** these were the
presumed authors of two widely read treatises urging men not to
marry; they often appeared in manuscripts along with antifeminist
treatises, some of which are listed below   682 **Tertulan** Tertullian
(d. 225), a church father who wrote in favor of chastity

Than been of goode wives in the Bible!
For trusteth well, it is an impossible
695 That any clerk wol speke good of wives,
But if° it be of holy saintes lives,
N'of noon other woman never the mo.
Who paintede the leon,° tell me who?
By God, if *women* hadde written stories,
700 As clerkes han within hir oratories,
They wold han written of men more wickednesse
Than all the mark of Adam° may redresse.
The children of Mercúrye and Venus
Been in hir werking full contrarious:
705 Mercúrye loveth wisdom and science,
And Venus loveth riot and dispence;
And for hir diverse disposicioun
Ech falleth in other's exaltacioun,
And thus, God wot, Mercúrye is desolat
710 In Pisces where Venus is exaltat,
And Venus falleth ther Mercúrye is raised:°
Therefore, no woman of no clerk is praised.
The clerk, whan he is old and may not do
Of Venus' werkes worth his olde shoe,
715 Than sit he down and write in his dotage
That women can not keep hir marriage!
  But now to purpose why I tolde thee
That I was beten for a book, pardee:
Upon a night Jankin, that was our sire,°
720 Reed on his book as he sat by the fire
Of Eva first, that for hir wickednesse,
Was all mankinde brought to wretchednesse,
For which that Jesus Christ himself was slain
That bought us with his herte blood again—

696 **But if** unless    698 **paintede the leon** the tale referred to is this:
a man shows a lion a picture of a man killing a lion; the lion replies,
"If the artist had been a lion, the picture would be different."
702 **mark of Adam** i.e., men    703–11 **The children . . . raised** Venus
and Mars are opposites, so that when one is in "exaltation" among
planets the other is "desolate," i.e., without influence. She is not
equating Mars with clerks and Venus with women; she is saying that
as Venus' influence wanes, Mars' increases    719 **our sire** my hus-
band

Lo, here express° of women may ye finde                          *725*
That woman was the loss of all mankinde!
  Tho reed he me how Samson lost his heres°—
Sleeping, his lemman kit° it with hir sheres,
Thurgh which treson lost he both his eyen.
  Tho reed he me, if that I shall not lien,                     *730*
Of Hercules and of his Dianire,
That caused him to set himself afire.
  No thing forgat he the sorrwe and the wo
That Socrates had with his wives two:
How Xantippa cast piss upon his heed—                           *735*
This sely man sat still as he were deed;
He wiped his heed, namore dorst he sayn
But "Ere that thonder stint, cometh a rain."
  Of Phasipha° that was the queen of Crete—
For shrewednesse him thought the tale sweete—                   *740*
Fy, speek namore! it is a grisly thing
Of hir horrible lust and hir liking!
  Of Clytermistra for hir lecherye
That falsely made hir husband for to die,
He reed it with full good devocioun.                            *745*
  He told me eek for what occasioun
Amphiorax at Thebes lost his lif:
Mine husband had a legend of his wif
Eriphylem, that for an ouche° of gold
Hath prively unto the Greekes told                              *750*
Where that hir husband hid him in a place,
For which he had at Thebes sorry grace.
  Of Livia told he me and of Lucie;
They bothe made hir husbands for to die,
That one for love, that other was for hate.                     *755*
Livia hir husband on an even late
Empoisoned hath for that she was his fo.
Lucia likerous loved hir husband so
That for he shold alway upon hir thinke,
She yaf him such a manner love-drinke                           *760*

725 **express** explicitly   727 **heres** hair   728 **lemman kit** lover cut
739 **Phasipha** Pasiphaë, who was enamored of a bull   749 **ouche**
ornament

That he was deed ere it were by the morrwe.
And thus algates° husbandes han sorrwe.
   Than told he me how one Latumius
Complained unto his fellaw Arrius
765 That in his garden growed swich a tree,
On which he said how that his wives three
Hanged hemself for herte despitous.
"O leve brother," quod this Arrius,
"Yif me a plant of thilke blessed tree,
770 And in my garden planted shall it be."
   Of latter date of wives hath he red
That some han slain hir husbands in hir bed
And let hir lechour dight hir all the night,
Whan that the corpse lay in the floor upright.
775 And some han driven nailes in hir brain
While that they sleep, and thus they han hem slain.
Some han hem yeven poison in hir drinke.
He spak more harm than herte may bithinke;
And therewithal he knew of mo proverbes
780 Than in this world there growen grass or herbes:
"Bet is,"° quod he, "thine habitacioun
Be with a leon or a foul dragoun
Than with a woman using for to chide."
"Bet is," quod he, "hye in the roof abide
785 Than with an angry wife down in the hous;
They been so wicked and contrarious,
They haten that hir husbands loven, ay."
He said, "A woman cast hir shame away
Whan she cast off hir smock." And furthermo,
790 "A fair woman, but she be chaste also,
Is like a gold ring in a sowes nose."
   Who wolde ween or who wolde suppose
The woe that in mine herte was and pine?
And whan I saw he wolde never fine°
795 To reden on this cursed book all night,
All suddenly three leves have I plight°
Out of his book right as he red, and eke
I with my fist so took° him on the cheeke

762 **algates** either way    781 **Bet is** it is better    794 **fine** cease    796
**plight** torn    798 **took** hit

That in our fire he fill backward adown.
And he up stirt as doth a wood leoun          800
And with his fist he smote me on the heed
That in the floor I lay as I were deed!
And whan he saw how stille that I lay,
He was aghast, and wold han fled his way—
Till atte last out of my swough I braide.°    805
    "O, hastou slain me, false theef," I saide,
And for my land thus hastou mordred me?
Ere I be deed yet wol I . . . kisse thee . . ."
And neer he came and kneeled fair adown
And saide, "Dere suster Alisoun,               810
As help me God, I shall thee never smite.
That I have done, it is thyself to wite.°
Foryeve it me, and that I thee beseeke."
And yet, eftsoones, I hit him on the cheeke,
And saide: "Theef, thus muchel am I wreke.°    815
Now wol I die; I may no lenger speke."
    But at the last with muchel care and wo
We fill accorded by us selven two.
He yaf me all the bridel in mine hand,
To han the governaunce of house and land,      820
And of his tonge and of his hand also;
And made him bren his book anonright tho.°
And whan that I had geten unto me
By maistry all the sovereignetee,
And that he said "Mine owne trewe wif,          825
Do as thee lust the term of all thy lif,
Keep thine honour, and keep eek mine estat"—
After that day we hadden never debat!
God help me so, I was to him as kinde
As any wife from Denmark unto Inde,             830
And also trew, and so was he to me.
I pray to God that sit in majestee,
So bless his soule for his mercy dere!
Now wol I say my tale, if ye wol heere.

*    *    *

805 out . . . braide I came out of my faint   812 to wite to blame
815 wreke avenged; it is evidently a feeble slap   822 And . . . tho
and I made him burn his book right then and there

835 The Frere lough whan he had herd all this.
"Now dame," quod he, "so have I joy or bliss,
This is a long preamble of a tale!"
    And whan the Somnour herd the Frere gale,°
"Lo," quod the Somnour, "Goddes armes two!
840 A frere wol entremette him° evermo!
Lo, goode men, a fly and eek a frere
Wol fall in every dish and eek mattere.
What spekestou of preambulacioun?
What, amble or trot or pees° or go sit down!
845 Thou lettest our disport in this mannere."
    "Ye? woltou so, sir Somnour?" quod the Frere.
"Now by my faith, I shall ere that I go
Tell of a somnour swich a tale or two
That all the folk shall laughen in this place."
850     "Now elles, Frere, I wol bishrew thy face,"
Quod this Somnour, "and I bishrewe me,
But if I telle tales two or three
Of freres, ere I come to Sidingborne,
That I shall make thine herte for to moorne.
855 For well I wot thy pacience is goon."
    Our Hoste cried, "Pees, and that anoon!"
And saide, "Let the woman tell hir tale.
Ye fare as folk that dronken been of ale!
Do, dame, tell forth your tale, and that is best."
860     "All redy, sir," quod she, "right as you lest—
If I have license of this worthy Frere."
    "Yis, dame," quod he, "tell forth and I wol heere."

838 **gale** sing out    840 **entremette him** stick his nose in    844 **pees**
hold your peace; or, perhaps, "pace"

# THE WIFE OF BATH'S TALE

In th'olde dayes of the King Arthour
Of which that Britons speken greet honour
All was this land fulfilled of faïrye:
The elf-queen with hir jolly compaignye
Daunced full oft in many a greene mede—                            5
This was the old opinioun as I rede°—
I speke of many hundred yeers ago.
But now can no man see none elves mo,
For now the grete charitee and prayeres
Of limitours,° and other holy freres,                             10
That serchen every land and every streem,
As thick as motes° in the sunne-beem,
Blessing halles, chambres, kitchens, bowres,
Citees, burghes, castles, hye towres,
Thropes, bernes, shipnes,° dayeries—                              15
This maketh that there been no fairies.
For there as wont to walken was an elf
There walketh now the limitour himself,
In undermeles° and in morweninges,
And saith his matins and his holy thinges                         20
As he goth in his limitacioun.
Women may go now saufly up and down:
In every bush or under every tree
There is noon other incubus° but he—
And he ne wol doon hem but° dishonour.                            25
    And so bifell that this King Arthour
Had in his house a lusty bacheler
That on a day came riding fro river,
And happed that, alone as he was born,
He saw a maide walking him biforn;                                30

6 **rede** understand   10 **limitours** see General Prologue, line 209
12 **motes** specks of dust   15 **Thropes . . . shipnes** villages, barns,
cowsheds   19 **undermeles** late mornings   24 **incubus** an evil spirit
which was supposed to lay with a woman while she slept, making her
pregnant with a demon child   25 **ne . . . but** won't do anything to
them except

Of whiche maid anon, maugree hir heed,
By very force he raft hir maidenheed.°
For which oppressioun was swich clamour,
And swich pursuit° unto the King Arthour,
35  That dampned was this knight for to be deed
By course of law, and shold han lost his heed
(Paraventure swich was the statute tho)
But that the queen and other ladies mo
So longe prayeden the king of grace,
40  Till he his life him graunted in the place,
And yaf him to the queen, all at hir wille,
To chese whether she wold him save or spille.°
    The queen thanked the king with all hir might,
And after this thus spak she to the knight
45  Whan that she saw hir time upon a day:
"Thou standest yet," quod she, "in swich array°
That of thy life yet hastou no suretee.
I graunt thee life if thou canst tellen me
What thing is it that women most desiren.
50  Be ware and keep thy necke-bone from iren.°
And if thou canst not tellen me anon,
Yet wol I yeve thee leve for to gon
A twelfmonth and a day to seech and lere
An answer suffisant in this mattere;
55  And suretee wol I han ere that thou pace,
Thy body for to yeelden in this place."
    Woe was this knight, and sorrwefully he siketh.°
But what!—he may not do all as him liketh;
And atte last he chees him for to wende
60  And come again right at the yeeres ende,
With swich answer as God wold him purveye,
And taketh his leve and wendeth forth his waye.
    He seeketh every house and every place
Where as he hopeth for to finde grace,
65  To lerne what thing women loven most.
But he ne coud arriven in no cost°
Where as he mighte find in this mattere

32 **raft hir maidenheed** took her virginity   34 **pursuit** suing for justice   42 **spille** let die   46 **array** condition   50 **iren** i.e., the ax   57 **siketh** sighs   66 **cost** coast, region

Two creatures according in fere.°
Some saiden women loven best richesse;
Some said honour, some saide jolinesse,          70
Some rich array, some saiden lust abedde,
And ofte time to be widow and wedde,
Some saide that our herte is most esed
Whan that we been y-flattered and y-plesed—
He goth full neigh the sooth, I wol not lie:          75
A man shall win us best with flatterye,
And with attendaunce and with bisinesse
Been we y-limed,° bothe more and lesse.
And some sayen that we loven best
For to be free, and do right as us lest,          80
And that no man repreve us of our vice,
But say that we be wise and nothing nice.°
For trewely, there is none of us alle,
If any wight wol claw us on the galle,°
That we nil kicke for he saith us sooth:°          85
Assay and he shall find it that so dooth.
For be we never so vicious withinne,
We wol be holden wise and clene of sinne.
And some sayn that greet delit han we
For to be holden stable and eek secree,°          90
And in oo purpose stedfastly to dwelle,
And not biwraye thing that men us telle—
But *that* tale is not worth a rake-stele.°
Pardee, we women conne no thing hele:°
Witness on Mida.° Wol ye heer the tale?          95
　　Ovid, amonges other thinges smalle,
Said Mida had under his longe heeres,
Growing upon his heed, two asses eres,
The whiche vice he hid as he best mighte
Full subtilly from every mannes sighte,          100
That save his wife there wist of it namo.
He loved hir most and trusted hir also.

68 **in fere** with each other　78 **y-limed** caught　82 **nice** foolish　84 **claw . . . galle** scratch us on a sore spot　85 **for . . . sooth** because he tells us the truth　90 **holden . . . secree** considered dependable and able to keep a secret　93 **rake-stele** rake-handle　94 **hele** conceal　95 **Mida** Midas

He prayed hir that to no creature
She sholde tellen of his disfigure.
105 She swore him nay, for all this world to winne,
She nolde do that villainy or sinne
To make hir husband han so foul a name—
She nold not tell it for hir owen shame.
But natheless, hir thoughte that she dyde,
110 That she so longe shold a conseil hide;
Hir thought it swal so sore about hir herte
That needely some word hir most asterte,°
And sith she dorst not tell it to no man,
Down to a maris° faste by she ran—
115 Till she came there hir herte was afire!
And as a bitore bombleth in the mire,°
She laid hir mouth unto the water down:
"Biwray me not, thou water, with thy soun,"
Quod she. "To thee I tell it and namo:
120 Mine husband hath long asses eres two!
Now is mine hert all whole, now is it oute!
I might no lenger keep it, out of doute."
(Here may ye see, though we a time abide,
Yet out it moot—we can no conseil hide.)
125 The remnant of the tale if ye wol heere,
Redeth Ovid, and there ye may it lere.
This knight of which my tale is specially,
Whan that he saw he might not come thereby—
This is to say what women loven most—
130 Within his brest full sorrweful was the gost.°
But home he goth, he mighte not sojourne;
The day was come that homeward most he turne.
And in his way it happed him to ride,
In all this care, under a forest side,
135 Where as he saw upon a daunce go
Of ladies four and twenty and yet mo;
Toward the whiche daunce he drow full yerne,°
In hope that some wisdom shold he lerne.

112 **asterte** escape   114 **maris** marsh   116 **bitore . . . mire** bittern
(a heron-like bird) makes booming noises in the mud (i.e., while
sticking his bill in mud). It used to be thought the bird made its
noise thus   130 **gost** spirit   137 **yerne** eagerly

But certainly, ere he came fully there,
Vanished was this daunce, he niste where!          *140*
No creature saw he that bare lif,
Save on the green he saw sitting a wif:
A fouler wight there may no man devise!
Again the knight this olde wife gan rise,
And said, "Sir knight, here forth ne lith no way.  *145*
Tell me what ye seeken, by your fay.
Paraventure it may the better be:
Thise olde folk kon muchel thing," quod she.
    "My leve moder," quod this knight, "certain,
I nam but deed but if that I can sayn             *150*
What thing it is that women most desire.
Coud ye me wisse, I wold well quit your hire."°
    "Plight me thy trouthe here in mine hand," quod she:
The nexte thing that I requere thee,
Thou shalt it do, if it lie in thy might,          *155*
And I wol tell it you ere it be night."
    "Have here my trouthe," quod the knight, "I
        graunte."
    "Thanne," quod she, "I dare me well avaunte°
Thy life is sauf, for I wol stand thereby.
Upon my life the queen wol say as I.               *160*
Let see which is the proudest of hem alle
That wereth on° a coverchief or a calle°
That dare say nay of that I shall thee teche.
Let us go forth withouten lenger speeche."
Tho rouned she a pistel° in his ere               *165*
And bade him to be glad and have no fere.
    Whan they be comen to the court, this knight
Said he had hold his day as he had hight,°
And redy was his answer, as he saide.
Full many a noble wife, and many a maide,          *170*
And many a widow (for that they been wise),
The queen hirself sitting as justise,
Assembled been his answer for to heere,
And afterward this knight was bode appere.

---

152 **Coud . . . hire** if you could teach me, I would pay you well
158 **avaunte** boast   162 **wereth on** has on   162 **calle** hairnet   165
**rouned . . . pistel** she whispered a little message   168 **hight** agreed

175  To every wight commanded was silence,
And that the knight shold tell in audience
What thing that worldly women loven best.
This knight ne stood not still as doth a beest,
But to his questioun anon answerde
180 With manly voice that all the court it herde:
"My liege lady, generally," quod he,
"Women desire to have sovereigntee
As well over hir husband as hir love,
And for to been in maistry° him above.
185 This is your most desire, though ye me kille.
Doth as you list: I am here at your wille."
    In all the court ne was there wife ne maide
Ne widow that contraried that he saide,
But saiden he was worthy han his lif.
190    And with that word up stert that olde wif,
Which that the knight saw sitting on the greene;
"Mercy," quod she, "my sovereign lady queene!
Ere that your court departe, do me right.
I taughte this answer unto the knight,
195 For which he plighte me his trouthe there
The firste thing I wolde him requere
He wold it do, if it lay in his might.
Before the court than pray I thee, sir knight,"
Quod she, "that thou me take unto thy wif;
200 For well thou wost that I have kept thy lif.
If I say false, say nay, upon thy fay."
    This knight answered, "Alas and weilaway!
I wot right well that swich was my biheste.
For Goddes love, as chees a new requeste:
205 Take all my good and let my body go."
    "Nay than," quod she, "I shrew us bothe two.
For though that I be foul, and old, and poore,
I nold for all the metal ne for ore
That under erth is grave or lith above,
210 But if thy wife I were, and eek thy love."
    "My *love!*" quod he, "nay, my dampnacioun!
Alas, that any of my nacioun
Shold evere so foul disparaged° be."

184 **maistry** mastery, domination    213 **disparaged** disgraced

But all for nought, the end is this, that he
Constrained was: he needes must hir wedde—          215
And taketh his olde wife and goth to bedde.
   Now wolden some men say, paraventure,
That for my negligence I do no cure
To tellen you the joy and all th'array
That at the feeste was that ilke day.          220
To which thing shortly answere I shall:
I say there nas no joy ne feest at all.
There nas but heviness and muche sorrwe.
For prively he wedded hir on morrwe,
And all day after hid him as an owle,          225
So woe was him, his wife looked so foule.
   Greet was the woe the knight had in his thought.
Whan he was with his wife abedde brought,
He wallweth° and he turneth to and fro.
His olde wife lay smiling evermo,          230
And said, "O dere husband, ben'dic'te!
Fareth every knight thus with his wife as ye?
Is this the law of King Arthoures hous?
Is every knight of his thus dangerous?°
I am your owne love and youre wif.          235
I am she which that saved hath your lif.
And certes yet ne did I you never unright.
Why fare ye thus with me this firste night?
Ye faren like a man had lost his wit.
What is my guilt? For Goddes love, tell it,          240
And it shall been amended if I may."
   "Amended!" quod this knight. "Alas, nay, nay,
It wol not been amended neveremo.
Thou art so lothly and so old also,
And thereto comen of so low a kinde,°          245
That litel wonder is though I wallwe and winde.
So wolde God mine herte wolde breste!"
   "Is this," quod she, "the cause of your unreste?"
   "Ye, certainly," quod he. "No wonder is."
   "Now sir," quod she, "I coud amend all this,          250
If that me list, ere it were dayes three,
So° well ye mighte bere you unto me.

229 **wallweth** tosses   234 **dangerous** sparing   245 **kinde** class, family
252 **So** so that

But for ye speken of swich gentilesse
As is descended out of old richesse°——
255 That therefore sholden ye be gentilmen——
Swich arrogance is not worth an hen.
Look who that is most vertuous alway,
Privee and apert, and most entendeth ay
To do the gentil deedes that he can,
260 Take him for the greetest gentilman.
Christ wol we claim of Him our gentilesse,
Not of our elders for hir old richesse.
For though they yeve us all hir heritage,
For which we claim to been of heigh parage,°
265 Yet may they not biquethe for no thing
To none of us hir vertuous living,
That made hem gentilmen y-called be,
And bade us follwen hem in swich degree.
Well can the wise poet of Florence,
270 That highte Dant', spoken in this sentence——
Lo, in swich manner rym is Dante's tale:
'Full selde up riseth by his braunches smalle
Prowess of man, for God of his prowesse
Wol that of him we claim our gentilesse.'
275 For of our elders may we no thing claime
But temporel thing that man may hurt and maime.
Eek every wight wot this as well as I,
If gentilesse were planted naturelly
Unto a certain linage down the line,
280 Privee and apert, than wold they never fine°
To doon of gentilesse the fair office——
They mighte do no villainy or vice.
Take fire, and beer it in the derkest hous
Bitwix this and the Mount of Caucasous,
285 And let men shet the doores and go thenne,
Yet wol the fire as faire lie and brenne
As twenty thousand men might it biholde:

253–54 swich . . . richesse such refinement and prestige as is de-
rived from inherited wealth. The hag's harangue which follows is an
amalgam of medieval commonplaces about true nobility, the false
value of youth, wealth, beauty, etc. The hag, like the Wife herself,
harangues her husband into submission  264 parage lineage  280
fine cease

His office naturel ay wol it holde,
Up peril of my life, till that it die.
Here may ye see well how that genterye°                    290
Is not annexed to possessioun,
Sith folk ne doon hir operacioun
Alway, as doth the fire, lo, in his kinde.
For God it wot, men may well often finde
A lordes son do shame and villainye;                         295
And he that wol han pris of his gentrye,
For he was boren of a gentil hous
And had his elders noble and vertuous,
And nil himselven do no gentil deedis,
Ne follwen his gentil auncestre that deed is,              300
He nis not gentil, be he duc or erl;
For villaines sinful deedes make a cherl.
For gentilesse nis but renomee°
Of thine auncestres for hir heigh bountee,°
Which is a straunge thing for thy persone.°               305
Thy gentilesse cometh fro God alone.
Than comth our veray gentilesse of grace:
It was nothing biqueth us with our place.°
Thenketh how noble, as saith Valerius,
Was thilke Tullius Hostilius                                         310
That out of poverte rose to heigh noblesse.
Redeth Senek, and redeth eek Boece:
There shull ye seen express that no drede is°
That he is gentil that doth gentil deedis.
And therefore, leve husband, I thus conclude:          315
Al were it that mine auncestres were rude,
Yet may the hye God—and so hope I—
Graunte me grace to liven vertuously.
Than am I gentil whan that I beginne
To liven vertuously and waive° sinne.                         320
   And there as ye of poverte me repreve,
The hye God, on whom that we beleve,

290 **genterye** gentility    303 **renomee** renown    304 **bountee** goodness
305 **straunge . . . persone** a thing foreign to your own person    308 **It
. . . place** it was not left to us with our social position    313 **express
. . . is** explicitly stated that there is no doubt    320 **waive** avoid

In willful poverte chees to live his lif;
And certes every man, maiden, or wif
325 May understond that Jesus, hevene King,
Ne wold not chese a vicious living.
Glad poverte is an honest thing, certain.
This wol Senek and other clerkes sayn.
Whoso that halt him paid of° his poverte,
330 I hold him rich al had he not a sherte;
He that coveiteth is a poore wight,
For he wold han that is not in his might.
But he that nought hath, ne coveiteth to have,
Is rich, although we hold him but a knave.
335 Veray poverte it singeth properly.°
Juvenal saith of poverte, 'Mirrily
The poore man, whan he goth by the waye,
Biforn the theves he may sing and playe.'
Poverte is hateful good, and as I guesse,
340 A full greet bringer out of bisinesse;
A greet amender eek of sapience
To him that taketh it in pacience.
Poverte is this, although it seem alenge,°
Possessioun that no wight wol challenge.
345 Poverte full often, whan a man is lowe,
Maketh his God and eek himself to knowe.°
Poverte a spectacle° is, as thinketh me,
Thurgh which he may his veray° freendes, see.
And therefore, sir, sin that I not you greve,
350 Of my poverte namore ye me repreve.
    Now sir, of elde ye repreve me:
And certes, sir, though noon auctoritee
Were in no book, ye gentils of honour
Sayn that men shold an old wight doon favour,
355 And clepe him fader for your gentilesse—
And auctours shall I finden, as I guesse.
    Now there ye say that I am foul and old:
Than dred you not to been a cokewold,

329 **halt . . . of** considers himself content with    335 **Veray . . . properly** true poverty sings naturally    343 **alenge** miserable    346 **Maketh . . . to knowe** causes him to know    347 **spectacle** eyeglass    348 **veray** true

For filth° and elde, also mote I thee,
Been grete wardeins° upon chastitee.                    360
But natheless, sin I know your delit,
I shall fulfill your worldly appetit.
    Chees now," quod she, "one of thise thinges tweye:
To han me foul and old till that I deye
And be to you a trewe humble wif                        365
And never you displese in all my lif;
Or elles ye wol han me yong and fair
And take your aventure of the repair°
That shall be to your house by cause of me—
Or in some other place, may well be.                    370
Now chees yourselven wheither that you liketh."
    This knight aviseth him,° and sore siketh;
But atte last he said in this mannere:
"My lady and my love, and wife so dere,
I put me in your wise governaunce:                      375
Cheeseth yourself which may be most plesaunce
And most honour to you and me also.
I do no fors° the wheither of the two,
For as you liketh it suffiseth me."
    "Than have I get of you maistry," quod she,          380
"Sin I may chees and govern as me lest?"
    "Ye, certes, wife," quod he, "I hold it best."
    "Kiss me," quod she. "We be no lenger wrothe.
For by my trouth, I wol be to you bothe—
This is to sayn, ye, bothe fair and good.               385
I pray to God that I mote sterven wood,°
But I to you be all so good and trewe
As ever was wife sin that the world was newe.
And but I be tomorn as fair to seene
As any lady, emperice, or queene,                       390
That is bitwix the est and eek the west,
Do with my life and deeth right as you lest:
Cast up the curtin, look how that it is."
    And whan the knight saw veraily all this,
That she so fair was and so yong thereto,               395

359 **filth** ugliness   360 **wardeins** guardians   368 **take . . . repair** take
your chance on the visiting   372 **aviseth him** thinks it over   378 **I
. . . fors** I don't care   386 **sterven wood** die insane

For joy he hent hir in his armes two,
His herte bathed in a bath of blisse!
A thousand time a-row he gan hir kisse.
And she obeyed him in every thing
400 That mighte do him plesance or liking.
    And thus they live unto hir lives ende
In parfit joy. And Jesu Christ us sende
Husbandes meeke, yong, and fresh abedde—
And grace to overbide° hem that we wedde.
405 And eek I praye Jesu shorte hir lives
That not wol be governed by hir wives.
And old and angry niggards of dispence°
—God send hem soon a veray pestilence!

---

404 **overbide** outlive    407 **of dispence** in spending

# THE CLERK'S PROLOGUE

"Sir Clerk of Oxenford," our Hoste saide,
"Ye ride as coy and still as doth a maide
Were newe spoused, sitting at the boord.
This day ne herd I of your tonge a word;
I trow ye study aboute some sophime.°                    5
But Salomon saith, 'Every thing hath time.'
For Goddes sake, as beth of better cheere!
It is no time for to studyen here—
Tell us some murry tale, by your fay!
For what man that is entered in a play,°                 10
He needes mot unto the play assente;
But precheth not, as freres doon in Lente,
To make us for our olde sinnes weepe—
Ne that thy tale make us not to sleepe.
Tell us some murry thing of aventures.                   15
Your termes, your colours, and your figures,°
Keep hem in store till so be ye endite
High style, as whan that men to kinges write.
Speketh so plain at this time, we you praye,
That we may understande what ye saye."                   20
    This worthy Clerk benignely answerde:
"Host," quod he, "I am under your yerde.°
Ye han of us as now the governaunce,
And therefore wol I do you obeisaunce
As fer as reson asketh, hardily.                         25
I wol you tell a tale which that I
Lerned at Padwe° of a worthy clerk,

5 **study . . . sophime** muse over some logic-chopping   10 **play** game
16 **termes . . . figures** terminology of rhetoric, your figures of speech,
and your rhetorical devices   22 **yerde** rule   27 **Padwe** Padua

As preved by his wordes and his werk.
He is now deed and nailed in his cheste—
30   I pray to God so yive his soule reste:
Frauncis Petrak,° the lauriat poete,
Highte this clerk, whose rhetorike sweete
Enlumined all Itaile of poetrye,
As Linian° dide of philosophye,
35   Or law, or other art particuler.
But deeth, that wol not suffre us dwellen heer
But as it were a twinkling of an eye,
Hem both hath slain; and alle shull we die.
But forth to tellen of this worthy man
40   That taughte me this tale, as I began,
I say that first with high style he enditeth,
Ere he the body of his tale writeth,
A prohemie° in which descriveth he
Pemond, and of Saluces° the contree,
45   And speketh of Appenin, the hilles hye
That been the boundes of West Lumbardye,
And of Mount Vesulus in special,
Wher as the Po, out of a welle small,
Taketh his firste springing and his sours
50   That estward ay encresseth in his cours
To Emeleward, to Ferrare and Venice,
The which a long thing were to devise.
And trewely, as to my judgement,
Me thinketh it a thing impertinent,
55   Save that he wol conveyen his mattere;
But this his tale, which that ye shall heere."

[*The Clerk's Tale, omitted here, is a long and
idealistic story of the young peasant girl Griselda,
whom a young nobleman, Walter, selects for his wife.*

31 **Frauncis Petrak** Petrarch (d. 1374) was the great humanist
scholar and poet. The Clerk's tale is based on his Latin translation
of a tale by Boccaccio; he translated it because, he said, it had
moved him to tears and he wished to preserve it for posterity. It is
sometimes imagined, on the basis of this line, that Chaucer met
Petrarch during his Italian voyage   34 **Linian** Giovanni di Lignano
(d. 1383), professor of canon law at Bologna   43 **prohemie** prologue
44 **Pemond, Saluces** Piedmont, Saluzzo

*He chooses her in response to the request of his people*
*that he marry and produce an heir; his choice seems*
*a mockery of their wishes, and he proceeds to abuse*
*Griselda cruelly. He even claims to send their children*
*off to be slain—because the fickle people wish it—*
*and finally pretends to renounce her and take another*
*wife. Griselda bears her fortunes with incredible pa-*
*tience, making Job-like and solemn, though increas-*
*ingly dogged, avowals of submission. Finally Walter*
*reveals that he has been testing her, and restores their*
*children out of hiding. Griselda swoons with joy and,*
*for the first time, weeps. They live happily after.*

*The interesting twist is the ending, in which the*
*idealistic young clerk adds—in the true spirit of the*
*university—an ironic admission that such ideals are*
*little followed. He mentions the Wife of Bath with*
*ironic deference, and ends by turning all into high*
*camp with an improbable song (called "L'Envoy de*
*Chaucer" in the manuscripts), using but three rhymes,*
*in praise of female domination. This ending follows*
*—Ed.]*

## THE CLERK'S EPILOGUE

This story is said not for that wives sholde
Follwen Grisilde as in humilitee—
For it were importable° though they wolde—
But for that every wight in his degree
Shold be constant in adversitee,                                    5
As was Grisilde. Therefore, Petrak writeth
This story, which with high style he enditeth.

3 were importable would be unbearable

For sith a woman was so pacient
Unto a mortal man, well more us oughte
10 Receiven all in gree° that God us sent.
For greet skile is, he preve that he wroughte:°
But he ne tempteth no man that he boughte,°
As saith Saint Jame, if ye his pistel° rede—
He preveth folk alday, it is no drede,

15 And suffreth us, as for our exercise,
With sharpe scourges of adversitee
Full ofte to be bete in sundry wise—
Not for to know our will, for certes he
Ere we were born knew all our freletee;°
20 And for our best is all his governance.
Let us than live in vertuous suffrance.°

But oo word, lordinges, herkneth ere I go:
It were full hard to finde nowadayes
In all a town Grisildes three or two,
25 For if that they were put to swiche assayes,°
The gold of hem hath now so bad allayes
With brass, that though the coin be fair at eye,
It wolde rather breste atwo than plye.°

For which, here for the Wives love of Bathe—
30 Whose life and all hir secte° God maintene
In high maistry, and elles were it scathe°—
I wol with lusty herte, fresh and greene,
Say you a song to glade you, I weene:
And let us stinte of ernestful mattere.
35 Herkneth my song that saith in this mannere:

10 **in gree** in stride, with good will    11 **For ... wroughte** for it is most reasonable that He test what He created    12 **boughte** saved 13 **pistel** epistle    19 **freletee** frailty    21 **suffrance** patience. The remainder of the passage is entirely original with Chaucer    25 **assayes** tests    28 **plye** bend. Good coin, containing enough gold, was pliable 30 **secte** sex, or sect    31 **scathe** a pity

## "L'ENVOY DE CHAUCER"

Grisilde is deed and eek hir pacience,
And both atones buried in Itaile,
For which I cry in open audience:
No wedded man so hardy be t'assaile°
His wives pacience in trust to finde                    40
Grisildis, for in certain he shall faile.

O noble wives, full of high prudence,
Let noon humilitee your tonge naile,
Ne let no clerk have cause or diligence
To write of you a story of swich merveile               45
As of Grisildis, pacient and kinde,
Lest Chichevache you swallwe in hir entraile.°

Follweth Ekko that holdeth no silence,
But ever answereth at the contretaile.°
Beth not bidaffed° for your innocence,                  50
But sharply take on you the governaile.
Emprenteth well this lesson in your minde
For commune profit, sith it may availe.

Ye archewives, stondeth at defence,
Sin ye be strong as is a greet camaile.°                55
Ne suffreth not that men you doon offence.
And sclendre wives, fieble as in battaile,
Beth egre° as is a tiger yond in Inde—
Ay clappeth° as a mill, I you conseile.

Ne drede hem not, doth hem no reverence;                60
For though thine husband armed be in maile,
The arrwes of thy crabbed eloquence
Shall perce his brest and eek his aventaile.°

39 assaile try   47 Chichevache . . . entraile Chichevache, the skinny
cow, feeds only on patient wives   49 contretaile counter tally
50 bidaffed made a fool of   55 camaile camel   58 egre fierce
59 Ay clappeth always clatter   63 aventaile chain mail attached to
helmet covering neck

303

In jalousy I rede eek thou him binde,
65 And thou shalt make him couche° as doth a quaile.

If thou be fair, ther folk been in presence
Shew thou thy visage and thine apparaile.
If thou be foul, be free of thy dispence;°
To get thee freendes ay do thy travaile.
70 Be ay of cheer as light as leef on linde,°
And let him care, and weep, and wring, and waile . . .

65 couche cower    68 dispence spending    70 linde linden tree

# THE MERCHANT'S PROLOGUE

"Weeping and wailing, care and other sorrwe
I know enough, on even and amorrwe!"
Quod the Marchant. "And so doon other mo
That wedded been! I trow that it be so,
For well I wot it fareth so with me!                          *5*
I have a wife, the worste that may be:
For though the feend to hir y-coupled were,
She wold him overmatch, I dare well swere.
What shold I you reherce in special
Hir hye malice? She is a shrew at all!°                        *10*
There is a long and large difference
Bitwix Griselde's greete pacience
And of my wife the passing° crueltee.
Were I unbounden,° also mote I thee,
I wolde never eft comen in the snare.                          *15*
We wedded men live in sorrwe and care:
Assaye whoso wol and he shall finde
I saye sooth, by Saint Thomas of Inde,
As for the more part—I say not alle;
God shilde° that it sholde so bifalle!                         *20*
    A, good sir Host, I have y-wedded be
Thise monthes two, and more not, pardee,
And yet I trowe he that all his live
Wifeless hath been, though that men wold him rive°
Unto the hert, ne coud in no mannere                           *25*
Tellen so muchel sorrwe as I now here
Coud tellen of my wives cursednesse."
    "Now," quod our Host, "Marchant, so God you
        blesse,

10 **at all** in every way   13 **passing** surpassing   14 **unbounden** sepa-
rated, freed   20 **shilde** forbid   24 **rive** stab

Sin ye so muchel knowen of that art,
30 Full hertely I pray you tell us part."
      "Gladly," quod he, "but of mine owne sore
For sorry hert I telle may namore."

# THE MERCHANT'S TALE

Whilom there was dwelling in Lumbardye
A worthy knight that born was of Pavie,
In which he lived in greet prosperitee;
And sixty yeer a wifeless man was he,
5 And follwed ay his bodily delit
On women, there as was his appetit,
As doon thise fooles that been seculer.°
And whan that he was passed sixty yeer—
Were it for holiness or for dotage
10 I can not say—but swich a greet corage°
Hadde this knight to been a wedded man,
That day and night he doth all that he can
T'espyen where he mighte wedded be,
Praying our Lord to graunten him that he
15 Might ones know of thilke blissful lif
That is bitwix an husband and his wif,
And for to live under that holy bond
With which that first God man and woman bond:
"Noon other life," said he, "is worth a bene!

7 As . . . seculer as these fools do who are secular—i.e., who are not
in monasteries but in "the world." Cf. line 78. These two lines suggest
that the tale was originally assigned to the Monk or Friar, although
it is possible that the Merchant is wishing he were in a monastery
10 corage desire

For wedlock is so esy and so clene°                    20
That in this world it is a paradis."
—Thus said this olde knight that was so wis.°
    And certainly, as sooth as God is king,
To take a wife, it is a glorious thing,
And namely whan a man is old and hoor.                    25
Than is a wife the fruit of his tresor:
Than shold he take a yong wife and a fair,
On which he might engendren him an heir,
And lede his life in joy and in solas;
Where as thise bacheleres sing "alas"                    30
Whan that they find any adversitee
In love, which nis but childish vanitee.
And trewely, it sit well to be so°
That bachelers have ofte pain and wo:
On brotel ground they build, and brotelnesse                    35
They finde whan they wene sikernesse°—
They live but as a brid or as a beest
In libertee and under noon arrest;
There as a wedded man in his estat
Liveth a life blissful and ordinat                    40
Under this yoke of marriage y-bounde:
Well may his hert in joy and bliss abounde.
For who can be so buxom° as a wif?
Who is so trew and eek so ententif
To keep him, sick and whole, as is his make?                    45
For wele or woe she wol him not forsake.

20 **esy . . . clene** enjoyable, righteous    22 **Thus . . . wis** the lines
which follow (23–148) are a bitterly ironic statement of the various
standard arguments in favor of marriage. It is possible that they are
spoken by January (line 22 being then parenthetical) and constitute
his self-deluded reasons for wanting to marry. Otherwise they are
spoken by the Merchant as a summary of January's reasons, or
indeed those of any idealist or naif. Whether January or the Mer-
chant himself is the speaker, the irony is suddenly dropped in line 148
and the section concluded with the cynical Merchant's true opinion.
(It has sometimes been thought that the lines are not ironical but a
serious statement meant for the Friar or Monk in an earlier version;
but it seems to the present editor impossible to imagine the lines as
anything but ironic in this context.)    33 **it . . . so** it is fitting
35–36 **On . . . sikernesse** on unsafe ("brittle") ground they build, and
they find insecurity when they expect security    43 **buxom** obedient,
humble

She nis not wery him to love and serve,
Though that he lie bedred till he sterve.°
And yet some clerkes sayn it is not so,
50 Of which he Theofrast is one of tho;
What fors though Theofraste liste lie?°
"Ne take no wife," quod he, "for husbondrye
As for to spare in household thy dispence.
A trewe servant doth more diligence
55 Thy good to keepe than thine owne wif,
For she wol claime half part all hir lif.
And if thou be sick, so God me save,
Thy veray freendes or a trewe knave
Wol keep thee bet than she that waiteth ay
60 After thy good,° and hath done many a day.
And if thou take a wife unto thine hold,
Full lightly maistou been a cockewold."
This sentence and an hundred thinges worse
Writeth this man—ther God his bones curse!
65 But take no keep of all swich vanitee—
Defye Theofrast, and herke me:
    A wife is Goddes yifte veraily.
All other manner yiftes hardily,
As landes, rentes, pasture, or commune,°
70 Or moebles,° all been yiftes of Fortune,
That passen as a shadwe upon a wall.
But drede not, if plainly speke I shall,
A wife wol last and in thine house endure
Well lenger than thee list,° paraventure.
75    Marriage is a full greet sacrament.
He which that hath no wife I hold him shent.°
He liveth helpless and all desolat—
I speke of folk in seculer estat.
    And herke why I say not this for nought
80 That woman is for mannes help y-wrought:
The hye God, whan he had Adam maked

48 sterve die   51 What . . . lie? What does it matter if Theophrastus
wanted to lie?   60 After thy good i.e., to inherit your property
69 commune the right to use common lands, like pastures   70 moe-
bles furnishings and any movable property   74 lenger . . . list longer
than you like (note the irony)   76 shent ruined

And saw him all alone, belly-naked,
God of his greete goodness saide than,
"Let us now make an help unto this man
Like to himself." And than he made him Eve.                85
Here may ye see, and hereby may ye preve
That wife is mannes help and his confort,
His paradise terrestre and his disport.
So buxom and so vertuous is she
They moste needes live in unitee:                          90
Oo flesh they been, and oo flesh, as I guesse,
Hath but one hert in wele and in distresse.
   A wife—a, Sainte Mary, *ben'dic'te!*
How might a man han any adversitee
That hath a wife? Certes, I can not saye.                  95
The blisse which that is bitwix hem twaye,
There may no tonge tell or herte thinke.
If he be poor, she helpeth him to swinke.°
She keepeth his good and wasteth neveradeel.
All that hir husband lust hir liketh well.                 100
She saith not ones "Nay" whan he saith "Ye."
"Do this," saith he. "All redy, sir," saith she.
   O blissful ordre of wedlock precious,
Thou art so murry and eek so vertuous,
And so commended and approved eek,                         105
That every man that halt him° worth a leek
Upon his bare knees ought all his lif
Thanken his God that him hath sent a wif,
Or elles pray to God him for to sende
A wife to last unto his lives ende—                        110
For than his life is set in sikernesse,
He may not be deceived, as I guesse,
So that he werk after his wives reed:°
Than may he boldly beren up his heed,
They been so trew and therewithal so wise—                 115
For which, if thou wolt werken as the wise,
Do alway so as women wol thee rede.
Lo how that Jacob, as thise clerkes rede,
By good conseil of his moder Rebekke

98 **swinke** work   106 **halt him** holds (considers) himself   113 **reed**
advice (again, certainly an ironic statement)

120 Bond the kides skin about his necke,
    For which his fadres benison he wan.
    Lo Judith, as the story eek telle can,
    By wise conseil she God's peple kepte,
    And slow him Olofernes while he slepte.
125 Lo Abigail, by good conseil how she
    Saved her husband Nabal whan that he
    Shold han been slain. And look Ester also
    By good conseil delivered out of wo
    The peple of God, and made him Mardochee
130 Of Assuere enhaunced for to be.
        There is nothing in gree superlatif,°
    As saith Senek, above an humble wif.
    Suffer thy wives tonge, as Caton bit.
    She shall command and thou shalt suffren it,
135 And yet she wol obey of curteisye.
        A wife is keeper of thine husbondrye:
    Well may the sicke man biwail and weepe
    Ther as there is no wife the house to keepe.
    I warne thee, if wisely thou wolt wirche,
140 Love well thy wife, as Christ loved his chirche.°
    If thou lovest thyself thou lovest thy wif.
    No man hateth his flesh, but in his lif
    He fostreth it; and therefore bid I thee,
    Cherisse thy wife or thou shalt never thee.°
145 Husband and wife, what so men jape or playe,
    Of worldly folk holden the siker waye.
    They been so knit there may noon harm bitide—
    And namely° upon the wives side.

                    *      *      *


    For which this January of whom I tolde
150 Considered hath inwith his dayes olde
    The lusty life, the vertuous quiete
    That is in marriage honey sweete;

---

131 **in gree superlatif** superior in degree    140 **as . . . chirche** The
mystical marriage between Christ and the Church, based on an
allegorical interpretation of the *Song of Songs*, was a medieval com-
monplace    144 **thee** prosper    148 **namely** especially

And for his freendes on a day he sente
To tellen hem th'effect of his entente.
With face sad this tale he hath hem told:                    155
He saide, "Freendes, I am hoor and old,
And almost, God wot, on my pittes° brinke.
Upon my soule somewhat most I thinke.
I have my body follily dispended—
Blessed be God that it shall been amended!            160
For I wol be, certain, a wedded man,
And that anon, in all the haste I can,
Unto some maide fair and tendre of age.
I pray you shapeth for my marriage
All suddenly, for I wol not abide;°                          165
And I wol fond° t'espyen on my side
To whom I may be wedded hastily.
But for as much as ye been mo than I,
Ye shullen rather swich a thing espyen
Than I, and where me best were to allyen.            170
    But oo thing warn I you, my freendes dere:
I wol noon old wife han in no mannere.
She shall not passe twenty yeer certain!
Old fish and yong flesh wolde I have full fain.
Bet is," quod he, "a pike than a pickerel,°                 175
And bet than old boef is the tender veel.
I wol no woman thrity yeer of age—
It is but bene-straw and greet forage.°
And eek thise olde widows, God is woot,
They kon so muchel craft on Wades boot,°             180
So muchel broken harm° whan that hem leste,
That with hem shold I never live in reste.
For sundry scoles maketh subtil clerkes:°
Woman of many scoles half a clerk is.
But certainly, a yong thing may men gie,°                  185

157 pittes graves   165 abide wait   166 fond try   175 pickerel a
young pike   178 bene-straw . . . forage refuse of bean plants and
coarse dry fodder   180 Wades boot Wade was a hero of Germanic
legend, and traveled by boat; but the reference remains a mystery
181 broken harm to make use of mischief   183 For . . . clerkes Cf.
Wife of Bath's Prologue, line 47; the Merchant has picked up several
echoes of her discourse   185 may men gie men may rule

Right as men may warm wex with handes plye.°
Wherefore I say you plainly in a clause,
I wol noon old wife han right for this cause:
For if so were I hadde swich meschaunce
190  That I in hir ne coud han no plesaunce,
Than shold I lede my life in avoutrye,°
And go straight to the devil whan I die.
Ne children shold I none upon hir geten—
Yet were me lever houndes had me eten
195  Than that mine heritage sholde falle
In straunge hand. And this I tell you alle—
I dote not—I wot the cause why
Men sholde wed, and ferthermore wot I
There speketh many a man of marriage
200  That wot namore of it than wot my page
For whiche causes man should take a wif:
If he ne may not live chaste his lif,
Take him a wife with greet devocioun,
Because of leveful° procreacioun
205  Of children, to th'honour of God above,
And not only for paramour or love;
And for they sholde lechery eschue,
And yeeld hir dette whan that it is due;
Or for that ech of hem sholde helpen other
210  In meschief, as a suster shall the brother,
And live in chastitee full holily
—But sires, by your leve, that am not I.°
For God be thanked, I dare make avaunt,
I feel my limes stark and suffisaunt
215  To do all that a man belongeth to.
I wot myselven best what I may do.
Though I be hoor, I fare as doth a tree
That blossmeth ere the fruit y-woxen be,
And blossmy tree nis neither dry ne deed:
220  I feel me nowhere hoor but on mine heed—
Mine hert and all my limes been as greene

186 wex . . . plye since wax was a traditional figure for fickleness
and instability, the line has a double meaning   191 avoutrye adul-
tery   204 leveful lawful   212 But . . . I Cf. Wife of Bath's Prologue,
line 118

As laurer thurgh the yeer is for to seene.
And sin that ye han herd all mine entente,
I pray you to my will ye wol assente."

Diverse men diversely him tolde                          225
Of marriage many ensamples olde.
Some blamed it, some praised it, certain.
But at the laste, shortly for to sayn,
As alday falleth° altercacioun
Bitwixe freendes in disputisoun,                         230
There fill a strife bitwix his brethren two,
Of which that one was cleped Placebo,
Justinus° soothly called was that other.

Placebo said: "O January, brother,
Full litel need had ye, my lord so dere,                 235
Conseil to ax of any that is here,
But that ye been so full of sapience
That you ne liketh, for your heigh prudence,
To waiven fro the word of Salomon:
This word said he unto us everichon,                     240
'Werk alle thing by conseil,' thus said he,
'And thanne shaltou not repenten thee.'
But though that Salomon spak swich a word,
Mine owne dere brother and my lord,
So wisly God my soule bring at reste,                    245
I hold your owne conseil is the beste.
For brother mine, of me take this motif:°
I have now been a court-man all my lif,
And God it wot, though I unworthy be,
I have stonden in full greet degree                      250
Abouten lordes in full high estat;
Yet had I never with none of hem debat—
I never hem contraried, trewely.
I wot well that my lord kan° more than I;
What that he saith, I hold it ferm and stable—           255
I say the same, or elles thing semblable.
A full greet fool is any conseillour
That serveth any lord of high honour

229 **alday  falleth** continually  occurs  232–33 **Placebo, Justinus**
Placebo means "I will please"—in short, they are the flatterer and
the just man  247 **motif** notion  254 **kan** knows

That dare presume or elles thenken it
260 That his conseil shold pass his lordes wit.
Nay, lordes be no fooles, by my fay.
Ye han yourselven shewed here today
So high sentence so holily and well,
That I consent and conferm everydeel
265 Your wordes all and your opinioun.
By God, there nis no man in all this town
Ne in Itaile coud bet han y-said.
Christ halt him of this conseil well apaid.°
And trewely it is an high corage
270 Of any man that stapen° is in age
To take a yong wife. By my fader kin
Your herte hangeth on a jolly pin!
Doth now in this matter right as you leste,
For, finally, I hold it for the beste."
275     Justinus that ay stille sat and herde,
Right in this wise he to Placebo answerde:
"Now, brother mine, be pacient I praye,
Sin ye han said, and herkneth what I saye.
Senek, amonges other wordes wise,
280 Saith that a man ought him right well avise
To whom he yiveth his land or his catel.°
And sin I ought avisen me right well
To whom I yive my good away fro me,
Well muchel more I ought avised be
285 To whom I yive my body for alway.
I warn you well, it is no childes play
To take a wife withouten avisement.
Men most enquere—this is mine assent°—
Wher she be wise, or sobre, or drunkelewe,°
290 Or proud, or elles otherways a shrewe,
A chidestere,° or wastour of thy good,
Or rich, or poor, or elles mannish wood.°
Al be it so that no man finden shall
None in this world that trotteth whole in all,°

268 **apaid** pleased    270 **stapen** advanced    281 **catel** possessions
288 **assent** opinion    289 **drunkelewe** a drunkard    291 **chidestere**
scold    292 **mannish wood** man-crazy    294 **trotteth . . . all** trots
perfectly in every way (choosing a wife is thus compared to buying
a horse)

Ne man ne beest swich as men coud devise;                    295
But natheless, it ought enough suffise
With any wife, if so were that she hadde
Mo goode thewes° than hir vices badde—
And all this axeth leiser for t'enquere.
For God it wot, I have wept many a tere                    300
Full prively sin that I had a wif:
Praise whoso wol a wedded mannes lif,
Certain I find in it but cost and care,
And observances of all blisses bare.
And yet, God wot, my neighebors aboute,                    305
And namely of women many a route,
Sayn that I have the moste stedfast wif,
And eek the meekest one that bereth lif—
But I wot best where wringeth me my sho.
Ye mowe for me right as you liketh do.                    310
Aviseth you—ye been a man of age—
How that ye entren into marriage,
And namely with a yong wife and a fair.
By him that made water, erth, and air,
The yongest man that is in all this route                    315
Is bisy enough to bringen it aboute
To han his wife alone. Trusteth me,
Ye shull not plesen hir fully yeeres three—
This is to sayn, to doon hir full plesance.
A wife asketh full many an observance.                    320
I pray you that ye be not yvel apaid."°
    "Well," quod this January, "and hastou y-said?
Straw for thy Senek, and for thy proverbes!
I counte not a panier full of herbes
Of schole-termes.° Wiser men than thou,                    325
As thou hast herd, assenteden right now
To my purpose. Placebo, what say ye?"
    "I say it is a cursed man," quod he,
"That letteth° matrimoigne, sikerly."
And with that word they risen suddenly,                    330

298 **thewes** virtues   321 **yvel apaid** displeased, offended   324–25 **I
. . . termes** I wouldn't give a basket of herbs for book-learning
329 **letteth** stands in the way of

And been assented fully that he sholde
Be wedded whan him list and where he wolde.

\*    \*    \*

High fantasy and curious bisinesse
Fro day to day gan in the soul impresse
335  Of January about his marriage.
Many fair shape and many a fair visage
There passeth thurgh his herte night by night:
As whoso took a mirrour polished bright,
And set it in a commune market place,
340  Than shold he see full many a figure pace
By his mirrour; and in the same wise
Gan January inwith his thought devise
Of maidens which that dwelten him beside.°
He wiste not where that he might abide.°
345  For if that one have beautee in hir face,
Another stant so in the peples grace
For hir sadness° and hir benignitee,
That of the peple greetest voice hath she;
And some were rich and hadden badde name.
350  But natheless, bitwix ernest and game,
He atte last appointed him° on oon
And let all other from his herte goon,
And chees hir of his own auctoritee—
For Love is blind alday, and may not see.
355  And whan that he was in his bed y-brought,
He portrayed in his hert and in his thought
Hir freshe beautee and hir age tendre,
Hir middle small, hir armes long and slendre,
Hir wise governance, hir gentilesse,
360  Hir womanly bering and hir sadnesse.
And whan that he on hir was condescended,°
Him thought his choice might not been amended.°
For whan that he himself concluded hadde,
Him thought ech other mannes wit so badde

343 **him biside** near him    344 **where . . . abide** which one to settle on
347 **sadness** gravity, earnestness    351 **appointed him** made up his
mind    361 **condescended** decided    362 **amended** improved upon

That impossible it were to replye                                365
Again his choice—this was his fantasye.
  His freendes sent he to at his instance,
And prayed hem to doon him that plesance
That hastily they wolden to him come.
He wold abredge° hir labour all and some:                        370
Needeth namore for him to go ne ride—
He was appointed ther he wold abide.
  Placebo came and eek his freendes soone,
And alderfirst he bade hem all a boone—
That none of hem none argumentes make                            375
Again the purpose which that he hath take,
Which purpose was plesant to God, said he,
And veray ground of his prosperitee.
He said there was a maiden in the town
Which that of beautee hadde greet renown.                        380
Al were it so she were of small degree,°
Suffiseth him hir youth and hir beautee.
Which maid he said he wold han to his wif,
To lede in ese and holiness his lif,
And thanked God that he might han hir all,                       385
That no wight his blisse parten° shall;
And prayed hem to labouren in this neede,
And shapen° that he faile not to speede—
For than he said his spirit was at ese.
"Than is," quod he, "no thing may me displese.                   390
Save oo thing pricketh in my conscience,
The which I wol reherce in your presence:
I have," quod he, "herd said full yore ago
There may no man han parfit blisses two—
This is to say, in erth and eek in hevene.                       395
For though he keep him fro the sinnes sevene,°
And eek from every branch of thilke tree,
Yet is there so parfit felicitee
And so greet ese and lust in marriage,
That ever I am aghast° now in mine age                           400
That I shall lede now so murry a lif,
So delicate, withouten woe and strif,

370 **abredge** shorten   381 **small degree** a lower social class   386
**parten** share   388 **shapen** arrange   396 **sinnes sevene** seven deadly
sins   400 **aghast** afraid

That I shall han mine heven in erthe here.
For sith that veray heven is bought so dere
405 With tribulacioun and greet penance,
How shold I than, that live in swich plesance
As alle wedded men doon with hir wives,
Come to the bliss ther Christ etern on live is?
This is my drede. And ye, my brethren twaye,
410 Assoileth me° this question, I praye."
   Justinus, which that hated his follye,
Answered anonright in his japerye.°
And for he wold his longe tale abredge,
He wolde noon auctoritee alledge
415 But saide, "Sir, so there be noon obstacle
Other than this, God of his high miracle
And of his mercy may so for you werche
That ere ye have your right of holy cherche,°
Ye may repent of wedded mannes lif
420 In which ye sayn there is no woe ne strif.
And elles God forbede but he sente
A wedded man him grace to repente
Well ofte rather than a single man.
And therefore, sir, the beste reed I kan:
425 Despair you not, but have in your memorye,
Paraunter she may be your purgatorye—
She may be Goddes mene° and Goddes whippe!
Than shall your soule up to heven skippe
Swifter than doth an arrwe out of a bowe!
430 I hope to God hereafter shull ye knowe
That there nis noon so greet felicitee
In marriage, ne never mo shall be,
That you shall let of° your salvacioun—
So that ye use, as skile is and resoun,°
435 The lustes of your wife attemprely,

<hr>

410 **Assoileth me** clear up for me   412 **japerye** mockery, irony.
Justinus' deft irony reflects the harsher irony of the Merchant him-
self. In line 441, for example, the Merchant has Justinus cite the
Wife of Bath as if she were one of the great "auctoritees" on mar-
riage!   418 **ere . . . cherche** before you get the last rites of the
Church   427 **mene** instrument   433 **you . . . of** will keep you from
434 **skile . . . resoun** proper and reasonable

And that ye plese hir not too amorously,
And that ye keep you eek from other sinne.
My tale is done, for my wit is thinne.
Beth not aghast hereof, my brother dere,
But let us waden out of this mattere.                      440
The Wife of Bath, if ye han understande,
Of marriage which we have on hande
Declared hath full well in litel space.
Fareth now well. God have you in his grace."
    And with that word this Justin and his brother    445
Han take hir leeve and ech of hem of other.
For whan they saw that it most needes be,
They wroughten so by sly and wise tretee
That she, this maiden—which that Mayus highte—
As hastily as ever that she mighte,                       450
Shall wedded be unto this Januarye.


                    *     *     *


    I trow it were too longe you to tarrye
If I you told of every scrit° and bond
By which that she was feffed in° his lond;
Or for to herknen of hir rich array.                      455
    But finally y-comen is the day
That to the chirche bothe be they went
For to receive the holy sacrament.
Forth comth the preest with stole about his necke,
And bade hir be like Sarah and Rebekke                    460
In wisdom and in truth of marriage,
And said his orisons as is usage,
And croucheth hem,° and bade God shold hem blesse,
And made all siker enough with holinesse.
    Thus been they wedded with solempnitee.               465
And at the feeste sitteth he and she
With other worthy folk upon the dais.
All full of joy and bliss is the palais,
And full of instruments and of vitaille,
The moste daintevous° of all Itaile.                      470

453 **scrit** deed   454 **feffed in** made heir to   463 **croucheth hem**
made the sign of the Cross over them   470 **daintevous** delicate

Biforn hem stoode instruments of swich soun
That Orpheus, ne of Thebes Amphioun,
Ne maden never swich a melodye.
At every course than came loud minstralcye,
475 That never trumped Joab for to heere,
Ne he Theodamas yet half so clere
At Thebes whan the citee was in doute.
Bacchus the wine hem shenketh° all aboute,
And Venus laugheth upon every wight:
480 For Januarye was become hir knight,
And wolde both assayen his corage°
In liberte° and eek in marriage—
And with hir firebrand in hir hand aboute
Dauuceth before the bride and all the route.
485 And certainly, I dare right well say this:
Ymeneus,° that god of wedding is,
Saw never his life so murry a wedded man!
Hold thou thy pees, thou poet Marcian,
That writest us that ilke wedding murrye
490 Of hir Philology and him Mercurye,
And of the songes that the Muses songe:
Too small is both thy pen and eek thy tonge
For to descriven of *this* marriage!
Whan tender youth hath wedded stouping age,
495 There is swich mirth that it may not be written.
Assayeth it yourself, than may ye witen
If that I lie or noon in this mattere.
   Mayus, that sit with so benign a cheere
Hir to behold it seemed faïrye—
500 Queen Ester looked never with swich an eye
On Assuer, so meek a look hath she.
I may you not devise all hir beautee,
But thus much of hir beautee tell I may,
That she was like the brighte morrwe of May,
505 Fulfill'd of alle beautee and plesaunce!
This January is ravished in a traunce
At every time he looked on hir face!

478 **shenketh** pours    481 **assayen . . . corage** try out his powers
482 **liberte** single life    486 **Ymeneus** Hymen

But in his hert he gan hir to manace°
That he that night in armes wold hir straine
Harder than ever Paris did Elaine.                                510
But natheless yet had he greet pitee
That thilke night offenden hir most he,
And thought, "Alas, O tender creature,
Now wolde God ye mighte well endure
All my corage, it is so sharp and keene.                          515
I am aghast ye shull it not sustene;
But God forbed that I did all my might!
Now wolde God that it were woxen night,
And that the night wold lasten evermo!
I wold that all this peple were ago."                             520
And finally he doth all his labour,
As he best mighte, saving his honour,
To haste hem fro the mete° in subtil wise.
The time came that reson was to rise,
And after that men daunce and drinken faste,                      525
And spices all about the house they caste.
And full of joy and bliss is every man.
—All but a squier highte Damian,
Which carf biforn the knight full many a day:
He was so ravished on° his lady May                               530
That for the veray pain he was ny wood;°
Almost he swelt and swouned ther he stood,
So sore hath Venus hurt him with hir brond,
As that she bare it dauncing in hir hond.
And to his bed he went him hastily.                               535
Namore of him at this time speke I,
But there I let him weep enough and plaine—
Till freshe May wol rewen° on his paine.
   O perilous fire that in the bedstraw breedeth!
O familier foe that his service bedeth!°                          540
O servant traitour, false homely hewe,
Like to the neddre° in bosom, sly, untrewe!
God shild us alle from your acquaintance!

_____

508 **manace** threaten   523 **mete** feast   530 **ravished on** enamored of
531 **ny wood** nearly mad   538 **rewen** have pity   540 **bedeth** offers
542 **neddre** adder

O January, drunken in plesance
545 In marriage, see how thy Damian,
Thine owne squier and thy borne man,°
Entendeth for to do thee villainye!
God grante thee thine homely° foe t'espye,
For in this world nis worse pestilence
550 Than homely foe alday in thy presence!
    Parfourmed hath the sun his ark diurne—
No lenger may the body of him sojourne
On th'orisont° as in that latitude.
Night with his mantle that is derk and rude
555 Gan overspred the hemispery aboute,
For which departed is this lusty route,°
Fro January with thank on every side.
Home to hir houses lustily they ride,
Where as they doon hir thinges as hem leste,
560 And whan they saw hir time, go to reste.
Soon after that this hastif Januarye
Wol go to bed—he wol no lenger tarrye.
He drinketh ipocras, claree, and vernage,
Of spices hot t'encreesen his corage,
565 And many a letuary° had he full fin,
Swich as the cursed monk Daun Constantin
Hath written in his book *De Coitu*.
To eten hem all he nas no thing eschu.°
And to his privee freendes thus said he:
570 "For Goddes love, as soon as it may be,
Let voiden all this house in curteis wise."
And they han done right as he wol devise:
Men drinken, and the travers° draw anon;
The bride was brought abed as still as ston;
575 And whan the bed was with the preest y-blessed,
Out of the chambre hath every wight him dressed.
And January hath fast in armes take
His freshe May, his paradise, his make:°
He lulleth hir, he kisseth hir full ofte—
580 With thicke bristles of his beerd unsofte,

546 **borne man** vassal from birth   548 **homely** domestic   553 **orisont** horizon   556 **route** company   565 **letuary** medicinal syrup   568 **eschu** hesitant   573 **travers** curtain around the bed   578 **make** mate

Like to the skin of houndfish, sharp as brere°
(For he was shave all new in his mannere)
He rubbeth hir about hir tender face,
And saide thus, "Alas, I mot trespace
To you, my spouse, and you greetly offende          585
Ere time come that I wol down descende!
But natheless, considereth this," quod he,
"There nis no werkman, whatsoever he be,
That may both werke well and hastily.
This wol be done at leiser parfitly.          590
It is no fors° how longe that we playe:
In trewe wedlock coupled be we twaye,
And blessed be the yoke that we been inne!
For in actes we mow do no sinne:
A man may do no sinne with his wif,          595
Ne hurt himselven with his owen knif,
For we han leve to play us by the lawe."
Thus laboureth he till that the day gan dawe;
And than he taketh a sop in fine claree,°
And upright in his bed than sitteth he,          600
And after that he sung full loud and clere
And kissed his wife and made wanton cheere.
He was all coltish, full of ragerye,°
And full of jargon as a flecked pie:°
The slacke skin about his necke shaketh          605
While that he sung, so chaunteth he and cracketh.
—But God wot what that May thought in hir herte
Whan she him saw up-sitting in his sherte,
In his night-cap and with his necke lene;
She praiseth not his playing worth a bene.          610
Than said he thus: "My reste wol I take.
Now day is come. I may no lenger wake,"
And down he laid his heed and sleep till prime.
And afterward, whan that he saw his time,
Up riseth January. But freshe May          615
Held hir chambre unto the fourthe day,

581 **brere** briars—being lately shaven, his beard is bristly    591 **no fors** no matter    599 **sop . . . claree** cake soaked in wine—a usual breakfast of nobles    603 **ragerye** wantonness    604 **jargon . . . pie** chitter-chatter as a spotted magpie

As usage is of wives for the beste.
For every labour some time mot han reste,
Or elles longe may he not endure—
620 This is to sayn, no lives° creature—
Be it of fish or brid or beest or man.

*     *     *

Now wol I speke of woeful Damian
That languisheth for love, as ye shall heere.
Therefore I speke to him in this mannere:
625 I say, "O sely Damian, alas,
Answer to my demand as in this cas:
How shaltou to thy lady freshe May
Telle thy woe? She wol alway say nay.
Eek if thou speke, she wol thy woe biwraye.°
630 God be thine help, I can no better saye."
    This sicke Damian in Venus' fir
So brenneth that he dieth for desir,
For which he put his life in aventure.
No lenger might he in this wise endure,
635 But prively a penner° gan he borrwe,
And in a letter wrote he all his sorrwe,
In manner of a complaint or a lay
Unto his faire freshe lady May.
And in a purse of silk heng on his sherte
640 He hath it put and laid it at his herte.
    The moone, that at noon was thilke day
That January hath wedded freshe May
In two° of Taur, was into Cancer gliden—
So long hath Mayus in hir chambre abiden,
645 As custom is unto thise nobles alle:
A bride shall not eten in the halle
Til dayes four, or three days atte leste,
Y-passed been—than let hir go to feeste.
The fourthe day complet fro noon to noon,
650 Whan that the heighe masse was y-doon,
In halle sit this January and May,

620 **lives** living    629 **biwraye** reveal    635 **penner** pen-case    643 **two**
two degrees

As fresh as is the brighte summer's day.
And so bifell how that this goode man
Remembred him upon this Damian,
And saide, "Sainte Mary! how may this be          *655*
That Damian entendeth not to me?°
Is he ay sick, or how may this betide?"
His squiers which that stooden there beside
Excused him by cause of his sicknesse,
Which letted him to doon his bisinesse—           *660*
Noon other cause mighte make him tarrye.
"That me forthinketh,"° quod this Januarye.
"He is a gentil squier, by my truthe.
If that he deid, it were harm and ruthe.
He is as wise, discreet, and eek secree            *665*
As any man I wot of his degree,
And thereto manly and eek servisable,
And for to be a thrifty man right able.
But after mete as soon as ever I may,
I wol myself visit him, and eek May,               *670*
To do him all the comfort that I can."
And for that word him blessed every man
That of his bountee and his gentilesse
He wolde so comforten in sicknesse
His squier, for it was a gentil deede.             *675*
    "Dame," quod this January, "take good heede,
At after-mete ye with your women alle,
Whan ye han been in chambre out of this halle,
That all ye go to see this Damian.
Doth him disport—he is a gentil man;               *680*
And telleth him that I wol him visite,
Have I no thing but rested me a lite;
And speed you faste, for I wol abide
Till that ye sleepe faste by my side"—
And, with that word, he gan to him to calle        *685*
A squier that was marshall of his halle,
And told him certain thinges what he wolde.
    This freshe May hath straight hir way y-holde
With all hir women unto Damian.

656 **entendeth . . . me** does not attend upon me    663 **me forthinketh**
I regret

690  Down by his beddes side sit she than,
     Comforting him as goodly as she may.
     This Damian, whan that his time he sey,
     In secree wise his purse and eek his bille,°
     In which that he y-written had his wille,
695  Hath put into hir hand withouten more—
     Save that he siketh wonder deep and sore
     And softely to hir right thus said he:
     "Mercy! and that ye not discover me;
     For I am deed if that this thing be kid."°
700  This purse hath she inwith hir bosom hid
     And went hir way—ye get namore of me.
     But unto January y-comen is she,
     That on his beddes side sit full softe,
     And taketh hir, and kisseth hir full ofte—
705  And laid him down to sleep and that anon.
     She feined hir as that she moste gon
     There as ye wot that every wight mot neede—
     And whan she of this bill hath taken heede,
     She rent it all to cloutes° at the laste,
710  And in the privee softely it caste.
          Who studieth° now but faire freshe May?
     Adown by olde January she lay,
     That sleep—till that the cough hath him awaked;
     Anon he prayed hir strepen hir all naked—
715  He wold of hir, he said, han some plesaunce;
     He said hir clothes did him encombraunce;
     And she obeyeth, be hir lief or loth.
     But lest that precious° folk be with me wroth,
     ·How that he wrought I dare not to you telle—
720  Or whether hir thought it paradise or helle.
     But here I let hem werken in hir wise
     Till evensong rung, and that they most arise.
          Were it by destinee or aventure,
     Were it by influence, or by nature,
725  Or constellacion, that in swich estat
     The heven stood that time fortunat

693 **bille** letter   699 **kid** known   709 **cloutes** shreds   711 **studieth**
thinks things over   718 **precious** prudish

As for to put a bill of° Venus' werkes
(For alle thing hath time, as sayn thise clerkes)
To any woman for to get hir love,
I can not say. But greete God above,                             730
That knoweth that noon act is causeless,
He deem° of all, for I wol hold my pees.
But sooth is *this:* how that the freshe May
Hath take swich impression that day
Of pitee on this sicke Damian                                    735
That from hir herte she ne drive can
The remembrance for to doon him ese!
"Certain," thought she, "whom that this thing displese,
I rekke not. For here I him assure
To love him best of any creature,                                740
Though he namore hadde than his sherte."
Lo, pitee renneth soon in gentil herte!
—Here may ye see how excellent franchise°
In women is whan they hem narrwe avise.°
Some tyrant is, as there be many oon,                            745
That hath an hert as hard as any ston,
Which wold han let him sterven° in the place
Well rather than han graunted him hir grace—
And hem rejoisen in hir cruel pride,
And rekke not to been an homicide.                               750
   This gentil May, fulfilled of pitee,
Right of hir hand a letter maked she,
In which she graunteth him hir veray grace—
There lacketh nought, only but day and place
Where that she might unto his lust suffise;                      755
For it shall be right as he wol devise.
And whan she saw hir time upon a day,
To visite this Damian goth May,
And subtilly this letter down she threste
Under his pillow—rede it if him leste.                           760
She taketh him by the hand and hard him twiste,°
So secreely that no wight of it wiste,

727 **put ... of** make a plea for   732 **deem** let Him judge   743 **franchise** liberality   744 **hem . . . avise** think things over carefully   747 **sterven** die   761 **twiste** squeezed

And bade him be all hoole and forth she wente
To January, whan that he for hir sente.
765   Up riseth Damian the nexte morrwe—
All passed was his sickness and his sorrwe.
He cembeth him, he preineth him and picketh,°
And doth all that his lady lust and liketh.
And eek to January he goth as lowe
770  As ever did a dogge for the bowe.°
He is so plesant unto every man
(For craft is all, whoso that do it can)
That every wight is fain to speke him good;
And fully in his lady grace he stood.
775  Thus let I Damian about his neede,
And in my tale forth I wol proceede.

\*      \*      \*

Some clerkes holden that felicitee
Stant in delit,° and therefore certain, he,
This noble January, with all his might
780  In honest wise as longeth to a knight,
Shop him to live full deliciously.
His housing, his array as honestly
To his degree was maked as a kinges.
Amonges other of his honest thinges,
785  He made a garden walled all of ston°—
So fair a garden wot I nowhere non.
For out of doute I veraily suppose
That he that wrote *The Romance of the Rose*
Ne coud of it the beautee well devise;
790  Ne Priapus° ne mighte not suffise,
Though he be god of gardens, for to telle

767 **cembeth . . . picketh** combs his hair, tidies himself up, and puts
on the finishing touches   769–70 **goth . . . bowe** bows as low as ever
a hunting-dog did   778 **Stant in delit** depends upon pleasure   785
**garden . . . ston** the "enclosed garden" described here has a very
ancient tradition, based upon allegorical interpretation of the *Song
of Songs*. It thus suggests the Garden of Eden and the Fall of Man,
the marriage between Christ and His Church, the Virgin, the soul's
union with God; its function here, needless to say, is ironic. On the
background see Stanley N. Stewart, *The Enclosed Garden*. And cf.
lines 894–906   790 **Priapus** fertility god

The beautee of the garden, and the welle
That stood under a laurer alway greene.
Full ofte time he Pluto and his queene
Proserpina and all hir faïrye                              795
Disporten hem and maken melodye
About that well, and daunced, as men tolde.
This noble knight, this January the olde,
Swich daintee° hath in it to walk and playe
That he wol no wight suffer bere the keye,        800
Save he himself: for of the smalle wicket°
He bare alway of silver a clicket,°
With which, whan that him lest, he it unshette.
And whan he wolde pay his wife hir dette
In summer seson, thider wold he go,                805
And May his wife, and no wight but they two.
And thinges which that were not done abedde,
He in the garden parfourmed hem and spedde.
And in this wise many a murry day
Lived this January and freshe May.                  810
But worldly joye may not alway dure
To January, ne to no creature.
—O sudden hap! O thou Fortune unstable,
Like to the scorpion so deceivable,°
That flatterest with thine heed whan thou wold stinge,  815
Thy tail is deeth thurgh thine enveniminge!
O brottel joy! O sweete venim quainte!
O monster, that so subtilly canst painte
Thy yiftes under hew of stedfastnesse,
That thou deceivest bothe more and lesse!        820
Why hastou January thus deceived,
That haddest him for thy full freend received?
And now, thou hast biraft him both his eyen;
For sorrwe of which desireth he to dien.
    Alas! this noble January free,                       825
Amid his lust and his prosperitee,
Is woxen blind, and that all suddenly.
He weepeth and he waileth pitously—
And therewithal the fire of jalousye,

799 **daintee** delight   801 **wicket** gate   802 **clicket** key   814 **deceivable** deceitful

830   Lest that his wife shold fall in some follye,
      So brent his herte that he wolde fain
      That some man bothe hir and him had slain.
      For neither after his deeth ne in his lif,
      Ne wold he that she were love ne wif,
835   But ever live as widwe in clothes blacke,
      Sole as the turtle° that hath lost hir make.
      But atte last, after a month or twaye,
      His sorrow gan assuage, sooth to saye:
      For whan he wist it may noon other be,
840   He paciently took his adversitee,
      Save, out of doute, he may not forgoon
      That he nas jalous evermore in oon.°
      Which jalousy it was so outrageous
      That neither in hall ne in noon other hous,
845   Ne in noon other place neverthemo,
      He nolde suffre hir for to ride or go,
      But if that he had hand on hir alway.
      For which full ofte weepeth freshe May,
      That loveth Damian so benignely
850   That she mot outher dien suddenly
      Or elles she mot han him as hir leste.
      She waiteth whan° hir herte wolde breste.
         Upon that other side Damian
      Becomen is the sorrwefulest man
855   That ever was; for neither night ne day
      Ne might he speke a word to freshe May,
      As to his purpose of no swich mattere,
      But if that January most it heere,
      That had an hand upon hir evermo.
860   But natheless, by writing to and fro,
      And privee signes, wiste he what she mente;
      And she knew eek the fine° of his entente.
      —O January! what might it thee availe
      Though thou mightest see as fer as shippes saile?
865   For as good is blind deceived be,
      As to be deceived whan a man may see.
      Lo Argus, which that had an hundred eyen,

836 **Sole . . . turtle** solitary as the turtledove   842 **evermore in oon**
constantly   852 **waiteth whan** expects that   862 **fine** aim

For al that ever he coude pour or pryen
Yet was he blent°—and God wot so been mo
That weenen wisly° that it be not so.                                    870
Pass over is an ese°—I say namore.

    This freshe May that I spak of so yore,
In warm wex hath emprinted the clicket
That January bare of the small wicket,
By which into his garden oft he wente.                                   875
And Damian that knew all hir entente
The clicket countrefeted prively.
There nis namore to say, but hastily
Some wonder by this clicket shall bitide,
Which ye shall heeren if ye wol abide.                                   880

    O noble Ovid! sooth saistou, God woot,
What sleight it is, though it be long and hot,
That he nil find it out in some mannere!
By Pyramus and Thisbe may men lere:
Though they were kept full longe strait overall,                        885
They been accorded rouning° thurgh a wall,
Ther no wight coud han found out swich a sleighte.

    But now to purpose: ere that dayes eighte
Were passed, ere the month of Juil, bifille
That January hath caught so greet a wille,                               890
Thurgh egging of his wife, him for to playe
In his garden, and no wight but they twaye,
That in a morrwe unto his May saith he:
"Rise up, my wife, my love, my lady free—
The turtles voice is herd, my dove sweete!                              895
The winter is gone with all his raines wete.
Come forth now with thine eyen columbin.
How fairer been thy brestes than is win!
The garden is enclosed all aboute:
Come forth, my white spouse, out of doute,                              900
Thou hast me wounded in mine hert! O wif,
No spot of thee ne knew I all my lif!
Come forth and let us taken our disport;

---

869 **blent** deceived   870 **weenen wisly** imagine for sure   871 **Pass . . . ese** closing your eyes to something is a convenience—i.e., what you don't know won't hurt you   886 **been . . . rouning** came to an agreement by whispering

        I chees thee for my wife and my comfort."°
905  —Swich olde lewed wordes used he.
        On Damian a signe made she
     That he sholde go biforn with his clicket.
     This Damian than hath opened the wicket,
     And in he stert, and that in swich mannere
910  That no wight might it see neither y-heere.
     And still he sit under a bush anon.
        This January, as blind as is a ston,
     With Mayus in his hand and no wight mo,
     Into his freshe garden is ago,
915  And clapte to° the wicket suddenly.
     "Now wife," quod he, "here nis but thou and I,
     That art the creature that I best love.
     For by that Lord that sit in heven above,
     Lever ich° had to dien on a knif
920  Than thee offende, trewe dere wif.
     For Goddes sake, thenk how I thee chees,
     Not for no coveitise, douteless,
     But only for the love I had to thee.
     And though that I be old and may not see,
925  Beth to me trew, and I wol tell you why.
     Three thinges, certes, shall ye win thereby:
     First, love of Christ; and to yourself honour;
     And all mine heritage, town and tower,
     I yive it you—maketh chartres° as you leste.
930  This shall be done tomorrwe ere sunne reste,
     So wisly God my soule bring in blisse.
     I pray you first in covenant ye me kisse.
     And though that I be jalous, wite° me nought:
     Ye been so deep emprinted in my thought,
935  That whan that I consider your beautee,
     And therewithal th'unlikely eld of me,
     I may not, certes, though I sholde die,
     Forbere to been out of your compaignye
     For veray love; this is withouten doute.

     894–904 Rise up . . . comfort January's words here are made up
     almost entirely of quotes from the *Song of Songs;* cf. line 785 and
     note   915 clapte to shut   919 Lever ich I'd rather   929 chartres
     deeds   933 wite blame

Now kiss me, wife, and let us rome aboute."                    *940*
    This freshe May, whan she thise wordes herde,
Benignely to January answerde—
But first and forward she began to weepe:
"I have," quod she, "a soule for to keepe
As well as ye, and also mine honour;                    *945*
And of my wifehood thilke tender flower
Which that I have assured in your hond
Whan that the preest to you my body bond.
Wherefore I wol answer in this mannere,
By the leve of you,° my lord so dere:                    *950*
I pray to God that never dawe the day
That I ne sterve as foul° as woman may
If ever I do unto my kin that shame,
Or elles I empaire so my name
That I be false. And if I do that lacke,                    *955*
Do strepe me, and put me in a sacke,
And in the nexte river do me drenche.
I am a gentil woman, and no wenche!
Why speke ye thus? But men been ever untrewe,
And women have repreve of you ay newe!°                    *960*
Ye han noon other countenance,° I leve,
But speke to us of untrust and repreve!"
—And with that word she saw where Damian
Sat in the bush, and coughen she began,
And with hir finger signes made she                    *965*
That Damian shold climb upon a tree
That charged was with fruit, and up he wente;
For verailly he knew all hir entente
And every signe that she coude make
Well bet than January, hir owne make;                    *970*
For in a letter she had told him all
Of this mattere, how he werken shall.
And thus I let him sit upon the pirye,°
And January and May rominge mirrye.
    Bright was the day and blew the firmament.                    *975*
Phebus hath of gold his streemes down sent

---

950 **By . . . you** i.e., "by your leave"   952 **foul** dreadfully   960 **re-**
**preve . . . newe** reproof from you over and over   961 **countenance**
constant habit   973 **pirye** pear tree

To gladden every flower with his warmnesse.
He was that time in Geminis, as I guesse,
But litel fro his declinacioun
980 Of Cancer, Joves exaltacioun.
And so befell that brighte morrwetide
That in that garden, in the ferther side,
Pluto, that is king of faïrye,
And many a lady in his compaignye,
985 Following his wife, the queene Proserpina—
Which that he ravished out of Etna
While that she gadred flowres in the mede
(In Claudian ye may the stories rede
How in his grisly carte he hir fette)
990 This king of fairy than adown him sette
Upon a bench of turves° fresh and greene,
And right anon thus said he to his queene:
"My wife," quod he, "there may no wight say nay:
Th'experience so preveth every day
995 The treson which that woman doth to man.
Ten hundred thousand tales tell I can
Notable of your untruth and brotelnesse.°
O Salomon, wise and richest of richesse,
Fulfill'd of sapience and of worldly glorye,
1000 Full worthy been thy wordes to memorye
To every wight that wit and reson kan:
Thus praiseth he yet the bountee of man:
'Amonges a thousand men yet foond I oon,
But of women alle foond I noon'—
1005 Thus saith the king that knoweth your wickednesse.
And Jesus *filius Syrak,*° as I guesse,
Ne speketh of you but selde reverence;
A wilde fire and corrupt pestilence
So fall upon your bodies yet tonight!
1010 Ne see ye not this honourable knight?
By cause, alas, that he is blind and old,
His owne man shall make him cokewold!
Lo where he sit, the lechour in the tree!

991 **bench of turves** presumably a terrace or mound fashioned in the
turf   997 **brotelnesse** instability   1006 **Jesus filius Syrak** presumed
author of *Ecclesiasticus*

Now wol I graunten of my majestee
Unto this olde, blinde, worthy knight                    1015
That he shall have ayain his eyen sight,
Whan that his wife wold doon him villainye.
Than shall he knowen all hir harlotrye,
Both in repreve of hir and other mo."
    "Ye shall?" quod Proserpine. "Wol ye so?          1020
Now by my modre's sire's soul I swere
That I shall yiven hir suffisant answere!
And alle women after for hir sake,
That though they be in any guilt y-take,
With face bold they shull hemself excuse,            1025
And bere hem down that wolde hem accuse—
For lack of answer none of hem shall dien!
All had men seen a thing with both his eyen,
Yet shall we women visage it hardily,°
And weep, and swere, and chide subtilly,             1030
So that ye men shull been as lewed° as gees.
What rekketh me of your auctoritees?
I wot well that this Jew, this Salomon,
Found of us women fooles many oon.
But though that he ne found no good woman,           1035
Yet hath there founde many another man
Women full trew, full good and vertuous.
Witness on hem that dwell in Christes hous:
With martyrdom they preved hir constaunce.
The Romain geests eek maken remembraunce            1040
Of many a veray, trewe wife also.
But sir, ne be not wroth, al be it so,
Though that he said he found no good woman;
I pray you, take the sentence of the man—
He mente thus: that in sovereign bountee             1045
Nis none but God, but neither he ne she.°
—Ey, for veray God that nis but oon,
What make ye so much of Salomon?
What though he made a temple, Goddes hous?
What though he were rich and glorious?               1050
So made he eek a temple of false goddes!

1029 **visage it hardily** boldly stare it in the face    1031 **lewed** foolish
1046 **he ne she** man nor woman

How might he do a thing that more forbode° is?
Pardee, as fair as ye his name emplastre,°
He was a lechour and an idolastre,°
1055 And in his eld he veray God forsook.
And if God ne had, as saith the book,
Y-spared him for his fadres sake, he sholde
Have lost his regne rather° than he wolde.
I set right nought, of all the villainye
1060 That ye of women write, a butterflye.
I am a woman: needes mot I speke,
Or elles swelle till mine herte breke.
For sithen he said that we been jangleresses,
As ever hoole I mote brouk my tresses,°
1065 I shall not spare for no curteisye
To speke him harm that wold us villainye."
     "Dame," quod this Pluto, "be no lenger wroth.
I yive it up. But sith I swore mine ooth
That I wold graunten him his sight again,
1070 My word shall stand, I warne you certain.
I am a king; it sit me not to lie."
     "And I," quod she, "a queen of faïrye.
Hir answer shall she have, I undertake.
Let us namore wordes hereof make.
1075 Forsooth, I wol no lenger you contrarye."
     Now let us turn again to Januarye
That in the garden with his faire May
Singeth full murrier than the papejay,
*You love I best, and shall, and other noon* . . .
1080 So long about the alleys° is he goon
Til he was come againes thilke pirye,°
Where as this Damian sitteth full mirrye
On high among the freshe leeves greene.
This freshe May, that is so bright and sheene,
1085 Gan for to sike° and said, "Alas, my side!
Now sir," quod she, "for aught that may bitide,

1052 **forbode** forbidden   1053 **emplastre** whitewash   1054 **idolastre**
idolater   1058 **rather** sooner   1064 **As . . . tresses** as sure as I ex-
pect to keep my hair (the point being that women do not go bald).
Note that she has herself the skill of giving a sufficient answer, with
which she proposes to endow the female race   1080 **alleys** paths
1081 **pirye** pear tree   1085 **sike** sigh

I most han of the peres that I see,
Or I mot die—so sore longeth me
To eten of the smalle peres greene.
Help, for hir love that is of hevene queene!          *1090*
I tell you well, a woman in my plit°
May han to fruit so greet an appetit
That she may dien but she of it have."
    "Alas!" quod he, "that I ne had here a knave
That coude climb! Alas, alas!" quod he,                *1095*
"For I am blind!" "Ye, sir, no fors," quod she,
"But wold ye vouche sauf, for Goddes sake,
The pirye inwith your armes for to take—
For well I wot that ye mistruste me;
Than shold I climbe well enough," quod she,           *1100*
"So I my foot might set upon your back."
    "Certes," quod he, "thereon shall be no lack,
Might I you helpen with mine herte blood."
He stoupeth down, and on his back she stood,
And caught hir by a twist,° and up she goth—           *1105*
Ladies, I pray you that ye be not wroth;
I can not glose,° I am a rude man—
And suddenly anon this Damian
Gan  pullen up the smock—and in he throng.°
    And whan that Pluto saw this greete wrong,          *1110*
To January he yaf again his sighte,
And made him see as well as ever he mighte.
And whan that he had caught his sight again,
Ne was there never man of thing so fain:
But on his wife his thought was evermo.                *1115*
Up to the tree he cast his eyen two,
And saw that Damian his wife had dressed
In swich manner it may not been expressed,
But if I wolde speke uncurteisly;
And up he yaf a roring and a cry                       *1120*
As doth the moder whan the child shall die—
"Out! Help! Alas! Harrow!" he gan to crye,
"O stronge lady store!° what dostou!"

1091 **plit** condition, i.e., pregnant   1105 **And . . . twist** pulled herself
on a branch   1107 **glose** talk around it, be euphemistic   1109 **throng**
shoved   1123 **O . . . store** Oh, shameless, shocking lady!

And she answerde, "Sir, what aileth you?
1125 Have pacience and reson in your minde.
I have you holp on both your eyen blinde.
Up peril of my soul, I shall not lien,
As me was taught, to hele with your eyen°
Was no thing bet to make you to see
1130 Than struggle with a man upon a tree.
God wot I did it in full good entente."
      "Struggle!" quod he. "Ye! algate in° it wente!
God yive you both on shames deeth to dien!
He swived° thee! I saw it with mine eyen,
1135 And elles be I hanged by the hals."°
      "Than is," quod she, "my medicine fals!
For certainly, if that ye mighte see,
Ye wold not sayn thise wordes unto me.
Ye han some glimsing,° and no parfit sighte."
1140      "I see," quod he, "as well as ever I mighte,
Thanked be God, with both mine eyen two;
And by my truth, me *thought*° he did thee so."
      "Ye maze,° maze, goode sir," quod she.
"This thank have I for I have made you see!
1145 Alas!" quod she, "that ever I was so kinde!"
      "Now dame," quod he, "let all pass out of minde.
Come down, my lief; and if I have missaid,
God help me so as I am yvel apaid.°
But by my fader soul, I *wende* have seen
1150 How that this Damian had by thee lain
And that thy smock had lain upon his brest."
      "Ye, sir," quod she, "ye may *ween* as you lest!
But sir, a man that waketh out of his sleep
He may not suddenly well taken keep
1155 Upon a thing, ne seen it parfitly
Till that he be adawed° veraily.
Right so a man that long hath blind y-be
Ne may not suddenly so well y-see,

1128 hele . . . eyen heal your eyes with   1132 algate in right in
1134 swived was laying   1135 hals neck   1139 glimsing glimpsing,
partial vision   1142 me thought it seemed to me. Compare this asser-
tion with "I saw it" (line 1134) and "I wende" (imagined, supposed,
line 1149). The progression comes to rest at line 1152   1143 Ye
maze you're confused   1148 yvel apaid sorry   1156 adawed con-
scious

First whan his sight is newe come again,
As he that hath a day or two y-seen.                    *1160*
Till that your sight y-sattled° be a while,
There may full many a sighte you beguile.
Beth ware, I pray you! For, by hevene king,
Full many a man weeneth to see a thing
And it is all another than it seemeth.                    *1165*
He that misconceiveth, he misdeemeth"°—
And with that word she leep down fro the tree.
    This January, who is glad but he?
He kisseth hir and clippeth hir full ofte,
And on hir womb he stroketh hir full softe,                    *1170*
And to his palais home he hath hir lad.
Now, goode men, I pray you to be glad.
Thus endeth here my tale of Januarye.
God bless us and his moder, Sainte Marye.

1161 **y-sattled** settled    1166 **misdeemeth** misjudges

# THE FRANKLIN ADDRESSES
# THE SQUIRE

"In faith, Squier, thou hast thee well y-quit°
And gentilly: I praise well thy wit,"
Quod the Franklain. "Considering thy youthe,
So feelingly thou spekest, sir, I allow° thee.
5  As to my doom,° there is none that is heer
Of eloquence that shall be thy peer,
If that thou live—God yeve thee good chaunce!°
And in vertu send thee continuance,
For of thy speech I have greet daintee.°
10  I have a son; and by the Trinitee
I had lever° than twenty pound worth land,°
Though it right now were fallen in mine hand,
He were a man of swich discrecioun°
As that *ye* been. Fy on possessioun
15  But if° a man be vertuous withall!
I have my sone snibbed,° and yet shall,
For he to vertu listeth not entende;°
But for to play at dees° and to dispende°
And lese° all that he hath is his usage.°
20  And he hath lever talken with a page
Than to commune with any gentil wight,
Where he might lerne gentilesse aright."
   "Straw for thy gentilesse!" quod our Host.
"What, Frankelain, pardee sir, well thou woost

1 **thee . . . y-quit** acquitted yourself well   4 **allow** commend   5 **As
. . . doom** in my judgment   7 **chaunce** fortune   9 **daintee** pleasure
11 **I . . . lever** I would rather have   11 **twenty . . . land** land which
produces £20 per annum income   13 **discrecioun** good judgment
15 **But if** unless   16 **snibbed** chided, scolded   17 **listeth . . . entende**
chooses to pay no attention   18 **dees** dice   18 **dispende** squander
19 **lese** lose   19 **usage** practice

340

That ech of you mot tellen atte leeste                    25
A tale or two, or breken his biheste."°
   "That know I well, sir," quod the Frankelain.
"I pray you, haveth me not in disdain,°
Though to this man I speke a word or two."
   "Tell on thy tale withouten wordes mo."              30
   "Gladly, sir Host," quod he, "I wol obeye
Unto your will. Now herkneth what I saye.
I wol you not contrarien° in no wise,
As fer as that my wittes wol suffise.
I pray to God that it may plesen you.                     35
Than wot I well that it is good enow."


# THE FRANKLIN'S PROLOGUE


Thise olde gentil Britons° in hir dayes
Of diverse aventures maden layes,°
Rymeyed° in hir firste Briton tonge;°
Which layes with hir instruments they songe,
Or elles redden hem for hir plesaunce.                     5
And one of hem have I in remembraunce,
Which I shall sayn with good will, as I can.
   But, sirs, by cause I am a burel° man,
At my beginning first I you beseeche
Have me excused of my rude° speeche.                      10
I lerned never rhetoric, certain;

26 **biheste** promise   28 **haveth . . . disdain** do not be offended with
me   33 **contrarien** go against   1 **Britons** Bretons, people of Brit-
tany in northern France   2 **layes** the Breton lays: short narrative
poems sung by minstrels, such as those composed by Marie de
France   3 **Rymeyed** rhymed   3 **firste . . . tonge** original Breton, a
Celtic language   8 **burel** plain   10 **rude** humble, rough

Thing that I speke it mot be bare and plain.
I sleep° never on the Mount of Parnaso°,
Ne lerned Marcus Tullius Scithero.°
15 Colours° ne know I none, withouten drede,
But swich colours as growen in the mede,°
Or elles swiche as men dye or painte;
Colours of rhetorike been too quainte.°
My spirit feeleth not of swich mattere:
20 But if you list, my tale shull ye heere.

# THE FRANKLIN'S TALE

In Armorik,° that called is Britaine,
There was a knight that loved and did his paine°
To serve a lady in his beste wise.
And many a labour, many a greet emprise°
25 He for his lady wrought, ere she were wonne;
For she was one the fairest° under sunne,
And eek thereto come of so heigh kinrede°
That well unnethes° dorst this knight for drede°
Tell hir his woe, his pain, and his distresse.
30 But atte last she for his worthinesse,
And namely° for his meek obeisaunce,°
Hath swich a pitee caught of his penaunce°

13 **sleep** slept   13 **Mount . . . Parnaso** Mount Parnassus, home of the
Muses   14 **Marcus . . . Scithero** Cicero   15 **Colours** rhetorical de-
vices   16 **mede** meadow   18 **quainte** strange   21 **Armorik** Armor-
ica (*ar* on + *mor* sea), Brittany   22 **did . . . paine** troubled himself
24 **emprise** enterprise   26 **one . . . fairest** one of the most beautiful
27 **kinrede** family   28 **well unnethes** with great difficulty   28 **for
drede** for fear   31 **namely** particularly   31 **meek obeisaunce**
humble submission, attention   32 **penaunce** suffering

That prively° she fill of his accord°
To take him for hir husband and hir lord,
Of swich lordship as men han over hir wives.          35
And for to lede the more in bliss hir lives°
Of his free will he swore hir as a knight
That never in all his life he day ne night
Ne shold upon him take no maistrye°
Again hir will, ne kith° hir jalousye,          40
But hir obey and follow hir will in all,
As any lover to his lady shall—
Save that the name of sovereignetee,°
That wold *he* have, for shame of his degree.°
      She thanked him, and with full greet humblesse          45
She saide, "Sir, sith of your gentilesse
Ye proffre° me to have so large° a reine,
Ne wolde never God bitwix us twaine,
As in my guilt, were outher wer or strif.°
Sir, I wol be your humble, trewe wif—          50
Have here my trouth—till that mine herte breste."°
Thus been they both in quiet and in reste.
      For oo thing, sires, saufly dare I saye:
That freendes everich other° mot obeye°
If they wol longe holden compaignye.          55
Love wol not be constrained by maistrye.
Whan maistry cometh, the God of Love anon
Beteth his wings and farewell—he is gone!
Love is a thing as any spirit free:
Women of kind° desiren libertee,          60
And not to been constrained as a thrall°—
And so doon men, if I sooth sayen shall.

33 **prively** inwardly   33 **fill . . . accord** came to an understanding
with him   36 **for . . . lives** in order to pass their lives in more happi-
ness   39 **maistrye** control   40 **kith** show   43 **sovereignetee** sov-
ereignty. The Franklin echoes the words of the Wife of Bath in her
tale (cf. lines 182–84), thus continuing the debate on marriage
44 **for . . . degree** out of respect for his rank   47 **proffre** offer
47 **large** free   48–49 **Ne . . . strif** would to God that there should
never, because of my fault, be war or strife between us   51 **breste**
should burst. The vow of humility here would satisfy the Clerk's
ideas on marriage   54 **everich other** each other   54 **obeye** i.e., make
compromise with   60 **of kind** by nature   61 **thrall** slave

Look who that° is most pacient in love:
He is at his avantage all above.
65 Pacience is an high vertu, certain,
For it venquisheth° (as thise clerkes sayn)
Things that rigour° sholde never attaine.
For every word men may not chide or plaine.
Lerneth to suffre, or elles, so mote I goon,°
70 Ye shull it lerne whereso° ye wol or non.
For in this world, certain, there no wight is
That he ne doth or saith sometime amiss.
Ire, sickness, or constellacioun,°
Wine, woe, or chaunging of complexioun°
75 Causeth full oft° to doon amiss or speken.
On every wrong a man may not be wreken.°
After the time must be temperaunce
To every wight that kan on governaunce.°
And therefore hath this wise worthy knight
80 To live in ese suffrance hir bihight,°
And she to him full wisly° gan to swere
That never shold there be defaute in here.°
—Here may men seen an humble wise accord:
Thus hath she take hir servant and hir lord—
85 Servant in love and lord in marriage.
Than was he both in lordship and servage.
Servage? Nay, but in lordship above,
Sith he hath both his lady and his love—
His lady, certes, and his wife also,
90 The which that law of love accordeth to.°
And whan he was in this prosperitee,
Home with his wife he goth to his contree

---

63 **Look who that** whoever    66 **venquisheth** outlasts, overcomes
67 **rigour** force    69 **so . . . goon** i.e., or I am mistaken    70 **whereso**
whether    73 **constellacioun** fate    74 **complexioun** the balance of
humors (hot, cold, moist, dry) which constitutes one's temperament
75 **full oft** frequently ("many a man" understood)    76 **wreken**
avenged    77–78 **After . . . governaunce** according to the situation
there must be moderation on the part of every man who knows how
to control himself    80 **suffrance . . . bihight** promised patience to
her    81 **wisly** certainly    82 **defaute . . . here** the lack in her, i.e.,
she promised to do the same    90 **accordeth to** agrees to. The Frank-
lin's elaborate compromise encompasses courtly love

Not fer fro Pedmark,° ther his dwelling was
Where as he liveth in bliss and in solas.°
  Who coude tell, but he had wedded be,       *95*
The joy, the ese, and the prosperitee
That is bitwix an husband and his wif?
A yeer and more lasted this blissful lif,
Till that the knight of which I speke of thus—
That of Kairrud° was cleped Arveragus—      *100*
Shop him° to goon and dwell a yeer or twaine
In Engelond, that cleped was eek Britaine,
To seek in armes worship° and honour
(For all his lust he set in swich labour)
And dwelled there two yeer—the book saith thus.  *105*

*       *       *

Now wol I stint° of this Arveragus
And speke I wol of Dorigen his wif,
That loveth hir husband as hir hertes lif.
For his absence weepeth she and siketh,°
As doon thise noble wives whan hem liketh.°    *110*
She mourneth, waketh, waileth, fasteth, plaineth;
Desire of his presence hir so distraineth°
That all this wide world she set at nought.
Hir freendes, which that knew hir hevy thought,
Comforten hir in all that ever they may.    *115*
They preechen hir, they tell hir night and day
That causeless she sleeth hirself, alas—
And every comfort possible in this cas°
They doon to hir with all hir bisinesse°—
All for to make hir leeve hir hevinesse.°    *120*
  By process,° as ye knowen everichon,
Men may so longe graven° in a ston
Till some figure therein emprinted be.

93 **Pedmark** Penmarch, the western extremity of Brittany, which has
a rocky coastline  94 **solas** comfort  100 **Kairrud** a village
101 **Shop him** prepared  103 **worship** renown  106 **stint** stop
109 **siketh** sighs  110 **whan . . . liketh** when they please (the con-
struction is impersonal)  112 **distraineth** oppresses  118 **cas** situa-
tion  119 **bisinesse** anxious attention  120 **hevinesse** sadness
121 **By process** in due course  122 **graven** engrave, scratch

So long han they conforted hir, till she
125 Received hath, by hope and by resoun,
Th'emprinting of hir° consolacioun,
Thurgh which hir greete sorrwe gan assuage—
She may not alway duren in swich rage.°
    And eek Arveragus in all this care
130 Hath sent hir letters home of his welfare
And that he wol come hastily again,
Or elles had this sorrwe hir herte slain.
Hir freendes saw hir sorrwe gan to slacke,
And prayed hir on knees, for Goddes sake,
135 To come and romen hir° in compaignye
Away to drive hir derke fantasye;°
And finally she graunted that requeste,
For well she saw that it was for the beste.
    Now stood hir castel faste° by the see,
140 And often with hir freendes walketh she
Hir to disport° upon the bank on heigh
Where as she many a ship and barge seigh°
Sailing hir course where as hem liste go.
But than was that a parcel° of hir woe,
145 For to hirself full oft, "Alas!" saith she,
"Is there no ship of so many as I see
Wol bringen home my lord? Than were mine herte
All warished of his° bitter paines smerte."
Another time there wold she sit and thinke
150 And cast hir eyen downward fro the brinke—
But whan she seigh the grisly rockes blacke
For veray fere so wold hir herte quake
That on hir feet she might hir not sustene.
Than wold she sit adown upon the greene
155 And pitously into the see biholde,
And sayn right thus, with sorrweful sikes colde:°
"Eterne God, that thurgh thy purveyance°
Ledest the world by certain governance,

126 **hir** their    128 **duren . . . rage** remain in such a passion    135
**romen hir** take a walk    136 **derke fantasye** gloomy imaginings
139 **faste** close    141 **Hir . . . disport** to amuse herself    142 **seigh** saw
144 **parcel** portion    148 **warished . . . his** relieved on its    156 **sikes
colde** unhappy sighs    157 **purveyance** providence

In idle,° as men sayn, ye nothing make.
But Lord, thise grisly feendly rockes blacke,                160
That seemen rather a foul confusioun
Of werk, than any fair creacioun
Of swich a parfit wise God and a stable,
Why han ye wrought this werk unresonable?
For by this werk south, north, ne west ne est          165
There nis y-fostred° man ne brid° ne beest:
It doth no good, to my wit, but annoyeth.
See ye not, Lord, how mankind it destroyeth?
An hundred thousand bodies of mankinde
Han rockes slain, al be they not in minde,              170
Which mankind is so fair part of thy werk
That thou it madest like to thine own merk.°
Than seemed it ye had a greet chiertee°
Toward mankind. But how than may it be
That ye swich meenes make it to destroyen,             175
Which meenes do no good but ever annoyen?
I wot well clerkes wol sayn as hem leste
By arguments that all is for the beste,
Though I ne can the causes not y-knowe.
But thilke° God that made wind to blowe,               180
As keep° my lord! This my conclusioun.
To clerkes let I all disputisoun°—
But wolde God that all thise rockes blacke
Were sunken into helle for his sake!
Thise rockes slain mine herte for the feere!"          185
    Thus wold she sayn with many a pitous teere.
Hir freendes saw that it was no disport
To romen by the see, but discomfort,
And shopen for° to playen somewhere elles.
They leden hir by rivers and by welles                 190
And eek in other places delitables;°
They dauncen and they playen at chess and tables.°
So on a day, right in the morrwetide,°

159 **In idle** in vain   166 **y-fostred** nourished   166 **brid** bird   172
**merk** image   173 **chiertee** fondness   180 **thilke** the same   181 **As
keep** protect   182 **let ... disputisoun** I leave all debate   189 **shopen
for** determined   191 **delitables** delightful   192 **tables** backgammon
193 **morrwetide** morning

Unto a garden that was there beside
195 In which that they had made hir ordinaunce
Of vitaille,° and of other purveyaunce,°
They goon and play hem all the longe day.
And this was on the sixte morrwe of May,
Which May had painted with his softe showres
200 This garden full of leves and of flowres;
And craft of mannes hand so curiously°
Arrayed had this garden trewely
That never was there garden of swich pris°
But if it were the veray paradis.°
205 The odour of flowers and the freshe sighte
Wold han maked any herte lighte
That ever was born, but if° too greet sicknesse
Or too greet sorrwe held it in distresse,
So full it was of beautee with plesaunce.
210 At after-dinner gonne they to daunce
And singe also, save Dorigen alone,
Which made alway hir complaint and hir mone,
For she ne saw him on the daunce go
That was hir husband and hir love also.
215 But natheless she most a time abide,
And with good hope let hir sorrow slide.
     Upon this daunce, amonges other men,
Daunced a squier before Dorigen
That fresher was and jollier of array,°
220 As to my doom,° than is the month of May.
He singeth, daunceth, passing° any man
That is or was sith that the world began.
Therewith he was, if men him shold descrive,
One of the beste faring man on live.°
225 Yong, strong, right vertuous, and rich, and wis,
And well-beloved, and holden in greet pris.°
And shortly, if the sooth I tellen shall,
Unwitting of this Dorigen at all,

195–96 ordinaunce . . . vitaille arrangement of foods   196 purvey-
aunce provisions   201 curiously carefully   203 pris excellence
204 veray paradis Paradise itself   207 but if unless   219 jollier. . .
array livelier in dress   220 As . . . doom to my way of thinking
221 passing surpassing   224 beste . . . live handsomest men alive
226 pris esteem

This lusty squier, servant to Venus—
Which that y-cleped was Aurelius—                               230
Had loved hir best of any creature
Two yeer and more, as was his aventure;°
But never dorst he tellen hir his grevaunce.
Withouten cup he drank all his penance.°
He was despaired—no thing dorst he saye,                       235
Save in his songes somewhat wold he wraye°
His woe, as in a general complaining.°
He said he loved, and was beloved no thing,
Of which mattere made he many layes,
Songes, complaintes, roundels, virelayes,°                     240
How that he dorste not his sorrow telle,
But languisheth as a fury° doth in helle.
And die he most, he said, as did Echo°
For Narcissus that dorst not tell hir woe.
In other manner than ye heer me saye                           245
Ne dorst he not to hir his woe biwraye,°
Save that paraventure some time at daunces
Ther yonge folk keepen hir observaunces,°
It may well be he looked on hir face
In swich a wise as man that asketh grace—                      250
But no thing wiste she of his entente.
Natheless, it happed ere they thennes wente,
By cause that he was hire neighebour
And was a man of worship and honour,
And had y-knowen him of time yore,°                            255
They fill in speeche,° and forth more and more
Unto his purpose drow Aurelius,
And whan he saw his time he saide thus:
    "Madame," quod he, "by God that this world made,
So that I wist it might your herte glade,                      260

232 as . . . aventure as it so happened   234 Withouten . . . penance
i.e., he experienced his suffering straight from the source   236 wraye
betray   237 complaining lament   240 complaintes . . . virelayes
love songs addressed to a lady based on courtly French models
242 fury an avenging spirit   243 Echo Echo could not tell Narcissus
of her love for him and died in despair   246 biwraye disclose
248 keepen . . . observaunces hold their ceremonies   255 of . . . yore
for a long time   256 fill . . . speeche got into a conversation

I wold that day that your Arveragus
Went over the see that I, Aurelius,
Had went ther never I shold have come again!
For well I wot my service is in vain—
265 My guerdon is but bresting° of mine herte.
Madame, reweth° upon my paines smerte,
For with a word ye may me sleen or save!
Here at your feet God wold that I were grave!
I ne have as now no leiser more to saye—
270 Have mercy, sweet, or ye wol do me deye!"°
    She gan to look upon Aurelius:
"Is this your will?" quod she, "and say ye thus?
Never erst,"° quod she, "ne wist I° what ye mente.
But now, Aurelie, I know your entente,
275 By thilke God that yaf° me soul and lif,
Ne shall I never been untrewe wif
In word ne werk as far as I have wit.
I wol be his to whom that I am knit°—
Take this for final answer as of° me."
280 But after that in play thus saide she:
"Aurelie," quod she, "by heighe God above,
Yet wold I graunte you to been your love,
Sin I you see so pitously complaine:
Look what° day that endelong Britaine°
285 Ye remove all the rockes, stone by stoon,
That they ne lette° ship ne boot° to goon.
I say, whan ye han made the coost so cleene
Of rockes that there nis no stone y-seene,
Than wol I love you best of any man—
290 Have here my trouth—in all that ever I can."
    "Is there noon other grace in you?" quod he.
    "No, by that Lord," quod she, "that maked me.
For well I wot that it shall never bitide.°
Let swich follies out of your herte slide!
295 What daintee° shold a man han in his lif

265 guerdon . . . bresting reward is only the bursting   266 reweth
take pity   270 do . . . deye cause me to die   273 erst before
273 ne wist I did I know   275 yaf gave   278 knit married   279 as
of from   284 Look what whatever   284 endelong Britaine all along
the coast of Brittany   286 lette prevent   286 boot boat   293 bitide
happen   295 daintee pleasure

For to go love another mannes wif
That hath hir body whan so that him liketh!"
   Aurelius full ofte sore siketh;
Woe was Aurelie whan that he this herde,
And with a sorrweful hert he thus answerde:      *300*
"Madame," quod he, "this were an impossible!
Than mot I die of sudden deeth horrible!"
And with that word he turned him anon.
   Tho come hir other freendes many oon,
And in the alleys° romeden up and down,      *305*
And nothing wist of this conclusioun.
But suddenly begonne revel newe
Till that the brighte sunne lost his hewe,
For th'orisont hath reft° the sun his light—
This is as much to say as, it was night—      *310*
And home they goon in joy and in solas.
   Save only wretched Aurelius, alas—
He to his house is gone with sorrweful herte.
He seeth he may not from his deeth asterte:°
Him seemed that he felt his herte colde.°      *315*
Up to the heven his handes he gan holde,
And on his knowes° bare he set him down
And in his raving said his orisoun.°
For veray woe out of his wit he braide.°
He niste what he spake, but thus he saide—      *320*
With pitous hert his plaint hath he begonne
Unto the goddes, and first unto the sunne:
He said, "Apollo,° god and governour
Of every plaunte, herbe, tree, and flower,
That yevest after thy declinacioun°      *325*
To ech of hem his time and his sesoun,
As thine herberwe° chaungeth, low or heighe:
Lord Phebus, cast thy merciable eighe°
On wretch Aurelie which that am but lorn!
Lo, Lord, my lady hath my deeth y-sworn      *330*

305 **alleys** walkways   309 **orisont . . . reft** horizon has taken away
314 **asterte** escape   315 **colde** grow cold   317 **knowes** knees   318
**orisoun** prayer   319 **braide** fled   323 **Apollo** Phoebus Apollo, god
of the sun   325 **That . . . declinacioun** who bestow (thy rays) accord-
ing to thy distance from the celestial equator   327 **herberwe** resi-
dence   328 **eighe** eye

Withouten guilt, but thy benignitee
Upon my deedly hert have some pitee.
For well I wot, Lord Phebus, if you lest,
Ye may me helpen, save my lady, best.
335 Now voucheth sauf that I may you devise°
How that I may been holpen, and in what wise:
Your blissful suster, Lucina the sheene,°
That of the see is chief goddess and queene
(Though Neptunus° have deitee in the see,
340 Yet emperess aboven him is she)
Ye knowen well, Lord, that—right as hir desir
Is to be quicked and lighted of° your fir,
For which she followeth you full bisily°—
Right so the see desireth naturelly
345 To followen hir, as she that is goddesse
Both in the see and rivers more and lesse.
Wherefore, Lord Phebus, this is my requeste:
Do this miracle—or do mine herte breste—
That now next at this opposicioun,°
350 Which in the sign shall be of the Leoun,
As prayeth° hir so greet a flood to bringe
That five fadme at the lest it overspringe°
The hyest rock in Armorik Britaine;
And let this flood endure yeeres twaine.
355 Than certes to my lady may I saye,
'Holdeth your hest,° the rockes been awaye!'
Lord Phebus, doth this miracle for me!
Pray hir she go no faster course than ye—
I say this, prayeth your suster that she go
360 No faster course than ye thise yeeres two.
Than shall she been even at the full° alway,
And spring-flood lasten bothe night and day.

335 **devise** explain   337 **Lucina the sheene** Diana, goddess of the
moon, who is called the "chaste goddess"   339 **Neptunus** Neptune,
chief god of the sea   342 **quicked . . . of** stimulated and lighted by
343 **bisily** constantly   349 **now . . . opposicioun** the next time the
moon and sun are in opposition, i.e., when the sun is in the sign of
Leo and the moon is in the sign of Aquarius—in about three months
351 **As prayeth** pray   352 **five . . . overspringe** that (the sea) over-
run by at least five fathoms   356 **Holdeth . . . hest** keep your
promise   361 **at . . . full** in a full moon

And but she vouche sauf° in swich mannere
To graunte me my sovereign lady dere,
Pray hir to sinken every rock adown                              365
Into hir owne derke regioun°
Under the ground ther Pluto dwelleth inne—
Or never mo shall I my lady winne!
Thy temple in Delphos° wol I barefoot seeke.
Lord Phebus, see the teres on my cheeke,                         370
And of my pain have some compassioun!"
And with that word in swoun he fill adown,
And longe time he lay forth in a traunce.
    His brother, which that knew of his penaunce,°
Up caught him, and to bed he hath him brought.                   375
Despaired in this torment and this thought
Let I this woeful creature lie—
Chese he for me wher° he wol live or die.

*        *        *

    Arveragus with hele° and greet honour,
As he that was of chivalry the flower,                           380
Is comen home, and other worthy men.
O, blissful artou now, thou Dorigen,
That hast thy lusty° husband in thine armes,
The freshe knight, the worthy man of armes,
That loveth thee as his own hertes lif!                          385
No thing list him to been imaginatif°
If any wight had spoke while he was oute
To hir of love; he had of it no doute.
He not entendeth° to no swich mattere
But dauncheth, jousteth, maketh hir good cheere.                 390
    And thus in joy and bliss I let hem dwelle,
And of the sick Aurelius wol I telle.
In langour and in torment furious
Two yeer and more lay wretch Aurelius,

363 **vouche sauf** sees fit   366 **derke regioun** Lucina in her mani-
festation as Proserpina, queen of hell   369 **Delphos** Delphi
374 **penaunce** suffering   378 **wher** whether   379 **hele** health   383
**lusty** joyous   386 **No . . . imaginatif** he is not at all the imaginative
(i.e., suspicious) sort   389 **not entendeth** pays no attention

395 Ere any foot he might on erthe gon,
Ne comfort in this time had he non—
Save of his brother, which that was a clerk:
He knew of all this woe and all this werk,
For to noon other creature, certain,
400 Of this matter he dorste no word sayn.
Under his brest he bare it more secree
Than ever did Pamphilus for Galathee.°
His breast was whole withoute for to seene,°
But in his hert ay was the arrow keene:
405 And well ye know that of a sursanure°
In surgery is perilous the cure,
But men might touch the arrwe or come thereby.
His brother weep and wailed prively,
Till at the last him fill in remembrance
410 That whiles he was at Orliens° in France—
As yonge clerkes that been likerous°
To reden artes that been curious,°
Seeken in every halk and every herne°
Particuler° sciences for to lerne—
415 He him remembered that, upon a day,
At Orliens in study a book he sey
Of magic naturel,° which his fellawe,
That was that time a bacheler of lawe
(Al were he there to lerne another craft)
420 Had prively upon his desk y-laft;°
Which book spak muchel of the operaciouns
Touching the eight and twenty mansiouns°
That longen to the moon—and swich follye
As in our dayes is not worth a flye
425 (For holy chirches faith in our bileve
Ne suffreth° noon illusion *us* to greve).

---

402 **Pamphilus . . . Galathee** the two lovers in a twelfth-century Latin
dialogue    403 **withoute . . . seene** to look at from the outside
405 **sursanure** a wound healed only on the surface    410 **Orliens**
Orleans, site of an old university    411 **likerous** zealous    412 **curious**
occult, out of the ordinary    413 **every . . . herne** every nook and
cranny    414 **Particuler** unusual    417 **magic naturel** i.e., magic op-
posed to "black" magic and necromancy    420 **y-laft** left    422 **eight
. . . mansiouns** the positions of the moon in relation to stars    426 **Ne
suffreth** does not permit

And whan this book was in his remembraunce,
Anon for joy his herte gan to daunce,
And to himself he saide prively,
"My brother shall be warished° hastily!          430
For I am siker that there be sciences
By whiche men make diverse apparences,°
Swich as thise subtile tregetoures° playe.
For oft at feestes have I well herd saye
That tregetoures within an halle large          435
Have made come in a water° and a barge,
And in the halle rowen up and down;
Some time hath seemed come a grim leoun,
Some time flowers spring as in a mede,
Some time a vine and grapes white and rede,      440
Some time a castel all of lime and ston,
And whan hem liked voided it° anon—
Thus *seemed* it to every mannes sighte!
Now than conclude I thus, that if I mighte
At Orliens some old fellaw y-finde            445
That had thise moones mansions in minde,
Or other magic naturel above,
He shold well make my brother han his love.
For with an apparence a clerk may make
To mannes sight that all the rockes blacke        450
Of Britaine were y-voided everichon,
And shippes by the brink comen and gon,
And in swich form enduren a day or two.
Than were my brother warished of his woe!
Than must she needes holden hir biheste,°        455
Or elles he shall shame hir at the leeste!"
    What shold I make a lenger tale of this?
Unto his brother's bed he comen is,
And swich comfort he yaf him for to gon
To Orliens, that up he stert anon              460
And on his way forthward than is he fare,
In hope for to been lissed° of his care.
    Whan they were come almost to that citee,

430 **warished** cured   432 **apparences** apparitions   433 **tregetoures**
magicians   436 **Have . . . water** have made water come in   422 **voided
it made** it disappear   455 **biheste** promise   462 **lissed** relieved

But if it were a two furlong or three,
465 A yong clerk roming by himself they mette,
Which that in Latin thriftily hem grette,°
And after that he said a wonder° thing:
"I know," quod he, "the cause of your coming."
And ere they ferther any foote wente,
470 He told hem all that was in hir entente.
This Briton clerk him asked of fellawes,
The which that he had know in olde dawes,°
And he answered him that they dede were—
For which he weep full ofte many a tere.
475 Down off his horse Aurelius light anon,
And with this magicien forth is he gon
Home to his house, and maden hem well at ese.
Hem lacked no vitaille° that might hem plese—
So well arrayed house as there was oon
480 Aurelius in his life saw never noon.
    He shewed him ere he went to supper
Forestes, parkes full of wilde deer—
There saw he hertes with hir hornes hye,
The greetest that ever were seen with eye;
485 He saw of hem an hundred slain with houndes,
And some with arrows bled of bitter woundes.
He saw, when voided were° thise wilde deer,
Thise fauconers° upon a fair river,
That with hir hawkes han the heron slain.
490 Tho saw he knightes jousting in a plain.
And after this he did him this plesaunce,
That he him shewed his lady on a daunce,
On which himself he daunced—as him thoughte.
And whan this maister that this magic wroughte
495 Saw it was time, he clapt his handes two,
And farewell—all our revel was ago!°
And yet removed they never out of the hous
While they saw all this sighte merveillous,
But in his study, ther as his bookes be,
500 They setten still, and no wight but they three!

466 **thriftily . . . grette** formally greeted them    467 **wonder** wondrous
472 **dawes** days    478 **vitaille** foodstuff    487 **voided were** had dis-
appeared    488 **fauconers** falconers    496 **ago** gone

To him this maister called his squier
And said him thus, "Is redy our supper?
Almost an hour it is, I undertake,
Sith I you bade our supper for to make,
Whan that thise worthy men wenten with me          505
Into my study ther as my bookes be."
"Sir," quod this squier, "whan it liketh you,°
It is all redy, though ye wol right now."
"Go we than soup,"° quod he, "as for the beste:
This amorous folk some time mot han hir reste."    510
    At after-supper fill they in tretee°
What summe shold this maistres guerdon° be
To removen all the rockes of Britaine,
And eek from Gerounde° to the mouth of Seine.
He made it straunge,° and swore, so God him save,  515
Less than a thousand pound he wold not have,
Ne gladly for that sum he wold not gon.
    Aurelius with blissful hert anon
Answered thus: "Fy on a thousand pound!
This wide world, which that men say is round,       520
I wold it yive, if I were lord of it.
This bargain is full drive,° for we been knit!°
Ye shall be payed trewely, by my trouthe!
But looketh now, for no negligence or slouthe,
Ye tarry us here no lenger than tomorrwe."          525
    "Nay," quod this clerk, "have here my faith to
        borrwe."°
To bed is gone Aurelius whan him leste,
And well neigh all that night he had his reste—
What for his labour and his hope of blisse,
His woeful hert of penaunce had a lisse.°           530
    Upon the morrwe, whan that it was day
To Britain tooke they the righte° way,
Aurelius and this magicien beside,
And been descended ther they wold abide.

---

507 it . . . you you like   509 Go . . . soup let's go to supper
511 tretee negotiation   512 guerdon reward   514 Gerounde the
river Gerounde   515 made . . . straunge made it difficult   522 full
drive fully made   522 knit agreed   526 to borrwe as a pledge
530 lisse relief   532 righte direct

535 And this was, as thise bookes me remembre,
The colde frosty seson of Decembre.
Phebus wax old,° and hewed like latoun,°
That in his hote declinacioun°
Shone as the burned gold with stremes brighte.
540 But now in Capricorn° adown he lighte,
Where as he shone full pale, I dare well sayn:
The bitter frostes with the sleet and rain
Destroyed hath the green in every yerd.
Janus° sit by the fire with double beerd
545 And drinketh of his bugle horn° the win,
Biforn him stant brawen° of the tusked swin,°
And "Nowell!" crieth every lusty man.
Aurelius in all that ever he can
Doth to this maister cheer and reverence,
550 And prayeth him to doon his diligence
To bringen him out of his paines smerte,
Or with a swerd that he wold slit his herte.
      This subtil clerk swich ruth had of° this man
That night and day he sped him that he can°
555 To waiten a time of his conclusioun°—
This is to sayn, to make illusioun
By swich an apparence or juggelrye°
(I ne kan no termes of astrologye)
That she and every wight shold ween° and saye
560 That of Britain the rockes were awaye,
Or elles they were sunken under grounde.
So at the last he hath his time y-founde
To maken his japes° and his wretchednesse
Of swich a supersticious cursednesse.
565 His tables Tolletanes° forth he brought,

537 **Phebus . . . old** i.e., the sun was near setting   537 **latoun** brass
538 **hote declinacioun** i.e., in Cancer, at the zenith north of the
Equator   540 **Capricorn** i.e., in opposition, or near the Equator
544 **Janus** Janus, the two-faced god ("with double beerd"), i.e.,
January   545 **bugle horn** horn of a wild ox for drinking   546 **brawen**
meat   546 **tusked swin** boar, wild pig   553 **ruth . . . of** had pity on
554 **sped . . . can** went as quickly as he could   555 **waiten . . . con-
clusioun** watch for a time to perform his operation   557 **juggelrye**
magic   559 **ween** believe   563 **japes** tricks   565 **tables Tolletanes**
Toledan astronomical tables

Full well corrected.° Ne there lacked nought,
Neither his collect ne his expanse yeeres,°
Ne his rootes,° ne his other geres°—
As been his centres° and his arguments,°
And his proporcionels convenients,°          570
For his equacions in every thing.
And by his eighte spere° in his werking
He knew full well how fer Alnath was shove°
Fro the heed of thilke fix Aries° above
That in the ninthe spere considered is—          575
Full subtilly he calculed all this.
Whan he had found his firste mansioun,°
He knew the remnant° by proporcioun,
And knew the arising of his moone well,
And in whose face and term, and every deel,°          580
And knew full well the moones mansioun
Accordant to° his operacioun,
And knew also his other observaunces°
For swich illusiouns and swich meschaunces°
As hethen folk useden in thilke dayes.          585
For which no lenger maked he delayes,
But, thurgh his magic, for a week or twaye
It seemed that all the rockes were awaye!

\*     \*     \*

566 **corrected** astronomical tables were frequently revised in the late Middle Ages    567 **collect . . . yeeres** i.e., "collect years" and "expanse years"—two ways of computing planetary movement based upon longer and shorter periods respectively    568 **rootes** tables for making other mathematical computations    568 **geres** equipment    569 **centres** mechanism on an astrolabe    569 **arguments** measurements from which other quantities may be derived    570 **proporcionels convenients** tables of proportions    572 **eighte spere** medieval astronomical theory conceived of nine spheres, or transparent shells, in concentric and eccentric motion around the earth. The fixed stars reside in the eighth sphere    573 **Alnath . . . shove** the star Arietes had moved    574 **fix Aries** i.e., the fixed star Aries, which was thought to reside in the ninth sphere and which served as a basis of other astronomical computations    577 **firste mansioun** the moon's first position, Alnath    578 **remnant** rest    580 **in . . . deel** in whose zodiacal sign and planet and every part    582 **Accordant to** having to do with    583 **observaunces** practices    584 **meschaunces** misguided occupations

Aurelius, which that yet despaired is
590 Wher° he shall han his love or fare amiss,°
Awaiteth night and day on this miracle.
And whan he knew that there was noon obstacle,
That voided were thise rockes everichon,
Down to his maistres feet he fill anon
595 And said, "I, woeful wretch Aurelius,
Thank you, lord, and lady mine Venus,
That me han holpen fro my cares colde!"
And to the temple his way forth hath he holde,°
Where as he knew he shold his lady see.
600 And whan he saw his time, anon-right° he
With dredful hert and with full humble cheere
Salued° hath his sovereign lady dere:
    "My righte lady," quod this woeful man,
"Whom I most drede and love as best I can,
605 And lothest were of all this world displese,
Nere it° that I for you have swich disese
That I most dien here at your foot anon,
Nought wold I tell how me is woe-bigon.
But certes outher must I die or plaine!
610 Ye sleen me guilteless for veray paine!
But of my deeth though that ye have no routhe,
Aviseth you° ere that ye breke your trouthe.
Repenteth you, for thilke God above,
Ere ye me sleen by cause that I you love.
615 For, Madame, well ye wot what ye han hight°
(Not that I challenge any thing of right
Of you, my sovereign lady, but your grace)—
But in a garden yond at swich a place,
Ye wot right well what ye bihighten me,
620 And in mine hand your trouthe plighten ye
To love me best. God wot ye saide so,
Al be that I unworthy am thereto.
Madame, I speke it for the honour of you
More than to save mine hertes life right now:
625 I have do so as ye commanded me,

590 **Wher** whether    590 **fare amiss** fail    598 **holde** gone    600 **anon-right** straight away    602 **Salued** greeted    606 **Nere it** were it not    612 **Aviseth you** think it over    615 **hight** promised

And if ye vouche sauf,° ye may go see.
Doth as you list, have your bihest in minde,
For quick or deed right there ye shall me finde.
In you lith all to do me live or deye:
But well I wot the rockes been awaye."                          630
    He taketh his leeve and she astoned° stood—
In all hir face nas a drop of blood.
She wende never have come° in swich a trappe.
"Alas," quod she, "that ever this shold happe!
For wende I never by possibilitee                               635
That swich a monstre° or merveil mighte be!
It is agains the process of nature."
And home she goth a sorrweful creature;
For veray fere unnethe° may she go.
She weepeth, waileth all a day or two,                          640
And swouneth that it routhe was to see.
But why it was, to no wight tolde she,
For out of town was gone Arveragus.
But to hirself she spak and saide thus,
With face pale and with full sorrweful cheere                   645
In hir complaint, as ye shall after heere:
    "Alas," quod she, "on thee, Fortune, I plaine,
That unware wrapped hast me in thy chaine,
For which t'escape woot I no succour
Save only deeth or elles dishonour—                             650
One of thise two bihoveth me° to chese.
But natheless yet have I lever to lese
My life than of my body to have a shame,
Or know myselven false, or lese my name;
And with my deeth I may be quit,° ywis.                         655
Hath there not many a noble wife ere this,
And many a maid y-slain hirself, alas,
Rather than with hir body doon trespass?
Yis, certes, lo, thise stories° beren witnesse:
    Whan thritty tyrants full of cursednesse                    660
Had slain Phidon in Athens atte feeste,

626 **vouche sauf** see fit    631 **astoned** astonished    633 **She . . . come**
she never thought she would fall    636 **monstre** wondrous thing
639 **unnethe** scarcely    651 **bihoveth me** I must    655 **quit** released
659 **thise stories** taken from Jerome's *Against Jovinian*

They commanded his daughtren for t'arreste,°
And bringen hem beforn hem in despit°
All naked, to fulfill hir foul delit;
665 And in hir fadres blood they made hem daunce
Upon the pavement—God yive him mischaunce!°
For which thise woeful maidens, full of drede,
Rather than they wold lese hir maidenhede,
They prively been stirt° into a welle
670 And dreint° hemselven, as the bookes telle.
    They of Messene let enquere and seeke
Of Lacedomye° fifty maidens eke,
On which they wolden doon hir lecherye.
But there was none of all that compaignye
675 That she nas slain, and with a good entente
Chees° rather for to die than assente
To been oppressed° of hir maidenhede.
Why shold I than to die been in drede?
    Lo, eek, the tyrant Aristoclides
680 That loved a maiden hight Stymphalides,°
Whan that hir fader slain was on a night,
Unto Dianes temple goth she aright
And hente° the image in hir handes two,
Fro which image wold she never go.
685 No wight ne might hir hands of it arace,°
Till she was slain right in the selve° place.
Now sith that maidens hadden swich despit°
To been defouled with man's foul delit,
Well ought a wife rather hirselven slee
690 Than be defouled, as it thinketh me.
    What shall I sayn of Hasdrubales wif
That at Cartage biraft hirself hir lif?
For whan she saw that Romains won the town,
She took hir children all and skipt° adown

---

662 **They . . . t'arreste** they commanded his daughters to be arrested
663 **in despit** in scorn   666 **God . . . mischaunce** God give them
misfortune   669 **been stirt** have jumped   670 **dreint** drowned
672 **Lacedomye** Lacedaemonia   676 **Chees** chose   677 **oppressed**
ravished   680 **hight Stymphalides** named Stymphalis   683 **hente**
seized   685 **arace** separate   686 **selve** same   687 **hadden . . . despit**
had such indignation   694 **skipt** threw herself

Into the fire, and chees rather to die                        695
Than any Romain did hir villainye.
    Hath not Lucrece y-slain hirself, alas,
At Rome whan that she oppressed was
Of Tarquin, for hir thought it was a shame
To liven whan that she had lost hir name?                     700
    The seven maidens of Milesie° also
Han slain hemself for veray drede and woe
Rather than folk of Gaul hem shold oppresse.
    Mo than a thousand stories, as I guesse,
Coud I now tell as touching° this mattere.                    705
Whan Habradate was slain, his wife so dere
Hirselven slow, and let hir blood to glide
In Habradates woundes deep and wide,
And said, 'My body at the leste way
There shall no wight defoulen, if I may!'°                    710
What shold I mo ensamples° hereof sayn?
Sith that so many han hemselven slain
Well rather than they wold defouled be,
I wol conclude that it is bet° for me
To sleen myself than been defouled thus.                      715
I wol be trew unto Arveragus,
Or rather slee myself in some mannere—
As did Demociones daughter dere,
By cause that she wold not defouled be.
O Cedasus,° it is full greet pitee                            720
To reden how *thy* daughtren deid, alas,
That slow hemselven for swich manner cas!°
As greet a pitee was it, or well more,
The Theban maiden° that for° Nichanore
Hirselven slow right for swich manner woe.                    725
Another Theban maiden° did right so—
For one of Macedonie had hir oppressed,
She with hir deeth hir maidenheed redressed.

701 **Milesie** Miletus, which was sacked by the Galatians in 276 B.C.
705 **as touching** concerning    710 **if . . . may** i.e., if I may (prevent it)
711 **ensamples** examples    714 **bet** better    720 **Cedasus** Scedasus of
Boeotia, whose two daughters killed one another after being violated
722 **swich . . . cas** such an occurrence    724 **Theban maiden** Nicanor
captured Thebes and fell in love with a virgin of the city    724 **for**
in fear of    726 **Another . . . maiden** this maiden killed the Mace-
donian first and herself afterward

What shall I sayn of Nicerates wif°
730 That for swich cas biraft hirself hir lif?
How trew eek was to Alcebiades
His love,° that rather for to dien chees
Than for to suffre his body unburied be?
Lo, which a wife was Alceste?"° quod she.
735 "What saith Omer° of good Penelopee?°
All Greece knoweth of hir chastitee.
Pardee, of Laodomia is written thus,
That whan at Troy was slain Protheselaus,
No lenger wold she live after his day.
740 The same of noble Porcia° tell I may:
Withoute Brutus coude she not live,
To whom she had all whole hir herte yive.
The parfit wifehood of Arthemesie°
Honoured is thurgh all the Barbarye.
745 O Teuta° queen, thy wifely chastitee
To alle wives may a mirrour° be!
The same thing I say of Biliea,°
Of Rodogone,° and eek Valeria."°
    Thus plained Dorigen a day or twaye,
750 Purposing° ever that she wolde deye.
    But natheless upon the thridde night
Home came Arveragus, this worthy knight,
And asked hir why that she weep so sore.

729 **Nicerates wif** when the Athenian leader Niceratus surrendered
his power to the Thirty Tyrants in Athens, his wife killed herself
rather than submitting to the Tyrants    731–32 **Alcebiades . . . love**
Timandra, Alcibiades' concubine, buried the dead body of her lover
734 **Alceste** Alcestis, who died in place of her husband    735 **Omer**
Homer    735 **Penelopee** Penelope was to choose a suitor on the
completion of an intricate tapestry, but to remain faithful to her
husband Odysseus she unraveled the work at night    740 **Porcia**
Portia is said to have choked on burning coals while being guarded
after her husband's death at Philippi    743 **Arthemesie** Artemesia,
wife to King Mausolus, built the "mausoleum" in his honor at his
death    745 **Teuta** Illyrian queen, whose success was in proportion to
her chastity    746 **mirrour** exemplar    747 **Biliea** Bilia, who defeated
the Carthaginians in a naval battle    748 **Rodogone** Rhodogune, the
daughter of King Darius, who killed her nurse for urging her to
remarry    748 **Valeria** suffered martyrdom for her fidelity    750 **Purposing** intending

And she gan weepen ever lenger the more°—
"Alas," quod she, "that ever I was born!          755
Thus have I said," quod she, "thus have I sworn . . ."
And told him all as ye han herd before;
It needeth not reherce it you namore.

    This husband with glad cheer in freendly wise
Answered and said as I shall you devise:          760
    "Is there ought° elles, Dorigen, but this?"
    "Nay, nay," quod she, "God help me so as wis,°
This is too much, and it were Goddes wille."
    "Ye, wife," quod he, "let sleepen that is stille.°
It may be well paraunter° yet today.          765
Ye shull your trouthe holden, by my fay,°
For God so wisly have mercy upon me,
I had well lever y-sticked° for to be,
For veray love which that I to you have,
But if ye shold° your trouthe keep and save.          770
Trouth is the highest thing that man may keepe."
But with that word he brast anon to weepe,°
And said, "I you forbed, up pain of deeth,
That never while thee lasteth life ne breeth,
To no wight tell thou of this aventure.          775
As I may best I wol my woe endure,
Ne make no countenance of hevinesse,
That folk of you may deemen harm or guesse."°
And forth he cleped a squier and a maide:
"Goth forth anon with Dorigen," he saide,          780
"And bringeth hir to swich a place anon."
They took hir leeve and on hir way they gon,
But they ne wiste why she thider wente:
He nolde no wight tellen his entente.
    Paraventure an heep° of you, ywis,          785
Wol holden him a lewed° man in this,
That he wol put his wife in jupartye.°

---

754 ever . . . more always more and more    761 ought nothing
762 God . . . wis as surely as God help me    764 let . . . stille i.e.,
leave alone what cannot be helped    765 paraunter perhaps    766 by
. . . fay by my faith    768 y-sticked stabbed    770 But . . . shold
rather than you should not    772 brast . . . weepe burst into tears
778 deemen . . . guesse think or guess evil    785 an heep a number
786 lewed foolish    787 jupartye jeopardy

Herkneth the tale ere ye upon hir crye!
She may have better fortune than you seemeth,°
790 And whan that ye han herd the tale, deemeth.°

\*    \*    \*

This squier which that hight Aurelius,
On Dorigen that was so amorous,
Of aventure happed hir to meete
Amid the town, right in the quickest° streete,
795 As she was bown° to goon the way forth right°
Toward the garden ther as she had hight.°
And he was to the gardenward also,
For well he spied whan she wolde go
Out of hir house to any manner place.
800 But thus they met of° aventure or grace,
And he salueth hir with glad entente,°
And asked of hir whiderward she wente.
And she answered half as she were mad,
"Unto the garden as mine husband bad,°
805 My trouthe for to hold—alas! alas!"
      Aurelius gan wondren on this cas,°
And in his hert had greet compassioun
Of hir and of hir lamentacioun,
And of Arveragus, the worthy knight,
810 That bade hir holden all that she had hight,°
So loth him was° his wife shold breke hir trouthe.
And in his hert he caught of° this greet routhe,
Considering the best on every side
That fro his lust yet were him lever abide°
815 Than doon so high a cherlish° wretchednesse
Agains franchise° and alle gentilesse.
For which in fewe wordes said he thus:
"Madame, sayeth to your lord Arveragus

789 **you seemeth** it seems to you   790 **deemeth** then judge   794
**quickest** most active   795 **bown** ready   795 **forth right** directly
796 **hight** promised   800 **of** by   801 **with . . . entente** cheerfully
804 **bad** requested   806 **cas** situation   810 **holden . . . hight** stick to
everything she promised   811 **So . . . was** so unwilling was he
812 **caught of** had on   814 **were . . . abide** he would rather leave off
815 **so . . . cherlish** such an ignoble   816 **franchise** generosity

That sith I see his greete gentilesse
To you, and eek I see well your distresse 820
That him were lever han shame—and that were
    routhe—
Than ye to me shold breke thus your trouthe,
I have well lever° ever to suffer woe
Than I depart° the love bitwix you two.
I you releese, Madame, into your hond.° 825
Quit every serement° and every bond
That ye han made to me as herebiforn,
Sith thilke° time which that ye were born.
My trouth I plight,° I shall you never repreve°
Of no bihest. And here I take my leeve, 830
As of the trewest and the beste wif
That ever yet I knew in all my lif.
But every wife be ware of hir biheste:
On Dorigen remembreth at the leste.
Thus can a squier doon a gentil deede 835
As well as can a knight, withouten drede."
She thanketh him upon hir knees all bare
And home unto hir husband is she fare,°
And told him all as ye han herd me said.
And be ye siker, he was so well apaid 840
That it were impossible me to write.
What shold I lenger of this cas endite?°
    Arveragus and Dorigen his wif
In sovereign blisse leden forth° hir lif—
Never eft° ne was there anger hem betweene. 845
He cherisheth hir as though she were a queene,
And she was to him trew for evermore.
Of thise two folk ye get of me namore.
    Aurelius, that his cost hath all forlorn,°
Curseth the time that ever he was born. 850
"Alas!" quod he, "alas that I bihighte
Of pured° gold a thousand pound of wighte°

823 have . . . lever would much rather   824 depart divide   825 into
. . . hond i.e., to yourself   826 serement oath   828 thilke that very
829 trouth . . . plight give you my word   829 repreve blame   838
fare gone   842 endite relate   844 leden forth pass   845 eft again
849 cost . . . forlorn has lost all his investment   852 pured refined
852 wighte weight

Unto this philosophre! How° shall I do?
I see namore but that I am fordo.°
855 Mine heritage° mot I needes selle
And been a begger. Here may I not dwelle
And shamen all my kinred° in this place,
But° I of him° may gete better grace.
But, natheless, I wol of him assaye°
860 At certain dayes yeer by yeer to paye,
And thank him of his greete curteisye.
My trouthe wol I keep, I wol not lie."
     With herte sore he goth unto his coffre
And broughte gold unto this philosophre
865 The value of five hundred pound, I guesse,
And him biseecheth of his gentilesse
To graunten him days of the remenaunt;°
And said, "Maister, I dare well make avaunt°
I failed never of my trouth as yit.
870 For sikerly my dette shall be quit°
Towardes you, how ever that I fare—
To goon abegged in my kirtel bare.°
But wold ye vouche sauf upon suretee°
Two yeer or three for to respiten° me,
875 Than were I well—for elles mot I selle
Mine heritage; there is namore to telle."
     This philosophre soberly answerde
And saide thus, whan he thise wordes herde,
"Have I not holden covenant unto thee?"
880 "Yis, certes, well and trewely," quod he.
"Hastou not had thy lady as thee liketh?"
"No, no," quod he—and sorrwefully he siketh.°
"What was the cause? Tell me if thou can."
Aurelius his tale anon bigan
885 And told him all as ye han herd before—
It needeth not to you reherce it more.
He said, "Arveragus, of gentilesse,

853 How what   854 fordo undone, lost   855 heritage inheritance
857 kinred relatives   858 But unless   858 him i.e., the magician
859 I . . . assaye I will try to arrange   867 of . . . remenaunt in which
to pay the rest   868 avaunt boast   870 quit paid back   872 To . . .
bare to go begging in my undershirt   873 suretee security   874
respiten give me an extension   882 siketh sighs

Had lever die in sorrwe and in distresse
Than that his wife were of hir trouthe fals."
The sorrwe of Dorigen he told him als,      890
How loth hir was to been a wicked wif,
And that she lever had lost that day hir lif,
And that hir trouth she swore thurgh innocence—
She never erst had herd speke of "apparence."°
—"That made me han of hir so greet pitee.      895
And right as freely as he sent hir me,
As freely sent I hir to him again.
This all and some, there is namore to sayn."
    This philosophre answered, "Leve brother,
Everich° of you did gentilly til other.      900
Thou art a squier, and he is a knight;
But God forbede, for His blissful might,
But if a clerk coud° doon a gentil deede
As well as any of you, it is no drede.
Sir, I relese thee thy thousand pound,      905
As thou right now were croppen° out of the ground
Ne never ere now ne haddest knowen me.
For sir, I wol not take a penny of thee,
For all my craft ne nought for my travaille.°
Thou hast y-payed well for my vitaille;°      910
It is enough. And farewell, have good day"—
And took his horse and forth he goth his way.
—Lordings,° this question wol I aske now:
Which was the moste free,° as thinketh you?
Now telleth me, ere that ye ferther wende.°      915
I kan namore, my tale is at an ende.

---

894 **apparence** illusion   900 **Everich** each   903 **But . . . coud** if a clerk could not (cf. line 770)   906 **were croppen** had crept   909 **travaille** labor   910 **vitaille** food   913 **Lordings** gentlemen. The Franklin ends in a courtly fashion by posing a question for discussion   914 **free** generous   915 **wende** travel

# THE HOST ADDRESSES
# THE PARDONER

"Thou *bel ami*,° thou Pardoner," he saide
"Tell us some mirth or japes° right anon."
   "It shall be done," quod he, "by Saint Ronion;
But first," quod he, "here at this ale-stake°
5  I wol both drink and eten of a cake."
  —And right anon thise gentils gan to crye,
"Nay, let him tell us of no ribaudye!°
Tell us some *moral* thing, that we may lere
Some wit, and thanne wol we gladly heere."
10   "I graunt, ywis," quod he. "But I mot thinke
Upon some honest° thing while that I drinke."

# THE PARDONER'S PROLOGUE

*Radix malorum est cupiditas.* 1 Timothy 6:10

Lordings (quod he), in chirches whan I preeche,
I paine me to han an hautein° speeche
And ring it out as round as goth a belle—
For I kan all by rote° that I telle.

1 **bel ami** pretty friend  2 **japes** jokes  4 **ale-stake** sign for a tavern
hung on a pole  7 **ribaudye** ribaldry  11 **honest** profitable
2 **hautein** lofty  4 **kan . . . rote** know all by heart

My theme is alway one,° and ever was:                         5
*Radix malorum est cupiditas.*°
First I pronounce whennes that I come,
And than my bulles° shew I all and some—
Our liege lordes seel on my patente,°
That shew I first, my body to warrente,°              10
That no man be so bold, ne preest ne clerk,°
Me to destourb of° Christes holy werk.
And after that than tell I forth my tales:
Bulles of popes and of cardinales,
Of patriarks and bishopes I shewe,                    15
And in Latin I speke a wordes fewe
To saffron with my predicacioun,°
And for to stir hem to devocioun.
Than shew I forth my longe crystal stones,°
Y-crammed full of cloutes° and of bones—              20
Relics been they, as weenen *they* echon!
Than have I in latoun° a shulder-bon
Which that was of an holy Jewes sheep:
"Good men," I say, "take of my wordes keep!
If that this bone be wash° in any welle,              25
If cow, or calf, or sheep, or oxe swelle,
That any worm hath ete or worm y-stonge,°
Take water of that well and wash his tonge,
And it is whole anon! And furthermor,
Of pokkes° and of scab and every sor                  30
Shall every sheep be whole that of this welle
Drinketh a draught. Take keep eek what I telle:

---

5 **theme . . . one** text is always the same    6 **Radix . . . cupiditas**
avarice is the root of evil. The Pardoner's theme is covetousness, or
greed, one of the Seven Deadly Sins. The other Sins are lust (lech-
ery), envy, anger (wrath), gluttony, sloth and pride. The greatest of
the Deadly Sins was thought to be pride, but the Pardoner cites
*1 Timothy* 6:10 (*Radix omnium malorum est cupiditas*) in favor of
greed, since it serves his purposes better    8 **bulles** certificates
9 **liege . . . patente** i.e., a bishop signed the papal decree    10 **warrente**
protect    11 **ne preest . . . clerk** there was general enmity among
parish clerks and pardoners    12 **destourb of** keep from    17 **To
. . . predicacioun** to spice my preaching    19 **crystal stones** glass
cases for displaying relics    20 **cloutes** rags    22 **in latoun** i.e., en-
cased in brass    25 **wash** washed    27 **That . . . y-stonge** that has
eaten or been stung by any snake    30 **pokkes** pustules

If that the good man that the beestes oweth°
Wol every wike, ere that the cock him croweth,
35  Fasting, drinken of this well a draughte—
As thilke holy Jew our elders taughte—
His beestes and his store° shall multiplye.
    And sirs, also it heeleth jalousye:
For though a man be fall in jalous rage,
40  Let maken with this water his potage,
And never shall he more his wife mistriste,°
Though he the sooth of hir defaute wiste
—Al had she taken preestes two or three.
    Here is a mittein° eek that ye may see:
45  He that his hand wol put in this mittein
He shall have multiplying of his grain,
Whan he hath sowen, be it whete or otes—
So that he offer pence or elles grotes.°
    Good men and women, oo thing warn I you:
50  If any wight be in this chirche now
That hath done sinne horrible, that he
Dare not for shame of it y-shriven° be;
Or any woman, be she yong or old,
That hath y-maked hir husband cokewold—
55  Swich folk shall have no power ne no grace
To offren to my relics in this place.
And whoso findeth him out of swich blame,
They wol come up and offre in Goddes name,
And I assoile° him by th'auctoritee
60  Which that by bull y-graunted was to me."
—By this gaude° have I wonne, yeer by yeer,
An hundred mark° sith I was pardoner.
I stande like a clerk in my pulpet,
And whan the lewed peple is down y-set
65  I preeche so as ye han herd before,
And tell an hundred false japes more.
Than pain I me to stretche forth the necke,

33 oweth owns  37 store stock  41 mistriste mistrust  44 mittein
mitten  48 grotes a groat was an English silver coin, worth four-
pence  52 y-shriven absolved, confessed  59 assoile absolve  61
gaude trick  62 hundred mark hundred marks, a large sum (mark
= ⅔ of a pound)

And est and west upon the peple I becke°
As doth a dove, sitting on a berne:°
Mine handes and my tonge goon so yerne°                    70
That it is joy to see my bisinesse!
Of avarice and of swich cursednesse
Is all my preeching, for to make hem free
To yiven hir pence—and namely, unto me.
For mine entent is not but for to winne,°                  75
And nothing for correccion of sinne—
I rekke° never, whan that they been beried,°
Though that hir soules goon a-blackeberried!°
For certes, many a predicacioun°
Cometh ofte time of yvel entencioun:                       80
Some for plesance of° folk and flatterye,
To been avanced° by hypocrisye;
And some for vaine glory; and some for hate.
For whan I dare noon otherways debate,
Than wol I sting him with my tonge smerte                  85
In preeching, so that he shall not asterte
To been defamed falsely—if that he
Hath trespassed to my bretheren° or to me;
For though I telle not his proper name,
Men shall well knowe that it is the same                   90
By signes, and by other circumstaunces.
—Thus quit° I folk that doon us displesaunces;
Thus spit I out my venim under hewe
Of holiness, to *seem* holy and trewe.
   But shortly mine entent I wol devise.°                  95
I preech of nothing but for coveitise:°
Therefore my theme is yet and ever was
*Radix malorum est cupiditas.*
Thus can I preech again that same vice
Which that I use—and that is avarice.                     100
But though myself be guilty in that sinne

68 **becke** nod   69 **berne** barn   70 **yerne** vigorously   75 **not . . .
winne** only to gain profit   77 **rekke** care   77 **beried** buried   78 **a-
blackeberried** wandering on a wild goose chase, i.e., to damnation
79 **predicacioun** sermon   81 **for . . . of** to please   82 **avanced** bene-
fited   88 **to . . . bretheren** against my fellow pardoners   92 **quit** pay
back   95 **devise** explain   96 **coveitise** covetousness

Yet can I maken other folk to twinne°
From avarice, and sore to repente
—But that is not my principal entente:
105 I preeche nothing but for coveitise.
Of this matter it ought enough suffise.
      Than tell I hem ensamples° many on
Of olde stories longe time agon.
For lewed° peple loven tales olde—
110 Swich thinges can they well report and holde.
What, trowe ye that whiles I may preeche
And winne gold and silver for I teeche,°
That I wol live in poverte *will*fully?
Nay, nay, I thought it never, trewely!
115 For I wol preech and beg in sundry landes:
I wol not do no labour with mine handes,
Ne make baskettes and live thereby—
Because I wol not beggen idelly.°
I wol none of the apostles countrefete;°
120 I wol have money, woole, cheese, and whete,
Al were it yiven of° the povrest page
Or of the povrest widwe in a village—
Al shold hir children sterve for famine!
Nay, I wol drinke licour of the vine
125 And have a jolly wench in every town!
      But herkneth, lordings, in conclusioun:
Your liking is that I shall tell a tale?—
Now have I drunk a draught of corny ale,
By God, I hope I shall you tell a thing
130 That shall by reson° been at your liking!
For though myself be a full vicious° man,
A moral tale yet I you telle can,
Which I am wont to preeche for to winne.°
Now hold your pees, my tale I wol beginne.

102 **twinne** turn     107 **ensamples** examples *(exempla)* of moral be-
havior     109 **lewed** ignorant     112 **for . . . teeche** for what I teach
(namely, poverty)     118 **idelly** in vain     119 **countrefete** imitate     121 **of**
by     130 **by reson** for (good) reasons     131 **vicious** wicked, given to
vice     133 **to winne** profit

# THE PARDONER'S TALE

In Flanders, whilom,° was a compaignye  
Of yonge folk that haunteden° follye—  
As riot, hasard, stewes,° and tavernes  
Whereas with harpes, lutes, and giternes°  
They daunce and playen at dees° both day and night,  
And ete also, and drink over hir might°— 140  
Thurgh which they doon° the Devil sacrifise  
Within that Devil's temple in cursed wise  
By superfluitee° abhominable!  
Hir othes° been so greet and so dampnable  
That it is grisly for to heer hem swere: 145  
Our blessed Lordes body they to-tere°—  
Hem thought that Jewes rent Him not enough!  
And ech of hem at other's sinne lough!°  
And right anon than comen tombesteres,°  
Fetis° and small, and yonge frutesteres,° 150  
Singers with harpes, bawdes,° wafereres°—  
Which been the veray devil's officeres  
To kindle and blow the fire of lecherye  
That is annexed unto° gluttonye.  

The Holy Writ take I to my witnesse 155  
That luxury° is in wine and drunkenesse:  
Lo, how that drunken Lot unkindely°  
Lay by his daughters two unwittingly—  
So drunk he was he niste what he wroughte.  

135 **whilom** once upon a time  136 **haunteden** practiced  137 **riot** . . . **stewes** revelry, gambling, whorehouses  138 **giternes** guitars  139 **dees** dice  140 **over** . . . **might** more than their capacity  141 **doon** make to  143 **superfluitee** overindulgence  144 **othes** oaths  146 **to-tere** tear apart. The Pardoner is concerned with the habitual swearing of gamblers and hedonists. Cf. Shakespeare's *'sblood! 'steeth!* (God's blood, God's teeth)  148 **lough** laughed  149 **tombesteres** dancing girls  150 **Fetis** pretty, neat  150 **frutesteres** fruit-sellers  151 **bawdes** prostitutes  151 **wafereres** wafer and cake vendors  154 **annexed unto** allied with  156 **luxury** (Lat. *luxuria*) lechery  157 **unkindely** unnaturally

160 Herodes,° who so well the stories soughte,
    Whan he of wine was replete° at his feste,
    Right at his owne table he yaf his heste°
    To sleen the Baptist John, full guilteless.
      Senec saith a good word, douteless:
165 He saith he can no difference finde
    Bitwix a man that is out of his minde
    And a man which that is drunkelewe°—
    But that woodness,° y-fallen in a shrewe,°
    Persevereth lenger than doth drunkenesse.
170 —O gluttonye, full of cursednesse!
    O cause first of our confusioun!
    O original° of our dampnacioun,
    Till Christ had bought us with his blood again!
    Lo, how dere, shortly for to sayn,
175 Abought was thilke cursed villainye:
    Corrupt was all this world for gluttonye!—
    Adam our fader and his wife also
    Fro paradise to labour and to woe
    Were driven for that vice, it is no drede:°
180 For while that Adam fasted, as I rede,
    He was in paradise, and whan that he
    Eet of the fruit defended° on a tree
    Anon he was out cast to woe and paine.
    O gluttony, on thee well ought us plaine!°
185 O, wist a man how many maladies
    Follwen of excess and of gluttonies,
    He wolde been the more mesurable°
    Of his diete, sitting at his table.
    Alas, the shorte throt, the tender mouth,
190 Maketh that est and west and north and south,
    In erth, in air, in water, men to swinke,°
    To get a glutton daintee° mete and drinke!
      Of this matter, O Paul, well canstou trete:
    "Mete unto womb, and womb eek unto mete,

160 **Herodes** Herod   161 **replete** full   162 **yaf . . . heste** gave his
order   167 **drunkelewe** falling-down drunk   168 **woodness** mad-
ness   168 **shrewe** scoundrel   172 **original** origin   179 **it . . . drede**
there is no doubt   182 **fruit defended** forbidden fruit (hanging)
184 **well . . . plaine** we should complain   187 **mesurable** careful,
restrained   191 **swinke** work   192 **daintee** choice

Shall God destroyen both," as Paulus saith.          195
Alas, a foul thing is it, by my faith,
To say this word, and fouler is the deede
Whan man so drinketh of the white and rede°
That of his throt he maketh his privee°
Thurgh thilke cursed superfluitee!          200
The apostle weeping saith full pitously,
"There walken many of which you told have I—
I say it now weeping with pitous vois—
That they been enemies of Christes crois,°
Of which the end is deeth: womb° is hir god!"          205
—O womb, O belly, O stinking cod,°
Fulfilled of dung and of corrupcioun!
At either end of thee foul is the soun.°
How greet labour and cost is thee to finde!°
Thise cookes, how they stamp, and strain, and grinde,          210
And turnen substance into accident°
To fulfillen all thy likerous talent!°
Out of the harde bones knocke they
The marry,° for they caste nought away
That° may go thurgh the gullet soft and soote.°          215
Of spicery° of leef and bark and roote
Shall been his sauce y-maked by delit,°
To make him yet a newer appetit.
But certes he that haunteth swich delices°
Is deed while that he liveth in tho vices.          220
   A lecherous thing is wine, and drunkenesse
Is full of striving° and of wretchednesse.
O drunke man, disfigured is thy face!
Sour is thy breeth, foul artou to embrace!
And thurgh thy drunke nose seemeth the soun          225
As though thou saidest ay "Sampsoun! Sampsoun!"—

198 **white . . . rede** i.e., wine   199 **privee** toilet   204 **crois** cross
205 **womb** stomach   206 **cod** bag, stomach   208 **soun** sound
209 **finde** satisfy   211 **turnen . . . accident** the terms are from
scholastic theology and refer to the arguments concerning forms
of things: essence (substance) versus appearance (accident)
212 **likerous talent** lecherous needs   214 **marry** marrow   215 **That**
(rel. pron.) what   215 **soote** sweetly   216 **spicery** spices   217 **by
delit** for delectation   219 **delices** delights   222 **striving** strife

And yet, God wot, Sampsoun drank never no win.
Thou fallest as it were a sticked swin;°
Thy tonge is lost, and all thine honest cure,°
230 For drunkeness is veray sepulture°
Of mannes wit and his discrecioun.
In whom that drink hath dominacioun
He can no conseil keep, it is no drede.
Now, keep you fro the white and fro the rede—
235 And namely, fro the white wine of Lepe
That is to sell in Fishstreet, or in Chepe:°
This wine of Spaine creepeth subtilly
In other wines growing faste by,
Of which there riseth swich fumositee°
240 That whan a man hath drunken draughtes three
And weeneth that he be at home in Chepe,
He is in Spain, right at the town of Lepe—
Not at the Rochelle, ne at Burdeux town°—
And thanne wol he sayn, "Sampsoun! Sampsoun!"
245    But herkneth, lordings, oo word I you praye—
That all the sovereign actes,° dare I saye,
Of victories in the Olde Testament,
Thurgh veray God that is omnipotent,
Were done in abstinence and in prayere:
250 Looketh the Bible and there ye may it lere.°
Look Atilla, the greete conquerour,
Deid in his sleep with shame and dishonour,
Bleeding at his nose in drunkenesse:
A capitain shold live in sobernesse!
255 And overall this, aviseth you° right well
What was commanded unto Lamuel°
(Not Samuel, but Lamuel, say I)—
Redeth the Bible and find it expressly,

228 **sticked swin** stuck pig    229 **honest cure** care for respectability
230 **veray sepulture** burial itself    236 **Fishstreet . . . Chepe** sections
of London; note the Pardoner's knowledge of such things    239 **fu-
mositee** wine vapor    243 **Not . . . town** i.e., the drinker of French
wines (Rochelle, Bordeaux) may find that Lepe, a more potent
Spanish wine, has been mixed in    246 **sovereign actes** important acts
250 **lere** learn    255 **aviseth you** consider    256 **Lamuel** a ruler told
not to drink wine as an example to his subjects

Of wine-yiving to hem that han justise.°              
Namore of this, for it may well suffise.           260
  And now that I have spoken of gluttonye,
Now wol I you defenden hasardrye:°
  Hasard is very moder of lesinges°
And of deceit and cursed foresweringes,°
Blaspheme of Christ, manslaughtre, and waste also   265
Of catel° and of time. And furthermo,
It is repreve° and contrary of honour
For to been hold a commune hasardour.
And ever the hyer he is of estat
The more is he holden desolat:°               270
If that a prince useth hasardrye,
In alle governance and policye
He is, as by commun opinioun,
Y-hold the less in reputacioun.
Stilboun, that was a wise embassadour,       275
Was sent to Corinth in full greet honour
Fro Lacedomye to make hir alliaunce,
And whan he came him happede° parchaunce
That all the greetest that were of that lond
Playing at the hasard he hem foond;        280
For which as soone as it mighte be
He stal him home again to his contree,
And saide, "There wol I not lese my name,
N'I wol not take on me so greet defame°
You to ally unto none hasardours.        285
Sendeth othere wise embassadours,
For by my trouthe, me were lever° die
Than I you shold to hasadours allye.
For ye that been so glorious in honours
Shall not allye you with hasadours        290
As by my will, ne as by my tretee."
This wise philosophre, thus said he.

---

259 **justise** judicial power    262 **defenden hasardrye** discourage gamb-
ling   263 **moder . . . lesinges** mother of lies   264 **foresweringes**
falsehoods   266 **catel** possessions   267 **repreve** a shame, reproach
270 **holden desolat** considered decadent   278 **him happede** it hap-
pened   284 **defame** dishonor   287 **me . . . lever** I would rather

    Look eek that to the king Demetrius
    The King of Parthes, as the book saith us,
295 Sent him a pair of dees of gold in scorn,
    For he had used hasard therebiforn;
    For which he held his glory or his renown
    At no value or reputacioun.
    Lordes may finden other manner play
300 Honest° enough to drive the day away.
      Now wol I speke of othes false and greete
    A word or two, as olde bookes treete:
      Greet swering is a thing abhominable,
    And false swering is yet more reprevable.
305 The heighe God forbade swering at all—
    Witness on Matthew. But in special
    Of swering saith the holy Jeremie,°
    "Thou shalt swere sooth thine othes and not lie,
    And swere in doom° and eek in rightwisnesse;°
310 But idle swering is a cursednesse."°
    Behold and see that in the firste table°
    Of heighe Goddes hestes honorable
    How that the second heste of him is this:
    "Take not my name in idle or amiss."
315 Lo, rather° he forbedeth swich swering
    Than homicide, or many a cursed thing.
    I say that, as by order, thus it standeth:
    This knoweth, that° his hestes understandeth,
    How that the second heste of God is that.
320 And ferther over, I wol thee tell all plat°
    That vengeance shall not parten from his hous
    That° of his othes is too outrageous:
    "By Goddes precious hert!" and "By His nailes!"
    And, "By the blood of Christ that is in Hailes,°
325 Seven is my chaunce, and thine is cink and traye!"°

---

300 **Honest** worthwhile    307 **Jeremie** Jeremiah    309 **doom** considered judgment    309 **rightwisnesse** righteousness    310 **cursednesse** wickedness    311 **firste table** of the Ten Commandments, i.e., the first five commandments    315 **rather** sooner    318 **that** he who 320 **all plat** flatly    322 **That** who    324 **Hailes** there was a tradition that some of Christ's blood was kept at Hayles abbey, Gloucestershire    325 **cink . . . traye** five and three (in craps)

"By Goddes armes, if thou falsely playe
This dagger shall thurghout thine herte go!"
—This fruit cometh of the bitched bones two:°
Forswering, ire, falseness, homicide.
Now for the love of Christ that for us dyde,                    *330*
Let° your othes, bothe greet and smalle.

    But sires, now wol I telle forth my tale.
Thise riotoures three of which I tell,
Long erst ere prime° rung of any belle,
Were set hem in a taverne to drinke.                            *335*
And as they sat they herd a belle clinke
Biforn a corse° was carried to his grave.
That one of hem gan callen to his knave—
"Go bet,"° quod he, "and axe redily
What corse is this that passeth here forby,                     *340*
And look that thou report his name well."

    "Sir," quod this boy, "it needeth neveradeel;
It was me told ere ye came here two houres.
He was, pardee, an old fellaw° of youres.
And suddenly he was y-slain tonight,                            *345*
Fordrunk,° as he sat on his bench upright:
There came a privee° thief men clepeth Deeth,
That in this contree all the peple sleeth,
And with his spere he smote his hert atwo,
And went his way withouten wordes mo.                          *350*
He hath a thousand slain this pestilence.°
And maister, ere ye come in his presence,
Me thinketh that it were necessarye
For to be ware of swich an Adversarye:
*Beth redy for to meet him evermore . . .*                     *355*
—Thus taughte me my dame; I say namore."

    "By Sainte Mary!" said this taverner,
"The child saith sooth. For he hath slain this yeer,
Henne over a mile,° within a greet village,
Both man and woman, child and hine° and page.                  *360*

---

328 **bitched . . . two** i.e., dice   331 **Let** leave off   334 **prime** six a.m.
337 **corse** corpse   339 **Go bet** go quickly   344 **fellaw** friend
346 **Fordrunk** thoroughly drunk   347 **privee** clandestine   351 **this
pestilence** during this plague   359 **Henne . . . mile** over a mile from
here   360 **hine** worker

I trow his habitacioun be there.
To been avised greet wisdom it were,
Ere that he did a man a dishonour."
    "Ye, Goddes armes!" quod this riotour,
365 "Is it swich peril with him for to meete?
I shall him seek by way and eek by streete,
I make avow to Goddes digne bones!
Herkneth, fellows—we three been all ones:
Let ech of us hold up his hand til other,
370 And ech of us become other's brother:
And we wol sleen this false traitour Deeth.
He shall be slain, he that so many sleeth,
By Goddes dignitee, ere it be night."
—Togidres han thise three hir trouthes plight.
375 To live and dien ech of hem for other,
As though he were his own y-bore brother.°
And up they stirt,° all drunken in this rage,°
And forth they goon towardes that village
Of which the taverner had spoke biforn.
380 And many a grisly ooth than han they sworn,
And Christes blessed body they to-rente:°
Deeth shall be deed, if that they may him hente!°
    Whan they han gone not fully half a mile,
Right as they wold han treden over a stile,
385 An old man and a povre with hem mette.
This olde man full meekely hem grette°
And saide thus: "Now, lordes . . . God you see! . . ."°
    The proudest of thise riotoures three
Answered again, "What, carl!° with sorry grace!
390 Why artou all forwrapped° save thy face?
Why livestou so long in so greet age?"
    This olde man gan look in his visage
And saide thus: "For I ne can not finde
A man, though that I walked into Inde°—

376 own . . . brother natural-born brothers    377 stirt lept    377 rage
fit    381 to-rente tore apart with swearing    382 hente catch    386
grette greeted    387 God . . . see God look (with favor) upon you
389 carl man, lout    390 forwrapped wrapped up    394 Inde India

Neither in citee, ne in no village—                           395
That wolde chaunge his youthe for mine age.
And, therefore, mot I han mine age stille,
As longe time as it is Goddes wille;
Ne Deeth, alas, ne wol not han my lif.
Thus walk I like a resteless caitiff,°                         400
And on the ground, which is my modres° gate
I knocke with my staff, both erly and late,
And saye, 'Leve moder, let me in!
Lo, how I vanish—flesh, and blood, and skin . . .
Alas, whan shall my bones been at reste?                       405
Moder, with you wold I chaunge my cheste°
That in my chambre longe time hath be,
Ye, for an haire-clout to wrap in me.'°
But yet to me she wol not do that grace;
For which full pale and welked° is my face.                    410
    But sires, to you it is no curteisye
To speken to an old man villainye,
But he trespass in word or else in deede.
In Holy Writ ye may yourself well rede:
*Agains an old man, hoor° upon his heed,*                      415
*Ye shold arise* . . . Wherefore I yive you reed,°
Ne doth unto an old man noon harm now,
Namore than that ye wolde men did to *you*
In age, if that ye so long abide—
And God be with you wher ye go° or ride;                       420
I mot go thider as I have to go . . ."
    "Nay, olde cherl!° By God thou shalt *not* so,"
Said this other hasardour anon,
"Thou partest not so lightly, by Saint John!
Thou spak right now of thilke traitour, Deeth,                 425
That in this contree all our freendes sleeth.
Have here my trouth, as thou art his espye,°
Tell where he is, or thou shalt it abye,°

400 **caitiff** wretch   401 **modres** mother's   406 **cheste** clothes-chest
408 **haire-clout . . . me** haircloth (for a shroud) to wrap me up in
410 **welked** withered   415 **hoor** white, old age   416 **reed** advice.
Note how his advice echoes the golden rule   420 **wher . . . go**
whether you walk   422 **cherl** rogue   427 **espye** spy   428 **abye** pay
for

By God and by the Holy Sacrament!
430 For soothly thou are one of his assent°
To sleen us yonge folk, thou false theef!"
     "Now, sires—" quod he, "if that ye be so leef°
To finde Deeth—turn up this crooked way.
For in that grove I left him, by my fay,
435 Under a tree—and there he wol abide . . .
Not for *your* boost he wol him no thing hide.
See ye that ook? Right there ye shall him finde!
God save you, that bought again mankinde,
And you amend . . ." Thus said this olde man;
440 And everich of thise riotoures ran
Till they came to that tree, and there they founde
Of florins° fine of gold y-coined rounde
Well ny an eighte bushels as hem thoughte—
No lenger thanne after Deeth they soughte,
445 But ech of hem so glad was of the sighte
For that the florins been so fair and brighte
That down they set hem by this precious hoord.
The worst of hem he spak the firste word.
"Bretheren," quod he, "take keep what that I saye;
450 My wit° is greet, though that I bourde° and playe.
This tresor hath Fortune unto us yiven
In mirth and jolitee our life to liven—
And lightly as it cometh so wol we spende.
Ey! Goddes precious dignitee! who wende°
455 Today that we shold han so fair a grace?
But might this gold be carried fro this place
Home to mine house—or elles unto youres—
For well ye wot that all this gold is oures—
Than were we in heigh felicitee.°
460 But trewely, by day it may not be—
Men wolde sayn that we were theeves stronge
And for our owne tresor doon us honge;°
This tresor most y-carried be by nighte,

---

430 **assent** party, faction   432 **leef** eager   442 **florins** gold coins,
originally Florentine   450 **wit** understanding   450 **bourde** play
tricks   454 **wende** would have thought   459 **heigh felicitee** great
happiness   462 **doon . . . honge** have us hanged

As wisly and as slyly as it mighte.
Therefore I rede that cut° among us alle                      465
Be draw, and let see where the cut wol falle;
And he that hath the cut with herte blithe
Shall renne to the town, and that full swithe,°
And bring us breed and wine full prively;
And two of us shall keepen subtilly                           470
This tresor well, and if he wol not tarrye,
Whan it is night we wol this tresor carrye
By one assent° where as us thinketh best."
    That one° of hem the cut brought in his fest°
And bade hem draw and look where it wol falle;              475
And it fill on the yongest of hem alle,
And forth toward the town he went anon.
And also soon as that he was agon
That one of hem spak thus unto that other:
"Thou knowest well thou art my sworen brother;            480
Thy profit wol I telle thee anon.
Thou wost well that our fellaw is agon;
And here is gold, and that full greet plentee,
That shall departed° been among us three.
But natheless, if I can shape° it so                          485
That it departed were among us two,
Had I not done a freendes turn to thee?"
    That other answered, "I noot how *that* may be.
*He* wot that the gold is with us twaye.
What shall we doon? What shall we to him saye?"              490
    "Shall it be conseil?"° said the firste shrewe.
"And I shall tellen in a wordes fewe
What we shull doon, and bring it well aboute."
    "I graunte," quod that other, "out of doute,
That by my truth I wol thee not biwraye."°                   495
    "Now," quod the first, "thou wost well we be twaye,
And two of us shall strenger° be than oon:
Look whan that he is set, that right anon
Arise as though thou woldest with him playe;

465 cut lots   468 swithe quickly   473 By . . . assent by common
assent   474 That one one   474 fest fist   484 departed divided
485 shape fix   491 conseil a secret   495 biwraye give away   497
strenger stronger

500 And I shall rive° him thurgh the sides twaye,
    While that thou strugglest with him as in game;
    And with thy dagger look thou do the same.
    And than shall all this gold departed be,
    My dere freend, bitwixe me and thee!
505 Than may we both our lustes° all fulfille
    And play at dees right at our owne wille!"
    And thus accorded° been thise shrewes twaye
    To sleen the thrid, as ye han herd me saye.
        This yongest, which that wente to the town,
510 Full oft in hert he rolleth up and down
    The beautee of thise florins new and brighte.
    "O Lord!" quod he, "if so were that I mighte
    Have all this tresor to myself alone,
    There is no man that liveth under the trone°
515 Of God that sholde live so murry as I!"
    And atte last the Feend, our enemy,
    Put in his thought that he shold poison beye°
    With which he mighte sleen his fellaws twaye;
    Forwhy° the Feend found him in swich livinge
520 That he had leve° him to sorrow bringe.
    For this was outrely° his full entente:
    To sleen hem both and never to repente.
    And forth he goth, no lenger wold he tarrye,
    Into the town unto a 'pothecarye,
525 And prayed him that he him wolde selle
    Some poison, that he might his rattes quelle,°
    And eek there was a polecat in his hawe°
    That (as he said) his capons had y-slawe,°
    And fain he wolde wreke him° if he mighte
530 On vermin that destroyed him by nighte.
        The 'pothecary answered, "And thou shalt have
    A thing that, also° God my soule save,

---

500 **rive** stick    505 **lustes** desires, ambitions    507 **accorded** agreed
514 **trone** throne    517 **beye** buy    519 **Forwhy** because    520 **leve**
permission. The rioter, though young, has forfeited his portion of
grace    521 **outrely** utterly, completely. "Outrely his full entente"
is a pleonasm suggesting the extent of his wicked purpose
526 **quelle** kill, control    527 **hawe** yard    528 **his . . . y-slawe** had
slain his capons    529 **fain . . . him** he would gladly avenge himself
532 **also** as

In all this world there is no creature
That ete or drunk hath of this confiture,° 534
Not but the montance° of a corn of whete,          535
That he ne shall his life anon forlete.°
Ye, sterve he shall, and that in lesse while
Than thou wolt goon a pas not but a mile,
The poison is so strong and violent."
    This cursed man hath in his hand y-hent°       540
This poison in a box, and sith he ran
Into the nexte street unto a man
And borrwed of him large bottles three.
And in the two his poison poured he—
The thrid he kepte clene for *his* drinke;         545
For all the night he shop him for to swinke°
In carrying of the gold out of that place.
And whan this riotour, with sorry grace,°
Had filled with wine his greete bottles three
To his fellaws again repaireth° he.                550
—What needeth it to sermon of it more?
For right as they had cast his deeth before,
Right so they han him slain, and that anon.
And whan that this was done, thus spak that oon:
"Now let us sit and drink and make us merrye,      555
And afterward we wol his body berye."
And with that word it happed him, *par cas*,°
To take the bottle ther° the poison was
And drank, and yaf his fellaw drink also:
For which anon they storven° bothe two!            560
    But certes I suppose that Avicen°
Wrote never in no canon ne in no *fen*°
Mo wonder signes° of empoisoning
Than had thise wretches two ere hir ending.
Thus ended been thise homicides two,               565
And eek the false empoisoner also.

---

534 **confiture** potion   535 **montance** amount, measure   536 **forlete**
give up   540 **y-hent** clutched   546 **shop . . . swinke** proposed to
work   548 **with . . . grace** let bad fortune be with him   550 **repair-
eth** returns   557 **par cas** by chance   558 **ther** in which   560 **storven**
died   561 **Avicen** Avicenna, Arabic physician   562 **fen** chapter
563 **signes** symptoms

O cursed sin of alle cursednesse!
O traitours homicide, O wickednesse,
O gluttony, luxury, and hasardrye!
570 Thou basphemour of Christ with villainye
And othes greete of usage and of pride!
Alas, mankinde, how may it bitide
That to thy Creatour which that thee wroughte,
And with his precious herte blood thee boughte,°
575 Thou art so false and so unkind, alas?
—Now, good men, God foryive you your trespass
And ware you fro the sin of *avarice!*
Mine holy pardon may you all warice,°
So that ye offer nobles° or sterlinges—
580 Or elles silver brooches, spoones, ringes;
Boweth your heed under this holy bulle!
Cometh up, ye wives, offreth of your woole!
Your name I enter here in my roll anon;
Into the bliss of Heven shull ye gon.
585 I you assoile, by mine heigh power—
Ye that wol offre—as cleene and eek as cleer°
As ye were born!—And lo, sirs, thus I preeche.
And Jesu Christ, that is our soules leeche,°
So graunte you *His* pardon to receive;
590 For that is best, I wol you not deceive.
    But sirs! oo word forgat I in my tale!
I have relics and pardon in my male°
As fair as any man in Engeland,
Which were me yiven by the Popes hand!
595 If any of you wol, of devocioun,
Offren and han mine absolucioun,
Come forth anon, and kneeleth here adown,
And meekely receiveth my pardoun;
Or elles taketh pardon as ye wende,°
600 All new and fresh at every miles ende—
So that ye offren alway new and newe°
Nobles or pence which that been good and trewe.

574 **boughte** redeemed   578 **warice** heal, absolve   579 **nobles** thin
gold coins   586 **cleer** pure   588 **leeche** physician   592 **male** bag
599 **wende** go along   601 **alway . . . newe** always again and again

It is an honour to everich that is heer
That ye mow have a suffisant° pardoner
T'assoile you in contree as ye ride,                        *605*
For aventures which that may bitide:
Paraventure there may fall one or two
Down off his horse and breke his neck atwo.
Look which a suretee° is it to you alle
That I am in your fellawship y-falle                        *610*
That may assoile you, both more and lasse,
Whan that the soul shall fro the body passe!
I rede that our Host here shall beginne,
For he is most envoluped° in sinne.
Come forth, sir Host, and offer first anon,                 *615*
And thou shalt kiss the relics everichon,
Ye, for a grote—unbuckle anon thy purs."
    "Nay, nay!" quod he, "than have I Christes curs!
Let be," quod he, "it shall not be, so th'eech!
Thou woldest make me kiss thine olde breech°               *620*
And swere it were a relic of a Saint—
Though it were with thy fundament depeint.°
But, by the crois which that Saint Elaine fond,
I wold I had thy coilons° in mind hond,
Insted of relics or of saintuarye:°                         *625*
Let cut hem off—I wol thee help hem carrye!
They shall be shrined in an hogges turd!"
    This Pardoner answered not a word.
So wroth he was, no word ne wold he saye.
    "Now," quod our Host, "I wol no lenger playe           *630*
With thee, ne with noon other angry man . . ."
    But right anon the worthy Knight began,
Whan that he saw that all the peple lough:
"Namore of this, for it is right enough!
Sir Pardoner, be glad and mirrye of cheere.                 *635*
And ye, sir Host, that been to me so dere,

---

604 **suffisant** competent    609 **which . . . suretee** what a protection
614 **envoluped** bound up, implicated    620 **breech** underclothes
622 **with . . . depeint** stained by your anus    624 **coilons** testicles
625 **saintuarye** box of relics

I pray you that ye kiss the Pardoner;
And Pardoner, I pray thee, draw thee neer,
And as we diden let us laugh and playe."
640 Anon they kist, and riden forth hir waye.

# THE PARSON'S PROLOGUE

By that° the Manciple had his tale all ended,
The sunne fro the south line° was descended
So lowe that he nas not to my sighte
Degrees nine and twenty as in highte.
Four of the clock it was, so as I guesse—                    5
For eleven foot, or litel more or lesse,
My shadow was at thilke time as there,
Of swich feet° as my lengthe parted were
In six feet equal of proporcioun.
Therewith the moones exaltacioun°—                           10
I mene Libra—alway gan ascende,°
As we were entering at a thropes ende.°
    For which our Host, as he was wont to gie°
As in this cas our jolly compaignye,
Said in this wise: "Lordings, everichon,                     15
Now lacketh us no tales mo than on!
Fulfilled is my sentence and my decree.
I trow that we han herd of ech degree°—
Almost fulfilled is all mine ordinaunce.
I pray to God, so yive him right good chaunce°               20
That telleth this tale to us lustily.°
Sir Preest," quod he, "artou a vicary,°

1 **By that** by the time that   2 **south line** meridian. Chaucer describes
the relation of the sun to its position at noon and also to his shadow
(lines 6–9)   8 **Of . . . feet** i.e., the ratio of Chaucer's height to the
cast of his shadow is 6:11   10 **exaltacioun** a planet's position in the
zodiac where the planet has greatest influence   11 **alway . . .
ascende** continued to ascend (above the horizon)   12 **a . . . ende**
the outskirts of a village   13 **gie** conduct, guide   18 **of . . . degree**
from each rank   20 **chaunce** fortune   21 **lustily** pleasantly   22
**vicary** vicar

Or art a person?° Say sooth, by thy fay!
Be what thou be, ne breek thou not our play,
25  For every man save thou hath told his tale.
Unbuckle and shew us what is in thy male!°
For trewely, me thinketh by thy cheere
Thou sholdest knit up° well a greet mattere.
Tell us a fable anon, for cockes bones!"
30      This Person answerede all atones,
"Thou gettest fable none y-told for me;
For Paul, that writeth unto Timothee,
Repreveth hem that waiven soothfastnesse°
And tellen fables and swich wretchednesse.
35  Why shold I sowen draff out of my fest°
Whan I may sowen whete,° if that me lest?
For which I say if that you list to heere
Moralitee and vertuous mattere,
And than that ye wol yive me audience,
40  I wol full fain,° at Christes reverence,
Do you plesance leveful,° as I can.
But trusteth well, I am a southren man—
I can not geste *Rum-Ram-Ruf,* by lettre;°
Ne, God wot, ryme hold I° but litel bettre.
45  And therefore, if you list, I wol not glose,°
I wol you tell a mirrye tale in prose
To knit up all this feest° and make an ende:
—And Jesu for his grace wit° me sende
To shewe you the way, in this viage,
50  Of thilke parfit glorious pilgrimage
That highte Jerusalem Celestial.°
      And if ye vouche sauf, anon I shall
Begin upon my tale, for which I praye

---

23 **person** parson   26 **male** bag   28 **knit up** bring together, wrap
up   33 **waiven soothfastnesse** neglect truthfulness (by concocting
fictions)   35 **draff . . . fest** chaff out of my fist   36 **whete** wheat
40 **full fain** very gladly   41 **plesance leveful** lawful pleasure
42–43 **southren . . . lettre** the Parson disclaims any inclination or
ability for romance (*geste*) or alliteration (*Rum-Ram-Ruff, by lettre*),
such as was popular in the North and West of England   44 **hold I**
can I keep up   45 **glose** hedge   47 **feest** feast (of stories)   48 **wit**
understanding, inspiration   49–51 **this viage . . . Celestial** the Par-
son compares the Canterbury pilgrimage to the larger pilgrimage
toward the New Jerusalem, or Heaven

Tell your avis:° I can no better saye.
But natheless, this meditacioun                              55
I put it ay under correccioun
Of clerkes, for I am not textuel°—
I take but the sentence,° trusteth well;
Therefore I make protestacioun
That I wol stande to correccioun."                           60
   Upon this word we han assented soone,
For, as it seemed, it was for to doone°
To enden in some vertuous sentence
And for to yive him space and audience;
And bade° our Host he sholde to him saye                     65
That alle we to tell his tale him praye.
   Our Host hadde the wordes for us alle:
"Sir Preest," quod he, "now faire you bifalle!
Telleth," quod he, "your meditacioun—
But hasteth you—the sunne wol adown!                         70
Beth *fructuous,*° and that in litel space
And to do well God sende you his grace.
Say what you list, and we wol gladly heere."

54 avis consent   57 textuel learned in texts   58 sentence the essen-
tial meaning   62 for . . . doone proper, fitting   65 bade we bade
71 fructuous fruitful

# "RETRACTION"

## Here taketh the maker of this book his leve:

Now pray I to hem all that herken this litel tretise
or rede, that if there be anything in it that liketh hem,
that thereof they thanken our Lord Jesu Christ, of
whom proceedeth all wit° and all goodness. And if
5 there be anything that displese hem, I pray hem also
that they arrette° it to the defaut of mine unkonning,°
and not to my will, that wolde full fain have said better
if I had the konning. For our Book saith,° "All that
is written is written for our doctrine"—and that is
10 mine intent. Wherefore I beseek you meekly, for the
mercy of God, that ye pray for me that Christ have
mercy on me and foryive me my guilts, and namely of
my translacions and enditings of worldly vanitees, the
which I revoke in my retraccions: as is the book of
15 Troilus, the book also of Fame,° the book of the
five and twenty Ladies,° the book of the Duchess, the
book of Saint Valentines Day of the Parlement of
Briddes, the tales of Canterbury (thilke that sounen
into° sin), the book of the Leon°—and many another
20 book, if they were in my remembrance, and many a
song and many a lecherous lay; that Christ for his
greet mercy foryive me the sin.

But of the translacion of Boece *De Consolatione*,°
and other books of legends of saints, and omelies,° and

---

4 **wit** knowledge, wisdom    6 **arrette** attribute    6 **defaut . . . unkon-
ning** my ignorance    8 **our . . . saith** the Bible says(*II Timothy* 3:16)
15 **book . . . Fame** Chaucer's *The House of Fame*    15–16 **book . . .
Ladies** Chaucer's *Legend of Good Women*    18–19 **sounen into** tend
toward    19 **Leon** Lion. The work is not known    23 **Boece . . . Con-
solatione** Boethius' *De Consolatione Philosophie* (*The Consolation
of Philosophy*)    24 **omelies** homilies

moralitee, and devocion, that thank I our Lord Jesu 25
Christ and his blissful Moder and all the saints of
heven, beseeking hem that they from henceforth unto
my lives end send me grace to bewail my guilts and to
study° to the salvacion of my soul, and graunt me
grace of veray° penitence, confession, and satisfaccion 30
to doon in this present life, thurgh the benign grace of
Him that is King of kings and Preest over all preestes,
that bought us with the precious blood of His hert, so
that I may been one of hem at the day of doom° that
shall be saved; *Qui cum patre et Spiritu Sancto vivit* 35
*et regnat Deus per omnia saecula. Amen.*

---

29 **study** give attention   30 **veray** true   34 **doom** judgment

# GLOSSARY OF BASIC WORDS

**Accorden** *v* agree; allow.
**Al** *conj* although.
**Algate(s)** *adv* at least; at any rate.
**Als** *adv* also.
**Also ... as** as ... as.
**Anon** *adv* immediately; right away.
**Apaid** *pp* pleased; satisfied; *yvele apaid* displeased; offended.
**Avisen** *v* consider; ponder.
**Axen** *v* to ask; ask for.
**Ay** *adv* ever; always.
**Been** *v* to be; *sg* am, art, is; *pl* are, been; *pt* was, were(n); *imp sg* be; *imp pl* beth; *pp* been, y-be(en); *neg* nis; *pt neg* nas, nere.
**Bet** *adj* & *adv* better.
**Blyve** *adv* quickly; *as blyve* as soon as possible.
**Brennen** *v* to burn; *pp* brend, brent.
**But** *adv* & *conj* only; *but as* except that; *but if* unless.
**Buxom** *adj* obedient, gracious
**Cas** *subst* event, happening; circumstance, situation; accident; *par cas* by chance, as it happened.
**Certes** *adv* certainly.
**Clepen** *v* to call, name; *pp* cleped, clept, y-cleped.
**Devise(n)** *v* to decide, determine; relate, explain.
**Digne** *adj* worthy; proud, haughty.
**Doom** *subst* judgment, opinion.
**Doon** *v* to do; cause, bring about; *pt* did; *pp* (y)-doon; *doon + inf* cause to + inf.
**Dorst, durst** *pt. subj* & *cond* dared, would dare.
**Drede** *subst* fear, anxiety; *withouten drede* without doubt.
**Duren** *v* to last, endure.

**Eek** *adv*   also.

**Eft** *adv*   again; *eftsoones* soon; again.

**Eld** *subst*   age, old age.

**Elles** *adv*   else, otherwise.

**Erst** *adv*   before; for the first time.

**Everich, everichon** *adj & pron*   each, each one, every one.

**Fain** *adj & adv*   glad, willing; gladly, willingly.

**Fele** *adj*   many.

**Fere** *subst*   companion; fellow.

**Fetis** *adj*   pretty, neat, elegant; dainty, small.

**For-** *intensive,* completely; *fordrunke* = very drunk; *for-straught* = distraught.

**Forsooth** *adv*   indeed.

**Forthy** *adv*   therefore.

**Fowel** *subst*   bird; *pl* foweles.

**Full** *adv*   very, entirely.

**Gay** *adj*   gay, carefree; bright, lively; well dressed.

**Ginnen** *v*   to begin; used as auxiliary verb in past tense, like "did"; *pt* gan, gonnen; did.

**Gentil** *adj*   noble, well-bred; courteous; **Gentilesse** *subst* nobility.

**Guise** *subst*   manner, custom, habit.

**He** *pron*   his, him; *pl* they; *gen* hire; *dat* hem, his; its.

**Henten** *v*   to seize, gain; *pt* hente, henten; *pp* hent, (y)-hent.

**Heigh, hye** *adj*   high.

**Herken, herknen** *v*   listen to; *imp* herkneth.

**Highte, hoten** *v*   to be called, named; command, bid; *pt* hatte, highte; *pp* hight, hoten.

**Honest** *adj*   respectable, proper; virtuous.

**Ilke, thilke** *adj*   same; the same.

**Kan** *v*   to know, to know how (to); *pp* koud.

**Keep, keepen** *v*   to take care, take heed, guard; *pp* kept, taken keep = take heed.

**Kinde** *subst*   birth; inclination, instinct; type; *by kinde* by nature.

**Lemman** *subst*   lover.

**Lesen** *v*   to lose; *pp* lorn, y-loren, y-lost.

**Leten** *v*   to let, permit; *let* + *inf* = cause to + inf.

**Leten** *v*   to hinder, prevent; shut off; delay; cause, desist; *pt* lette, letted; *pp* let.

**Leve, lief** *adj*   dear, beloved.

**Lever** *adj*  rather, more willing, more agreeable; *me were lever*  I would rather.

**Lewed** *adj*  ignorant; rude, coarse.

**List, lest** *3 sg imp v*  it pleases; *pt*  liste, leste.

**Lite, litel** *adj*  little, small.

**Lorn** *pp*  of lesen = to lose; *I nam but lorn*  I am lost for sure.

**Lust** *subst*  pleasure, desire.

**Meten** *v*  to dream; *me mette (impersonal)* = I dreamed

**Mo** *adj & pron*  more, others.

**Moot, mot** *v*  must, should, may; *pt*  most(e), must(e).

**Morrwe** *subst*  morning; next morning; *a-morrwe*  next morning, in the early morning.

**Muchel, mickel** *adj*  much.

**Murry(e), mirry, merry** *adj*  merry.

**Namo, namore** *adj & pron*  no more, no other.

**Nas** *neg*  (he) was not.

**Natheless** *adv*  nonetheless.

**Nere** *pl neg*  (we, they) were not.

**Nice** *adj*  foolish.

**Nis** *neg*  (he) is not.

**Niste** [from *witen = ne wiste*]  (he) did not know; *he niste what he wroughte*  he didn't know what he did.

**Nolde** [from *will, woll = ne wolde*] *pt neg*  (he) would not.

**Nones**  for the nonce, for the occasion.

**Noot** [from *witen = ne wot*]  (I) do not know; *I noot not where thou art*  I don't know where you are.

**Nought** *subst*  nothing; **Not** [unstressed form of *nought*] *adv*  not.

**Oo** *adj*  one.

**Or** *adv*  ere, before.

**Outher** *adj & conj*  either.

**Over all** *adv*  everywhere.

**Parde** *excl*  par Dieu, by God.

**Pas** *subst*  pace, step; distance.

**Propre, proper** *adj*  own, one's own; special; good-looking, well-grown.

**Quaint** *adj*  curious, strange; skilful, crafty.

**Quod** [from *quethen*] *pt*  said, quoth.

**Rathe** *adv*  soon; early.

**Reden** *v*  to counsel, advise; study; *pp*  red, rad.

**Reed, rede** *subst*  advice, plan.

**Rennen** *v*  to run.

**Repairen** *v* to return, go.

**Save** *prep* except.

**Sely** *adj* 1. happy, good; poor 2. wretched, unfortunate.

**Shrew** *subst* scoundrel, bum.

**Siken** *v* to sigh.

**Siker, sikerly** *adv* surely, certainly.

**Sin** *conj* since.

**Sithen** *conj & adv* afterwards; since.

**Somedeel** *adj* somewhat.

**Sooth** *subst* truth; *adj* true.

**Sterven** *v* to die; *pt 3 sg* starf; *pp* storven, y-storve.

**Stinten, stenten** *v* to stop, restrain.

**Sufferen** *v* to endure, suffer; permit, allow.

**Sweven** *subst* dream.

**Swich** *adj & pron* such; such a (one).

**Swinken** *v* to work, labor; *pp* swonken, y-swonke.

**Swithe** *adv* quickly.

**That** *rel pron* that, that which.

**Ther** *rel adv & conj* where; *theras* = whereas, where.

**Thilke** *adj* the same, that.

**Thinken** *impers v* it seems to me (her, him); *sg* me (hir, him) thinketh; *pt* thoughte.

**Thise** *pron* = the general sense of "those" or "your," as "these pilgrimages."

**Tho** *pron* those.

**Tho** *adv* then.

**Thries** *adv* three times, thrice.

**Till** *prep* until.

**Til** *prep* to.

**To-** *intensive* completely =, entirely =, "to pieces"; *to-hewen,* cut to pieces; *to-shred* all shredded up.

**Trowen** *v* to believe, think.

**Twaye** *adj* two; *tweyne* twaine.

**Unnethe(s)** *adv* scarcely.

**Wenden** *v* to wend, go; *pt* wente; *pp* (y-)went.

**Wenen** *v* to think, suppose, imagine; *pt* wende, wenden; *pp* wend, y-went.

**Wher** *conj* whether.

**Whilom** *adv* once upon a time.

**Wight** *subst* man, person; creature; *adj* strong; *a lite wight* a short time.

**Will, woll** *v* to will, wish; intend (to); would like (to); *pl* wollen; *pt* wolde.

**Wis, wisly** *adv*  certainly, surely.

**Witen** *v*  to know; *sg* wost, woot; *pl* witen; *pt* wiste, wisten; *pp* wist; *neg* noot, nist, etc.

**Wood** *adj*  crazy, insane.

**Y-** *prefix*  [sign of past participle].

**Yeven, yiven** *v*  to give; *pt* yaf; *pp* yeven, yiven.

**Yfere** *adv*  together.

**Ywis** *adv*  certainly.